Unnatural States

Unnatural States

The International System and the Power to Change

Peter Lomas

Routledge
Taylor & Francis Group

LONDON AND NEW YORK

First published 2014 by Transaction Publishers

2 Park Square, Milton Park, Abingdon, Oxfordshire OX14 4RN
711 Third Avenue, New York, NY 10017

Routledge is an imprint of the Taylor & Francis Group, an informa business

First issued in paperback 2017

Library of Congress Catalog Number: 2013039628

Library of Congress Cataloging-in-Publication Data

Lomas, Peter, 1948-
  Unnatural states : the international system and the power to change / Peter Lomas.
    pages cm
    ISBN 978-1-4128-5399-6 (cloth : alk. paper)
    1. International organization--Philosophy. 2. International relations--Philosophy. 3. State, The--Philosophy. 4. Human rights--International cooperation. 5. Weapons of mass destruction--International cooperation. 6. Developed countries--Foreign economic relations--Developing countries. 7. Developing countries--Foreign economic relations--Developed countries 8. Environmental protection--International cooperation. I. Title.
    JZ1308.L66 2014
    320.1--dc23
                                                        2013039628

ISBN 13: 978-1-4128-5399-6 (hbk)
ISBN 13: 978-1-138-51765-3 (pbk)

Contents

Introduction

Toward the millennium Chris Brown wrote: "International Relations today is a theoretically sophisticated and challenging social science, the location of important debates on, for example, agency-structure, gender, identity, and the further reaches of post-modern and post-structural thought." The point needed making, he said, to counter the impression that international theory was merely "higher journalism" or "current-affairs-with-a-twist."

That was a striking declaration of faith by one of the leading lights of the discipline, after half a century of discipline-querying debates. My own teachers in the 1980s urged me to question whether there was such a discipline as International Relations, as opposed to a space where several established fields of inquiry (history, political theory, economics, anthropology) fortuitously and perhaps transiently converged. For my part, even today, I would not be so sanguine about the sophistication of IR debates or the force of their intellectual challenge. As the end of the Cold War showed, events can overturn our settled beliefs about the world and make accepted tools of analysis look inadequate. Then there is the inevitable element of politics in analysts' work. We are all subjects, as well as observers, of the *activity* of international relations—all implicated on one level or another; that alone seems to make it controversial ever to argue that a social science is mature, or for that matter to disparage "higher journalism" on international themes. Chris Brown himself would settle for a broad-minded stance, "denying a privileged position to any one theory or set of theories."[1]

But beyond these controversies, it seems to me that fundamental misconceptions still pervade discussions, professional or otherwise, of human relations in the world as a whole; and I have made them the focus of this book. I take as my starting point the practice, in what I call the conventional wisdom of international relations, of treating states as agents—that is, able to take action—in their own right, a practice which I think has no basis in reality or common sense. Close examination of this practice reveals a yawning void where true human concerns should be. These are moral concerns. Refuting the convention of state agency leads to the conclusion that international theory should be defined by moral concerns.

The elements of my argument are as follows.

- Talk of states acting in their own right is so widespread as to constitute the conventional wisdom of international relations. This is, however, a dubious assumption. Normally only individual persons are held to be agents, with wills of their own.
- Conceivably, states could be *collective* agents, if they were perfectly identifiable with the societies inscribed under them. But existing states fail in any number of ways to represent "their" peoples, and assets are unequally distributed over the system. These are linked controversies, since the system is universal. All states must be equal for a shared conception of the state to prevail.
- It is, in addition, morally wrong to treat states as agents, in a context where agency is political freedom made manifest. The ubiquity and the permanence of states mean that international theory must be normative in practice.
- Morality is the distinguishing trait of human beings. Only human beings are able to imagine everything there is. This places us in a dominant position on earth—a fact which gives rise to morality itself, and means that international theory must be normative in principle as well.
- International theory must therefore be recast, with morality as central, to guide and to assist historic change.
- A practical way to begin this task is to confront persistent moral concerns in the world, to see what kind of society emerges from the attempt to resolve them in an integrated way. These concerns include human rights, weapons of mass destruction, relations between rich and poor peoples, and human life in the natural environment.
- In this venture philosophers and international theorists may make common cause, for the domain of human relations is, for all intents and purposes, the world, and the tasks of philosophy and international theory are the same.

Plan of the Book

In Section I of the book the conventional wisdom of international relations is set out. Chapter 1 is a survey of Anglo-American writing since about 1960, showing the widespread assumption that states are agents—or more commonly, "actors."

In chapter 2 I turn to the state-actor cliché, an ambiguous formula conflating two meanings of "to act." States, I point out, cannot *take action* in their own right—this happens only in some mechanistic account of events—and actors only pretend. Hobbes blurred the distinction deliberately, to argue, in a melodramatic portrayal of human life, that actors and agents, appearance and performance, are the same. Hence his theory of state-formation, as a kind of symbolic politics. Hence too his state agent, the "Artificiall Man" of the collectivity embodied and ruled by an absolute monarch—a synthesis Hobbes achieves by fusing the imagery of the theater and public advocacy and extending it to the world as a whole. In the end I come down against his procedure, but it is seminal for understanding the Realist accounts of international relations that prevailed during the Cold War and are still influential today.

Hobbes's state actor/agent is personal after a fashion, and still (if minimally) accountable, in his doctrine of social order through autocracy. By contrast, I argue in chapter 3, in the system we live under, even these gestures to legitimacy are absent. We are left with an unstable, problematic entity, the constituted state, in which the subjective and objective components of human identity are routinely muddled. Seen in this light, international theory must be reformed simply in order to make sense of our lives.

In part II of the book I set out some philosophical supports for a new approach. In chapter 4 I argue that international theory must be normative in practice, because the ubiquity and the permanence of states provide a direct challenge to human values. This rules out Naturalism, a view of things with no place for abstractions, minds or shared social ideas, all of which are essential to the conception of states and the understanding and practice of morality.

In chapter 5 I argue that international theory must be normative in principle, because of the unique character and powers of human beings. Only human beings can imagine everything there is, and order the whole of reality—a capacity which makes for human dominance and ultimately morality itself.

In chapter 6 I show how we think hierarchically, to make judgments which enhance our vision of reality and define its parts with precision—allowing a clear idea of the world with all human relations in it, and so prescriptions for change.

In Part III of the book I ask what kind of collective agency is conceivable in the unreformed states system of today. In chapter 7

I stress the inequality, discontinuity, and rigidity of the system. The peoples captured by its borders and institutions are, I say, not effective communities, and so are unable to be metamorphosed as collective (state) agents.

This position is supported, in chapter 8, by a survey of contemporary theories of nationhood, which fail comprehensively to agree. And since it is people in the form of nations who are held to give life to states, I argue that there is no agreed conception of states either.

In chapter 9 I outline the various functions that the state-as-agent is conventionally held to fulfill, and refute them in turn.

In Part IV of the book I appraise some debates in international theory in the light of my thesis. In chapter 10 I consider the most recent writing, where I find a failure to come to grips with practical problems and a neglect of normative thinking.

Next I examine Kantian approaches, first as political idealism (chapter 11), then as the metaphysics of Enlightenment underlying modernity (chapter 12).

In my Conclusion I turn to prescription, addressing the moral concerns I have set out. I also inquire what would be needed to make states more like human agents, and the consequences of such change.

What Kind of Normative Theory?

Some analysts would be inclined to call my approach Kantian or cosmopolitan, following the work of the great eighteenth-century philosopher. Kant foresaw in remarkable detail the evolution of the states system. Crucial questions were asked by him, or are implicit in the paradoxes he raised, about the influence of war on political development and the possibility of a peace-loving community of all humankind. Yet Kant was also rather ambivalent about the future of institutions—a position seen, perhaps unfairly, to reflect a deeper ambivalence in his thinking.

In any case we already live, to my mind, in a Kantian world, where the challenges Kant foresaw have come to fruition. The states system in particular cannot be an end in itself. For if societies are naturally—culturally—distinct, there is little hope for a system of divisions to represent us all uniformly to each other; and if there is a common humanity transcending cultural differences, then to give those divisions rights and powers of their own is pointless, even destructive. This is the problem of state agents. The idea is a cul-de-sac on the road of human evolution.

What exacerbates the dilemma into a cause of conflict is that the states system reinforces original inequalities. The logical next step would be for the states themselves to evolve, to become more alike and equal in material terms and the human potential they contain. But that is easier said than done, when state agency itself goes inadequately examined.

One way forward is to focus on the moral concerns that this impasse throws up. I have named four. International theorists, I suggest, should lead the way to a better world by investigating what kind of society emerges from the attempt to resolve them in an integrated way. In the process we may link arms with philosophers, who come at the question from the opposite direction, that of individuals and human nature. I can imagine no clear outcome to this enterprise, though I have no doubt our thinking would together be transformed.

I begin this book with the commonest commonplace of international theory, to expose it as a meaningless cliché. In the masterly hands of Hobbes, it was elaborated into a shock formula for organized society, a reading of history as civilization's failure. Kant sought to rescue morality from Hobbes and create the structures of modernity, but Kant's influence is coming to an end. In the Cold War, politicians disagreeing over another philosopher almost brought the world to an end. Hence the challenges of our time. These are primary and profound. Philosophers have done much to define the modern world. The point of international theory is to change it.

Note

1.   Chris Brown, *Understanding International Relations* (Basingstoke: Macmillan, 1997), pp. vii–viii and 18.

I

Against the Conventional Wisdom

1

A Troublesome Abstraction

What do we mean by international relations? Well, in the first place, surely, we think of events in the lives of people in other countries, especially those distant, and so different, from our own. When I heard, from my peaceful Scottish home, of soldiers sent onto the streets of Rangoon to silence the people's call for the government they elected, the difference between my life and life in Burma was forcefully laid bare.

On another level, we think of our actual relations with people in other countries, and by extension with everyone else on earth. What this entails can mean many things. It began, for me, as soon as I grasped the significance of events in Burma, by an involuntary act of imaginative sympathy with Burmese people, and thought of other outsiders' reaction as being the same. Also, however passive outsiders might have remained toward events in Burma, however slight their sense of a tie to people there, it is actions that give life to the inquiry. This understanding first took root in the minds of those reporting events in that country, in the hope of attracting outsiders' attention, and could only grow with outsiders' identification with the people most directly concerned.

The effect on others, near and far, of these openings in the fabric of human consciousness may be great (galvanizing some to action on their own account) or small (some may simply think themselves lucky not to face hard challenges), but will certainly be unavoidable. No one's thinking will afterward be the same, as these contrasts in the human condition crop up, again and again, over the surface of the earth. Some people will put their comfort, even their lives, at risk on behalf of distant strangers.[1] All this is surely why we speak of international *relations* in the first place.

What we do not, as a rule, consider (though in my view we should) is whether there is something inherently problematic—some cultural issue around difference—which draws our attention to life in other countries and leads to the concerns I have mentioned. In the example I began with, it is whether things indispensable for me ("human rights") are indispensable for people elsewhere; and if not, why not. Beneath this question lies the deeper one of whether human nature is, or is not, fundamentally the same everywhere. But while anthropologists come at the question theoretically, to ponder how different humans can be, in time as well as space, in the present the answer is political: it matters, potentially, for all of us what humans in their differences *do*. And that is why, when I examine the differences between my life and life elsewhere, it is collective actions and shared destinies that I light upon; they have meaning in some wider world that eventually includes us all.

By contrast, the modern theory of international relations seems to have been ruled by something else entirely: the idea of relations between—even actions by!—states. Take this Reader from 1989, in which Marc Williams offered an overview of the field:

> Writers on international relations frequently assert that the state is the main actor in world politics. Most studies of world politics or international politics begin from the assumption that the object of study is the political interactions of sovereign states. . . . Indeed, if we focus, primarily, upon the "actors" in world politics it is difficult to challenge the assumption of the primacy of the state since state forms, and organisations composed of states, not only appear to take the major decisions in international relations but also reserve for themselves the right to do so.[2]

Or take this view from 1961, referring to

> the national state—our primary actor in international relations. This is clearly the traditional focus among Western students, and is the one which dominates almost all of the texts employed in English-speaking colleges and universities.[3]

Take the view from the year 2000:

> Despite a number of trends to the contrary, the state (or the nation-state) has been, and remains, the primary actor in the global system.[4]

Take Hedley Bull's renowned work, *The Anarchical Society* (1977):

> [S]tates are the main actors or agents in world politics.[5]

Or take Olson and Groom's historical survey, in which the object of study is defined, from antiquity, as inter-state relations.[6] Or the so-called English School of theorists, whose first tenet is that there is a "society" of states, based on respect for treaties and the rule of law.[7] Common to all these accounts is the assumption that states are well-defined human entities (who or what else can act?)—either individuals, or groups of individuals acting as one. The assumption is more obvious when *nation*-states are referred to, though this is not always the practice. In addition, it supports the global status quo, since states are the traditional protagonists of diplomacy and international law.[8] But the question remains how state "actors or agents" can conceivably represent us all to each other, and what is to be gained from this way of picturing the world.

1.1 Toward Complexity

During the past half-century, reservations about the traditional focus in international studies have certainly not been lacking. We find them in J. David Singer's 1961 essay, just quoted, on the "level-of-analysis problem." Singer enquired whether the best approach for theorists lay at the level of states or the system of states. In posing this question he made a complex contribution. First, he drew on a discussion by Kenneth Waltz of the causes of war, in which three concentrations of power (individual, state, and states system) were identified. Second, he implicitly criticized the abstract modelling approaches in vogue among his fellow Americans. In addition, he complained that

> in overemphasizing the differences among the many national states, the observer is prone to attribute many of what he conceives to be virtues to his own nation and the vices to others, especially the adversaries of the moment. That this ethnocentrism is by no means an idle fear is borne out by perusal of the major international relations texts published in the United States since 1945. Not only is the world often perceived through the prism of the American national interest, but an inordinate degree of attention (if not spleen) is directed toward the Soviet Union; it would hardly be amiss to observe that most of these might qualify equally well as studies in American foreign policy.[9]

A close examination of Singer's position, however, shows him failing to follow his own reservations through. He begins by observing that whether one opts for the "micro- or macro level of analysis" (the "national state" or the "international system") is "ostensibly a mere matter of methodological or conceptual convenience." And he ends: "the scholar may be more interested in one level than another at any given time and will undoubtedly shift his orientation according to his research needs. So the problem is really not one of deciding which

5

level is most valuable to the discipline as a whole and then demanding that it be adhered to from now unto eternity." Between Singer's opening *ostensibly* and his closing *undoubtedly* there is no deepening of the initial critique. Then he goes astray by couching his argument in terms of systems theory, which means taking states themselves as given. Finally, the easy assumption of states as unified polities may fairly be put in doubt, but a deeper approach is required to show how they cannot be key agents in the system and at the same time varyingly effective, as Singer also contrives to suggest.[10]

Two years earlier Arnold Wolfers had proposed, more simply, "supplements to the [traditional states-as-actors approach] rather than substitutes for it." He suggested introducing analyses of foreign policy and of the activity of intergovernmental organizations (giving the United Nations as an example).[11] This view proved influential. But in retrospect what is still missing is some explanation of how states themselves might act.

Foreign-Policy Analysis

The first proposed supplement was pioneered in the United States by James Rosenau, who went on to lead the field for decades in both theory and empirical studies.[12] From the very beginning, however, foreign-policy analysis seems to have been poorly coordinated with international theory. Otherwise, Wolfers's terms would soon have been exceeded—for example, through the highlighting of divisions within societies, or the effects of diversity (ethnic, cultural, political) between them. But in the event, writers slipped back and forth between the *process* of foreign-policy making and "actor accounts" (of states) in which complexity and diversity scarcely figured. This they did, on occasion, while presenting themselves as critics of both. In 1962 Snyder, Bruck, and Sapin declared:

> We need to carry the actor-situation scheme one step further in an effort to rid ourselves of the troublesome abstraction "state." It is one of our basic methodological choices to define the state as its official decision-makers—those whose authoritative acts are, to all intents and purposes, the acts of the state. *State action is the action taken by those acting in the name of the state.* Hence, the state is its decision-makers.[13]

But this assumption, of course, is open to the challenge that states are more than that—"their" people, for instance—or that the decision-making is influenced by impersonal factors, like territory and resources, as Rosenau stressed. These authors' reductive "methodological choice" for the sake of obtaining effective "actors" deprived them of theoretical subtlety from the outset.

Perhaps inevitably, foreign-policy analysis itself soon became the focus of attention. Graham Allison, in a celebrated study, attacked the image of a "rational" or "unitary" state "actor" on the grounds that this gave a simplistic, over-harmonious image of the making of foreign policy.[14] Allison's was a groundbreaking work, with its detailed, insider-informed account of the Cuban missile crisis a decade earlier. The agents of his version often turned out to be the American government and its bureaucracy *imperfectly* interacting. Hence, in part, the crisis. Yet despite his emphatic demonstrations of complexity, theorists continued to portray states as the actual implementers of these deliberations—figuring by implication in a domain of their own, with an autonomy only a unified entity can display.

In the end, the resolution of the Cuban imbroglio seems to have owed most to a factor not weighed in any of Allison's models: the courage of a few highly-placed individuals (the Kennedy brothers and their helpers) in restraining American retaliation to the Soviet provocation till the Soviet leadership saw sense. For a few days in 1962, they *were* the American state, exactly as Snyder, Bruck, and Sapin imagined. But surely the deeper lesson, which only those few individuals grasped, was the potential of the states system itself to become a problem in human relations; for the dispute over Soviet installations in Cuba arose less from the right to defend people with weapons of mass destruction than from the putative limits of that right.

Foreign-policy analysis after *Essence of Decision*, then, implicitly needed a sense of the world as a whole, conceptually and geographically—an international theory—to enlighten it, or monolithic state "actors" would continue to prevail by default. Wolfers's intervention was misleading, or inadequate. Yet despite their interlocking concerns, the two areas of study have remained largely separate ever since. In this regard, the Cold War and awareness of growing American prominence seem to have had an ambiguous effect—practically stimulating, but intellectually stifling—on a discipline increasingly dominated by Americans.[15] From now on, if authors were to call the unity and autonomy of states into question, this would often be for reasons of *self*-interest—an interest, paradoxically, in reinforcing those attributes, rather than explaining them. Hence Martin Wight's dismissal of the "intellectual and moral

7

poverty" of the international theory of the time. It could be reduced, he said, to "the theory of survival."[16]

Non-state Actors

As for those other "actors" whose study Wolfers had recommended, writers began from the late 1960s to appraise their diversity and range of influence. Most went beyond him, to study the actions and inter-actions of multinational companies and the many informal pressure groups in modern society, and on to supra- and sub-state institutions.

In retrospect, the study of complexity has had enduring but ambigu-ous consequences. First and foremost, the definition of certain "actors" as *non*-state merely added perspective to the traditional "state actor" norm of reference. New and numerous forces might make the world more "interdependent" (a key jargon term of the time[17]), but this leaves unclear how a state—in practice, a state *government*—might exercise the power left over, so to speak, from their activity.

This question lay at the heart of Edward Morse's account of the strengthening of "low" (economic and welfare) policies at the expense of "high" (security) ones, against a background of reduced US-Soviet tensions and expanding trade.[18] Morse's were fluent, confident studies. Yet his focus was on Northern older-industrialized societies, where democracy made for stability as well as transparency. Where theorists perceived a wider challenge to the international status quo they were less sanguine. Seyom Brown veered between empirical observation and strategic anxiety in the face of a new "polyarchy" of power.[19] Talk of "pluralization" and "complex" (Keohane and Nye) or "systemic" interdependence (Morse) suggested a domain where power was more diffused, but the fairness of its distribution was not gone into. More "actors" in international relations does not mean more equal relations.

Or more effective politics. The new accounts failed precisely to locate the capacity for autonomous human action which political theorists seek. "Transnationalism" (Keohane and Nye), evoking heightened cross-border transactions, brought little of substance to the debate. Qualitatively, this new "ism" fell short of the older *inter*nationalism—referring to a breaking-down of all barriers between peoples, not just tariff ones.

Unsurprisingly, "interdependence" itself soon came under fire. How was it to be measured—quantitatively, in terms of human exchange, or qualitatively, in terms of human trust? Was it a real phenomenon, or an idea; a descriptive or a prescriptive term; or just one of many "woolly and redundant blanket concepts" in fashion, as Reynolds and McKinlay argued?[20] Reynolds inquired into how various "non-state actors," from multinationals to trade unions, might affect the behavior of state governments. But as he admitted, the result was a snapshot which took little account of effects over time and was practically limited to speculation about what went on in decision-makers' heads. His conclusion merely restates the "level-of-analysis problem" in more sophisticated terms:

> the problem needs to be examined at two levels: first at the level of direct interplay between non-state actors and state decision-makers, including the influences that each may be able to bring to bear on the decision-making processes and environments of the other; and secondly at the level of the international system, when technological change, political relationships, and systemic structures all condition the outcome that would otherwise result from state and non-state actor interplay.

International theory emerging like this, as the sum of all transactions, implied a research agenda as wide as the world itself. As Reynolds wrote, "[interdependence] was used to cover such wide and disparate ranges of phenomena that it virtually became a summary description of the current state of the international system, in which it was impossible to disentangle cause, consequence, and manifestation."[21]

Cold War Ambivalence and Détente

The ambiguities of interdependence and its related concepts owe much, in my view, to their promoters' ambivalence toward new-fangled complexity in international relations. This was a logical reaction, as far as it went. *Inter*-dependence, between societies set up as *in*-dependent states, must simultaneously batten on and undermine the established structure of their relations. States are required for the mechanisms by which cross-border transactions are both stimulated and regulated; but proliferating human exchange, and the entrusting of transactions to non-state organizations, can unsettle the system of borders and state possessions altogether. To most people this might seem no bad thing. But in the Cold War the need to maintain stable deterrence as the central structure of policymaking was the major concern. The test, therefore, of the mainly American promoters of interdependence was how far they would accept the dilution of power concentrated in states, including their own.

In the practical domain of foreign policy, after all, power struggles went on as before. The nightmare prospect of nuclear war was manipulated with increasing sophistication by Northern politicians, fed by an ever-growing supply of deterrence doctrine condoned, if not actually produced, by international theorists. And what was the balance of nuclear terror itself but a self-serving US-Soviet mutual dependence, alternately reflecting and disguising a bipolar concentration of state-related power? In the area of trade, transactions in continuous expansion since the Second World War took on an overtly political character, following the emergence of large numbers of former-colonial societies under the guise of newly independent states—the fulfilment of the original UN plan of 1945. Intergovernmental institutions gained in size and importance as a result. The 1970s were the heyday of the New International Economic Order—a move by post-colonial regimes to gain better terms for their raw-material exports, and technological imports, than their colonial predecessors had supported.[22] Yet these newcomers evidently lacked power beyond the closed milieux of UN institutions. The NIEO raised consciousness, rather than income. Against this background interdependence became, for the economist Susan Strange, "a persuasive euphemism for asymmetric independence"—a persistent inequality between North and South in wealth, technology, and influence.[23] Under the US policy of détente, trade was pursued even across the Cold War divide, to defuse flashpoints like the Middle East. Soviet imports of American grain showed the failure of Communist regimes to feed their citizens, while Soviet trade in gold and diamonds with the racist South African regime made Soviet pronouncements on behalf of the world's poor sound hollow. Interdependence as a commercial phenomenon overtook even Communism in the long run.

As both a slogan and a phenomenon, then (the distinction was never properly made), interdependence expressed a pervasive sense of moral compromise, like the stalemate at the heart of the Cold War. It blurred the policy/theory distinction for that reason. The Soviet leadership's image was long damaged by stories of domestic repression; in the United States Kissinger, as National Security Adviser and Secretary of State (1973–77), ruled over weak presidents, one of them paralyzed by corruption. Though Kissinger fulminated against strategic parity, it did nothing to weaken the US-Soviet condominium. On the contrary, détente could confirm it. Détente was his project, whimsically related to *entente* (rapprochement between the older "great powers" of Britain and France). But whereas the latter referred to friendship of a kind, détente merely means relaxation, leisure. The new policy mix was deceptive—compatible, as the European historian Kissinger well understood, with shared strategies of national power.[24] Reversing, but only nominally, Clausewitzian priorities, it was the Cold War conducted by other means. For this scenario American theorists could be seen to write the script, while their Soviet counterparts went through a charade of disagreement.[25]

The functional, economistic bias of interdependence as a concept also gave a highly selective view of the Cold War world. Depicting states as merely one set of "actors" among many meant downplaying the oppression being exercised in their name, through the nuclear balance of terror and sphere-of-influence competition among formerly colonized peoples. As international theory this was morally bankrupt if not actively misleading. It did exactly what its exponents pretended not to do: it took state "actors" for granted. Before long, in any case, the sight of state governments upstaging each other in greed, over a commodity they claimed to own, put paid to the alleged benignity of international economic exchange. After the oil-price shocks of the 1970s, the twin prophets of interdependence came out as apologists for American power.[26]

1.2 Dependency Theory

The point can be made clearer still by showing what interdependence theory and its offshoots excluded: critical scrutiny of the instruments and effects of state-related power in the changing climate of international relations. That is precisely what writers from a broadly Marxist school of thought, also in its heyday in the late 1960s and 1970s, set themselves to achieve.

Dependency theorists, as we now call them, took for granted the political implications of an expanding world economy, as the numbers of registered states grew in leaps and bounds from former British, French, and Portuguese Africa. But they shared neither the premises nor the popularity of the dominant Western commentators. They saw the world economy as unequal and unfair, and their culprit was capitalism. One outcome was the New International Economic Order pursued in the name of former-colonial states in United Nations fora. The NIEO declaration read: "The gap between the developed and the developing countries continues to widen in a system which was established at a time when most of the developing countries did not even exist as independent states and which perpetuates inequality."[27] Dependency theorists, both in and out of government, differed only on the degree of deliberateness behind this conjuncture. With their aid, a sophisticated debate developed on themes originally opened up by Lenin but now relevant in a wholly changed institutional setting.[28]

Interdependence as a concept arose from Northerners debating mainly Northern exchanges, and their objects of study ranged so widely that the result was bound to be impressionistic.[29] No new frameworks of insight emerged, only a superficially more complicated and optimistic image of the global status quo. Dependency theorists, by contrast, were disinterested and internationalist by design: committed to a world of greater equality, not just greater interaction, between societies and individuals, North and South. They also conducted proper research—often dealing in the same data as liberal economists, while arriving at opposite conclusions. The objects of their critique were precise and identifiable in the burgeoning global economy—firms, their employees, and the wages they earned; and the prices of products, including raw materials in the post-colonial South that Northern governments and firms were showing a renewed interest in procuring. What was proposed in dependency theory was nothing less than a comparison of the material circumstances of ordinary people across the world, and the mechanisms by which their daily strivings were controlled. This was the fundamental, the qualitative difference from interdependence theory. But in judging the respective legacies one must again note the influence of the Cold War.

Because the Soviet Union was a closed society, run by a blinkered and sclerotic cabal, the contribution to international theory from that direction was next to nil. Soviet propagandists took the line that Sovietism was an extension of Marxist doctrine, but no one believed them. Soviet "internationalism" in practice, especially after the Second World War, meant competition with Western governments for influence and materials in the former-colonial areas. Economically, however, it was no contest; the power of Western finance was too great.[30] Any real debate, therefore, about justice in international relations, once the system entirely comprised formally independent nations, had to be conducted in the open societies of the West—but also under the shadow of the Cold War, which meant everyone was on one side or the other, like it or not. As a result, though interdependence and dependency theorists were contemporaries with a common theme (the implications of the growing world economy), their writings developed separately, with little debate between them. Interdependence specialists were, and remained, transactionist or functionalist theorists; dependency theorists were, and remained, radical economists and political activists, and never the twain would meet.

After Marx

One question that the radicals asked, and that remains open despite the end of the Cold War, was the continuing relevance of Marx's doctrine, with its emphasis on exploitation and liberation from exploitation. The more dogmatic among them might preach that only a world revolution would put right the injustices of capitalism, but this solution was ruled out from the first by the danger of nuclear war. Yet merely to question the potential for abuse of power in the new, universal system of states was to bring Marxist doctrine up to date and to situate it on its proper—philosophical—level.

Marx had argued that industrial development would lead to the dispossessed uniting everywhere to seize state power. He was saved from a full test of this view by the uneven development of industry in nineteenth-century Europe—which impeded the spread of syndicalism—and by the fact of colonial empires. For the same reason he was saved from a test of his views on human nature—views moralistically inclined but imbued with biological determinism. His ideas were in any case put forward at a time when most people in the world lived in rural or colonial, not centralized or industrial, societies. All this has changed. Everyone alive today has grown up under the aegis of a centrally organized, nominally independent state; and the norm of this system is industrial economic development, fostered or actually run in the name of personal and political progress.

Dependency theorists drew the logical conclusion, mapping Marx's theory of classes onto international relations through an image of "center" and "periphery." The workers of the older-industrialized countries, at the center of the world economy, were portrayed as fatally compromised: at war simultaneously with "their" capitalists at home and with their working-class coevals in the ex-colonial periphery, who had every interest in industrial development of their own. In this picture of the world as an single, exploitative society there was also room for a collaborator class of individuals who, with the help of inherited wealth or power, sought to promote private, export-linked growth and so unite periphery and center—lining their own pockets while contributing to the worldwide depression of wages.

This was a proper theory of international relations, if still an economistic one; it had the symmetry of a logical and comprehensive vision of the world. It brought to birth, and humanized, the stilted doctrine of Marx's own writings, trapped between prophecy and determinism.[31]

Its protagonists were real people—capitalists and their servants in state governments or firms, bound together by a shared, though unequally shared, aim. Naturally this included the *nomenklatura* of Communist societies, who affected to abhor the developing conjuncture while benefiting personally and politically from it.

The dependency theorists also acted as conscience keepers for the official critics of the system in the South. It went without saying, after 1945, that colonial frontiers would form the boundaries of the new states, enclosing marketable assets. The governments lobbying for the New International Economic Order were all too conscious of their newly bestowed sovereignty, a windfall of pure power with material windfalls in its train. The 1974 declaration, perhaps the most ambitious reparations claim in history, insisted on "the right of all States, territories and peoples under foreign occupation, alien and colonial domination or *apartheid* to restitution and full compensation for the exploitation and depletion of, and damages to, the natural resources and all other resources of those States, territories and peoples."[32] But the putative rights of *states* did not then, and do not now, include a promise of fair redistribution among wrongly deprived *peoples* of any wealth recovered, any assets revalued, after the desired overthrow of colonial rule. Justice between states does not mean justice within them. To most dependency theorists, the NIEO was merely bourgeois nationalism writ large. State capitalists were just profiteers of a different kind.

These radical critics, then, whether Marxist or merely *Marxisant*, gave to international theory a picture of genuine moral complexity and a notional position of impartiality from which to judge it. By identifying an unjust global conjuncture, they enlarged the scope of international theory and deepened its thrust. Single-handedly, they founded political economy for the machine age.[33] Following the end of the Cold War and the disappearance of Communism, their theme of inter-capitalist rivalry mediated by state governments became the core preoccupation of liberal economics (ironically turned, in a spirit of triumphalism, to improving the efficiency of capitalism itself).

In retrospect, what is missing from their work is some sense of how East-West and North-South relations interacted in the Cold War—a perspective uniting economic and security concerns in a single vision. If Marxism is a conspiracy theory applied to all human relations, they supplied ample material evidence for it; yet no more than Marx did they address the question of human nature itself. That omission is perhaps as accountable to the oppressive political climate of the times as to the economic focus of their work—at least if, as Martin Wight implied, international theory was impossible before the Cold War was over.

As political thinkers, the dependency theorists were marginalized, often written off as Communists—akin to being called a traitor or subversive. But if some of them failed to overcome Marx's determinism, they did so for understandable reasons. One is that they saw themselves as economists rather than international theorists. The other, far more important, is that their approach had a moral orientation in a political environment hostile to such thinking. The only real divergence between them turned on Marx's own ambivalence toward capitalism: whether its expansion should be grimly welcomed as leading to its own destruction or condemned for the short-term social harm.[34] But this was a divergence about means, not ends. Their concerns were always broadly moral—more so, in a sense, than Marx's own, because they had to confront a world in which his prediction of universal capitalist development came true.

Most obviously, it came true through the universal states system, which settled states as exploitable possessions on the whole of humankind—a formalization of property in land which helped to trigger the worldwide struggle of the Cold War. The subsequent nuclear standoff forced everyone for decades into different camps. Under these conditions, a critique of moral complexity was unlikely to receive support from those who thought of themselves as professional international theorists first. Some of them drew strength precisely from rejecting moral complexity; the Cold War was their cause.

1.3 Realism and Its Critics

Realist international theory (in older language, "power politics" or *realpolitik*) is characterized by scepticism about the place of morality in a world ostensibly ruled by brute force. Wars, and the failure of diplomacy to avert or resolve them, supply the root justification for this scepticism, best seen before 1945 in the work of E. H. Carr, with Thucydides, Machiavelli, and Hobbes in the historical background.[35] The relevant picture of international relations is of a disordered competition between societies, in contrast to the underlying order of life within them. In this precarious domain, political accountability is limited to the ability of leaders to act effectively. To act, if necessary, brutally: better to be strong than to be a fool, even at the risk of appearing a knave.

State "actors" occupy a logical, indeed central place in this view of things. It is a commonplace that no one, in the absence of unified thinking, can act effectively in his or her existence. Without unified *collective* thinking, there can be no effective action on behalf of society as a whole. In Realism the emphasis is compounded: without unified action at the global level there is no power to keep the peace, and prevent disorder, among all humankind. For this purpose, created states are taken as identical to the societies housed by them. States *can* be "the main actors or agents" in international relations, because they *must.*

Still, many might feel something important is being glossed over in this remorseless progression: the possibility, however faint, of a general interest in peace which would eliminate the need for a special *state* power of intervention in human affairs. The Realist reply is once again to stress expediency: an absolute ordering concentration of power is required, at the best of times as at the worst, in a domain beset by extraordinary uncertainty and dissent. But of course such a domain is exactly what the systematic, but unequal, distribution of assets among autonomous "actors" is likely to turn into—a process initiated for the world as a whole in 1945. Pursuing the Realist thesis beyond this point threatens to turn it into tautology and the Realist claim to preeminence into arrogance.

Tautology

A tautology is a logical error: a thought, or form of words, with ostensibly different components which are semantically the same. The classic example from philosophy is "All bachelors are unmarried men." Or consider: "All university teachers are lecturers." Insofar as university teaching means to lecture, this sentence says the same thing twice. Its import is unstable. When we have read it we have effectively read nothing.

Taking states and their inhabitants to be identical without qualification is a form of tautology. Clearly, states represent some kind of human thing—but ask yourself what kind of thing. To my mind, only societies as a whole can conceive of states; but who knows, since 1945, whether this is not just a reaction to the fact of the universal states system? Sometimes a tautology is singled out as a platitude, an assertion which is banal because self-evident. Certainly we can say of both a platitude and a tautology that they contain nothing new. But only in a tautology can the components be reversed (all unmarried men are bachelors, all lecturers are university teachers). This verbal sleight of hand may be likened to the tenet of conventional international theory that all states are "actors," and all (or for Realists, the most effective) "actors" are states. But again, this is equivalent to saying nothing at all.

Real political action in any case can hardly be so lightly conceived. People in a divided society may for a number of reasons come drastically to undermine their own, or their leaders', freedom to act, despite all the attempts of the politicians or the prescriptions of political thinkers. Multiple instances of such undermining may, even harmlessly, be at work in the world at any one time, giving rise to the image of a disorderly domain. But this image relates to the effect of a phenomenon, not its cause. If international Realists ever stop to consider this fact, they do so only to reject it as either too troubling or too complicating. Yet what, you might ask, are states, if not something social; and may not the disorder that Realists perceive be simply the sign of a legitimate desire for change?

The Attack on Realism

With the end of the Cold War in sight two authors, Richard Ashley and Rob Walker, began a campaign along these lines. Both claimed that sovereignty, the archetypal feature of states and the basis of their attributive autonomy, had no deep justification; it was merely a device to control competition over territory and the speed of social and technological change. In Walker's view, to distinguish rigidly between "a locus of authentic politics within and a mere space of relations between states" meant underplaying the life opportunities offered by modern society.[36] For David Campbell, Realism encouraged an unjustified "faith in the autonomy of the international and its contempt for the normative."[37] Ashley specifically accused "neo"-Realists of fostering "the state-as-actor illusion in their conception of the international system."[38]

Justin Rosenberg focused his attack on classic works by Carr, Morgenthau, and Waltz. The idea of autonomous states, he said, was undermined by transnational capitalism, and the idea of unitary ones by progressive social movements—a trend, moreover, that was older than the twentieth century. The state of Realist doctrine could be preserved only by a conspiracy in which theorists were complicit with political practitioners, themselves complicit with seekers after private gain. In his analysis Rosenberg combined the practical insights of interdependence with the political thrust of dependency theory, placing international realism alongside economic neoliberalism in a world where the manipulation of power had never ceased to grow. The result, in its crudest (Morgenthau's) form, was "frankly a diplomats' manual of statecraft"—in general, an ideology of raison d'état (attachment to states for their own sake, out of insecurity or greed for power). The domestic domain could not be separated from the international, or the political from the economic—or from the moral, when it came to judging the use of power.[39] Or as Kimberly Hutchings put it, in Realism one should see not just a domestic/international, but a "morality/politics" divide.[40]

Attacks on Realism in its own terms, like these, had their effect. Almost all variants of the approach lost the dominant position they had had since the end of the Second World War. Morgenthau, once a canonical author, slipped down the scale of esteem. Carr was rehabilitated as someone who had distanced himself both from Realism and from the naive idealism that Realists condemned.[41]

A Pervasive Orthodoxy

The unmasking of Realist preconceptions must count as one of the most significant steps forward in international theory since its foundation as an academic discipline in the early twentieth century. Yet paradoxically, the new counter-Realist approaches still fell short of eliminating the "actor" role conventionally attributed to states. It is implicitly there, for instance, in Walker's allowance for "relations between states." (Physicists may study the relations of atoms, but that is not the same thing). Ashley rather confusingly wrote:

> Succinctly put, the state is *not the only actor* whose conduct makes a difference in the determination of consequential international political outcomes, and upon inspection, even the social entity to which the signifier "state" might be appended is seen to be a complex amalgam of potentially contesting individuals and agencies, each of which can be understood as an actor in its own right.[42]

What this comment leaves unclear is how "potentially contesting individuals and agencies" might fuse in Ashley's state "actor," and even whether their contesting is directed at the state as "social entity" or at each other. Nor is it evident how a "complex amalgam" might bring about "consequential international political outcomes." In this way the whole idea of effective political action is called into question—perhaps more than Ashley intended.

Meanwhile, Realists still had their champions. In Britain, Alan James argued:

> Whenever human beings band together to act collectively, the collectivity which is so created must, if it is to fulfil its purpose, be deemed to have the capacity to act as a unit. Some decision-making procedure

must then be established, and authority given to certain persons to speak in the unit's name. In these ways the abstraction, the notional entity, can be seen as having a quasi-independent life, and can engage in relations with others of its kind. There is no other way in which collective entities can operate. Accordingly, the collective entities known as sovereign states may properly, and must, be conceived as single units. Any attempt, therefore, to ignore or deny the unitary nature of states is an attempt to ignore or deny the conceptualizing device which is crucial for the very existence of inter-state relations . . . the fact that externally the state is deemed to be a single entity, a notional person, in no way contradicts the insight that within the state there is much competitive activity.[43]

On closer inspection, however, key questions go unanswered here. A unified state might be necessary for "inter-state relations," but what first gives life to these relations? Exactly what form of *human* relations are possible between a "notional person" and "others of its kind"? And if effective action requires "authority given to certain persons to speak in [the state]'s name," surely this delegation of power to those real persons is intended precisely to *avoid* states acquiring "a quasi-independent life." Meanwhile, individuals and groups in society may have good and sincere reasons to be, and to remain, divided in themselves; in which case mere expediency, not authority, is involved in calling on a "unitary actor" to embody them politically.

In fact, as becomes clear, James's approach is absolutely dependent on the Realist paradigm of international relations, in a precise illustration of the tautological element in it. For Realists, concentrated state power depends on "the capacity to act as a unit," while unity and personality, as mutually reinforcing, are taken for granted. Now "the Realists speak this way," according to James, "because that is how states have chosen [*sic*] to play the international game." Here state "persons" and political unaccountability are together assumed. "And indeed, if there is to be such a game, there is no other way in which it could be played." Here an identity of views between international theorists and Realist governments is assumed—placing the theorists, controversially, on the side of the powers that be. Yet "[Realist theorists] are in step both with what is logically necessary and with international practice in deeming states to be notional persons." Here the rightness of the *status quo ante* is assumed. But that is precisely what no one of independent mind should do.[44]

Surely then the radical critics had a point: what passed for a Realist description of international relations was a self-fulfilling prophecy.

The only question is why the critics did not have more success. Partly, perhaps, because of their inability to believe in their own instincts. Even Rosenberg could write: "states do perforce routinely pursue [*sic*] strategies in the international arena which must take into account the interests and behaviour [*sic*] of other states." This was to admit through his language what he took such pains to avoid (Carr's "irreducible category" of "the agency of the state"). He went on to explain in more Marxist terms that state "actors" really could exist, but only when states were monopolized for oppressive ends—which Realists pretended not to notice, or tried by other means to justify. What was needed, he argued, was an explicit counter-theory to "the one extrapolated from normative political theory" by Realists:

> there appears to be no parallel as yet within IR with the way in which the tradition of normative political theory was overtaken by political sociology. On the day that IR scholars too break with the Hobbesian problematic of "why must we support the coercive activities of the state." . . . [O]n that day the stranglehold of Realism on IR as a social science will begin to loosen.[45]

The political theorist Roy Jones, however, would have none of this. Reviving arguments from Raymond Aron and Martin Wight, he attacked the idea of international relations as a discipline with terms and principles of its own. He accepted Wight's question ("Why is there no international theory?") but rejected Wight's pessimism about the times. On the contrary, Jones argued, the development of democracy in Europe and North America had led, as Kant hoped, to "a large network of perpetual peace," as against "the crude environment of mutually hostile, discrete sovereigns to which [international theory] is mistakenly required to refer. . . . The answer to Wight's special case question is not Wight's. There is no international theory because there is no need for international theory." Politics was part of the normal and not-unsuccessful search for social order at the state, interstate, and cross-state levels, through myriad forms of human striving and exchange. States were the end of this process, not its instigators. "The state, as such, is not an international actor," said Jones, "because it is not itself an actor of any kind."[46]

1.4 Flights to Abstraction

Still, this was not a lesson that international theorists appeared ready to absorb. In the late Cold War a new discussion developed, again from a critique of Realism, on the relative autonomy of states and the states system. This was the "level-of-analysis problem" approached via a distinction from social theory, between "agents" and "structures."[47]

Again the key starting point was a work by Kenneth Waltz.[48] In the process, an established philosophical term was recovered: actions in society, or international relations, as the product of agents. The "structure" here was the states system, in which Waltz saw the concentration of power as conditioning—or rather, in a contradiction of classical views, emasculating—the independent action of states in the mass (hence the "neo" attached to his Realism). If all is structure, what place is left for (state) agents?

On this point the debate's founding father, Alexander Wendt, might differ, but only through an anthropomorphic account in which states figured literally as human individuals, like persons, at liberty in the world. State agency was already assumed by him; one of his titles tells us so.[49] In the end he went further, asserting:

> For even empirically-oriented IR scholars . . . there is a question of whether states *should* be persons. Relative to the alternatives, I believe that a strong argument can be made that they should, notwithstanding its potential costs: states help bring order, and yes, even justice to the world, and if we want to have states then it is better they take the form of persons rather than something more amorphous, because this will help make their effects more politically accountable.

Yet this was a strange, almost ironic proposal, in a strange passage. For a start, among "IR scholars" it is precisely the "empirically oriented" who have shown the least interest in opening up the question of state agency, still less in asking "whether states *should* be persons" (notice how Wendt smuggles in the modal). At this point, however, so far from explaining how states might act, Wendt took refuge in an implausible detachment. "IR scholars," he wrote (carefully avoiding presenting himself as one), "routinely treat state persons 'as if' they were real. Given IR's claim to authoritative knowledge about world politics, the continual performance of this narrative in IR theory contributes importantly to making this 'fantasy' a reality." So why not take the scholars at their word?[50]

This camp approach to human social action explained nothing about what kind of beings "state persons" might be. And it is hard to see how any international theorist—even one wanting dubiously to pose as a "scholar" or exponent of "authoritative knowledge" in an overtly political domain—could justify his or her pursuit of "fantasy."[51] For the rest, Wendt's contribution, introducing ideas from outside international studies (social theory, constructivism, scientific realism) set off a complex discussion that continues today—but one largely devoid of references to real people and events.[52]

On Wendt and state "personhood," Patrick Thaddeus Jackson later remarked: "If states are persons, and the principal persons in world politics, then elements of world politics not having to do with states and state action are necessarily backgrounded; likewise, if the state is not a person, or not the principal person in world politics, other actors or forces may emerge as more prominent factors."[53] But here again comes the Realism-inspired slide between state actors/agents and states as primary actors/agents, in which the issue of how states themselves might act is glossed over.

The real challenge at the time, I would say, was to overcome not just the aggressive mind-set of Realism but its impact on the structure of theory itself, namely the normalization of state agency even in the minds of those who would distance themselves from moral scepticism. It is power, rather than agency, that preoccupies Realists; for them the burning question is not how states can act, but how some states can concentrate more power than others. In this view state agency, as the mere *capacity* for action, is taken for granted. So for Jackson even to have inquired after the principal "person in world politics" was to fall into the trap of Realist closed thinking. Persons did not come into it at all.

Waltz's critics in the debate, in fact, missed the obvious explanation of his grand depiction of immobility in the relations of powers—that it was not theory proper, but merely a description of the international status quo of the late Cold War. From an early stage, Waltz had been one of the few Realists to push deterrence doctrine to its logical limit, seeing in the growth of nuclear arsenals the result of policies since 1945— which included the weapons' "success" in keeping the peace internationally. By the late 1970s, the interdependence theorists were evoking the expanded opportunities for trade and human exchange under the US-Soviet condominium—and in their stress on the new vibrancy of *non*-state actors, sidelining traditional state ones. Waltz in his doctrine turned interdependence upside down, to focus on those sidelined states—but to make the case for deterrence, indefinitely. As he revealed in dedicated tracts, he favored nuclear proliferation as a means of slowing (and therefore controlling) the pace of international change.[54] In his vision of the world, states move as flies trapped on flypaper do—futilely, to demonstrate the pointlessness of all politics for the yawning god-kings of nuclear strategy like himself.

Still, Waltz did not follow up his own depressing formula to advocate the immediate worldwide distribution of nuclear weapons—merely a gradual, impersonal "spread." This captious reservation, postponing Utopia to the Greek calends, allowed for a few advanced societies, like his own, to stay technologically, indefinitely, ahead of the rest. Not so *neo*-Realist, then, nor so radical, after all: just another blueprint for great-power hegemony, but one even more sinister and dangerous than before.

"Post"-

Beyond the agent-structure debate, the end of the Cold War itself contributed to the erosion of Realism's security-oriented premises. Support for new thinking in international theory became widespread. Steve Smith claimed that post-modernism offered

> alternatives to the dominance of a very restrictive positivism, a methodology licensed by a stark empiricist epistemology that combines with it to *determine* the ontology of the world of international relations. These, after all, are the people who brought you the "state as actor" and "war as a natural phenomenon."[55]

The longer-term effect of the post-modern turn, however (with its own post-posts), seems to have been to weaken empiricism in general, to the detriment of practical social study and political change. Large numbers of people, breathing the intellectual laughing-gas of Derrida and Deleuze, have found themselves transported, like Alice in Wonderland, into a surreal game of dissidence where words are twisted into curiouser and curiouser forms, and an addiction to neologism weakens the victim's will to escape. But in my view, the original flight from political reality was a dereliction of duty in itself, when everyone else was struggling, like Alice, with torpid geriatrics and slashing Red Queens.[56]

Even Smith, while enthusiastically supporting new developments in international theory, and blaming the dominance of Realism on US hegemony, seemed unable quite to break the conventional mold. In his 2003 address to the International Studies Association, he declared:

> International Relations theory has almost been defined by its worship of the state-as-actor, and the consequent downplaying of the role, or

fate, of individuals or other actors. And, of course, there is a powerful circularity in all of this. The state becomes reified, and its centrality to how the discipline sees the world becomes tautological. There is no space for other actors, except as amendments or additions to the rule that the state is the core actor in international relations.

"Space for other actors," however, still implies states as "actors" in their own right.[57]

Following the peaceful, almost accidental resolution of the Cold War, there is good reason to regard Realist international theorists, whether in or out of power, as inherently shortsighted or in bad faith. All of which suggests there was no need to take refuge in abstraction to oppose them in the first place. The truth of this argument was demonstrated by Peter Willetts, who extended his earlier empirical research on non-state actors into an attack on Realist state-centrism and state agency itself. This was a logical step. The members of any non- or sub-state body, from local councils to charities and international pressure groups like Greenpeace and Amnesty International, must show quantifiable results from their state-*independent* activity, to justify their existence to their members and governments alike, and qualify to take part in broad political debate. At the same time, in an ever more institutionalized setting we may well ask what is left of states' own political rationale (this was the question that the interdependence theorists had neglected to pursue).

Willetts made four points. First, "the state as a legal person" was "a highly abstract fiction" often confused with governments and "countries." Second, there was a lack of similarity between countries/states in many practical respects, and so no typical actor/agent among them. Third, the Realist image of an "anarchical international system" encouraged the false idea of unified agents, misrepresenting "transnational relations and intergovernmental relations" simultaneously. Fourth, the universal assumption of nation-states glossed over the conceptual difference between a state and a nation. A nation-state, said Willetts, "would exist if nearly all the members of a single nation were organized in a single state, without any other national communities being present. Although the term is widely used, no such entities exist."[58]

1.5 Globalis/zation

Despite this comprehensive and, in its own way, persuasive attack, state agents have remained in widespread intellectual currency in international theory—coming under different emphases, but neither deeply doubted nor fully explained. With the rise of the globalis/zation thesis they were threatened again.[59]

This thesis, however, is in many respects just an updated interdependence. (Compare definitions: Globalization: "a process of increasing interconnectedness between societies such that events in one part of the world increasingly have effects on peoples and societies far away." Interdependence: "a condition where states (or peoples) are affected by decisions taken by others."[60]) The updating consists chiefly in an image of information communicated, and transactions conducted, electronically and near instantaneously—with consequences for everyone, but largely bypassing the mediation of state governments. How far a real phenomenon is involved, however, is debatable, just as the parameters of interdependence were never properly defined. Meanwhile, the recurrent pressures for social controls on specific Internet subjects, and local Internet controls imposed by governments for their own ends, have worked, and continue to work, against the ideal image of unlimited worldwide communication.

Besides, in this discussion state agency is once again neither excluded nor necessarily downplayed. For example, the recession-fuelling credit crunch of 2007–8 was generally blamed on the failure of certain governments to control cross-border financial activities for which their states were the putative lenders of last resort. These activities had been opportunistically seized and manipulated by a relatively small number of individuals exploiting developments in electronic communication (one of those "accelerative tendencies" of modernity to which Walker referred). Seen in this light, the economic crisis was a failure of the states system itself, through either an excess of interdependence, or an insufficiency of regulation of cross-border activity, which state governments might subsequently remedy. Moreover, the crisis was concentrated in one particular geographical area, what has been called the North Atlantic community. Not only is this the most highly inter-linked area in the world electronically, and therefore untypical of the world as a whole; but public debate in these societies is marked by a diversity of opinion on the socioeconomic purpose of states (regulation or deregulation; restraint or stimulus; Milton Friedman or Maynard Keynes?) So all in all, one might ask whether the crisis was global or less than global; accidental or caused; even, in some imaginary long term, "good" or "bad."

Anthony McGrew, attempting a definition of globalis/zation, evokes "a multidimensional process" taking place on the economic, military,

legal, ecological, cultural, and social levels at once;[61] a set of changes
in which everything seems to happen faster and more widely—*than
before*, is the implication. But what is before, in this context, and how do
we measure the changes? What unites them in one "process"? The very
term (globalis/zation) implies unity, because there is only one globe,
only one earth, and if what is being referred to were not in some sense
a single process it would hardly be identifiable against the historical
past. A neologism, however, does not prove a phenomenon.

Next, McGrew admits to the controversial nature of his definition,
to qualify it further: as a diffusion of power from the state to the global
level, involving many individuals and groups in institutional contexts of
varying formality. Yet this shift (from "globalization" to "global politics")
is a fundamental change of perspective, from empirical/sociological
to political/philosophical; from observable, quantifiable phenomena
to subjective, accountable human actions. And even then problems
persist, such as: what kind of politics is global politics? where does it
take place as an organized activity?—if everywhere, surely nowhere.
Significantly, one of McGrew's favoured terms ("space"[62]) suggests
emptiness, rootlessness.

In a further shift, he extends his (already polysemic) definition to
include a lack of democracy or fairness: "as with globalization, inequality and exclusion are endemic features of contemporary global politics."

> [T]hree factors in particular are crucial: first, enormous inequalities
> of power between states; second, global governance is shaped by
> powerful interests and global capital; third, the technocratic nature
> of much global decision-making, from health to security, tends to
> exclude many with a legitimate stake in the outcomes.[63]

Now the first factor evoked here implies state agency as the continuing
practice of choice among international theorists (who include, in this
context, McGrew himself[64]). The second points, as the dependency
theorists did, to disguised human agents undermining the general interests of citizens, including through state governments. The third refers
to the anomic impact on society of non-human agents (machines). No
clear picture of agency emerges. In the same place McGrew condemns
the "distorted" nature of "global politics"—distorted, that is, in favor
of "those states and groups [*sic*] with greater power, resources and
access to key sites of global decision-making"—a situation that "sits
in significant tension with a world in which democracy is generally
valued." This fuzzy declaration once made, however, he shuffles off the

discussion to another set of colleagues: "Whether a more democratic or just global politics is imaginable, and what it might look like, is the concern of normative theorists examined in later chapters in this volume."[65] Dividing up the subject in this way rather goes against the idea of global concerns and concepts in the first place.

One might also refer here in passing to the obvious tautology in Jan Aart Scholte's definition of globalis/zation, to the effect that "the global sphere is a web of transborder networks."[66] For a globe is a sphere, and a sphere is a globe—not to mention that a web is also a net. Errors like Scholte's occur when the theorist lacks a clear sense of the world.

1.6 The Textbook View

In any event, most academic teachers of International Relations, in the age of globalis/zation, have continued to write as if the idea of state agents still meant something. Nor has the convention been dethroned among political practitioners; nor, as a result, has the awkward relation between the two groups been greatly clarified.

Along quasi-reformist lines Baylis, Smith, and Owens warn, in the sixth edition of their textbook, as Baylis and Smith did in the first, against seeing relations "between states," Realist style, as primary: "Our focus is on the patterns of political relations, defined broadly, that characterize the contemporary world. Many will be between states, but many—and perhaps most—will not."[67] But of course "political" relations are relations between human subjects—people accountable to others, and to their own consciences, for their actions. Such relations are between states only insofar as states themselves are seen as species of humans. State agency lurks as an unexamined assumption under this statement of intent.

More generally these authors have placed a pervasive emphasis on globalis/zation, beginning with their book's title. But confusingly: they subtitled it an "introduction to international relations"—as if these relations, not globalis/zation or their alternative, world politics, formed the focus of interest. Besides, though what makes a nation is debatable, the term undoubtedly refers to some kind of voluntary human group, capable in theory of collective action, including toward other such groups. So international relations are by implication political and of interest to us all. We never needed to be told that they were global.

Determined, nevertheless, to avoid traditional terminology, the authors stuck with their title, inviting study through one edition after another of *The Globalization of World Politics*. But this merely means, does it not, the worldization of world politics. When we have read this title we have read nothing.

In the light of these uncertainties, most textbook writers will settle for outlining other people's theories. So for Baylis, Smith, and Owens again, international Realists hold that "the main actors on the world stage are states," while Liberals "question the idea that the state is the main actor on the world political stage"; and Marxists, preoccupied by the "world capitalist economy," think that "the most important actors are not states but classes."[68] Meanwhile, Steans and Pettiford outline a "Critical Theory" model in which "states are not privileged as the only significant actors in IR."[69] Dunne, Kurki, and Smith define "state-centric" approaches as "theories that take as their key onto-logical objects state actors. Mainstream IR theories such as realism, neorealism, and neoliberalism take the state-as-actor as their point of departure."[70] Lake argues that "states are likely to remain central actors in world politics,"[71] while for Kegley and Blanton "the concept of state sovereignty . . . identifies the state as the primary actor today."[72] And in the entry for *state* in Evans and Newnham's International Relations Dictionary, we read: "sometimes called the nation-state, this is the main actor in international relations."[73]

Still—"main actor"; "most important actor"; "significant actor"; "state actors [as] key ontological objects" or as a theoretical "point of depar-ture"; "central actor"; "primary actor"—in these academic presentations the *primacy* of the state actor/agent may be called into question but state agency itself is not.[74] Many of these commentators, moreover, are either from, or based in, Western Europe, unlike the predominantly North American ones quoted earlier—which shows "state-as-actor premises" to be widely tolerated on both sides of the Atlantic.[75]

Around this theme, in fact, Colin Wight has discerned a conspiracy to preserve International Relations as a distinct discipline, especially in the light of the frank suggestion by his older namesake that there need not be one. But look more closely, and you can see his punches being subtly pulled.

> The first step for IR theory, and one upon which its identity might be said to depend, is the construction of the "state-as-agent." . . . Indeed, any denial of the "state-as-agent" thesis might seem to pres-age the end of IR as an academic discipline. There are good reasons, then—reasons related to the division of academic labour—for the widespread acceptance of the "state-as-agent" thesis within the IR academic community. For without the notion of the "state-as-agent,"

> IR appears to be little other than a macro-sociological exercise in political theory or history. Devoid of the notion of the "state-as-agent" the answer to Martin Wight's search for international theory is clear: if the state is not an agent, then international theory just is political theory—although perhaps with a wider spatial remit. Without a notion of the "state-as-agent" the distinction between political theory and international theory collapses.[76]

Yet surely this outcome would not be dire for international theorists—political people of a sort? Their ostensible reluctance, then, to criticize *each other* for clinging to "the 'state-as-agent' thesis" must be due to something more than a mere "division of academic labour." (So tell us, Professor Wight: how many charlatans does it take to change a light bulb?).

1.7 After Realism

As I have recounted, a great deal of effort has been expended in academic International Relations to overcome the influence of Realism. This effort, as part of an attempt at self-criticism from inside the discipline, predates the end of the Cold War. Both then and since, the oppressive "might-is-right" associations of Realism have come under fire. In time, growing numbers of writers have been emboldened to attack Realism's formal characteristics as well—including, from various standpoints, state agency. Yet they have found nothing substantial to put in its place. In any case, in international relations, as the phrase implies, the assumed agent is and always was something else: the nation. Somewhere in the evolution of our studies over the past hundred years, this idea and its implications—of real communities acting with effect on their own behalf, and interacting with others in the process—has been lost.

Lost, or discarded: systematic thinkers at the origin of the Realist vision of the world arguably did no more than take to extremes the impersonality emerging in the structures of modern society. Contemporary Realism is a caricature, not a subversion, of this trend. State agents, as I have pointed out, are enshrined in international law and the traditional diplomatic theory from which politicians take their collective cue. Then in 1945 states were openly made the protagonists of the new universal system—holders of rights without distinction as to culture or values, and so without specific social reference. By contrast, older ideas of nationalism and internationalism date from a time—the European nineteenth century—when nation building and liberal democracy could be portrayed as complementary forms of social progress.

More than anything, it was the Nazi and Soviet-Communist forms of organized human association which put paid to the benign conception of nationalism, and hence to inter-, or shared, national expression as a basis for peaceful relations. So on the eve of the Second World War Carr could assert that historians and diplomats had lost their way by not facing up to reality: gentlemanly suppositions about the willingness of foreigners to keep to agreements and pacifically debate differences did not apply to dictators like Hitler and Stalin. International theorists, in this situation, were not being Realistic enough. In a long tradition rooted in Aristotle and Machiavelli, Carr sought to expose unpleasant truths about human nature linked to the concentration of political power. That was not all he said, but a caricature of the former diplomat's evolving thought opened the door to the hijacking of Realism by Cold Warriors.

The Cold War was the heyday of the monolithic, impersonal, faceless state. Even before 1945, industrialization and closed-boundary jurisdictions had begun to have a dehumanizing effect on social relations. The impact of the nuclear weapon took this further, sealing the new universal system against itself. Realists were the first to understand this development and to reinvent themselves as deterrence theorists— seeing in the global balance of terror an idealized version of their narrow, controlling conception of social order. Under deterrence, there is no practical difference between the state and "its" people: from a victim's point of view, because nuclear weapons are indiscriminate in their effects; from a possessor's point of view, because control of the weapons necessitates a political elite who for all practical purposes *are* the state. Down this road comes the practice of "blackboxing"— "seeing complex structures as simple unitary phenomena" and "states as unitary rational textbook actors."[77] As inhuman "actors" too—open to manipulation by governments for their own ends, including the portrayal, through fear or disdain, of states as independent *of them*. And so to the unaccountable state agent of conventional international theory, hidden somewhere between government and the governed: unreal protagonist of the unreal Cold War world.

As the number of created states multiplied, the world economy grew and the Cold War settled into institutionalized forms, the dominance of Realism-as-deterrence weakened, and complexity entered international theory. By itself this undermined the monolithic state agency to which Realists, didactically, laid claim, but it also left unclear what action for change was possible; hence the minimal and confused import of interdependence and its offshoot, globalis/zation. The ultimate result, in the post-modern turn, was an outright reaction to the epistemological simplicities of Realism. And overreaction: it is not simply the primacy of state agents that is implausible but the whole idea of an inanimate mover in human society. Since the decline of deterrence, which became obvious with the collapse of the Cold War, the problem has had to be addressed anew, in a world left damaged by that conflict, and with the institutions that preceded—and in part caused—it still in need of reform.

What do we mean by international relations? I think that because of the Cold War, theorists have had to begin again to find the answer—and they have not got very far. As I shall show, theorists of the nation comprehensively and often profoundly disagree on what one is. The original protagonist of International Relations is controversial and may be defunct. Yet who is to give life to states, except human beings in some organization larger than the village and the family? Now we all live under states, but it seems there is no agreed conception of them either. A picture, then, of the world as inhabited and run by nation-state agents is so far from reality as to be positively dangerous for the future of our kind.

Unless, as Hobbes suggested, it is all a show, got up for public instruction. So first we have to discover—as the language of the conventional wisdom itself seems to demand—how actors and agents can be the same.

Notes

1. "A British democracy activist arrested in Burma has been sentenced to 17 years in prison. James Mawdsley, 26, from Lancashire, was arrested in the city of Tachilek in north-east Burma, also known as Myanmar, on Tuesday. It was the third time he had been arrested in the country, in which he served a jail term last year, and from which he has been deported twice. This time, Mr Mawdsley was accused of carrying hundreds of pro-democracy leaflets and entering the country illegally." "British activist jailed in Burma," BBC World News Online 2 September 1999. On Burma further see Thant Myint-U, *The River of Lost Footsteps: A Personal History of Burma* (London: Faber and Faber, 2007).

2. Marc Williams, Introduction to chapter 3, "The state in the contemporary world" in Marc Williams (ed.), *International Relations in the Twentieth Century: A Reader* (Basingstoke: Macmillan, 1989), p. 78.

3. J. David Singer, "The level-of-analysis problem in international relations" [1961] in James N. Rosenau (ed.), *International Politics and Foreign Policy: A Reader in Research and Theory* (New York: Free Press, 1969), p. 24.

4. Bruce Russett, Harvey Starr, and David Kinsella, *World Politics: The Menu for Choice* (6th ed. Boston/New York: Bedford/St. Martin's, 2000), p. 47.

5. Hedley Bull, *The Anarchical Society: A Study of Order in World Politics* (Basingstoke: Macmillan, 1977), p. 82.

6. William C. Olson and A. J. R. Groom, *International Relations Then and Now: Origins and Trends in Interpretation* (London: HarperCollins Academic, 1991), pp. 1, 2 and 3.

7. See Alex J. Bellamy (ed.), *International Society and its Critics* (Oxford: Oxford University Press, 2005).

8. G. R. Berridge, Maurice Keens-Soper, and T. G. Otte, *Diplomatic Theory from Machiavelli to Kissinger* (Basingstoke: Palgrave, 2001), p. 1.

9. Singer, "The level-of-analysis problem," p. 24.

10. *Ibid.*, pp. 20, 24, 27, 28.

11. Arnold Wolfers, "The actors in international politics" in William T. R. Fox (ed.), *Theoretical Aspects of International Relations* (Notre Dame, IND: University of Notre Dame Press, 1959), p. 84.

12. Starting, for example, with James N. Rosenau, *The Scientific Study of Foreign Policy* (New York: Free Press, 1971).

13. Richard H. Snyder, H. W. Bruck and Burton Sapin, 'The decision-making approach to the study of international politics' [1962] in Rosenau (ed.), *International Politics and Foreign Policy*, p. 202, emphasis in original.

14. Graham T. Allison, *Essence of Decision: Explaining the Cuban Missile Crisis* (1st ed. Boston: Little, Brown, 1971); 2nd ed. Graham T. Allison and Philip Zelikow (Reading, MA: Addison-Wesley, 1999).

15. Cf. Stanley Hoffmann, *Gulliver's Troubles: or, the Setting of American Foreign Policy* (New York: McGraw-Hill, 1968).

16. Martin Wight, "Why is there no international theory?" in Herbert Butterfield and Martin Wight (eds.), *Diplomatic Investigations* (London: Allen & Unwin, 1966), pp. 20 and 33.

17. See Robert O. Keohane and Joseph S. Nye, *Transnational Relations and World Politics* (Cambridge, MA: Harvard University Press, 1972); (eds.), *Power and Interdependence: World Politics in Transition* (Boston: Little, Brown, 1977).

18. Edward L. Morse, "The transformation of foreign policies: modernization, interdependence, and externalization," *World Politics* 22 (3), April 1970, pp. 371–92; and *Modernization and the Transformation of International Relations* (New York: Free Press, 1976).

19. Seyom Brown, *New Forces in World Politics* (Washington: The Brookings Institution, 1974). More critically, from this time, see Carey B. Joynt and Percy E. Corbett, *Theory and Reality in World Politics* (Basingstoke: Macmillan, 1978).

20. Philip A. Reynolds and Robert D. McKinlay, "The concept of interdependence: its uses and misuses" [1979] in Kjell Goldmann and Gunnar Sjöstedt, *Power, Capabilities, Interdependence: Problems in the Study of International Influence* (Beverly Hills, CA: Sage, 1999), p. 159. See also R. J. Barry Jones and Peter Willetts, *Interdependence on Trial: Studies in the Theory and Reality of Contemporary Interdependence* (London: Frances Pinter, 1984).

21. P. A. Reynolds, "Non-state actors and international outcomes," *British Journal of International Studies* 5 (2), April 1979, pp. 91, 99, 111.

22. See Lars Anell and Birgitta Nygren, *The Developing Countries and the World Economic Order* (London: Methuen, 1980), and Hans W. Singer and Javed A. Ansari, *Rich and Poor Countries: Consequences of International Disorder* (4th ed. London: Unwin Hyman, 1988).

23. Susan Strange, *The Retreat of the State: The Diffusion of Power in the World Economy* (Cambridge: Cambridge University Press, 1996), p. xiii.

24. See Henry A. Kissinger, *A World Restored: Metternich, Castlereagh and the Problems of Peace, 1812–1822* [1957] (London: Phoenix, 2000).

25. G. Shakhnazarov, "Effective factors of international relations," *International Affairs* (Moscow), February 1977, pp. 79–87, clearly shows the influence of "interdependence" and "pluralism."

26. Joseph S. Nye, *Bound to Lead: The Changing Nature of American Power* (New York: Basic Books, 1990) and *Soft Power: The Means to Success in World Politics* (New York: Public Affairs, 2004); Robert O. Keohane, *Power and Governance in a Partially Globalized World* (London/NY: Routledge, 2002). On this phase see also James N. Rosenau (ed.), *Linkage Politics: Essays on the Convergence of National and International Systems* (New York: Free Press, 1969), and *Turbulence in World Politics: A Theory of Change and Continuity* (Princeton: Princeton University Press, 1990), pp. 97–100, 249–52; and Reynolds's review of the latter, "The world of states or the state of the world," *Review of International Studies* 18 (3), July 1992, pp. 261–269.

27. UN General Assembly Resolution 3201 (S-VI), 1 May 1974, para 1.

28. A debate expertly analysed in Anthony Brewer, *Marxist Theories of Imperialism* (2nd ed. London: Routledge, 1990).

29. An early experiment was Karl W. Deutsch, *Political Community and the North Atlantic Area: International Organization in the Light of Historical Experience* [1957] (New York: Greenwood Press, 1969).

30. As argued by Philip Windsor, "The Soviet Union in the international system of the 1980s," Adelphi Paper 151, *Prospects of Soviet Power in the 1980s: Part I* (London: International Institute for Strategic Studies, 1979).

31. See further R. N. Berki, *Insight and Vision: The Problem of Communism in Marx's Thought* (London: Dent 1983).

32. UN General Assembly Resolution 3201 (S–VI), para 4 (3).

33. See especially Adrian Wood, *North-South Trade, Employment and Inequality: Changing Fortunes in a Skill-Driven World* (Oxford: Clarendon Press, 1994); Ethan B. Kapstein, "Workers and the world economy: breaking the postwar bargain," *Foreign Affairs* 75 (3), May/June 1996, pp. 16–37; Manuel Castells, "The informational mode of development and the restructuring of capitalism," and Gary Gereffi, "Rethinking development theory: insights from East Asia and Latin America (1989/1994)," in J. Timmons Roberts and Amy Bellone Hite, *The Globalization and Development Reader: Perspectives on Development and Global Change* (Oxford: Blackwell, 2007).

34. Frank condemned the exploitativeness of trade, while Laclau and Warren insisted that Marx had focused on relations of production, rather than exchange. See Brewer, note 28 above.

35. E. H. Carr, *The Twenty Years' Crisis 1919–1939: An Introduction to the Study of International Relations* [1939] (2nd ed. London: Macmillan, 1946).

36. R. B. J. Walker, *Inside/Outside: International Relations as Political Theory* (Cambridge: Cambridge University Press, 1993), pp. 6 and 20.

37. David Campbell, "International engagements: the politics of North American international relations theory," *Political Theory* 29 (3), June 2001, p. 436.

38. Richard K. Ashley, "The poverty of neorealism," *International Organization* 38 (2), spring 1984, p. 285.

39. Justin Rosenberg, "What's the matter with realism?," *Review of International Studies* 16 (4), Oct 1990, pp. 285–303.

40. Kimberly Hutchings, "The possibility of judgement: moralizing and theorizing in international relations," *Review of International Studies* 18 (1), January 1992, p. 57.

41. Graham Evans, "E. H. Carr and international relations," *British Journal of International Studies* 1 (2), 1975, pp. 77–97; Paul Howe, "The Utopian Realism of E. H. Carr," *Review of International Studies* 20 (3), July 1994, pp. 277–97; Carr, *The Twenty Years' Crisis*, Preface to 2nd edition (1946), p. x.

42. Richard K. Ashley, "Untying the sovereign state: a double reading of the anarchy problematique," *Millennium* 17 (2), summer 1988, p. 244, emphasis added.

43. Alan James, "The realism of realism: the state and the study of International Relations," *Review of International Studies* 15 (3), July 1989, pp. 220–221.

44. *Ibid.* In a clumsy joke about "overkill" in closing (p. 227), James acknowledged an affinity with Realism as deterrence theory, which he then attempted rather unsuccessfully to disguise (p. 229, n. 22).

45. Rosenberg, "What's the matter with realism?," pp. 286, 290, 297, 298.

46. Roy E. Jones, "The myth of the special case in International Relations," *Review of International Studies* 14 (4), October 1988, pp. 269 and 271.

47. Generally dated back to Alexander Wendt, "The agent-structure problem in international relations theory," *International Organization* 41 (3), autumn 1987, pp. 335–70.

48. Kenneth N. Waltz, *Theory of International Politics* (New York: McGraw-Hill, 1979).

49. Alexander Wendt, "Anarchy is what states make of it: the social construction of power politics," *International Organization* 46 (2), 1992, pp. 391–425.

50. Alexander Wendt, "The state as person in international theory," *Review of International Studies* 30 (2), April 2004, p. 316, original emphasis. See also "Forum on the state as a person" in the same volume, pp. 255–87.

51. Peter Lomas, "Anthropomorphism, personification and ethics: a reply to Alexander Wendt," *Review of International Studies* 31 (2), April 2005, p. 355, n. 17.

52. The debate can be traced in the *Review of International Studies*, e.g., Alexander Wendt, "Bridging the theory/meta-theory gap in international relations"; Martin Hollis and Steve Smith, "Beware of gurus: structure and action in international relations," vol. 17 (4), October 1991. Wendt, "Levels of analysis vs. agents and structures: part III"; Hollis and Smith, "Structure and action: further comment," 18 (2), April 1992. Hollis and Smith, "Two stories about structure and agency," 20 (3), July 1994. Vivienne Jabri and Stephen Chan, "The ontologist always rings twice: two more stories about structure and agency"; Hollis and Smith, "A response: why epistemology matters in international theory," 22 (1), January 1996. Hidemi Suganami, "On Wendt's philosophy: a critique," 28 (1), January 2002. Jonathan Joseph, "Hegemony and the structure-agency problem in International Relations: a scientific realist contribution"; Patrick Thaddeus Jackson, "Foregrounding ontology: dualism, monism, and IR theory," 34 (1), January 2008.

53. Patrick Thaddeus Jackson, "Forum introduction: Is the state a person?" *Review of International Studies* 30 (2), April 2004, pp. 257–58.

54. Waltz first propounded this thesis in Adelphi Paper 171, "The Spread of Nuclear Weapons: More May Be Better," (London: International Institute for Strategic Studies, autumn 1981). See also Scott D. Sagan and Kenneth N. Waltz, *The Spread of Nuclear Weapons: A Debate Renewed* (2nd ed. New York/London: Norton, 2005).

55. Steve Smith, "Epistemology, post-modernism and international relations theory: a reply to Østerud," *Journal of Peace Research* 34 (3), 1997, p. 335, emphasis in original.

56. The illness, old age, and conservatism of successive General Secretaries explain the drift in Soviet policymaking from the late 1960s: the relentless nuclear arms buildups, the disastrous invasion of Afghanistan in 1979, and the economic ruin which eventually put paid to the Soviet state and ended the Cold War by default. But not before the US presidency (1980–88) of Ronald Reagan, a reactionary who joked about starting a nuclear attack on the Soviet Union; who as NATO commander-in-chief accepted that a nuclear war "limited to Europe" (and sparing Americans) was possible; and who delayed the end of the Cold War by seeking to undermine the reformist Soviet leader, Gorbachev—countering the Soviet offer of general nuclear disarmament, at Reykjavik in 1986, with the US Strategic Defense Initiative for space-based weapons. On a more charitable view, Reagan's advanced age and ignorance exposed him to manipulation by more articulate and aggressive officials. US diplomacy was eventually rescued by separate support for Gorbachev from British Prime Minister Margaret Thatcher (in office 1979–90), who nevertheless, within two years of coming to power, connived at a 2m increase in British unemployment in the name of liberal economics.

57. Steve Smith, "Singing our world into existence: international relations theory and September 11," *International Studies Quarterly* 48 (3), September 2004, p. 505.

58. Peter Willetts, "Transnational actors and international organizations in global politics," in John Baylis and Steve Smith (eds.), *The Globalization of World Politics: An Introduction to International Relations* (1st ed. Oxford: Oxford University Press, 1997), pp. 287, 289, 290–291.

59. Spelt with an *s* by Europeans, and a *z* by Americans, but given the unstable definition I choose to spell it with both.

60. John Baylis, Steve Smith, and Patricia Owens (eds.), *The Globalization of World Politics* (6th ed. Oxford: Oxford University Press, 2014), pp. 9, 536.

61. Anthony McGrew, "Globalization and global politics" in *ibid.*, p. 21 and box 1.4.

62. E.g., the world as "a shared social space" (3 times); "national economic and political spaces"; "National economic space . . . is no longer coterminous with national territorial space"; "the world literally is transformed into a single social space"; "the entitlement of states to rule within their own territorial space"; "the politics of state and non-state actors within a shared global social space." *Ibid.*, pp. 18, 19, 22, 23, 27, 29.

63. *Ibid.*, p. 29.

64. E.g., "led by the world's emerging powers"; "These emerging BRIC states . . . are driving a South to South globalization and increasingly seeking to alter the rules and institutions of world order to reflect their new found influence and power"; "for many, especially weak states, sovereignty . . . has not always

translated into effective control within their territories"; "the entitlement of states to rule within their own territorial space"; "a more activist state"; "the politics of state and non-state-actors"; "a politics of domination, competition, and contestation amongst powerful states and transnational non-state forces." *Ibid.*, pp. 22, 24, 27, 28, 29.

65. *Ibid.*, p. 29.
66. Jan Aart Scholte, "The globalization of world politics" in John Baylis and Steve Smith (eds.), *The Globalization of World Politics* (2nd ed. Oxford: Oxford University Press, 1997), p. 15.
67. Baylis, Smith, and Owens (eds.), *The Globalization of World Politics* (6th ed. 2014), p. 3; cf. Baylis and Smith (eds.), *The Globalization of World Politics* (1st ed. 1997), p. 3.
68. Baylis, Smith, and Owens (eds.) (6th ed. 2014), pp. 4–5. Elsewhere and earlier, Smith had written that differing views of international anarchy in "neorealism and neoliberalism . . . mask a much wider agreement about the nature of international politics: It involves states as actors; it focuses on patterns of cooperation and conflict; actors are unitary and rational; and state interests, determined by the state's position in the international political system, drive foreign policy behavior." "Foreign policy is what states make of it: social construction and international relations theory" in Vendulka Kubálková (ed.), *Foreign Policy in a Constructed World* (Armonk, NY: M. E. Sharpe, 2001), p. 42.
69. Jill Steans and Lloyd Pettiford, *Introduction to International Relations: Perspectives and Themes* (2nd ed. Harlow: Pearson Educational, 2005), p. 109.
70. Tim Dunne, Milja Kurki, and Steve Smith (eds.), *International Relations Theories: Discipline and Diversity* (3rd ed. Oxford: Oxford University Press, 2013), p. 358.
71. David A. Lake, "The state in international relations" in Christian Reus-Smit and Duncan Snidal (eds.), *The Oxford Handbook of International Relations* (Oxford: Oxford University Press, 2008), p. 56.
72. Charles William Kegley and Shannon Lindsey Blanton, *World Politics: Trend and Transformation* (13th ed. Boston, MA: Wadsworth, 2011), p. 16.
73. Graham Evans and Jeffrey Newnham, *Penguin Dictionary of International Relations* (London: Penguin, 1998), p. 512.
74. However, an "ontological object" cannot be an actor/agent, which implies choice, will, subjectivity. See below, section II.
75. Ashley, "The poverty of neorealism," p. 279.
76. Colin Wight, *Agents, Structures and International Relations: Politics as Ontology* (Cambridge: Cambridge University Press, 2006), p. 177.
77. Ken Booth, "Human wrongs and international relations," *International Affairs* 71 (1), January 1995, p. 115.

2

Hobbes's Symbolic Politics

"Actors and agents are treated synonymously [in international theory],"
says Colin Wight, "and attributions of agency can change, not only
within theories, but also within the space of a sentence. Rarely is it
clear what agency is, what it means to exercise agency, or who and
what might do so." The problem, he adds, is "endemic to the discipline."[1]

Both nouns relate to a verb, "to act," but with widely differing if not
opposing meanings: to do and, as in a play, to pretend to do. Better
then, surely, to reserve *actor* for our traditional use, for those engaged
in professional pretence in Hollywood, the West End, the Opéra, and La
Scala? These individuals, as they always remain, enter only tangentially
into international relations. By contrast, ordinary people like you and
me—people making breakfast, teaching a lesson, or ploughing a field,
voting together in an election (or taking to the streets instead)—are
usually described in philosophical debate as *agents*: the doers of literal,
necessary, prosaic actions, or actions in general. Repeated across the
world, these constitute the true material of international relations; and
it is the idea of states as the protagonists, or merely the agonists, in this
domain that amounts, in Wendt's word, to "fantasy."

Surely too the renowned Luciano, or Julia, or Gérard, when singing
or feigning for their supper, are being agents in their own cause—their
offstage, offscreen lives consisting of ordinary actions and encounters,
were it not that celebrity seems to undermine the epithet. Nowadays,
moreover, at least in the West, politics as an expression of collective
life tends to be firmly differentiated from dramatizations of it—why
else are politicians condemned, when they seem to be pretending?

Perhaps things are not so simple. Events like the choice of a ham
actor to command the most powerful armed forces on earth, at a time
of insistent global peril, can make us all doubt our grip on reality (it
happened, to my mind, in 1980). In Italy, people joke that only bad
actors go on the stage. What then should we think of the world, when

bad actors go into politics? Perhaps politicians ought to be better actors, and those who think that "all the world's a stage" have something to teach us.[2] Still, look what happens when the cliché is followed through, as Philip Reynolds did in closing his own *Introduction to International Relations*:

> The stage on which these actors perform was depicted [in this book] as one where action was always based on uncertainty—about the nature of the set and the other players, and so about the consequences of movement, or of doing nothing; where all actors perceived their roles as being primarily in conflict with those of others, but that in reality, though it was not always so perceived, roles could in most cases be better played with some degree of cooperation, and with none at all the play could not proceed; and where actions rarely, if ever, led to clear advantage and no disadvantage, but that normally all possible actions had some elements of gain and some elements of loss, and the choice of action was to be determined by judgment of the respective mixes of gains to be won and losses to be suffered by selection of the various courses open.[3]

Imagine having a part in *that* play! It makes *Waiting for Godot* look like *Die Hard with a Vengeance*.

Certainly the men and women who act on stage or screen succeed by symbolizing some *type* of person or situation with which everyone can identify; likewise, it is a symbolic importance that actions in the name of states assume. ("Politicians," wrote Galbraith, "play roles that are larger than life and not their own."[4]) Power, whether emotional or political, can be conjured up through an appeal to the collective imagination. But equally, if "acting" in the one sense is symbolic, public action in the other, to do with poverty and prosperity, war and survival, is literal, real. They are neither the same nor equivalent. Ignoring this distinction leads, I shall argue, to false descriptions of human relations, either mechanistic or melodramatic.

The political theorist David Runciman tells how, in the land of Shakespeare, early in the twentieth century, some writers deliberately (creatively, as they saw it) blurred the agent/actor distinction, adopting a metaphor of masks for disparate groups in competition for influence under existing states. But very soon the experiment was abandoned in disarray.[5] Much earlier, Hobbes had recourse to dramatic imagery for his political doctrine—but as I shall show, not without paradox either.

2.1 Mechanistic

In the "agent-structure debate," in the wake of Cold War Realism, the participants set out to discover how agents (notably states) and structures (notably the states system) could be co-determined and co-influencing: a relation which implicitly would limit states' power and room for maneuver. But I reject the very idea of state agency. Surely it is obvious that states have no volition—no will of their own. Men and women have their own individual wills; a group of people engaged in a joint action may be said to have a common will. They, and they alone, take action. But they are not states.

The state of human conception and, potentially, constitution is something distinct from individuals, or groups of people in communities or nations—words which contain their own meaning for the togetherness, the group-ness, of the members. It is simply the device through which relations between these groups, and the individuals in them, may be conducted. Even when this arrangement covers the whole inhabitable earth, the point remains the same. Political devices are abstractions, ideas about people—not people as such. So they cannot be agents. It is never right to say that states act.

In our common speech—perhaps especially in the hybrid tongue of English—we often express ourselves loosely, adopting an anthropomorphic or quasi-metaphorical description for events. We do so in scientific contexts when we say, in another variation on the verb, that a certain chemical "acts on" another. We do so familiarly, informally when we say that a bus "goes" down the street. This is shorthand for saying that a chemical change is taking place, or a bus is being driven down the street. Our general meaning is clear, and that is usually enough. Experience in its infinite variety is imperfectly defined by language, and imagination is often called upon to fill the gaps in understanding. But as for metaphors, we can get by without them altogether for the actions of people—the doers, the subjects, of actions. Scientists induce chemical changes; bus drivers drive buses; governments govern us. States do nothing. We have no need of a verb for them.

Social or collective actions certainly require some special form of description to distinguish them from individual ones, but those descriptions must also be recognizably human. Patrick Thaddeus Jackson forgets this, when he writes of the "social actors . . . empowered to speak on behalf of (or "in the name of") an entity, *thereby making that entity an actor*" (his emphasis). In this sentence the actor/agent distinction has already been dashed over. He goes on to evoke "social actors" alongside—that is, in addition to—both individuals and states, and so muddy the waters of explanation completely:

> a house, a social relationship, and a state are not "things" at all, but *patterns of activity* organized around certain regulative ideals. *But so are "individuals,"* which [*sic.*] are socially empowered to speak and act on their own behalf—never absolutely, but always in particular circumstances, with particular social entailments, able to do particular things and not others.[6] (Author's emphasis)

Not only are the individuals apostrophised here obviously not the same as a house (or a state); they are not the same individuals either, because their behavior is not the same in the "patterns of activity" evoked. Nor is it helpful to define all these objects so abstractly; a "pattern of activity" will not keep off the rain. Despite Jackson's complicated system of distinctions, we still end up with people as inanimate things.

Some concept of the literal and prosaic must always ground us in society, but it needs to be more precisely defined. When representing, or taking action on behalf of, someone or something external to ourselves, our wills are always in some sense subjected to that person or thing. By contrast, when taking action in our own persons, with our own inner purpose, our wills are active, open-ended, freely choosing, in a freedom we hold dear—especially, perhaps, when engaged in a joint endeavor with others. Yet between these two modes of being there is no necessary contradiction like the one Jackson is seen wrestling with. We can always choose, as individuals, to be agents of our own destiny.[7]

By the same token, when we say, as we sometimes do, of an abstract entity like "the market" (another of Jackson's "social actors"[8]) that it "seems to have a will of its own," we mean to evoke an anomaly: only conscious, deciding people have wills of their own. The difference is between a mechanistic description of society, with people viewed purely externally, as actors are, and a fully human one involving morality and the possibility of change.

2.2 Melodramatic

Despite his rejection of Hobbes's "final solutions," Jackson's approach here is not unlike that of his great seventeenth-century counterpart. Both, for example, profess to value social "empowerment" as the basis of political action. In fact, the most famous of political theorists conflated actors and agents by design.

The culpable loss of humanity in conventional international theory is due, I have said, to a mechanistic approach. Our self-image is impoverished by making states, instead of people, agents. Hobbes, by contrast, wants to make states, instead of people, actors. He wants to explain us to ourselves through melodrama, where a collective self is realised at the cost of individual will.

All social order is insecure, says Hobbes, without a state; but with a state, order in society is possible; in fact, states are the origin of shared meaning and morality itself. In his account, the two key forms of public representation—acting in the sense of public *action*, and acting in the sense of public *portrayal*—are merged in a drama of collective experience.

A special choice of language is involved here, to the explanation of which Hobbes devotes an entire chapter in *Leviathan* before embarking on political prescription. It turns on an archaic use of "personation" for "representing the words and actions of an other": first, in theatrical portrayal,

> as *Persona* in latine signifies the *disguise,* or *outward appearance* of a man, counterfeited on the Stage. . . .

Second, in the sense of *standing in for* someone in a real-life position of responsibility—a role which

> from the Stage, hath been translated to any Representer of speech and action, as well in Tribunalls, as Theaters. So that a *Person,* is the same that an *Actor* is, both on the Stage and in common Conversation; and to *Personate,* is to *Act,* or *Represent* himselfe, or an other; and he that acteth another, is said to beare his Person, or act in his name [...] and is called in diverse occasions, diversly; as a *Representer,* or *Representative,* a *Lieutenant,* a *Vicar,* an *Attorney,* a *Deputy,* a *Procurator,* an *Actor,* and the like.[9]

Hobbes's approach, like his language, is deliberately ambiguous and suggestive. It operates conflation on two levels—on the one hand, to merge the professional representative in public affairs with the dramatic actor on the stage ("as well in Tribunalls, as Theaters"); on the other, to merge their activity: joining the figurative evocation of human life to literal actions. This is where the melodrama comes in.

Certainly, insofar as actors symbolize other people or things to us, and public representatives exert themselves on others' behalf, both are involved in vicarious actions. They stand in someone else's stead; they have to think beyond themselves as individuals when carrying out their tasks. So of a man acting on the stage, or an advocate in court, we might say, in the traditional expression, "he is not his own man." At the same time (and against Hobbes's claim), these individuals do what they do differently, from different training, and with different results. The actor's task is to be colorful, the representative's to be faithful. The actor succeeds by portraying a recognizable type of person or situation; the representative promotes a unique individual or cause. The actor's domain is fantasy, the representative's reality. We value and hold on to these distinctions, even in moments of great difficulty and tension. To let go of them is to slip into melodrama, exaggerating the emotional import of real-life situations and risking the loss of our sense of self—succumbing to the power of our imaginations, instead of controlling it. Similarly, when we describe a person's behavior as "theatrical," we mean forced, insincere; attention-seeking rather than considered.

In his double use of "personation," Hobbes deliberately conflated the two different meanings of "to act." For the same purpose, he deliberately conflated "author" with "authorise." It is the author, he said, who gives the actor his instructions, as we do to our representative in real-life situations. But again this was, to say the least, playing fast and loose with language, even allowing for less clear-cut conceptions of these roles and functions in Hobbes's time than ours. The *moral* responsibility of one who instructs an actor, or a representative, is engaged; the instructor him/herself is the first to know the difference between what is likely to ensue. If I encourage my lawyer, or an actor in a play I have written (or am directing), to "use his imagination," I commit myself to results for which the ultimate responsibility will be mine. But equally, the results will not be the same. This distinction was overridden by Hobbes, in his insistence on a "Covenant" between "authors" and the "Actors, Representers, or Procurators, that have authority from them."[10]

2.3 Hobbes's Design

Hobbes, however, had a purpose behind this elaborate structure of meanings, which was the formulation of a universal political doctrine. Human relations in the mass, he argued, were competitive, unpredictable, potentially violent. The solution was the social contract: the surrender of all personal wills to a ruler for the sake of social peace—a process seen literally as the construction of a collective Self in the institution of government. Yet the planned outcome for Hobbes was not representative government as we understand it today—a group institution—but a single ruler, a monarch, on the grounds that only individual persons are, as the word suggests, undivided, and able to act decisively, with a single will.

Hobbes's reasoning here resembles that behind the idealized state agent of Realist international theory. The aim in each case is unified public action—perceived as an urgent necessity in the chaotic, confused, and dangerous domain of human relations in the mass. Yet the monarchical ruler, while undivided in his own will, would also, Hobbes insisted, be "authorised"—given the right to act—by the people, with whom ultimate responsibility lay ("by this Institution of a Common-Wealth, every particular man is Author of all the Soveraigne doth"[11]). The people would always "own" his actions, in the double sense of possessing and bearing responsibility for (as in our modern usage of "own up to")—just as Hobbes's Author is the instructor of his Actor. In this way the ruler, while a real person, would also stand as a surrogate person (an "Artificiall Man") for the people; like a character on the stage enacted ("personated") by a flesh-and-blood actor, who is both symbolic and real.

The culmination of this reasoning, at which Hobbes quickly arrived, is government not just by monarchy but by absolute monarchy. Such a ruler, being an individual, would be able to act effectively, without practical limits, and being unaccountable would also be free to act impartially—without the restrictions imposed by personal debts of interest or honor. As Hobbes put it, "a Monarch cannot disagree with himselfe, out of envy, or interest; but an Assembly may."[12] And an absolute monarch is the purest form of monarch to represent his subjects, both symbolically and, in terms of their surrendered wills, literally—to make a third thing beyond them all, the social institution of a state.

Purposeful Conceit

The name for this reasoning is a conceit: a compressed ambiguity, containing both literal and figurative elements. A conceit works—if it works—through our imaginative engagement with it. Hobbes depicted his own idea in the frontispiece to the first edition of *Leviathan*, showing an earth-straddling, crowned ruler whose torso, on closer inspection, is made up of a mass of tiny human figures, in the manner of a trompe l'oeil painting. The artist who adopts this style thinks in more than one dimension at once. Some well-known works by Arcimboldo, for example, purport to be a still-life tableau of fruit and vegetables. But pull back the perspective, and you can see the same objects shaped and arranged like facial features—eyes, nose, mouth—with the whole making up a face, as in a portrait head. Such paintings depend on our using our imaginations to "see," in the mind's eye, both the everyday objects and the living person artfully concealed in their assemblage. Likewise, Hobbes's political conceit depends on people's ability to see themselves embodied, both literally and figuratively, in the person of the monarch.

Two Forms of Reification

A conceit also involves reification. This word (literally, "making a thing") means the conjuring-up of an entity that does not self-evidently exist. We may reify semiconsciously, when unclear about the object of our thought—for example, in daydreaming; or by self-deception, through wishful thinking. The latter is the usual, critical sense in which the word is used: people should not pretend that unreal things exist, or set up more levels of reality than there truly are. Reification in philosophy often carries these negative connotations of gratuitousness, prolixity. A whole school of thinkers in the twentieth century, tracing their lineage from Leibniz and Hume, devoted themselves to an intellectual battle on this terrain—seeking to establish once and for all the things that were real in order to banish those that were not.

But we may also reify deliberately, by the exercise of our imaginations— even creatively, as when we imagine an actor representing a real person. And we may do these things together with other people, as when we imagine a group of which we are part to be united for some common purpose—any group, that is, large enough not to be consulted on all matters of concern, as nations arguably are. On such leaps of faith Hobbes's doctrine depends for its conception of society as both embodied and governed by the ruler in the personalized state.

> This done, the Multitude so united in one Person, is called a COMMON-WEALTH, in latine CIVITAS. This is the Generation of that great LEVIATHAN, or rather (to speake more reverently) of that *Mortall God*, to which wee owe under the *Immortal God*, our peace and defence.[13]

"Generation" here is Hobbes's word for reification, the collective gesture by which a state is conjured up, suggesting the giving of life to an imagined object. All this time, of course, as members of society, people know in the literal part of their minds that the personalized state is an imagined thing; but they also know that the impulse to order and the impulse to freedom naturally conflict; for they know their natures—so

Hobbes's argument runs. Unlike other creatures, he says, "men are continually in competition for Honour and Dignity"; "when there is no common enemy, they make warre upon each other, for their particular interests."[14] The ever-present danger of generalized violence can be staved off only through a supreme effort of collective will—to reify, and then submit to, the monarch as state incarnate. As Runciman puts it: "The state can be a person, but only if its members are already prepared to believe in the personality of the state."[15]

Arcimboldo, before the mind's eye, conjured up a human face; Hobbes proposed a whole political play, "translated," as he put it, "from the Stage." Implicitly, people could live with the paradoxes as they could with the creations of their own imaginations at work on the stage.

From the Reified State to a System of State Actors

What further reinforces the Hobbesian doctrine, as has become abundantly clear in our own time, is international relations. States conceived as bulwarks against social conflict gain added meaning in a context where everyone is a stranger.

As Hobbes explains it, the division of the population of the world is necessary for general order. Each monarch has the "Authoritie" over his citizens "to conforme the wills of them all, to Peace at home, and mutuall ayd against their enemies abroad."[16] In this way the processes of social formation and state-formation telescope into each other, to generate a complete system of personalized states, each able to take action on the citizenry's behalf in a world on the edge of chaos and violence. On this view of things, the Hobbesian state is still mechanistic ("Artificiall") but moves in a very public melodrama of all human life. Embodied in the persons of monarchs, it exists in an imaginative domain where actors and agents are effectively the same. This, for Hobbes, is the price of peace and perhaps survival itself: the social contract existentially, because universally, conceived.

> For if we could suppose a great Multitude of men to consent in the observation of Justice, and other Lawes of Nature, without a common Power to keep them all in awe; we might as well suppose all Man-kind to do the same; and then there neither would be, nor need to be any Civill Government, or Common-wealth at all; because there would be Peace without subjection.[17]

Here, though, real difficulties set in. It is expected of Hobbesian monarchs that they be impartial, above the fray, in their dealings with their subjects, but the same does not apply to their dealings with each other, where they represent the interests of their states. Yet without some quality of impartiality exercised simultaneously within and between these same rulers, order in the system, in the world as a whole, can hardly be relied on. At this point, Hobbes's runaway logic runs off the map.

Hobbes saw the potential for contradiction; after all, the special burden of "Kings, and Persons of Soveraigne authority," he said, is to be permanently in a "posture of War." His overriding concern here is with legitimacy. Still, the potential for conflicts of interest between rulers themselves is not removed. Expediency is never without complications. The Hobbesian ruler must be someone of superhuman strength and judgment, or the monarchical role itself will be hollowed out, becoming merely symbolic. Also, the symmetry of Hobbes's system depends on an atomized conception of fundamental human relations (beyond an acknowledged monarch, he says, there is only "the confusion of a disunited Multitude"[18]). Atomization presupposes no difference, or none worth having, between people's private and public selves, or their individual and collective ones. Human identity is apt to dissolve in instability, when people see themselves simultaneously embodied and governed by someone else.

Again Hobbes anticipated this criticism, insisting: "men cannot distinguish, without study and great understanding, between one action of many men, and many actions of one multitude . . . and therefore are disposed to take for the action of the people, that which is a multitude of actions done by a multitude of men, led perhaps by the perswasion of one."[19] People in general, that is, can be misled, and so should be properly led. Individuals must be subject to social imperatives, and social imperatives to global ones. These elaborations, however, put a further strain on his scheme. Is there really nothing more to life than this miasmic unfreedom? Fear, it is true, is a great solvent of individual identity and social bonds; but is fear as all-pervasive and extreme as Hobbes would have us believe? We are back with the problems of melodrama.

Hobbes was aware, too, of the danger of exaggeration in his approach. His language is full of oxymorons ("Artificiall Man," "mortall God") suggesting strained credibility or excessive emotion. And as Runciman points out, the organic parallels that he sought to draw, in a literal fleshing-out of his thesis, between the "Artificiall Man" of the state and the parts of the human body, break down.[20] Yet there is more at stake here than language. A refutation of Hobbes must work on several levels at once—individual/social; state/system; literal/figurative—and make a logical whole. A judgment of human nature is required.

2.4 Facing the Hobbesian Challenge

One way to respond is anthropologically: arguing that turmoil and bloodshed are not necessary or typical features of life for humankind in general. Evidence from history, showing periods of peace as well as war; evidence from premodern societies among whom war has not been endemic; and evidence of order in certain localized groups and communities today—all these may be invoked against Hobbes's elaborate justification for autocracy.

On the question of contemporary experience, it is striking how little value Hobbes attached to the traditional institutions and small settled communities of his own country and time. Villages, guilds, and churches occupied then, as their modern equivalents do now, a median position in organized society: between individuals and higher, more formal, more impersonal institutions, up to and including central institutions of state. Face-to-face communities of all kinds anchor people in a culture of familiarity, counteracting social atomization and reducing the possibility of uncontrolled violence; in them, one may say, no one is a stranger. Even families, social groups predetermined by biology, arguably partake of a long-established moral hierarchy in which peace is the norm. That these real social groups and the order they provide had no force in Hobbes's mind underlines the fact that, as Runciman says, *Leviathan* was "above all, a book against civil war."[21]

Hobbes and Human Nature

In any case, Hobbes set out to meet all criticisms of his doctrine by placing it on the level of human nature and moral argument. The political thesis of *Leviathan* is only part of a wider philosophical scheme. Human nature, in his stated conception, is dynamic. Distrust arises, and ambition is formed, from individuals' perception of their fundamental equality as human beings. ("From Equality proceeds Diffidence—From Diffidence Warre"; diffidence here in its older meaning of distrust).[22] Hence equality is not a social ideal but an original and inescapable condition—in fact, the root problem in human affairs. It boils down to the ease with which one man may kill another, through either physical strength or mental ingenuity. In turn, honesty and sincerity are reduced to an admission of this unpleasant fact of life. There is, Hobbes said—brutally demonstrating his own maxim—no behavioral norm strong enough to prevent our striking against others first in a perceived clash of interests.

That, ostensibly, is why he set so little store by the cultural norms and hierarchical order of traditional society, or arguments from experience that human nature is inclined to peaceful behavior—in England or elsewhere; now or in the past. In fact, he took great pains to argue that human nature is always and everywhere fundamentally the same—the same, that is, in being dominated by "a perpetuall and restlesse desire of Power after power, that ceaseth onely in Death."[23] In these circumstances, it is states which supply the solution of overarching order, provided that the resulting arrangement is not based on equality but subverts what Hobbes calls "natural" human equality. Hence absolute monarchy. At the same time, he insisted, there could be no injustice in living under such rulers, since security and order in society, in the world as a whole, were guaranteed by them.

As it happens, the passage from *Leviathan* in which Hobbes explicitly links internal and external state security immediately follows one in which he comes close to depicting the states system itself as part of the problem in human relations. First he insists that people in premodern societies—without organized states, and living only in traditional or tribal communities—were in a general condition of war. This is in support of his general pessimistic argument from human nature. Then relaxing his position, he acknowledges that historical reports on this score might not be accurate—before shifting his ground back again, from possible ignorance to certain refutation:

> But though there had never been any time, wherein particular men were in a condition of warre one against another; yet in all times, Kings, and Persons of Soveraigne authority, because of their Independency, are in continuall jealousies, and in the state and posture of Gladiators . . . But because they uphold thereby, the Industry of their Subjects; there does not follow from it, that misery, which accompanies the Liberty of particular men.[24]

This is tantamount to saying that the states system justifies states—a circular argument. In the same passage Hobbes defends himself against the charge of cynicism. Citing the measures a man takes to secure his life and property when "he rides armed," or "locks his dores . . . and chests," he expostulates:

> Does he not there as much accuse mankind by his actions, as I do by my words? But neither of us accuse mans nature in it. The Desires,

and other Passions of man, are in themselves no Sin. No more are the Actions, that proceed from those Passions, till they know a Law that forbids them; which till Lawes be made they cannot know: nor can any Law be made, till they have agreed upon the Person that shall make it.[25]

To this one could reply that the states system justifies states only if we all "accuse mans nature." Hobbes's invocation of "Sin" is a red herring.

2.5 Dissembling and Democracy

There is, moreover, a great deal of lived social life in established states, in our own times, that weighs against Hobbes's view of things—and since his approach purports to be practical and concrete, counterarguments from experience must weaken it accordingly. Consider again his conceit centered on "acting." Without the order imposed by states, this implies, any appearance of social order is *only* appearance—the result of individuals' dissembling to mask their inner aggression and fear. By this logic, we are all actors in public, potentially engaged in a hypocritical pretence—which is why the law may be compared to a show ("as well in Tribunalls, as Theaters"); and why, by extension, people may be brought to see, in the threatening symbolism of absolute monarchy, the source of all social obedience. Equally, Hobbes's thinking relies on an assumption of the ruler's peculiar integrity—his ability to know at all times the difference between right and wrong, truth and lies—since the ultimate tribunal is his own judgment. People in general, meanwhile, are assumed to have no morality of their own, independently of that imposed by the upholding of their states, and little pride of self.

Quite the opposite, in fact, could be argued: that people hold on to their sense of self to the point of seeing state institutions, on occasion, as a threat to them, while it is in unfree or corrupt—but still organized—societies that individuals are inclined to dissemble to each other. In such circumstances one rarely learns people's true opinions about anything, because they cannot "be themselves." Social relationships become constricted and confused; it becomes routine to doubt the good faith of anyone, even in one's own family, so far has lying become the norm. But this is due to the nature of the established institutions, rather than to a lack of them.

The problem was diagnosed first secretly, then publicly, even clamorously, by dissidents under Soviet Communist rule in the Cold War. In Eastern Europe a whole literature of political rebellion grew up around identity and sincerity.[26] Before Communism, East Europeans had already endured a long history of absolutism under tsars, Habsburgs, or Ottomans. Communist rule itself entailed a near-total eradication of traditional communities and institutions through mass purges, forced migration, centralized planning, and cultural force-feeding—a kind of ideological civil war. Meanwhile, the rulers themselves, in the Soviet heartland and beyond, relied on personality cults, expressed in militarism and public show, including show trials of dissenters. Those regimes were not, of course, literal monarchies, but like monarchies they functioned by presenting a monolithic face of government while behaving dynastically and nepotistically (see the Ceausescus in Romania, the Kims in North Korea, or the oligarchs of Communist China). Arguably this is Hobbesian absolutism put into practice, albeit disguised as dictatorship of the proletariat.

Again, on the question of political corruption, even the ideally upright monarch imagined by Hobbes would be unable to govern without some apparatus of state, and in this regard Hobbes rather too lightly depicts the "Officers" of state as either ideally uncorrupt like their monarch, or correctable by his power to punish. And Hobbes's own conception of monarchy, as I shall show, was expedient, preferring the simple stability of autocracy even over the dynastic principle.

On the level of social relations, he sought to justify an individual's distrust of his fellows as a necessary form of self-help—a reason to ignore, if perversely, the "Lawes, and publike Officers, armed, to revenge all injuries shall bee done him."[27] But as we know, the laws and "publike Officers" embodying Communism were inimical to social life in their own right; the officers themselves were far from incorruptible, which is why *nomenklatura* has entered all languages for a rotten apparatus of state. While accepting that his sovereign would, as a human being, be corruptible, Hobbes denied that he should be accountable ("It is true that they that have Soveraigne power, may commit Iniquity; but not Injustice, or Injury in the proper signification"[28]). But as the victims of Communism learned to their cost, that is a distinction without a difference. In the end, the dictatorships of the proletariat lost credibility for the same reason that all dictatorships down the ages have done, through a generalized distrust in the impartiality of their institutions.

A social condition of ingrained dissembling may therefore signify not, as in Hobbes's vision of society without a state, the absence of an organized, hierarchical political structure, but precisely the obtrusive *presence* of one—with an uneven, inefficient, or unfair reach. The truth then would not be, as Hobbes asserts, that no one knows morality before he knows law, and states define social morality; but rather, people already possess a morality, whether instinctive or instilled, which leads them to judge existing laws, and perhaps even the whole of officially promulgated values, to be wrong.

The lesson from this is that only democracy is an end in itself, because it allows us to take the risk of our natures. Only under conditions of open social relations can we trust other people—including our leaders—to be themselves, and so really get to know them, which is essential to social learning and the progress of morality. The preciousness of democracy flows precisely from this: it has the inalienable value of real life even with its imperfections, so enabling us to form a true society, with its potential for higher things than individuals can realize by themselves. On this basis we can distinguish between submission to a state that is the reification of fear, and provisional acceptance of states as instruments of positive shared goals.

2.6 Literary Lessons

Hamlet

In Hobbes's own lifetime, moreover, these questions had begun to be explored on the literal stage, in Elizabethan and Jacobean theaters. First came the historical plays of Shakespeare and Marlowe, depictions of the ideals and dilemmas of monarchical rule. Then came *Hamlet*, a drama of high politics and international relations, marked by intrigue and bloodshed, in which the two senses of acting, imaginative and literal, are laid bare in an exegesis of sincerity and honor among elites. In this play the protagonist becomes, temporarily, an actor on behalf of a state—and dies in the attempt.

Heir apparent to the throne of Denmark, Prince Hamlet discovers that the king, his uncle Claudius, is a usurper and his mother an adulteress; together they conspired to kill Hamlet's father and seize the throne. Now Hamlet himself, on discovering the crime, is in peril of losing his royal inheritance and even his life. His response is to temporize while deciding on the best course of action—and to disguise this subversive reflection, to feign madness in public at the court. On this risky experiment all the double meanings and dramatic irony of the play turn.

As spectators, we see the prince's personal crisis, whose resolution will determine whether he will become an actual (and a just) monarch in recovery of his throne—a decisive man of action rather than a dreamy intellectual. But Hamlet's public pretence is also vacillation; he has become an actor because he cannot yet be (because it is too dangerous for him to be) an agent, in his and the kingdom's cause. As time goes on, however, doubts arise. Can anyone dissemble continuously and not go mad? Is this not what subtle politicians play on, when they cultivate an image of themselves as in the grip of events that they struggle heroically to control? Is not even the best of rulers obliged to become what Machiavelli advised: "a great dissembler and deceiver"[29]—trapped, like King Claudius, in his own conception of necessary evil?

Then there is the character of Hamlet himself. His inner life, laid bare to us through his self-questioning soliloquies, is precisely what makes him credible, a figure with whom we can identify; a man, moreover, reluctant to assume the trappings of monarchical power. Hamlet's choice, finally, of the ignoble course of public pretence is for liberating reasons. This is brought home by the play within a play: a drama of antique ritual put on at the Danish court, with Hamlet himself as director, but also, as it turns out, an allegory of the intrigue leading to the old king's death. After this revelation of the truth, Hamlet has no choice but to "come out of character" and take action in justice and revenge.

At the end of *Hamlet* the hero loses his life but removes the corruption at the heart of the Danish state: this is our gain as spectators of the drama, Aristotelian catharsis purging our pent-up emotions to release us back wiser into our everyday lives. We are able to experience reality more fully and become what Hamlet fails to be (because the play is a tragedy), makers of our own destiny. That, too, is a lesson Shakespeare intends. Through our glimpses into Hamlet's mind, and his need to dissemble, the play shows us the difference between the actor and the man of action, as between appearance and reality, lies and truth. Meanwhile the real, corrupt dissemblers, the usurper king and queen, will perish at Hamlet's hands in his last act of sacrifice. Thus, it is legitimate to *impersonate* someone temporarily, for exemplary ends, as the fictional Hamlet does (and actors ideally do); but no one can literally *become* another, on a permanent basis. That way, *Hamlet* tells us, mortal deception and moral suicide lie. We must be ourselves in life in general, above the complications and temptations of power. Actors and agents are not the same.

The play's dénouement reveals Denmark's new ruler to be a foreigner; the effort to cleanse the dynastic state has led to its destruction. But there is also (and this is Shakespeare's modernity, his originality over Aristotle) hope of better things.[30] The future is open, which is why *Hamlet*, though a tragedy, is not a melodrama—aimed not to intimidate but to ennoble and instruct. Reality prevails over pretence at the hero's first casting aside of his mask. Yet Prince Hamlet's momentary embodiment of the Danish state is also the last decision of his life. The monarch-as-actor is shown sacrificed to national redemption and historic change.

The Prisoner of Zenda

By the end of the nineteenth century, to "personate" had become an archaic usage close to our modern "impersonation"—implying a clear difference between drama and real life, falsehood and truth. In Europe, the symbolism of the personalized state had long been shattered by revolution. In *The Prisoner of Zenda* (1894), it became the pretext for a whimsical political thriller.

'Personation" here refers to the hero's temporary substitution for the king of Ruritania, helped by the accident of their resemblance. Unbeknown to the people, the real king has been kidnapped, and while the loyal soldiery struggle to free him, his lookalike Rassendyll assumes the appurtenances of monarchy amid the throng of nobles, princes, and courtiers. As the king's enemies, and Rassendyll privately, assert, this is a fake king—more than an actor, an impostor—among multiple references to tricks, games, and the playing of parts.[31]

The novel is also an international-political drama, full of asides on diplomacy and statecraft, but in a tone of genial banter; the story of a private jaunt in a vanishing pastoral milieu where power is concentrated, and national identity symbolized, by single individuals on whom the fates of entire unwitting peoples depend. Behind the derring-do, Balkan society is reduced to the status of scenery. As in Dumas previously and Buchan subsequently, this is the source of the novel's drama and its nostalgic charm. Ruritania itself has since come to stand for fantasy international relations in a fairy-tale world ruled by aristocratic gentlemen and their devoted servants.

Hamlet and *The Prisoner of Zenda*, in different ways, are allegories in which the symbolic workings of monarchy are contrasted with its real-life alternatives, and the latter win out, as truth triumphs over lies. At the end of *Hamlet* the Danish monarchy is broken and Danish independence is lost; at the end of *Zenda* the hero relinquishes his borrowed Arcadian kingdom for banal domestic life in London (an abdication foreshadowing the fate of many real-life European monarchs). History's egregious challenges have been met; the masks of royal rule are cast aside. The Hobbesian monarch may bestride the earth, but in *Hamlet* the institution itself disappears. In *Zenda*, whichever king you identify with, monarchy is a prisoner of flawed reality. For us, spectators of these scenes, the ease with which appearances of state have been dismantled merely reinforces the impression of states themselves as colossal inventions of social order.

In Hobbes's political doctrine there is no point at which these illusion-destroying revolutions can take place. Which brings us to his metaphysical arguments.

2.7 Metaphysical Hobbes

Hobbes imagined the workings of democracy, only to reject it because it could not guarantee the security of society. At the same time, he acknowledged the artifice of his chosen alternative, monarchy. His first solution was to reinforce it externally, with an imagined world in which all states would be absolute monarchies. Still, the problem of securing the institution over time remained. His answer was further artifice.

> Of all these Formes of Government, the matter being mortall, so that not onely Monarchs, but also whole Assemblies dy, it is necessary for the conservation of the peace of men, that as there was order taken for an Artificiall Man, so there be order also taken, for an Artificiall Eternity of life; without which, men that are governed by an Assembly, should return into the condition of Warre in every age; and they that are governed by One man, as soon as their Governour dyeth. This Artificiall Eternity, is that which men call the Right of *Succession*.[32]

In practice, however, all Hobbes envisaged was control of the process so that whoever succeeded a dying absolute monarch would preserve the institution of monarchy itself. His reasoning here is tautological when not actually cynical.[33] Some further, even more unaccountable source of power was therefore called for. This he found in divine right. Absolutism in this form meant that

> [the Monarch's] Power cannot, without his consent, be Transferred to another: He cannot Forfeit it; He cannot be Accused by any of his Subjects, of Injury: He cannot be Punished by them: He is Judge of what is necessary for Peace; and Judge of Doctrines: He is Sole Legislator; and Supreme Judge of Controversies; and of the Times, and Occasions of Warre and Peace: to him it belongeth to choose Magistrates, Counsellours, Commanders, and all other Officers, and Ministers; and to determine of Rewards, and Punishments, Honour, and Order.

These powers Hobbes binds together under a single divine sanction, based on Old Testament precedents for kingly rule and some New Testament ones. The precedents themselves, however, are dubious, almost ironic. He takes "Render unto Caesar" literally, to hold up Christ as an exemplary taxpayer, and Israel's many tribes as models for kingly rule in a states system where war is both endemic and patriotic. "Here is confirmed," says Hobbes, "the Right that Soveraigns have, both to the *Militia*, and to all *Judicature*."[34] But this is *post hoc* justification based on myth.

In any case, key principles of kingly rule are missing from this ostensibly Christian account. One is that Christian kings should be not merely impartial but saintly, as in early medieval French tradition, where the corollary of a perfect absolute monarchy was perfection in the persons of monarchs themselves. Hobbes knew the Frankish tradition of natural law, but he could not, and did not, argue for it, having already accepted that monarchs could "commit Iniquity" unaccountably.[35] A second Christian principle is the unity of humankind under God. But Hobbes could not invoke this either, as it would undermine the rights of rulers, on which he insisted, to maintain their separate secular domains, if necessary by waging war with each other. These omissions expose the system-building bias in his political doctrine.

2.8 Strangers in History

Seen as a whole, Hobbes's scheme for states in *Leviathan* is overwhelmingly reliant on his personal preconceptions about human nature. He rejected democracy not because he failed to understand it, but because he would not trust it. Human beings could never, he argued, establish a peaceful social order without some overarching apparatus of control.

Still, even Hobbes could not completely avoid self-doubt and contradiction, as his own honesty in places reveals. And on the fundamental level—that of judgment of one's fellow human beings—while self-doubt may not be fatal, self-contradiction certainly is. Few would disagree that there is ample evidence that "in the nature of man, we find three principall causes of Quarrell. First, Competition; Secondly, Diffidence; Thirdly, Glory."[36] But it takes only one person to identify all these causes at once to suggest that they need not persist indefinitely in human affairs. Understand the problem, and you are halfway to the solution. There is enough evidence in Hobbes's work to suggest he grasped that logic too. Else why defend the "Desires, and other Passions of man" as "in themselves no Sin"; why trouble to believe that previous societies might *not* always have been "in a condition of warre one against another"?

A decade before *Leviathan*'s first publication, moreover, Hobbes noted the hazards of generalizing from records of past events.

> Though words be the signs we have of one another's opinions and intentions; yet, because the equivocation of them is so frequent according to the diversity of contexture, and of the company wherewith they go (which the presence of him that speaketh, our sight of his actions, and conjecture of his intentions, must help to discharge us of): it must be extreme hard to find out the opinions and meanings of those men that are gone from us long ago, and have left us no other signification thereof but their books; which cannot possibly be understood without history enough to discover those aforementioned circumstances, and also without great prudence to observe them.[37]

This approach, which comes normal to us today, is more ingenuous and open to trust than most of *Leviathan*. The fact remains, however: a Hobbesian admission that violence and anarchy may *not* be inevitable in human relations weakens his case for an authoritarian personalized state.

Suggestively, one of Hobbes's modern interpreters argues that we should see him as a philosopher of existential paradox: someone with a singularly modern and agile mind, who could be both adaptable in the light of events and strongly focused on system-building. By implication, no interpretation of his politics as damned by his contradictions is likely to be adequate: neither the "traditional view"—stressing dichotomies between his espousal of science and his moral opinions—nor the "natural law view" of his scientism at odds with his professed Christian inspiration. Rather, Hobbes's own advice would be for us to live with contradictions as they appear in the course of time, and which even ambitious, systematic philosophers are unable to resolve.[38]

Even so, this collaboration in paradox could never be fully lucid. It has nothing of the human complexity of Shakespearean tragedy; it is just the acting-out of a fundamental condition. People who "cannot distinguish, without study and great understanding, between one action of many men, and many actions of one multitude" will have only a dim perception of government. Still less will they be able to perceive order among humankind as a whole. On this highest level—the level beyond individual states—Hobbesian scepticism persists at its strongest; his international theory has a metaphysics of its own, or none. As the quotation suggests, for Hobbes all men may be strangers and destined to remain so. And if strangers in history call for "great prudence to observe them," we may never be able to enter into a relationship of trust with our contemporaries whom we never meet and whose lives we will never fully share.

Idols Cannot Be Authors

During the Cold War international Realists, invoking Hobbes, pushed this view to the limits—challenging all who criticized the status quo to prove that the world was not the place of instability and mortal danger they themselves claimed it to be. They thought in effect of the world as one state, ruled into some indefinite future by the balance of nuclear terror. Not all of them, however, can have been sincere, or sincere all of the time; deterrence always entailed a flirtation with cataclysmic violence. The end of the Cold War called that particular bluff, by proving that the great majority of people do not live on fantasies of Armageddon.

In *Leviathan* Hobbes challenges us, more precisely, to say what kind of social order we would put in states' place; and lacking a satisfactory answer, to admit that there must be some freedom of maneuver for states themselves. At the same time, all freedom for him is paradoxical: human beings use it only to lose it. The freedom of states itself, then, has only an attributive or ideal character. Unlike in the system of today, where states are the formal, unchallenged protagonists; and unlike in the conventional wisdom of international relations, state agency for Hobbes is always artificial. Since we must, he says, obey a ruler, we should do so consciously, for an extraordinary purpose—ultimately, to preserve the productive "Industry" of human beings manifest in art, science, and technology.[39] But states are merely the beginning of this process, not its end; not to be celebrated, still less venerated, even as cultured images of our social selves. As Hobbes in his own distinctive vocabulary made clear: "Idols cannot be Authors: for an Idol is nothing."[40]

Naturally enough, the most intractable problem with this dynamic conception of human relations comes in its extension from the level of state-formation to the level of state preservation, from the securing of one society to the securing of all humankind. In *Leviathan* state-formation is legitimized by a social surrender, and state preservation is effected by the ruler who represents each society and, through his succession, ensures its continuity. International relations is the generalization of these principles to the world as a whole. But in the first place, as Hobbes himself concedes, the impartiality which enables a ruler to stand above society is always hard-won. The real man at the apex of power will struggle to persuade the mass of people to be citizens.

The state thus conceived is an idealization, an imagined forceful solution to conflictual human relations.

Still less, moreover, can political impartiality be guaranteed over a number of such entities (and geography alone seems to call for a number indefinitely). Hobbesian rulers seeking to preserve many states as a system cannot risk being impartial toward each other without jeopardizing the interests of their subjects, and they cannot do the latter and still remain legitimate rulers. Unless, that is, there is order both *within* separate states and *between* the rulers held, in Hobbesian fashion, to embody them. But this is, to say the least, an improbable prospect of human conformity. In the real world, conflicts of interest are likely to break out between Hobbesian rulers and, Hamlet-style, within them, between their internal legitimacy and their external instrumentality, their actor role and their agent role; between their need to keep their own counsel even on pain of dissembling, and their need to be true to others in the higher cause of states. To some extent this is the dilemma of all politics, but above the level of states it leaves only a "posture of War': an institutionalized situation, like the Cold War, both mechanistic and melodramatic, and intolerable in the long term.

Hobbes's final prescription, dictated by his own hyperbolic vision, lay in divine right—in absolute rulers accountable to God alone. Yet in the event this was a relation for which he argued with scant evidence and perhaps scant conviction. This underlines the idealized nature of his scheme, and of all systems of states likely to follow it. We can be loyal to our human rulers, or to all humankind, but we cannot be loyal to both.

The final flaw in Hobbesian idealism foreshadows the core problem of life under the states system of today, from which the transcendent aura of monarchy has vanished but where conflict and competition persist by virtue of the system's own divisions. That problem is state agency: a reification too far.

2.9 The Hobbesian Legacy

What Hobbes explained, and at the same time dispelled, is the mystique of the personalized state. States' original purpose, he argued, was order and peace in society. The authority given to the monarch to take action in everyone's name derived from this. But only from this. The Hobbesian social contract is with a monarch, not with God. That is the first reason why the Hobbesian state is artificial: not society's puppet, but certainly society's creation.

For state continuity, Hobbes turned the tables of these power relations, stipulating how each ruler should gerrymander the monarchical arrangement beyond his own mortal span. He should decide his successor personally, like a Roman emperor, and fix the institutions of social control with a slew of invented justifications. So the Hobbesian state over time is artificial too.

Both steps are explained through the author-actor extended metaphor. The Hobbesian monarch symbolically represents individuals in society to themselves, by putting into effect their desire for order and peace. And as there are many societies in the world, so there will be many monarch-states. In this way state actors become state agents too. But actors, Hobbes has already pointed out, are artificial persons, with no wills of their own. At this point his metaphor runs out of reality. What is more, by intervening in social relations to secure monarchy indefinitely, the Hobbesian ruler arguably becomes an author in his own right—stealing the collective will, instead of enacting it. At this point Hobbesian accountability runs out as well.

This becomes obvious when we compare his panacea with the idealized state of Christian divine-right tradition. There too monarchs would hold the wills of individuals in trust, while their actions were symbolic before the people at large. But *anointed* monarchs' authority, and their own freedom of action, were God-given, and the entire arrangement depended on the monarch's manifest personal virtue. Even state continuity depended on it, for monarchs could be martyrs too. "In my end is my beginning," said Mary, Queen of Scots, and in Hobbes's own lifetime another Stuart died for this ideal.

In the divine-right tradition, there is no precise focus for political will. Monarchs' own wills, like those of individuals and peoples, must ultimately conform with the will of God. But free will, like morality, subsists nonetheless. In their anointed kings and queens, individuals could find the most natural and most perfect extension of themselves, partaking in this way of the moral ideal of society under God. Hobbes's image of the king as actor-representer reflects this imaginative longing, and replicates the structure of the divine-right state in which society is symbolically represented by one person. But that is far as the parallel goes. The Hobbesian state, unlike the monarchy by divine right, is always *something less than* a person (or moral ideal), because the shared values providing its authority are self-regarding (in practice, self-preserving) rather than transcendent. And arguably when the Hobbesian monarch, in the crisis of his succession, acts to promulgate monarchy against peradventure, he no longer represents shared values of any kind but merely his own. Hobbes takes the structure of the divine-right state and leaves its mystical core. State agency after him is simply an attempt to revive the mystique of states, and without an overarching set of values doomed to fail.

Imaginary Persons

By the same token, the "state person" idea floated by Wendt has long since been killed off by Hobbes. Personal rule as divine-right rule is already dead for him. What is left? he asks. The state can be a person, but only an imaginary one (an "Artificiall Man"). Leaving aside the justifiable scepticism to which Hobbes's own political inclinations give rise, for most of us today there is no such thing as an imaginary person anyway. There are only real persons, individuals, who may or may not combine in society. But these are also irreducible, indivisible people with self-knowledge and the capacity to be agents in their own right. The Hobbesian extreme of fundamental unfreedom, refuting all original sources of human identity, has not prevailed.

Obviously, states are not physical persons, natural individuals. Equally, on some level we like to think that there can be both individuals and real societies made up of them. So there is no place for imaginary persons at all (except, as Runciman points out, in fiction[41]). Or as I have previously put it,

> the commonsense view of reality can accommodate *both* persons (human individuals) *and* the state (as something like, but also unlike, a human individual). Hence, it is not necessary to argue that the state actually *is* a person.[42]

For the rest, we already have a term of "personality" for the character traits of individuals, and more controversially, "national character" for the traits of certain social groups that are traceable in the world. Together these make up the identity of "international relations," if anything does. What we, international theorists and everyone else, now need to know is how individuals in society—as *nations*—can be effective collective *agents* in the universal *states system*. Now of these three entities, the first is the object of a debate going back some time. On nationhood, nationality, and nation-formation, we have a copious literature to consult. It is states and agency that present new, inscrutable objects of inquiry in a system which combines them by fiat and muddles the case even for nations, so that Willetts can say that "no such entities [as nation-states] exist."[43]

There is of course the hypothetical possibility, in the system as it is, that conscious choosing individuals—in democracies, or in consensual societies in general—will act in real harmony with each other, with their inherited institutions and territorial legacies, for the sake of shared aims. Then, and only then, might we say that states were agents. And since individuals are moral agents, we would tend to think of this as an exercise of moral will, but one different from—greater than—the wills of individuals.

The failure in the conventional wisdom of international relations— the travesty everyone alive today faces—is the uncritical assumption that this happens routinely and everywhere; that today's created states and their peoples really are (or can be made to seem) synonymous. We find this assumption in the structure of Realist international theory, and it is implicit in most other international theorists' language, as I have shown; when it is the conditions under which societies can be sufficiently democratic, or sufficiently consensual, to be real collective agents—with or without their inherited states—which is of interest in the first place. As I argue in the next chapter, this means rethinking morality itself.

Notes

1. Colin Wight, *Agents, Structures and International Relations*, p. 178.
2. William Shakespeare, *As You Like It*, Act II Scene VII. See also: "For realists, the main actors on the world stage are states," Baylis, Smith, and Owens (eds.), *The Globalization of World Politics* (6th ed. 2014), p. 4; "the globe is a stage, and the players in the drama are many," Kegley and Blanton, *World Politics: Trend and Transformation*, pp. 15–16; and John T. Rourke, *International Politics on the World Stage* (12th ed. New York: McGraw-Hill, 2007).
3. P. A. Reynolds, *An Introduction to International Relations* (2nd ed. London: Longman, 1980), p. 306.
4. John Kenneth Galbraith, *A Life in Our Times: Memoirs* (London: Andre Deutsch, 1981), p. 43.
5. David Runciman, *Pluralism and the Personality of the State* (Cambridge: Cambridge University Press, 1997).
6. Patrick Thaddeus Jackson, "Hegel's House, or 'People are states too'", *Review of International Studies* 30 (2), April 2004, pp. 286–287.
7. Animals can act purposively, but only human beings have "future intentions"—an "ability to commit oneself to do things in the future"—Carlos J. Moya, *The Philosophy of Action: An Introduction* (Cambridge: Polity Press, 1990), p. 167.
8. Jackson, "Hegel's House," p. 287.

9. Thomas Hobbes, *Leviathan* [1651], ed. Richard Tuck (Cambridge: Cambridge University Press, 1996), ch. XVI, pp. 111–112, original italics, spelling and capitals (as in all following quotations unless otherwise stated). Jackson ignores the theatrical associations of Hobbes's "Personation," merely arguing that he "calls for an all-powerful Leviathan to impose some consistency on our social and linguistic usages" ("Hegel's House," p. 287).
10. Hobbes, *Leviathan*, ed. Tuck, p. 112.
11. *Ibid.*, p. 124.
12. *Ibid.*, pp. 135 and 132.
13. *Ibid.*, p. 120.
14. *Ibid.*, pp. 119, 118.
15. Runciman, *Pluralism and the Personality of the State*, p. 31. See also Carl Schmitt, *The Leviathan in the State Theory of Thomas Hobbes* [1938] tr. George Schwab and Erna Hilfstein (Chicago: University of Chicago Press, 2008), ch. III.
16. Hobbes, *Leviathan*, ed. Tuck, pp. 120–121.
17. *Ibid.*, pp. 118–119.
18. *Ibid.*, p. 122.
19. *Ibid.*, p. 73.
20. Runciman, *Pluralism and the Personality of the State*, p. 24 and pp. 20–24 generally.
21. *Ibid.*, p. 12.
22. Summary to ch. XIII, reproduced in Kenneth Minogue (ed.), Hobbes, *Leviathan* (London: Dent, 1973), p. xxix.
23. Hobbes, *Leviathan*, ed. Tuck, p. 70.
24. *Ibid.*, p. 90.
25. *Ibid.*, p. 89.
26. E.g., from the former Czechoslovakia, in fiction Milan Kundera, *The Unbearable Lightness of Being* (1984) and in non-fiction Václav Havel, *The Power of the Powerless* and *Living in Truth* (London: Faber and Faber, 1987). See also Anne Applebaum, *Iron Curtain: The Crushing of Eastern Europe 1944–56* (London: Allen Lane, 2012), Part Two.
27. Hobbes, *Leviathan*, ed. Tuck, p. 89.
28. *Ibid.*, p. 124.
29. "gran simulatore e dissimulatore': Niccolò Machiavelli, *Il Principe* ch. XVIII [1513–] in *Il Principe/Scritti Politici* ed. Luigi Fiorentino, (Milano: Mursia, 1988), p. 89.
30. As famously argued in A. C. Bradley, *Shakespearean Tragedy* [1904] (3rd. ed. Basingstoke: Macmillan, 1992).
31. At one point, the real king's aide-de-camp says to the narrator: "Do you think that the nobles and the people will enjoy being fooled as you've fooled them? Do you think they'll love a King who was too drunk to be crowned, and sent a servant to personate him?" Anthony Hope, *The Prisoner of Zenda* (London: Penguin Popular Classics, 1994), p. 39.
32. Hobbes, *Leviathan*, ed. Tuck, p. 135.
33. Ideally, for Hobbes, a reigning monarch should designate his successor by "expresse Words, or Testament . . . as the first Emperours of *Rome* declared who should be their Heires"; or custom should be followed. "But where neither Custome, nor Testament hath preceded, there it is to be understood,

First, that a Monarchs will is, that the government remain Monarchicall; because he hath approved that government in himselfe. Secondly, that a Child of his own, Male, or Female, be preferred before any other; because men are presumed to be more enclined by nature, to advance their own children, than the children of other men; and of their own, rather a Male than a Female; because men, are naturally fitter than women, for actions of labour and danger. Thirdly, where his own Issue faileth, rather a Brother than a stranger." *Ibid.*, pp. 136–137.

34. *Ibid.*, pp. 139, 144, 143. See I Samuel:20, quoted (loosely) by Hobbes.
35. He was also selective in his examples. See his (inaccurate) references to "Chilperique," *ibid.*, pp. 86 and 396. On this subject see further Pierre Riché, *The Carolingians: A Family Who Forged Europe* [1983] tr. Michael Idomir Allen (Philadelphia: University of Pennsylvania Press, 1993), especially part V.2.
36. Hobbes, *Leviathan*, ed. Tuck, p. 88.
37. Thomas Hobbes, *The Elements of Law, Natural and Politic* [1640] ed. Ferdinand Tönnies (Cambridge: Cambridge University Press, 1928), p. 52.
38. W. H. Greenleaf, "Hobbes: the problem of interpretation" [1969] in Maurice Cranston and Richard S. Peters (eds.), *Hobbes and Rousseau: A Collection of Critical Essays* (New York: Doubleday, 1972), pp. 5–35. See also Raia Prokovnik and Gabriella Slomp (eds.), *International Political Theory after Hobbes: Analysis, Interpretation and Orientation* (Houndmills: Palgrave Macmillan, 2011).
39. Hobbes, *Leviathan*, ed. Tuck, pp. 88–89.
40. *Ibid.*, p. 114.
41. David Runciman, "The concept of the state: the sovereignty of a fiction" in Quentin Skinner and Bo Stråth (eds.), *States and Citizens: History, Theory, Prospects* (Cambridge: Cambridge University Press, 2003), p. 37.
42. Lomas, "Anthropomorphism, personification and ethics," p. 351, emphasis in original.
43. Willetts, "Transnational actors and international organizations in global politics."

3

Despite Philosophical Reason

In the absence of personalized institutions or a doctrine like Hobbes's to justify them, the raison d'être of states as expressions of collective will is inevitably called into question. Personalized institutions and Hobbesian doctrine were themselves called into question following the creation in 1945 of a universal system of states with its own self-regarding secular law. This leaves the nature of modern states essentially under challenge. How much more risky, then, must it be to attribute autonomy and independence to them without some overarching set of values? Ultimately, international theory makes sense only if it is normative. That is the argument of this chapter.

3.1 Reality and Ontology

The first set of problems arises as states shift shape, in the conventional wisdom of international relations. This is an issue for ontological inquiry—the philosophy of what reality is made up of. What kind of entity *is* a state, in the human interactions being evoked? Something like, and unlike, a person? A legal organization outlasting individual governments? A territorially based (and defined) group of people? Those people acting together, among other groups of people doing the same? Territory itself? A set of linked (including human) resources? Some or all of these elements seem to be in use at any given point. How they fit together, however, is unclear, and some may be mutually incompatible.

States mean different things for different international theorists too, especially when they begin to question the conventional wisdom. Marjo Koivisto, for example, casts a critical eye over a range of theories, including recent ones. Simplifying somewhat, and in order of examination, I find her queries touch on whether a state

- is an autonomous unit
- changes over time
- is a person
- has causal power
- is subject to global social forces
- is more than the sum of its institutional parts
- is more than the actions of its leaders
- is a territorially settled nation.

She also writes as if states are, and are not, agents in their own right.[1]

3.2 The Norm in Normative

A second, deeper set of problems arises from states' unrepresentativeness, for the peoples governed in their name. This is, it turns out, a universal challenge to human values, in the all-encompassing system created in 1945. The state-agent convention holding the system together entails a perfect identification between existing states and the people inscribed under them. But nothing justifies this step. So far from being (as it was, when first proposed) a solution to humankind's problems, the states system is part of them. It divides, as much as it unites. It confuses, as much as it clarifies. This is a moral concern in its own right. To argue otherwise is, I say, a way of avoiding moral concerns. International theorists should abandon this illusion and focus on moral concerns.

Such an approach is usually described as normative, which I take to mean *aimed to develop morality through norms, or accepted social practices.* Since the origin of the word refers to a measure, we might say a norm is a tangible measure of shared social values—of what people in society agree is right conduct.[2] An illustrative use of the term occurred in a debate in 2007–8 on the question of whether the Anglican Church should ordain as priests individuals who were avowedly homosexual; this had happened in North America, and the resulting controversy threatened to split the worldwide Anglican Communion. Desmond Tutu, the archbishop of Cape Town, took the view that God did not discriminate between people according to their sexual orientation and that Anglicans, accordingly, should not make an issue of recent developments in their church. An American Anglican cleric replied that this would be a dereliction of duty on the part of a body basing moral teaching on the Bible, where homosexuality was condemned. For the Church to ordain avowedly homosexual people would, he argued, send a public message that homosexuality was normative—a practice that anyone might advisedly adopt.

When we say that a particular human practice represents, or goes against, the norm—is or is not *normal*—we speak from some preconception of general or typical human behaviour. Most people, moreover, would argue that morality is meaningful only if it is social—showing membership of, and responsibility to, a human group including, but going beyond, biological families. That after all is the basis of contemporary debates about sexuality. When homosexuality was declared, in Britain, in 1967, to be no longer illegal, it was conditionally defined as taking place "between consenting adults"—as a private practice between individuals which did not impinge on society as a whole. However, it is for two reasons that my interest here is in social norms.

First, in order to stress that the ambit of study in international theory, rightly or wrongly, is anthropocentric—I think rightly. I shall have to defend this position later, but here it means I am not concerned with norms in respect of non-human creatures, or inanimate things, as scientists are when they measure the length of giraffes' necks or the electrical charge of lightning.

Second, to repeat the view I stated at the outset, the study of international relations is overwhelmingly concerned with peoples and societies rather than individuals. I take this to be fairly uncontroversial as a starting assumption; that is, when each of us thinks about "foreign" countries, this implies whole societies whom we do not, or do not fully, know. So, naturally I am going to start from a premise of norms as (human) social practices. At the same time, this is not the whole story. Most obviously, it asks, but does not answer, the question of whose morality one is seeking to develop: the societies we define as the populations of particular countries, or a single society of everyone on earth?

3.3 Justifying the Normative

A more immediate difficulty arises from the fact that in modern international theory, the normative strain has been rather neglected. It "has often been treated as lying at the periphery of the discipline," according to Toni Erskine.[3] Even "critical" social theorists see it as "a separate activity which they do not have to practise," says Mervyn Frost. "It can, on their view, be left to a specialist class of political philosophers."[4] Friendly commentators reflect this bias even while appearing to oppose it. Steve Smith and Patricia Owens, for example, once asserted that

> all theories reflect values, the only question being whether or not we are explicit about what they are ... In our view, all theories have values

67

running through their analysis, from what they choose to focus on as the "facts" to be explained, through the methods they use to study these "facts," down to the policy prescriptions they suggest. Thus, it is not that normative theory is odd, or optional.[5]

Yet the same authors, in editing the same book on international relations, classified normative theory as an "alternative approach" and in shaping the next edition effectively ignored it.[6] We would not say, in life in general, that something was "not optional" and at the same time an "alternative approach," or go on to forget about it altogether—let alone something as important as values.

The long marginalization of normative theory in international studies also seems indefensible when one considers that influential governments have claimed moral leadership in their own way. The US Carter administration (1976–80) promoted universal human rights; the UK Labour government, at the turn of the twenty-first century, proposed an "ethical foreign policy." There has been little of an integrated response to such initiatives; most normative international theory has been produced on specific topics, like nuclear disarmament or global poverty-relief, by individuals not calling themselves international theorists. Baylis, Smith, and Owens even contrive to suggest that "making the world a better place" has gone out of fashion.[7]

Now a certain reserve in this area is understandable. If our theme is the totality of relationships between people in the world, then the vastness of the world, and the diversity of cultures in it, should add a special element of caution—one might even say modesty—to our approaches. There may therefore be virtue in not wanting to appear thoughtlessly prescriptive (advocating specific courses of action) in international theory.

In fact, an element of personal accountability seems to be at stake here, insofar as we all live in separate societies and have distinct relations and responsibilities within them. If I express a judgment, in my own inherited society, of the way I am governed, or on some generalized problem, then I am going to be answerable for it in the most direct of ways. Others in society are likely to see in my assertions a challenge to agree or disagree, and will respond in kind. And if I have particular influence—through education, experience, seniority (over children, at least), or a position affording special insights—then I have an extra duty to make my judgments as wisely as possible (and some may assume that I have this influence even in its absence). In such circumstances, political judgments *are* moral judgments. They have implications for society's norms; the debates to which they give rise can force all of us to revise our personal views. Accountability as immediate as this there is no escaping. But, some would say, these terms cease to apply in respect of societies where we do not have—or perhaps do not choose—to live; so judgments of *them* should not be made in the first place, or made in only the most general of terms. That, too, is what modesty in international theory may mean.

Last but not least, there is a difficulty with the word "normative" itself, often used for something less than, though related to, morality. When a philosopher feels the need to define "normative ethics" as lying between "metaethics" and "applied ethics," we are in more than linguistic trouble;[8] and these distinctions are quoted by Kimberly Hutchings as typical of academic philosophy.

> Meta-Ethics is concerned with the most abstract foundational questions, such as the possibility of moral truth or the meaning of moral agency. Normative Ethics, which always relies on certain meta-ethical assumptions, is concerned with the elaboration and defence of substantive moral theories that provide answers about how to determine moral rightness and wrongness in general. . . . Applied Ethics is concerned with applying Normative Ethics to particular issues and situations.[9]

Yet while different forms of the *study* of morality can be argued for, surely it is the *practice* of morality that matters, in life in general. Over-formalizing and dividing up morality unhelpfully suggests that there is some area of human life to which morality might not apply—an area beyond (meta) ethics. Meanwhile, Applied Ethics gives us the relevant change-effecting aspect of the study, but without mentioning that the effect is, like all morality, social—a meaning that the "norm" part of "normative" carries. Left to itself in the middle, Normative Ethics simply says ethics twice.

In fact one could argue that some norms or accepted social practices ought to be considered *un*acceptable. Nationalism is an example—acceptable when a people's survival is at stake, but unacceptable when it leads to ethnic cleansing. On the other hand, normative theory as morality-in-the-making, as an attempt to create new and better social practices, is definitely what I am about. (In this respect, too, I am following common usage: we may praise a person by saying she is moral but not by saying she is normative.) Still, I have to overcome the impression that this approach is, for most international theorists, just another branch of their subject (and one that they would not touch with a bargepole), and for philosophers a rather narrower undertaking.

The way I overcome all these difficulties is to argue, as I shall do in detail in what follows, that international theorists and moral philosophers, in the modern world, have a common cause. Same world, same subject. My overriding aim is to prove that the task before us is less one of arguing doubtfully about how to include morality in international theory than to decide which courses of action to advocate through the medium of that theory. In other words, "normative" here implies, complex and daunting though the task may seem, aimed to develop morality through norms, or accepted social practices, *in the world as a whole.* The society that is the object of this activity is the society of us all.

As for the "modesty" caveat—dissuasive of judgments of people in distant places on the grounds that their circumstances are not well-known to us, or that the judgments themselves are unaccountable—I think this is a powerful but not a decisive argument. For one thing, it is not self-evident that everyone in the world thinks that way. More important, what is being judged?—the human condition, I think, over and above unknown strangers; and when the strangers themselves become known, it is often because they are contributing forcefully, for good or ill, to the human condition—and so inviting judgment of themselves. In addition, there are beyond doubt societies which have more influence, collectively, than others—through wealth, weapons, or reputation—so that to live in them and *not* form judgments about humankind in general, at least on behalf of its weaker members, is irresponsible in its own right. (I have met people in other societies who thought me unlucky to have been born in Britain, but that was not how my governors taught me to see things.) Finally, as I shall argue in the next chapter, the universal states system itself constitutes a de facto society of all humankind—in which, therefore, moral judgments can be seen as normal.

3.4 Anonymous Agents

To return to the unrepresentativeness of states—which I argue invalidates the state-agent convention and gives rise to the need for normative theory—it should be obvious that I am not referring to a simple question of "internal" political accountability. To say that not all contemporary states are democracies by standards on which all can agree is to express a truism. Meanwhile, there are well-known instances of attempts to set up essentially democratic states, like the provision by which the US Congress is authorized to inhibit US governments' freedom to wage war in the people's name, or the more ambitious claim that the existing United States is an original democratic state.

Here I mean, rather, the objective unrepresentativeness of a given state, in the sense that "its" people may not be represented by it almost regardless of their views. People, for example, are not objectively responsible for events occurring before they were born, so they are not represented—even in democracies—by a state which is nominally the same as the one in whose name certain historical actions were taken. In my own inherited case of the United Kingdom, this would include its very constitution as a grouping of different older societies. Or one could refer to the lack of responsibility borne by women today, more or less everywhere, for aspects of political life dating from before women were allowed to vote in public elections. The historical argument, moreover, cuts both ways, making for intense debates which cannot be impartially resolved. To take another issue, reparations for slavery or colonialism: whether people alive today benefit, or suffer, as a result of some colonial past, they will all do so involuntarily. And if such impacts are conceivable (in terms of racial sensitivities, for example, or economic inequality), it is because the states of today are, in concrete ways, projections from that past.[10]

Whether people live under unaccountable regimes, therefore, or with the consequences of events long past, they will be imperfectly represented by "their" state, and to that extent actions undertaken in their name are not their actions. In later chapters I shall give further examples of this normative disconnection. It does much to explain the different and incompatible roles that states, in conventional international theory, are held to play, and the sleight-of-hand shape-shifting that goes on there.

IR-Talk

Nevertheless, some continue to think that a certain neutrality in this area is possible—that one can, in effect, take or leave normative international theory, at least at the level of language. Opening his study of states in international relations, John M. Hobson writes:

> Across the spectrum of the social sciences a variety of theorists in different disciplines have situated theories of the state within two generic frameworks. The first comprises *normative* theories of the state, which consider what the most desirable or appropriate form

of state and political community might be. The second comprises *explanatory* theories of the state, which consider who controls, or what forces shape, the state and its behaviour.[11]

But is such a distinction possible—taking the morality out of the politics, as it were, and the politics out of the international? Hobson in any case promptly forgets his own rule, when reporting the views of others on the role/function/place of states in international relations. Consider the following twenty observations—paraphrases of theorists' positions—taken from his survey (all emphases and apostrophes are his):

> minimalist liberal states are not envious of each other . . . states voluntarily prefer to conform to international law . . . a "bottom-up" approach which begins with the intentions of states . . . states wish to establish and maintain "a good reputation" . . . states do not know, and therefore do not trust, the intentions of others . . . state *A* will gladly forgo any gains . . . states cannot afford to be indifferent or insensitive to others' gains . . . states are interested in getting to the "Pareto Frontier" . . . states do not want to be classified as acting outside the bounds of "civilized" international society . . . states often come to tolerate limits on their sovereignty . . . these norms lead states to subconsciously choose to cooperate . . . states tend to create the appearance of a *threatening* "other," against which the "self" is defined negatively . . . Japan has refused to share its economic technology . . . [Japan has] been highly intransigent and inflexible . . . "anarchy is what states make of it" . . . developments in the international system [. . .] pushed states to increase expenditures . . . the state is what I call "territorially promiscuous" . . . the ultimate Bonapartist balancing act that states can achieve . . . states have promoted (intentionally and unintentionally) the development of an increasingly integrated global spatial architecture.[12]

Hobson, let me repeat, is merely summarizing the views of others here. Still, anyone can see that this is nonsense-talk. All these affective expressions involve assertions about states not just as agents—as the subjects of actions—but as moral agents, fully like persons. Surely a *"sic."* ought to be stuck onto every one of them—even onto single words ("subconscious" states?—not Freudian individuals, please note, but whole Freudian societies are being implied!). What is the reality in everyday, literal terms, being evoked here? Who, precisely, can be identified as the individual or group engaged in the supposed actions? Where can we go to see the attitudes and emotions expressed? And though value judgments are obviously involved, how can we engage with them, to support or oppose the underlying positions? Earlier I acknowledged that one could be tentative in formulating moral judgments in international relations, but the kind of writing Hobson alludes to is not at all cautious in that respect: it expresses value judgments boldly at every turn, in the clear language of human emotion. Yet at the same time it is devoid of clear human subjects or a clear social context—and so devoid of a credible foundation.

Or consider Andrew Linklater writing in his own person—as it happens, on a normative international theme:

> States have developed laws of war that limit the harm they do to each other and to their respective populations, but they have not had the same success in creating a system of cosmopolitan law that protects the rights of persons everywhere. Difficulties in the latter domain have arisen because rival conceptions of human rights exist in international society and because new states in particular have been anxious to ensure that support for the international protection of human rights does not become a pretext for intervening in their internal affairs.[13]

Again, this is clearly wrong, since the relations in question are not analytically portrayed, as between the "minds" of states; which in any case I would say is implausible. All too obviously this passage was written with no forethought as to the entities involved and the actions being described. How can states do harm to each other *and* to "their respective populations"? Are not human populations precisely what makes up states, to engage in relations, harmful or otherwise? If not, what kind of entities are these, so "anxious" to block the interventions of (equally ill-defined) others in their "internal affairs"—in the name, of all things, of the protection of "human rights"? Human agents as subjects and objects of actions are being muddled together here, to make a third, redundant, and meaningless thing (a state agent) beyond them all.

Or consider Baylis, Smith, and Owens attempting a multifaceted definition of states: as something like a "legal person," as conceptualized for companies in domestic law; as a "country" or "a community of people who interact in the same political system"; or as "the apparatus of government, in its broadest sense"—depending, the authors say, on whether the disciplinary perspective is that of the lawyer, political theorist, philosopher, or sociologist. Arguably this is ducking the definitional question altogether. Then under "state autonomy" we read that "in a more interdependent world, simply to achieve domestic objectives national governments [*sic*] are forced to engage in extensive multilateral collaboration and cooperation." They go on:

> But in becoming more embedded in frameworks of global and regional governance states confront a real dilemma: in return for more effective public policy and meeting their citizens' demands . . . their capacity for self-governance—that is state autonomy—is compromised.

With this authorial slippage from government (real agent) to state (false agent), the drama of governments' "dilemma" in trying to act freely in a complex tug of loyalties in the world is elided. With the reification of the state agent as something separate from the peoples and institutions trapped in the web of interdependence, a whole structure of relations is set up in which no conscious, judging humans figure.

Again, "state-sponsored terrorism exists," say these authors, "when individual states provide support to terrorist groups including funding, training, and resources, including weapons," though in such situations "states go to great lengths to ensure that their involvement is as clandestine as possible so that their leaders have a degree of plausible deniability when they respond to such charges." Here again we find reified state agents making separate choices, and taking separate actions, from the choices and actions of "their leaders"—a political and conceptual nonsense. Later, the "original connotation of terrorism" is said to be "the use of violence by the state to keep its own citizenry fearful"—thus positing state agents acting separately from the people as well.[14] No wonder terrorists are so hard to track down, if they are able to hide from both governments and citizens in some mysterious space called "the state." But of course, this is nothing more than the empty conceptual space occupied by the state (agent) in the authors' projections. Impersonal, anonymous, a law unto itself, this pointless invention of theorists only feeds the mystique of terrorist fear.

3.5 Agents and Proxies

In the previous chapter I distinguished between two key meanings of "to act"—the dramatic or imaginative, and the literal or prosaic. Actors, I said (adopting the usual term from stage and screen), go "outside" or "beyond" themselves in pretending to be other, usually imaginary, people; while agents (adopting the usual term from philosophy) are simply the doers of ordinary everyday actions, or actions in general. Now I want to stress the moral difference between these conceptions of agency, which Hobbes deliberately overrides: one is free and the other is not.

A free agent (again, according to common usage) is someone who takes action in his or her own right; with his or her own volition; whose actions are synonymous with his/her own will—in order to express or extend his or her own person. I am being a free agent when I lift up this book in front of me and open it to read. I am doing exactly what I will: exercising metaphysical freedom, the property of everyone. Agency, as used by philosophers, often includes this sense of capacity: the capacity to choose one's actions absolutely. By contrast, there are people whose actions serve or reproduce the will of another, but are still, unlike the actor's, literal. A lawyer retained on our behalf, to carry out our instructions, is such a person: our servant, with no effective will of his/her own. Diplomats or politicians occupy this position temporarily, when they sign treaties in the name of states. This is Hobbes's "Representer," but without his confusing theatrical overtones. The usual word for such a person is a proxy.

Confusingly, in some social contexts the word "agent" remains in use in this sense. Estate (in America, real-estate) agents are employed by people who wish, perhaps anonymously, to buy or sell property in a legally recorded transaction. Theatrical or performance agents serve the actors and singers of stage and screen, to win contracts for them, to gain (or save) them publicity. Travel agents can arrange journeys for us. Literary agents try to get their clients' writings into print. All of these, moreover, can be agents on behalf of groups—performance agents for theatrical troupes, travel agents for group travel, literary agents for joint authors, lawyers representing firms in court.

Agents of this kind are go-betweens, putting themselves forward for us in situations where we cannot be present or, perhaps, have all the relevant information at our fingertips. Their only raison d'être is faithfully to carry out our wishes, their only exercise of personal autonomy when they choose to be, or to cease to be, our representatives. Their choices are made within preordained rules, and within those rules they bear no responsibility for consequences. This enables them to remain separate individuals in their own right; they have merely placed their personal wills in abeyance while acting professionally on others' behalf. To put it differently, they have artificially and temporarily divided up their wills between their own and others'. Married lawyers could not also be divorce lawyers, unless these rules of representation held.

Proxies, then, are important real people, but not what we normally call free agents. They take action, but with no, or insignificant, autonomy. Their purpose, like the actors of stage and screen, is precisely *not* to enact their own persons; but unlike those feigners, they have no subjectivity either. Actors retain an irreducible quantum of subjectivity in interpreting their assigned roles, where they are prompted, by authors, producers, and directors, to deeper and richer imaginings of persons and situations beyond their surroundings and even their own experience. Still, in the end no one's will is divisible. Even actors can never forget (on pain of madness, as *Hamlet* shows) that they are real people, with personal causes, behind the mask of invention—sometimes perversely, when, to the frustration of audiences and critics, they misrepresent their authors' intentions; sometimes inadvertently, when they forget their lines, perhaps because a love affair, or the shopping, suddenly seems more important. But as for proxies, they are not in any real sense the subjects of the actions they carry out. It is precisely in that lack of subjectivity that their usefulness to others consists.

These understandings, however, seem scarcely to figure in the way the workings of the modern states system are depicted. In international law and diplomacy, and in much of international theory, states are held to do things in their own right, in accord with their own "wills." They take initiatives; they are not proxies. They comprise the membership of international organizations, starting with the chief inter-state body, the UN, and conclude agreements among themselves which are binding on whole populations: a role of corporate agent (not servant) in law. They embody the distributed "ownership" of territory and resources: a role of proprietor. They perpetuate "their" people's continuity with the past, as custodians of history and inheritance. They "recognise" each other, which means bestowing a form of legitimacy. By implication, they get into the domain of values—exercising moral agency in their own right. Yet this involves no direct consultation of the wishes of the peoples concerned. How could it, on the scale of all states at once? This is where all the problems of international theory begin.

As David Runciman puts it:

> The moral agency of the state depends upon individuals suspending their disbelief, and acting as though the state has a moral agency that it in fact lacks. It so happens that individuals seem to be quite able to do this, and modern political life is founded on just this kind of wishful thinking, but it has been achieved for the most part despite

rather than with the aid of philosophical reason, which cannot be expected to let the matter rest there.[15]

States cannot be agents in their own right a) literally, because they are not individual human beings, and b) because they are not, either, societies acting "as one," "like a person," which they conceivably could be only if they embodied—were perfectly identical with, in all cases—"their" peoples: a condition which, I shall argue, is neither possible nor desirable. The present states system is a purely formal arrangement in which each component state figures as, at best, a metaphor. What happens in reality is that each of the several roles or functions formally ascribed to states is enacted piecemeal by each government of the day, while other activities go on which may, or may not, be fairly ascribed to the peoples implied. International relations viewed holistically, as an empirical activity, is the shapeless sum of these parts.

What the state-agent/actor convention, by its very falsity, teaches is that we must find a way to incorporate into international theory the subjective element which is integral to human nature, or that theory will encourage representations of our situation on earth which strip us of our humanity and our freedoms at a time when statehood has become a fact of life for everyone. This is the real, underlying crisis of modernity. There is one hypothetical community of humankind, but it is confused and made inherently conflictual by the states system—or at least more so than need be the case. Yet this is not the same as anarchy, the lack of overarching government in the world that international Realists evoke. Rather the problem, as Rousseau remarked, is that government is everywhere, and everywhere contestable.[16]

Notes

1. "The state, in its institutional ensemble, has a variety of strategies available to both resist institutionalisation by other actors . . . and to pursue multiscalar strategies in [an] attempt to articulate new state space . . . the state in its institutional specificity must be understood as relatively autonomous of the national scale . . . the state makes successful (or unsuccessful) claims to institutionalise state space at various scales, and so do other social forces." Yet she concludes that "state power . . . is specific to the strategies and activities that its officials reflexively mobilise in the context of the state's strategically selective institutions." Marjo Koivisto, "State theory in International Relations: why Realism matters" in Jonathan Joseph and Colin Wight (eds.), *Scientific Realism and International Relations* (Basingstoke: Palgrave Macmillan, 2010), pp. 69–87, quoting here from pp. 84 and 86.

2. Latin *norma*, "carpenter's square, pattern, rule" (*Shorter Oxford English Dictionary*, 1983).

3.   Toni Erskine, "Normative international relations theory" in Dunne, Kurki and Smith (eds.), *International Relations Theories*, p. 55.
4.   Mervyn Frost, *Ethics in International Relations: A Constitutive Theory* (Cambridge: Cambridge University Press, 1996), p. 33.
5.   Steve Smith and Patricia Owens, "Alternative approaches to international society" in John Baylis and Steve Smith (eds.), *The Globalization of World Politics* (3rd ed. Oxford: Oxford University Press, 2005), p. 279.
6.   Baylis, Smith and Owens (eds.), *The Globalization of World Politics* (4th ed. Oxford: Oxford University Press, 2008).
7.   They attribute the deliberate taking of "a normative position," or a "commitment to change the world" in IR theory to the period 1919–1939, sometimes called the period of Idealism. They go on: "[The] debate between idealism and realism has continued to the present day, but it is fair to say that realism has tended to have the upper hand." Baylis, Smith and Owens, "Introduction," *The Globalization of World Politics* (6th ed. 2014), pp. 3–4.
8.   The reference is to Shelly Kagan, *Normative Ethics* (Boulder, Colo.: Westview Press, 1998), p. 2.
9.   Kimberly Hutchings, *Global Ethics: An Introduction* (Cambridge: Polity Press, 2010), p. 6.
10. On this last point see Thomas Pogge, *Realizing Rawls* (Ithaca: Cornell University Press, 1989); D. K. Fieldhouse, *The Colonial Empires: A Comparative Survey from the Eighteenth Century; Economics and Empire 1830–1914*, and *Colonialism 1870–1945: An Introduction* (London: Weidenfeld and Nicolson, 1966, 1973, and 1981).
11. John M. Hobson, *The State and International Relations* (Cambridge: Cambridge University Press, 2000), p. 2, emphasis in original.
12. *Ibid.*, pp. 70, 93 (twice), 99 (twice), 100 (three times), 153, 154, 155, 159, 170 (twice), 172, 205, 230 (twice), 234.
13. Andrew Linklater, "Cosmopolitan harm conventions" in Steven Vertovec and Robin Cohen (eds.), *Conceiving Cosmopolitanism: Theory, Context and Practice* (Oxford: Oxford University Press, 2002), p. 260.
14. Baylis, Smith and Owens (eds.), *The Globalization of World Politics* (6th ed. 2014), pp. 544–545.
15. David Runciman, "Moral responsibility and the problem of representing the state" in Toni Erskine (ed.), *Can Institutions Have Responsibilities?* (Basingstoke: Palgrave Macmillan, 2003), p. 47.
16. "L'homme est né libre, et partout il est dans les fers." Opening of Jean-Jacques Rousseau, *Du Contrat Social* [1762].

II

Talk about the World

4

All International Theorists Now

In this section I investigate the best philosophical basis that can be found for a reformed—a normative—international theory.

To recapitulate, there are two sets of problems arising from the uncritical assumption of state agency. First is our apparent inability to give a final answer to the ontological question: what kind of entity is a state—where does it fit into our overall vision of reality? Second, we need to know how states can represent us fully and fairly, since we are all forced to live under one.

Clearly, international theory must be normative in practice, to answer the second question alone. But the first opens up, in its own right, the basis of reality on which the populations of the world must live. It is therefore necessary to go back to philosophical first principles and rethink international theory with their help. In this chapter I consider and reject Naturalism as a way to proceed.

4.1 Naturalism

Naturalism is the view that there is nothing beyond the physical domain, the one detectable by our senses—in Anthony Quinton's definition, "any philosophy which sees mind as dependent upon, included within, or emergent from, material nature, and not as being prior to or in some way more real than it."[1] Reinhardt Grossmann argues that there are Naturalists *and then* ontologists, because the former deny the possibility of mental events altogether.[2]

Whatever states are, they exist and serve the purposes they do only insofar as humankind shares some conception of them. International theory itself relies on what Karen Fierke calls an "intersubjective ontology," implying a domain of shared ideas.[3] Some of these may be unrealizable *ideals*, but the effect is the same: Naturalism will not do as a version of international relations, even a partial one.

Grossmann declines to argue the case against Naturalism analytically, on the grounds that there is "a battle between two temperaments":

> There is, on the one hand, the scientific temperament which favors a conception of philosophy as, at worst, a brother of poetry, and at best a servant of science. On the other hand, there is the ontological spirit, according to which ontology has a completely different perspective from the sciences and offers glimpses of truths scientists never dream of. According to the naturalist, everything that is not scientific smacks of mysticism. Ontology can be nothing but poetry in disguise. To leave science is to travel through a night without stars, through a blackness without light. According to the ontologist, to abandon ontology is to desert a field that grows the most fascinating flowers of truth. I describe the battle in these emotional terms, because it is an emotional battle. In all such battles, the choice is never merely between two rational positions.[4]

But surely the problems that revolve around the states system decide the issue even more firmly, because this is an important—perhaps the most important—locus of human contestation and conflict, over territory and material resources, over cultural values, over power itself and its legitimacy; and states now cover, physically and conceptually, the whole inhabitable earth. In the face of this challenge, only a vision which incorporates moral concerns in its essence can cope, and this rules out from the start approaches with no place for minds or shared ideas. I divide the challenge into the ubiquity and the permanence of states.

4.2 The Ubiquity of States

In 1945 the United Nations Organization introduced a universal principle: everyone in the world shall have a state. This meant two things: the physical enclosure and division of the earth.

These developments are two sides of the same coin. On one side, the rule that there is no longer any inhabitable part of the earth that does not "belong to" someone or other, through the putative nations so united. As R. N. Berki put it:

> [The concept of sovereignty] has come to signify the nation's absolute supremacy to conduct its relations, external and internal, according to its own will and without any obligation to a higher, more comprehensive community. Most significantly, it refers also to the nation's unlimited right to use and dispose of its material wealth, natural resources, scientific know-how, skill, manpower, and so forth. It

confirms, in other words, the position of the nation as *owner*—owner of property which, in the context of a community of nations, appears as "private property" pure and simple.[5]

On the other side is the rule that there is no longer anyone on earth who does not "belong to" some formally constituted nation-state. This is clearly visible in the founding principle of the UN that colonialism should come to an end everywhere. The predecessor organization, the League of Nations, coexisted with empires and entrusted whole populations to imperial regimes.[6] Within empires, nation-states (including, in some aspects, the metropolitan one) could still be portrayed as fluid, their parameters blurred by transcontinental identities and aims. But in a system formally dedicated to the abolition of empires, only nation-states could subsist as the leading concentrations of political power.

The new conjuncture is evident in other, less grandiose but no less effective ways. There are, for example, powerful twin legal dispositions against individuals' being stateless, and against their belonging to more than one state at once (nation-belonging apparently being less decidable in law). The first means no legal protection for the victims, except under the UN itself; for in order to be recognized as UN refugees, stateless individuals must surrender any previous citizenship they have held. Yet the UN is also the supreme organization of states, and its own identity and freedom of maneuver depend on that fact. As for "dual nationality," this in theory enables individuals to transcend the jurisdiction of any one state, except that state governments have the legal right to recognise only one of the formal identities claimed—commonly that of an individual's birth. Potentially, this is a right of life or death.[7]

To the physical ubiquity of states we should add their cultural or conceptual ubiquity, as manifested by the Enlightenment legacy of the scientific worldview, implicit in Berki's comment that the earth's material resources are to be not only owned, but also used and even expanded with the help of human intelligence and its product, technology. This predominantly European model is now universal, owing to the impact of European colonial regimes. In its wake come the ideals of technical "modernization" and "development," prevalent now in all non-Western societies under the impetus of people's aspirations to Western standards of living, which governments everywhere encourage and varyingly serve. Where once it was the practice to refer to the margins of the "known world," remote places explored only by adventurers and colonials, now the known world is effectively the whole world.

No part is considered beyond the power of science, within the framework of the states system, to explore and to exploit.

4.3 The Permanence of States

The introduction of a spatially comprehensive states system is not the only significant innovation in human social arrangements since 1945. The other is the prescribed permanence of states themselves. In this way it is given to states through their governments to dominate not only all territorial space but all future time as well. The onset of the Cold War after 1945, its length, its apocalyptic dangers and apparent insolubility obscured for decades the far-reaching implications of the new world constitution. Until the early 1960s, moreover, the UN's founding principles remained unfulfilled for millions of people born under the European empires. But the rapid decolonization which then began is more or less complete; and the Cold War is over.

The effect of all this has been to push onto a universal plane the secularization of society promoted in Europe since the Enlightenment. Religious belief can help to assuage people's uncertainty about the future. Until 1945 this could include uncertainty about the survival of states and the fulfilment of hopes associated with them, notably people's hopes of material security for themselves and their descendants. The modern states system stands in principle for the removal of this uncertainty (but only in principle; for many it has meant the opposite, as material security has gone unrealized, cultural development distorted, and personal fulfilment denied).

4.4 Unnatural States

These two features—the all-encompassing character of states and their dominance over all other formal institutions—derive from a deeper feature, their artifice, the fact of being "man-made."[8]

This includes, but means more than, artificiality when we say, as we sometimes do, that this or that state is artificial, because its population is not a "natural" community—or worse, is inherently prone to conflict. Some states could quite plausibly be seen as harboring natural communities (say, island states, or where there is a perception of long-lived ethnic continuity). Nor am I referring here to the elaborate product of Hobbes's doctrine, whose very logic rests on the artificiality of individual states. Rather, it is the states *system* which is artificial—the ubiquity and the permanence of states together. Implicitly, the system is an end in itself.

To repeat, everyone on earth "belongs to" a state; everyone is supremely represented to everyone else through a state. All higher institutions are inter-state institutions, modifiable and ultimately revocable by actions in the name of states. All lower institutions are accountable on a sliding scale that has states, or the system of states, at its apex. In the case of non-governmental organizations, this hierarchy is a legal one even though they may exist to contest governments and laws; their "consultative status" under the UN organization means that in practice their access and influence are subject to the wishes of state governments.

States, in short, have been made the sovereign human institution not only immediately, practically, but also existentially, timelessly. Yet in this system which depends essentially on states as its units, the units are unalike. This is uncharacteristic of the systems of nature as we interpret them. It is also unnatural, in terms of *human* nature, that any institution should be held to represent all human society for the whole of time and space without itself being open to change.

The product of a single decision after the Second World War, this is an innovation with totalitarian implications. In the conventional wisdom of international relations the states system is taken as given, or interpreted anthropologically, as a development from the human past leading seamlessly to a kind of politics of state agents. But I want to stress the circularity of this reasoning and the unreality, in terms of lives lived, of this first truly global institutional step. In practice, as I shall show, states mean different things for different people in different places, even though the ideals people seek through—and beyond—them may be the same.

States cannot, or cannot easily, be naturalized; and this is more of a problem than the conventional wisdom suggests. The societies established under the system are not, after all, voluntary. Modern states are not—with the tortuous productions of Hobbes's imagination behind us—electable, accountable, replaceable, disposable, punishable, as the human members of their governments (in theory) are. If they were, who knows how many people would not choose to belong to a different state, or to none at all? Our political theory, and by extension our theory of international relations, is worth nothing unless it takes account of this fact.

4.5 Four Moral Concerns

If we live in a wholly known, or at least wholly claimed, world, divided up between organs of political power to which all other instruments and forms of power are formally subordinated, yet with deep

85

inconsistencies, then the universal states system itself begins to look like an anomaly. International theory must be normative, to face the challenges that arise.

Normative international theory was forced underground in the Cold War, during which time the danger of human extinction took precedence over everything else. But this danger too was man-made. Virtually all morality, in fact, was obfuscated by politicians in the Cold War; for the result of their response—in both North and South—to the general threat of extinction implicit in nuclear weapons was the bloc system in which the territorial and conceptual borders of states, with their imprisoned peoples, were blurred, in a caricature of deontological, morally chosen cosmopolitanism. The unity of humankind was invoked by subjection, as leaders placed their feet on our collective neck.

This generalized moral evil, in which many international theorists were complicit, at last began to be abolished in 1989; yet international theory, especially normative international theory, has still to catch up, to realize the full implications of the universal states system in the light of the moral challenges of the Cold War; which includes finding forgiveness for what was done in the Cold War to hold back humankind's search for happiness and peace.

This task is now, naturally enough, a task for everyone. The classical thinkers of ancient times brought systematic philosophy, including moral philosophy, into being by generalizing from their personal perceptions to the whole of humankind. At the same time, their practical knowledge of the earth, and of humankind's diverse and expanding cultures, was circumscribed by the limits of travel. Today the wheel has come full circle: in science we have a potential practical knowledge of the whole earth, and the diversity of culture has narrowed, yet there are moral concerns which are discernibly those of all humankind. They include (to mention the four which seem to me the easiest to define) the unequal enjoyment of political freedoms across the earth; material inequality between "Northern" older-industrialized societies and "Southern" rural or former-colonial ones, where poverty may threaten human life itself; the continuing existence of weapons of mass destruction and strategies for their use; and a troubled relationship with the natural environment, in which human overpopulation figures prominently but also confusedly, as both cause and effect.[9] Already, some modern philosophers have begun to adapt classical traditions of thought to specific problems like these.[10] Yet we still await efforts of similar determination and rigor from the side of international theory.[11]

In any case, a disciplinary division of labor on matters of concern to all humankind is a contradiction in terms.

The universal states system has turned states into a metaphysical object; we are all international theorists now. But a paradoxical one; so philosophers must extend their ambit to human relations in the world as a whole. What is needed above all is a return to a holistic form of reasoning which emerged after the Second World War, only to fall out of favor with the rise of professional international theory. In briefly more optimistic times, the philosopher F. S. C. Northrop argued that the intensification of international relations should lead to a fusion of cultures—Eastern and Western, scientific and aesthetic—and the reconciliation of differences between peoples.[12] As his collaborator put it: "The next step forward is a world order, doing for the world as a whole what the legal order in the state has achieved for the state."[13] And by implication, what the states system had so far, in terms of peace and justice, failed to achieve.

In turn, we need a more precise and expansive conception of reality than Naturalism affords, and which, unlike Naturalism, includes moral ideas as normal. In the next chapter I shall attempt to set one out.

Notes

1. Entry in Alan Bullock, Oliver Stallybrass and Stephen Trombley (eds.), *The Fontana Dictionary of Modern Thought* (2nd ed. London: Fontana Press, 1988), p. 562.
2. Reinhardt Grossmann, *The Existence of the World: An Introduction to Ontology* (London: Routledge, 1992), ch. I.
3. Karen Fierke, "Constructivism" in Dunne, Kurki and Smith (eds.), *International Relations Theories*, p. 172.
4. Grossmann, *The Existence of the World*, p. 9.
5. R. N. Berki, "On Marxian thought and the problem of international relations," *World Politics* 24 (1), October 1971, pp. 102–103, original emphasis. The International Covenants on Economic, Social and Cultural Rights and on Civil and Political Rights (1966) have identical articles (I/2) that "All peoples may, for their own ends, freely dispose of their natural wealth and resources without prejudice to any obligations arising out of international economic co-operation, based upon the principle of mutual benefit, and international law." Texts in Ian Brownlie and Guy S. Goodwin-Gill (eds.), *Basic Documents on Human Rights* (6th ed. Oxford: Clarendon Press, 2006).
6. On this topic see further Øyvind Østerud, "The narrow gate: entry to the club of sovereign states," *Review of International Studies* 23 (2), April 1997, pp. 167–184.
7. In an extreme example of a state government exercising its sovereign right to judge its "own" people, even after they have left for other jurisdictions, in 2009 the Iranian authorities arrested and subsequently executed an

Iranian-born Dutch citizen on a domestic criminal charge (drug smuggling; see "Iran hangs Iranian-Dutch woman Sahra Bahrami," BBC World News Online 29 January 2011). Ms Bahrami had first been arrested while taking part in protests against contentious Iranian presidential elections, which doubtless constituted her real offence in the eyes of the government that emerged from them.

8.   I am using this as a merely conventional expression. I would not be opposed to its interpretation in a feminist historical sense, to condemn centuries of male domination of political life—provided this is seen as resulting in the same artificial product.

9.   "Older-industrialized" seems to me a useful dual description for the European and North American societies whose industry is physically older than in the "newly industrialized/industrializing" societies of Latin America and East Asia, and also whose secular institutions go back further than in the traditional or rural societies now developing them.

10.   E.g., Charles R. Beitz, *Political Theory and International Relations* [1979] (2nd ed. Princeton, NJ: Princeton University Press, 1999); Michael Walzer, *Spheres of Justice: A Defense of Pluralism and Equality* (Oxford: Martin Robertson, 1983) and *Just and Unjust Wars: A Moral Argument with Historical Illustrations* (4th ed. New York: Basic Books, 2006); Charles R. Beitz, Marshall Cohen, Thomas Scanlon and A. John Simmons (eds.), *International Ethics: A Philosophy and Public Affairs Reader* (Princeton, NJ: Princeton University Press, 1985); Onora O'Neill, *Faces of Hunger: An Essay on Poverty, Justice and Development* (London: Allen & Unwin, 1986); John Finnis, Joseph M. Boyle, Jr., and Germain Grisez, *Nuclear Deterrence, Morality and Realism* (Oxford: Clarendon Press, 1987); Thomas W. Pogge, *World Poverty and Human Rights: Cosmopolitan Responsibilities and Reforms* (2nd ed. Cambridge/Malden, MA: Polity Press, 2008); Henry Shue, *Basic Rights: Subsistence, Affluence and US Foreign Policy* (2nd ed. Princeton, NJ: Princeton University Press, 1996); Gordon Graham, *Ethics and International Relations* (Oxford: Blackwell, 1997); Nigel Dower, *World Ethics: The New Agenda* (Edinburgh: Edinburgh University Press, 1998); John Rawls, *The Law of Peoples* (Cambridge, MA: Harvard University Press, 1999); Simon Caney, *Justice beyond Borders: A Global Political Theory* (Oxford: Oxford University Press, 2002); Nigel Dower and John Williams (eds.), *Global Citizenship: A Critical Reader* (Edinburgh: Edinburgh University Press, 2002); Peter Singer, *One World: The Ethics of Globalization* (New Haven: Yale University Press, 2002); Seyla Benhabib, *Another Cosmopolitanism*, commentaries by Jeremy Waldron, Bonnie Honig and Will Kymlicka, ed. Robert Post (New York: Oxford University Press, 2006); Thomas W. Pogge and Darrel Moellendorf (eds.), *Global Justice: Seminal Essays* and Thomas W. Pogge and Keith Horton (eds.), *Global Ethics: Seminal Essays* (St. Paul, MN: Paragon House, 2008).

11.   Honorable exceptions include Chris Brown, *International Relations Theory: New Normative Approaches* (Brighton: Harvester Wheatsheaf, 1992); Terry Nardin and David R. Mapel (eds.), *Traditions of International Ethics* (Cambridge: Cambridge University Press, 1992); Mervyn Frost, *Ethics in International Relations: A Constitutive Theory* (Cambridge: Cambridge University Press, 1996), and (ed.), *International Ethics* (Los Angeles: Sage,

2011); Moorehead Wright (ed.), *Morality and International Relations: Concepts and Issues* (Aldershot: Avebury, 1996); Molly Cochran, *Normative Theory in International Relations: A Pragmatic Approach* (Cambridge: Cambridge University Press, 1999); *How Might We Live? Global Ethics in a New Century*, special issue of *Review of International Studies* 26, December 2000; Joel H. Rosenthal and Christian Barry (eds.), *Ethics and International Affairs: A Reader* (3rd ed. Washington, DC: Georgetown University Press, 2009); Patrick Hayden (ed.), *The Ashgate Research Companion to Ethics and International Relations* (Farnham, Surrey/Burlington, VT: Ashgate, 2009); Kimberly Hutchings, *Global Ethics: An Introduction* (Cambridge: Polity Press, 2010); Richard Shapcott, *International Ethics: A Critical Introduction* (Cambridge: Polity Press, 2010); and Duncan Bell (ed.), *Ethics and World Politics* (Oxford: Oxford University Press, 2010).

12. F. S. C. Northrop, *The Meeting of East and West* (New York: Macmillan, 1946); (ed.), *Ideological Differences and World Order: Studies in the Philosophy and Science of the World's Cultures* (New Haven: Yale University Press, 1949).

13. Roscoe Pound, "Towards a new jus gentium" in Northrop (ed.), *Ideological Differences and World Order*, p. 1.

5

The Human Domain

International theorists take for granted that they should talk about the world; but what justifies this assumption in the first place? The superficial answer is anthropocentrism. But what justifies anthropocentrism, apart from simple human self-interest? My answer is human distinctiveness. Only human beings are capable of imagining everything there is. This places us in a dominant position in nature, on the earth—a fact which gives rise to morality itself, by showing us our power over, and responsibility to, all living things, including ourselves. If this is true, only human beings are moral, and international theory must be normative in principle.

Ontology

I said "if this is true"; I need first to show that human beings are capable of imagining everything there is. This I propose to do by an excursion into ontology. That is the first major theme of this chapter. Human beings define the world, against the background of reality as a whole.

Morality

The second follows from it: the explanation of morality, as the application of human dominance. Here I find significant that we use "integrity" both for moral uprightness and for a holistic sense of ourselves.[1] By implication, it is possible to be both happy and good.

Action

Still, morality even as the application of human dominance is social—realised in action toward, in company with, other people: doing good, or the right thing, for its own sake; when necessary, in others' interest at the expense of our own; not as the proxy of another person, or under duress, but freely, willingly, with our own inner purposes and desires, as an expression of our power to change—both the world and our own selves.

5.1 Ontology: Realism

Ontology is the attempt to form a general theory of reality, as Empedocles (fifth century BCE) did when he asserted that everything was
made up of earth, air, water, or fire, or some combination of these "elements." His account reflects the simple metaphysics we all cultivate, as
we grow out of childhood and try to put together a meaningful picture
of what surrounds us. That this is a would-be comprehensive picture
is often lost sight of, as we learn to live with practical limitations—
perhaps allowing ourselves, in these modern times, some amusement
at the ancient Greek's naive physics. Yet the challenge for us is the
same as it was for him: how to determine what everything is made up
of while being sure that nothing, in our working hypotheses, is left
out. Modern ontology is the attempt to take up the challenge with the
greatest rigor and incorporating all the gains in perception owed to
science. Among its exponents, the so-called Realists (nothing to do
with Realism in international theory) make the most ambitious claims
for human powers.

In the last chapter I referred to Reinhardt Grossmann's dismissal
of Naturalism as the belief that "there are no abstract things."[2] Most
of us, I suggested, would reject Naturalism on these grounds, arguing
that there really are minds, and ideas formed by them, even if we do
not understand everything about them or agree on an identical view of
them. There are even shared ideas, attesting to the existence of communicating minds. The universal states system we live under would
not have come into existence at all, as an assemblage of ideas about
human social organization, if that were not the case.

The general argument for ontological Realism originates elsewhere,
in the observation that material things exist independently of our
thoughts about them. What we think about material things is not without consequences *for them*; obviously, down the centuries, the human
impact on nature has never ceased to grow. But equally, we can, and
do, acknowledge the independent existence of material things in nature
and allow the operations of nature to take place "on their own." Most
of the time they will do so anyway: the winds will blow, the clouds will
form, and rain will fall, the tides will rise up on the shore whatever we
do, as King Canute legendarily sought to show.

On this basis we say that the operations of nature, and material things
in general, are real. Turning this perception on its head, we may say
that our thoughts about nature and material things are in their own

right real, even though they cannot be directly observed. Realism in ontology begins from here. There are material things, and non-material things, and both make up reality. Empedocles's account, portraying everything as either earth, air, water, or fire, is incomplete. It is a materialist (or a Naturalist) account. In international theory, moreover, we are interested so much in the society of human beings that it is often non-material things that dominate our thinking. This, too, means we will incline toward Realism in ontology.

Universals

The core of this approach, as developed by philosophers, is the finding of common characteristics—"universals"—in things, enabling their classification into categories or most-general types of entity. As biologists classify all living things by their observed common characteristics, so ontological Realists categorize literally everything there is, to build up a comprehensive picture of reality. (In the next chapter I consider how this works out concretely and in detail in international theory.)

Some philosophers, called Nominalists, have denied the existence of universals, arguing that human beings perceive each thing separately and as it were for the first—and last—time, so that to give expression to experience is nothing more than the act of naming (hence Nominalism). Hobbes stood out for this view, declaring there was "nothing in the world Universall but Names; for the things named, are every one of them Individuall and Singular."[3] To a Nominalist, the classification of things by their commonly perceived properties is impossible, because the perception itself is an illusion. By the same logic, a vision of reality as a whole is beyond reach. For reasons which will become clear, I choose to adopt a Realist approach not only over a Naturalist one but over a Nominalist one as well.

From the distinctions made by Grossmann, I arrive at the following conclusions of interest for my argument.

1) Ontological Realists, unlike Naturalists, claim that there is such a thing as mind and therefore abstraction, judgment, and power over material things.
2) Ontological Realists, unlike Nominalists, claim that it is possible to form a philosophical theory which (hypothetically) encompasses everything which really exists and happens.

"Hypothetically" is an important qualifier here. The ontological-Realist claim is not that someone may encompass, Godlike, in his or her mind every single thing there is—only that a theory is possible which encompasses every *type* of thing, and orders experience according to this principle.

In his account Grossmann distinguishes between the world and the universe. The latter is "one gigantic spatio-temporal whole. . . . *The universe is a concrete thing, and so is every part of it.*" The world is the domain that we humans inhabit, against the background of the concrete, spatio-temporal universe. Though materially concentrated in Planet Earth, it obviously extends beyond, whether directly (since humans have travelled into space), or indirectly (since humans have observed and made sense of further parts of the universe). Above all, though part of the spatio-temporal universe, the world is conceptually distinct from it through our reasoning, in particular our capacity to conceive abstractions—mental orderings not limited in time and space. The properties of things by which we categorize them exemplify this capacity, and this domain.[4]

A Common Definition of the World

Clearly, philosophy has moved on since Empedocles's time, when categories of matter could be held to cover everything there is. We now routinely hold that there are material things and non-material things, and both make up reality. So much for Naturalism. There are real abstract things.

By the same token, the categories by which we classify everything, in our search to make sense of experience, are themselves real. After all, on one level these are no more than organized thoughts, and we have established that thoughts are real. But if, in addition, our categories correspond to real distinctions *between* things, we will have the potential to order things by them—in fact, to order everything (since to define a thing is also to say what it is not). An account of reality assembled in this way will be both material and non-material, comprising material things and our thoughts about them. That is what ontological Realists set out, in the most thorough and systematic way, to do. Nominalists—at least, committed ones—deny its feasibility, in my view wrongly. The proof turns on the common properties of things, and our ability to form a comprehensive and ordered vision of reality with their aid.

More to the point, Nominalists deny a way of thinking quite familiar and ordinary to us, the very conception of the world as we live in it and imagine others to do the same. How modern this is is debatable; suffice to say that it is as old as organized society. Without a statement of our common perception of things, organized society would be impossible; for while an isolated individual may confirm to him/herself the reality of abstractions (by the correspondence between material things and his/her thoughts about them), we need others to confirm those logical divisions of reality which enable us to form a picture of the *whole* of experience, and so define the world. Seen in this way, ontological Realism is no more than philosophers' attempt to spell out systematically, on the basis of shared ideas, what all our common experience is. In the history of Western philosophy this is said to have begun with the ancient Greeks, but we may surmise that precedence in this area is largely a matter of the record that has survived.

Common sense, in fact, so far seems to tell us ontological Realism is true that for anyone to be a committed Nominalist at all must be implausible and wilful, unless Nominalism is seen as a series of errors which, corrected, yield a Realist vision. ("Common" sense and "common" experience here are related: referring to what is experienced by humans together—and so confirmed as the same—and what has been repeatedly experienced, and so bearing the authority of history).

We take for granted, then, I say, that our thoughts are real, just as material things are real. We take for granted that this thinking can be applied in general, to sort out categories of reality and order our experience. And eventually, abstracting from the mass of known and unknown things, we arrive at the most complete and ordered thought of all. It was Plato, says Grossmann, who first discovered that "there is a world and not just a universe."[5] Modern ontologists set out to secure the evidence for this position.

Civilization and Modernity

There are, in addition, independently positive reasons for us to maintain it. In the first place, human civilization in general seems to rest on the assumption that an ordered world is possible, regardless of whether the universe itself is so ordered.

Second, it is clear that modern, Western civilization is built on ontological Realism, where it is taken for granted that we humans do the ordering of the world, for the sake of freeing ourselves to act within it. This includes even action to resolve the problems, such as environmental pollution or climate change, that modern civilization itself throws up.

Third, the institutions and values which shape intellectual debate about international (i.e., all human) relations are largely those of modern Western civilization, in application worldwide since 1945—most visibly in the universal states system.

So it is not surprising that Colin Wight argues that international theorists must be (and generally are) ontological Realists. "Every theory of knowledge," he writes,

> must logically presuppose a theory of what the world is like (ontology), for knowledge (epistemology) to be possible. In which case, all philosophies, cognitive discourses and practical activities presuppose a realism—in the sense of some ontology or general account of the world—of one kind or another. The question is not whether to be a realist, but of what kind.[6]

5.2 Ontology: The Rivals to Realism

Nominalism

Grossmann seems to falter, when he lists all the categories of thing which in his view are real, while remarking that "there may be more or there may be less." On the face of it, this is giving ground to Nominalism, by implying that a philosophical theory which potentially encompasses the whole of human experience is unachievable. Such a concession would mean that our sense of the real is itself uncertain, since this depends, Realistically, on the whole as well as the parts.

The idea, however, that there are more things in heaven and earth than are dreamt of in Grossmann's philosophy stems simply, as he makes clear, from the finite extent of philosophers' energies.

> There is no "decision procedure" that allows us to decide once and for all, by some mechanical method, how many categories [of thing] there are. Nor are categorial (ontological) inquiries of a more sublime and indubitable nature than ordinary ones, as many philosophers used to think. All we can do is to argue piecemeal that things of a certain kind do not belong to a given category, because things of this kind have properties different from the properties of the things of the category. . . . To sort out the categories is a painstaking chore.[7]

Realist ontology, in other words, is expansive, open-ended. We do not know all there is to be known, or how knowing more could affect our overall picture of reality. At the same time, it is in our nature to proceed as if a fuller picture would be no less ordered than the one we already have.[8] Progress in our thinking will lead us not away from Realist ontology but toward completer and finer visions of reality. To resume my earlier analogy, biologists are continually discovering new species, or new things about known species from bacteria to elephants, which modify their picture of the living world. But this alters nothing in their assumption that the whole domain of nature is in principle knowable and susceptible to organization in their minds. And in fact it seems to me that to argue for common properties in things even on a piecemeal basis is part of our successful affirmation of the real.

This is different from arguing, as Nominalists do, that the whole enterprise is illusory. The Nominalist approach could be described as open-ended insofar as new objects of experience are treated as unique, so that there will always be an infinity of things to accommodate. This surely reflects some basic truth about the universe. But nothing positive in the process has been said for Nominalism itself; in fact nothing stable has been shown to exist at all. As Ralph Church once put it:

> Those who assert that no two experiences can be strictly the same do not seem to realize one of the consequences of their assertion. If no two experiences are the same in any respect, then any experience is unique in every respect [. . .] Thus the fond husband who kissed his wife good-bye as he went off to work would be parting with her literally forever, as she would be parting with him. Returning that evening to a home that was quite different from the one he knew that morning he might presume to find someone there, though whether she would answer to the same name, or even be a woman at all would be more than doubtful in a world in which nothing were the same as anything else. In such a world there could not be two pins that were the same in any respect, or two needles. There could only be one pin and one needle. And the pin would be different in all respects from everything else, as would the needle.[9]

A Nominalist approach is not open-ended in a deeper sense, toward the properties of things which allow us to order them hierarchically, and so expand even the dimensions of our understanding. This only ontological Realism lets us do, notably by going beyond the Empedoclean approach, which explains everything in material terms, to one including abstractions, like our thoughts—and so to make sense of the subjects, as well as the objects, of perception: ourselves.

On the Nominalist/Naturalist position that as spatio-temporal beings, we perceive only spatio-temporal (i.e., concrete) things, Grossmann argues that our routine abilities prove this false.

> I believe that perception is judgmental in character: one always perceives *that* such and such is so-and-so.. . . In perceiving that [billiard ball] A is white, I perceive, not only the billiard ball A, but also the

color white. And while the billiard ball is spatio-temporal, the color is not. Thus it is simply not true that we can perceive nothing but spatio-temporal things. We can and do perceive abstract things as well.[10]

Science in general is understood like this: as an effort to understand not only how things work and fit together under the "laws of nature," but also what those laws themselves mean.[11] Going to the limits of our knowledge of the universe, we learn to define things which are *not* concrete, or not apparently knowable at all, and so live more fully in the world. In this way science foreshadows the order in our thinking that we aspire to in respect of everything. Besides, the Nominalist criticism that the order of Realist ontology is imposed by human minds is not in itself an argument against our capacity to order. Quite the opposite is true. The world is a place we inhabit and define.

Hobbes as a Nominalist

Taking Hobbes at his word and for a consistent Nominalist, one might be tempted to read his political doctrine as an elaborate exercise in irony, he having assumed that a comprehensive and ordered vision of reality is beyond human capacity and perhaps even nothing is assuredly real. At first sight this suggests a cautious pragmatism, by which we think of everyone beyond our immediate neighborhoods as diverse and even exotic beings whose language, culture, and values are strange, possibly incomprehensible, or even inimical to us. Better, if that is the case, to think from the word go that we know nothing and can only give names—invented, self-regarding names—to people and things as we encounter them; which supposes no coherent vision on which to base international theory.

Two reservations, however, arise before we can follow Hobbes down this road. The first is the obvious one that it is not modern. In our time, I have argued, a real world of order, knowledge, and unity is postulated—by many people actually taken for granted. Of course these expectations are far from being ideally fulfilled, but the point is that they exist, are socially supported and widely understood. Even on the level of language there are strong unifying forces across societies and cultures; just as Latin was once the language of the most developed part of the world, now English is becoming the common language of the world as a whole.

The second reservation lies in Hobbes's own ambiguities. While Nominalism seems to rule out even the simplest speculative generalization about humankind, Hobbes engaged forcefully in such generalization, with his prescription for permanent, universal, and imposed social order as the alternative to endless violence. He could also, as I have shown, be fascinatingly inconsistent in doing so; and in these doubts, his consciousness of potential contradictions, lies his strength as a thinker. That, after all, is how he came to be considered one of the great theorists of state-building, the founder of the "liberal tradition [of] Locke, Rousseau, and John Stuart Mill";[12] and to be adopted, during the Cold War, as the great architect of deterrence-based world order, seen as the logical end of competition in such building. The Hobbesian state is the prime theater of human choice, reflecting our nature back to us to offer the gains of social peace. But equally, he seems to say, that is all there is. Life, the great drama of competing human relations, is not a rehearsal for anything else. We know he thought this way, because when he wrote a universal states system did not exist; his attribution of a metaphysical character to states involved a leap in the dark.

Hobbes, then, is revealed as a philosopher of both human potential and human limitations; and for this reason he anticipates, almost despite himself, the kind of world-consciousness that ontological Realism and, in international theory, Kantian cosmopolitanism enshrine.

Conceptualism

Finally on ontology, there is, as Grossmann stresses, no "third way" between Realism and Nominalism; if one is right, the other must be wrong. This is self-evidently the case in principle: we may say that a comprehensive and logical categorization of the whole of reality is possible, or equally that such a categorization is impossible, but not that a partial categorization is either possible or impossible.

In the history of philosophy, such a compromise view has in fact been argued for. On a Conceptualist view, universals exist as mere concepts, not the real properties of things. In turn, an ordered vision of reality must be literally "all in the mind."[13]

Against this, Grossmann argues:

> In so far as things *have* properties, properties cannot exist, by definition so to speak, *separated* from their things. . . . It is obvious that things would have the colors they have, the shapes they have, etc., even if there were no minds at all and, hence, no concepts. This is not to say, of course, that anyone would *know* those colors, shapes, etc., if there existed no minds.

Similarly, a white billiard ball is "an instance of whiteness [which] is completely independent of what we call it." To deny this means denying the existence of universals, so Conceptualists, for Grossmann, are merely Nominalists in disguise.[14]

Still, for our purposes in international theory this is only half the story, because Grossmann's argument refers only to material things. If there were "no minds at all, and, hence, no concepts," then socially contrived objects like states, which depend on shared ideas, would cease to exist. If human beings were wiped out, states would vanish too, insofar as their identity pertains to them as units of human organization.

Certainly it may be said of human *relations* that they are concrete. In this way Colin Wight tries to get round Conceptualism, quoting Marx to the effect that a state is a "real-concrete object," a "structured institutional ensemble."[15] But it is not self-evident that these definitions, insofar as they are intelligible at all, refer to the same thing: surely a state is primarily a social *idea*, and actual social relations are something different. Nor is it immediately clear what kind of *social* relations international relations, implicating all states and human beings together, are.

My own view is that Conceptualism is imaginable only in the complete absence of normative thinking—something unnatural if not impossible. I have argued that the conventional wisdom of international relations rests on a false, reductive, and trivializing imagery of state agents in a "politics" of inter-state relations explainable only by its complete moral emptiness; that in reality, states are imperfect reflections of the societies they nominally represent, and therefore nothing like the expression of those societies' collective wills. (I shall argue this case in detail in section III.) This leads directly to the notion of states existing solely "in people's heads," as described in Conceptualism—but as anomalies, inchoate concepts that we struggle with and ultimately, from our vision of reality, discard.

The real existence of states is dependent on agreement on what they are—not just as a social idea, but as the same social idea; since 1945, this agreement has had to be worldwide and therefore ontological. But in practice, I say, there is no such agreement; and for good reason, like the differences between promulgated states in both their abstract (political) and their concrete (territorial) dimensions. If this view is correct, doubts about Conceptualism should begin to emerge from the study of international relations properly—that is, normatively—conceived; and it is in international theory that we shall find the solution to this traditional philosophical dispute.

5.3 The Status of Moral Ideas

Fundamentals

After universals, fundamentals. When Empedocles argued that everything was made up of earth, air, water, or fire, or some combination of these four elements, he was making a statement of philosophical first principles or fundamentals: a statement not about things which existed for him alone, on that day or the next, but about things which must *always* exist, for everyone. As MacIntyre put it: "The truths about beings that are deduced from indubitable first principles are all necessary truths. Thus, ontology has nothing to do with the contingent order of the world."[16] Loose talk from international theorists about this or that ("positivist," "constructivist") ontology, as a mere method to be adopted for the purpose of argument, is misleading. It means ignoring the question of what is fundamental, the second half of Empedocles's concerns.

Holism

Loose talk from international theorists about paradigms or worldviews also misleads, by implying that international theory, because it takes as its object the world and all the people in it, has a metaphysics of its own which needs no particular justification. But international theory needs its own metaphysical justification, simply because everything does. If individuals are embedded in society, the world is embedded in the universe, and on these facts we base all our approaches to life. Which brings me back to the first half of Empedocles's concerns; for he appears to have held that his categories of what must exist covered *everything* that must exist. This is the requirement of holism we find in Realist ontology.

Updating Empedocles, we could point out that earth, air, water, and fire, or some combination of these elements, fails to account for what goes on in our minds—our thoughts and ideas, which are abstractions; the reasoning process itself. The ancient Greek's version of reality is incomplete. Not only are the things around us our concern, but the things "within" us as well.

This much is intuitively clear from our memories of growing up and making sense of what we find. In the process we strive against the odds, by virtue of being human, to make sense of literally everything there is—classifying it not only quantitatively but also qualitatively, assigning each thing a place in an overall order. The sense of personal reality built up in this way must be both externally consistent, corresponding to the common experience we undergo, and internally coherent, reconcilable with our sense of order. Holism and first principles are mutually reinforcing. We cannot assert the fundamental identity of anything without taking account, conceptually, of everything; otherwise, it would be impossible to establish how fundamental any given thing was.

Integrity

This may, as I have mentioned, be literally too much to ask. Demands on our time by other people; the need to maintain a livelihood; the shocks and accidents that lie in wait for us along the course of our lives, all can get in the way of organised thinking. Even some elements of our own consciousness may defy definition.[17] Then as the waggish Mr. Rumsfeld pointed out, there will always be things that we do not know we do not know.[18] St Paul, on the other hand, could make light of such concerns.[19] And Kant developed a complete personal philosophy, including a working theory of international relations, while scarcely going more than a day's journey by horse and carriage from his home. All through life, the impulse persists for us to make sense of experience as a whole, and to people it with fully grasped truths, even if we fall short of our aim. In the meantime, we make do with defining at least what *type* of thing any given thing is (the requirement of first principles or fundamentals); and though uncertain of the status of some things, we cannot doubt that they must have some place in the whole, if our account of the whole is to work (the requirement of holism).

This is most clearly seen in our moral sense. It governs all our decisions and our image of ourselves. We may hold contradictory views on natural phenomena, pleading an inadequacy of empirical knowledge. We may even hold contradictory views about our own relation to material things; again, fuller data may be prayed in aid. But what we cannot do is hold contradictory opinions on the right course of action in a given situation, or our ideal image of ourselves. This is because morality always implies action, as the *end* of thought (in both senses: the purpose and the goal). To hold to contradictions on this level means denying our very selves.

David Hume once famously queried whether morality was logical at all. To move seamlessly from facts to moral judgments, he said—from an "is" to an "ought'—involved a form of deception, including, very likely, self-deception.[20] But later he came to see morality itself as evolutionary, a natural form of human learning helped, in social exchange, by shared customs and culture.[21]

So much more then must this reasoning apply in the world as a whole, as the place of all social exchange. The "secret union of soul and body" at which Hume marvelled, and makes decisive action, including moral action, possible, finds its most perfect expression in a community of all humankind. Hume said as much, in language prescient of modern international theory:

> The mutual dependence of men is so great, in all societies, that scarce any human action is entirely compleat in itself, or is performed without some reference to the actions of others, which are requisite to make it answer fully the intention of the agent. [. . .] Nor have philosophers ever entertained a different opinion from the people in this particular. For not to mention, that almost every action of their life supposes that opinion; there are even few of the speculative parts of learning, to which it is not essential. What would become of *history*, had we not a dependence on the veracity of the historian, according to the experience, which we have had of mankind? How could *politics* be a science, if laws and forms of government had not a uniform influence upon society?[22]

And how could international theory not be philosophical, in a world wholly organised by human beings? The "ought" in *normative* international theory is there from the start.

5.4 Human Dominance, or the Sovereignty of Human Relations

The connection between ontology and international theory should now be clear. Ontology—at least Realist ontology—points the way to a conception of reality as a whole, of which the world is part. International theory includes potentially everything in the sphere of living human relations. But above and beyond this, I say, the domain of human relations *is* to all intents and purposes the world—encompassing, strange though this may seem, even those parts of it which have some claim to be independent of us.

First, because there is a de facto society of all humankind, formed by the ubiquity and the permanence of states. Second, because human beings are dominant in the world.

These reasons, moreover, are related. The de facto society of all humankind has been brought about by the dominance of the human species. In the beginning of history, so far as we can discern it at all, human society may have developed out of a solidarity necessary for survival in the face of some external threat. If so, that is a millennial effort that we now assume (rightly or wrongly, but we still assume it) to be over, replaced by the prospect that we humans alone control the future of our species and, in fact, of all life on earth. So successful has our species proved that even beasts of prey like tigers, whose ancestors could have wiped out all humans, have had to be taken under our protection because threatened with extinction by the extension of our powers and our demands.

Of course we do not know what kind of human society will evolve out of the present de facto society of all humankind. That is one of the problems we face. In international theory, it is expressed in the dilemma of the future of states. Will they become more important in our lives, or less? Will they change, and perhaps disappear? (These have been central questions of international theory at least since Kant.) Similarly, we do not know what kind of world, or what kind of "human nature," will evolve out of human dominance. Will we continue to dominate other species, and perhaps even wipe them out? Will we destroy ourselves, through the destruction of supportive nature? Will human nature itself change, through evolution or planned changes to human institutions? (These have been central questions of philosophy since philosophy began). But human dominance is real. It binds our ontology (our vision of reality) and our morality (our chosen actions) together. In the face of human mastery, explanation and justification, theory and metaphysics form a single conceptual chain. Human relations subsume all other relations, and the concerns of philosophy and of international theory are the same.

No Metaphors

Human dominance, however, also implies human uniqueness, the most literal form of solitude. This means there are no true metaphors for human experience in general—a fact which decreases the prospects for the survival of the states system as currently conceived.

A system of ubiquitous and permanent states requires a common definition of the world to work—implying, I have argued, a de facto society of humankind in respect of which all judgments are made. States already ratify human society, insofar as people under them are led to think beyond their individual, family, and local identities. Under a universal states system, everyone on earth is induced to think beyond the societies defined by states. In that sense the present system is emblematic of some higher form of social relations than it routinely allows. Which already suggests that, as representing hard-and-fast divisions of humankind, it is obsolescent, and states cannot hold except as metaphors for something else.

A society of all humankind, meanwhile, as a metaphysical entity, is unique in its own right, as an expression of the world, that human abstraction from the concrete, all-encompassing universe. Only human beings could make such an abstraction. On this level no metaphors at all apply; in this sense (and this sense only) the states system, as a human creation, *is* the world. But this simple convergence is belied when a superfluous item, the state agent, is postulated within the world; which is what happens when states themselves are conceived as independent.

Independence, or sovereign action, is the first rule of the contemporary, universal states system. This means autonomy and self-sufficiency for all its units alike, or state-shaped societies acting in uniform ways. Now, self-sufficiency implies that each unit is a microcosm of the whole—each "nation-state"(-agent) as a world in itself. But that is a contradiction in terms. One cannot have the world as a whole and the world in parts—at least, not at the same time. To do so is to divide humankind against itself. People cannot be independent of each other twice over—once as individuals and once as members of parts of humankind. Unless, that is, the parts (states) are metaphors for something else. But on the fundamental level no metaphors apply; there is only unique and literal human experience. On this level nothing, *pace* Hobbes, is necessarily a metaphor for anything else. The conception of states that he articulated so vividly cannot hold.

We can have the world-as-world, or the world as (states) system— human division seen as an end in itself. But we cannot have both. The notion is a walking tautology, a double definition of the same thing— ourselves. Which is why the state as a general idea is so divisive, and in our efforts to define it so fleeting and unstable. In fact it seems to me the most fleeting and unstable thing of all. Even God is easier to define, because we can at least say what God is not (not the universe, not the world, not ourselves). The states system as currently conceived turns the human condition into a predicament. International theory must be normative, to help out in this contingency and bring historic change. And since it is philosophy, or rather philosophy as ontology, that leads us to this lesson, international theorists must be philosophers too.

5.5 Reality and Reification in International Theory

Grossmann distinguishes usefully, for the purposes of this argument, between facts and states of affairs. "A mere state of affairs is something that would be a fact if it existed."[23] A state of affairs may also be referred to as a contingency—something that is the case by chance, rather than as an established truth or a constituent fact of the world. In international theory there are many examples—I have quoted some—of the political entities we call states being talked about as if they were agents in their own right, "behaving" like individual people or like societies acting together. But this is, I have said, merely a convention—a contingent agreement between some people to speak in a certain way.

States in the form we know them today, with clear and in-principle unrevisable borders, enclosing strictly defined natives and non-natives together, have not always existed and so plainly not been essential to the survival of the human race. The ubiquitous and permanent states system is therefore, in Grossmann's terms, a mere historical state of affairs. This is not to say that states in general are a chimera, that they do not exist. Clearly, states exist in all our minds, in the form of ideas. That is why I have insisted on the need for an ontology sophisticated enough to accommodate abstraction. But as Ernest Barker put it, "ideas are not persons, any more than they are fictions,"[24] and as persons ourselves we should not find it hard to know the difference.

Grossmann deals with reification by saying that "there exist relations that are abnormal, that is, which connect what is there with what has no being at all."[25] He describes the latter as "intentional objects of the mind." I can, for example, imagine Hamlet the Prince, or a character in a novel, as a real person; or that the earth is flat. This is an intentional action on my part—what literary theorists call the suspension of disbelief. While I am knowingly collaborating with a fiction in this way, there is a state of affairs in my mind connected with an object which does not exist. Grossmann describes this as a "unique relation, characteristic of minds and only of minds."[26] But more than unique, it is unstable, because I can change my mind if I wish, and revert to thinking realistically (Hamlet does not exist; the earth is round, etc.)—and vice versa, indefinitely. So it is not surprising that Grossmann describes as abnormal our ability to manipulate our thoughts between, for example, socially established facts, like wars and revolutions, and fantasy, like the "events" of *The Lord of the Rings*. Nevertheless, there is no need to dress this up in the language of ontology; what Grossmann is referring to is the workings of the imagination. Thus, I can imagine (something like) state agents. But I do not believe that they exist.

Quine sought to portray the matter differently, remarking: "we commit ourselves to an ontology containing centaurs when we say there are centaurs."[27] But this is to trivialize the issue. We would feel no need to make such an assertion at all except in a context of the suspension of disbelief. Moreover, we attach practical and even moral importance to absolute lucidity, in a range of everyday situations. No one, for example, faced with a frightened child, would deny that nightmares are real experiences. Yet at the same time we (adults) know, and take pains to show to frightened children, that the content of nightmares is unreal.

As Hume put it:

> Nothing is more free than the imagination of man; and though it cannot exceed that original stock of ideas, furnished by the internal and external senses, it has unlimited power of mixing, compounding, separating, and dividing these ideas, in all the varieties of fiction and vision. It can feign a train of events, with all the appearance of reality, ascribe to them a particular time and place, conceive them as existent, and paint them out to itself with every circumstance, that belongs to any historical fact, which it believes with the greatest certainty. Wherein, therefore, consists the difference between such a fiction and belief? It lies not merely in any peculiar idea, which is annexed to such a conception as commands our assent, and which is wanting to every known fiction. For as the mind has authority over all its ideas, it could voluntarily annex this particular idea to any fiction, and consequently be able to believe whatever it pleases; contrary to what we find by daily experience. We can, in our conception, join the head of a man to the body of a horse; but it is not in our power to believe, that such an animal has ever really existed.[28]

What Hume is describing here is the human capacity for the suspension of disbelief—which can only be based, paradoxically enough, on an underlying, unbreakable sense of reality. In international relations, moreover, we are dealing not with the existence or nonexistence of Hamlet the prince, or unicorns, or the smile of the Cheshire Cat, but with matters of serious consequence—life and death, happiness and suffering—for literally everyone in the world. Once this is understood, not believing in state agency becomes a matter of not willing to be deluded or delude others, and of minding our language accordingly.

The world, in short, is a necessity; the states system is contingent; and state agency arises out of an inability or unwillingness to accept the difference.

5.6 Summary

Ontology

What is required of international theorists is an account of the world as human beings live in it and imagine others to do the same. It stands to reason that this will be focused on the common ground between human beings in founding their perceptions, rather than their differences. An account of the world is an account of how humans define it, against the background of reality as a whole. Why so fundamental? Because the world is now full of man-made things, and it is necessary to distinguish between them and everything else in order to establish what exists in its own right.

Morality

What is required of all of us is to know how best to live with each other in the world. This question arises not only out of our need, but also out of our power, to define the world. Only human beings are able to imagine everything there is. This places us in a dominant position over other, especially living, things. Human dominance is therefore the origin of morality. If we had not always had the potential to dominate other living things, the question of our difference from them would not have arisen. The modern world itself, in a kind of finality, is the fulfilment of this difference; which makes human dominance the essence of morality as well.

Action

How does all this relate, specifically, to states in international theory? First, because of the ubiquity and the permanence of the states system. Its order and divisions are laid across all our view of things. Second, because of the widespread working assumption, among theorists and defenders of the system, that states are agents—with the implication that they are in some sense moral agents as well. This is, I have argued, a mistaken assumption. But what is not mistaken is that agency—the capacity for free human action—is what matters in the world. In fact, *right* human action is *all* that matters in the world. This must lead us on to query whether states are not among the man-made things to be dispensed with, or at least radically reformed, in the cause of what is both just and real.

Notes

1. "**Integrity**. **1**. The condition of having no part or element wanting; unbroken state; material wholeness, completeness, entirety. **2**. Unimpaired or uncorrupted state; original perfect condition; soundness. **3**. **a**. Innocence, sinlessness. **b**. Soundness of moral principle; the character of uncorrupted virtue; uprightness, honesty, sincerity." *Shorter Oxford English Dictionary* (3rd. ed. Oxford: Clarendon Press, 1973.)

2. Grossmann, *The Existence of the World*, p. 9.

3. Hobbes, *Leviathan*, ed. Tuck, p. 26.

4. Grossmann, *The Existence of the World*, p. 8, emphasis in original, and chs. I and II generally. Here is a summary of the Naturalist, Nominalist, and Realist theses, broadly following Grossmann's account. The Naturalist denies outright that there are abstract things, existing outside space and time—which goes against the possibility of universals, itself an example of a socially shared idea. The Nominalist is likely to be a more sophisticated form of Naturalist, who accepts that common, or at least similar, properties can be identified in plural things but argues that this is because those things and their properties happen to exist in the same space and time; and space and time is all there is. Properties themselves, on this view, are concrete, and only concrete. According to Nominalists, all that Realists are doing is collecting every instance of the similarities in things and making them, falsely, into a rule of sameness that holds indefinitely. So the whiteness or redness that we discern in white or red billiard balls would be no more than many observed cases, in space and time, of something we agree to call white or red; there can be no "real" universal quality of whiteness or redness outside space and time—and so no abstract things either. The Realist response may be explained using Grossmann's own color example. We take it for granted that midnight blue is darker than canary yellow. But where, in space and time, do we locate this thought? Nowhere; it holds everywhere and indefinitely. This conclusion represents a real abstract thing—a fact. Properties, then, are concrete insofar as they are "in" things, as colors are "in" billiard balls or flowers; but equally, properties as the distinguishing characteristics of things, by which we order them, exist in our minds, not "in" any temporal thing. Our experience routinely accommodates both abstract and concrete dimensions. Incidentally, the ability to distinguish shades of color is an exception allowed by Hume to his rule that all ideas in the mind arise from sense impressions: David Hume, *An Enquiry Concerning Human Understanding* [1748], ed. Peter Millican (Oxford: Oxford University Press, 2007), sec. II. On property instances and possible minor inconsistencies in Grossmann's position see Ramon M. Lemos, *Philosophy and Phenomenological Research* 55 (2), June 1995, p. 483. See also J. P. Moreland, "Naturalism and the ontological status of properties" in William Lane Craig and J. P. Moreland (eds.), *Naturalism: A Critical Analysis* (London: Routledge, 2000), pp. 67–109.

5. Grossmann, *The Existence of the World*, p. 8, emphasis removed.

6. Wight, *Agents, Structures and International Relations*, p. 26. This assertion is repeated almost verbatim in the joint introduction to Joseph and Wight (eds.), *Scientific Realism and International Relations*, p. 9.

7. Grossmann, *The Existence of the World*, pp. 46–47.

8. Cf. *ibid.*, pp. 85–86.

9. Ralph Withington Church, *An Analysis of Resemblance* (London: Allen & Unwin, 1952), p. 13. But see also Gonzalo Rodriguez-Pereyra, *Resemblance Nominalism: A Solution to the Problem of Universals* (Oxford: Clarendon Press, 2007).

10. Grossmann, *The Existence of the World*, p. 34, original emphasis, and pp. 20–24, 41–45. See also Meyrick H. Carré, *Realists and Nominalists* (Oxford: Oxford University Press, 1946), p. 15; and Bertrand Russell, *History of Western Philosophy* [1946] (2nd ed. London: Allen & Unwin, 1961), ch. XVIII, pp. 166–167.

11. Cf. Richard Holmes, *The Age of Wonder: How the Romantic Generation Discovered the Beauty and Terror of Science* (London: HarperCollins, 2008).

12. Katrin Flikschuh, *Kant and Modern Political Philosophy* (Cambridge: Cambridge University Press, 2000), p. 2.

13. Abelard (1079–1142) is a key figure, based on his "Glosses on Porphyry" ed. and tr. Richard McKeon, reprinted in Arthur Hyman and James J. Walsh (eds.), *Philosophy in the Middle Ages: The Christian, Islamic and Jewish Traditions* (Indianapolis: Hackett, 1973). For informed analysis see Peter King, "Metaphysics" in *The Cambridge Companion to Abelard* ed. Jeffrey E. Brower and Kevin Guilfoy (Cambridge: Cambridge University Press, 2004), pp. 65–125.

14. Grossmann, *The Existence of the World*, pp. 17, 37, 36 and 23, original emphasis. Or as Ayer argued in a slightly different context: "It happens to be the case that we cannot, in our language, refer to the sensible properties of a thing without introducing a word or phrase which appears to stand for the thing itself as opposed to anything which may be said about it." But, he added, this was no reason to see things and their properties as materially separate. Alfred Jules Ayer, *Language, Truth and Logic* (2nd ed. London: Gollancz, 1946), p. 42. Here is my own illustration, elaborating on note 4 above. Imagine I have a window box with two pansy plants, one with flowers of midnight blue and the other of canary yellow. These colors are an integral part of those physical things, the flowers, at a particular time and in a particular place; they were not there when the plants were mere (grey-brown) seeds or (green) seedlings, and will disappear in their turn, when the flowers that display them wither and die. Yet it is no less the case that midnight blue is darker than canary yellow in all conceivable instances, independently of anyone's observation of the things that display them—and in that sense, the darker-than relation is not limited in time or space. In the same way, universal properties can exist both "in" material things and in our minds as the ordering principle of reality, both simultaneously and independently; and in that respect Conceptualism—the argument that universals exist as thoughts alone—is wrong.

15. Wight, *Agents, Structures and International Relations*, p. 185.

16. Alasdair MacIntyre, "Ontology" in Paul Edwards (ed.), *The Encyclopedia of Philosophy* (New York/London: Collier Macmillan, 1967).

17. See "The ontology of evanescent point-instants" in Randal Collins, *The Sociology of Philosophies: A Global Theory of Intellectual Change* (Cambridge, MA/London: Harvard University Press, 1998) pp. 237–38 and 233–52 generally.

18. "There are known knowns. There are things we know that we know. There are known unknowns. That is to say, there are things that we now know we

don't know. But there are also unknown unknowns. There are things we do not know we don't know." US Secretary of Defense Donald Rumsfeld, 12 February 2002 (based on viewing original briefing; text differs slightly at www.defense.gov/transcripts/transcript.aspx?transcriptid=2636). Despite the controversial context (drawing hypothetical links between Islamic terrorism and hypothetical weapons of mass destruction in Iraq), these remarks seem to me an admirably concise statement of the extent of human knowledge.

19. I Corinthians 13:2.

20. David Hume, *A Treatise of Human Nature* Book III, part I, section I [1740], ed. L. A. Selby-Bigge, 2nd ed. revised P. H. Nidditch (Oxford: Clarendon Press, 1978), pp. 469–470.

21. Hume, *An Enquiry Concerning Human Understanding* [1748], ed. Peter Millican (Oxford: Oxford University Press, 2007), sec. VII (I), p. 48 and sec. V (I), pp. 32, 34–35. "All inferences from experience," says Hume, "are effects of custom, not of reasoning" ; but later: "We learn the influence of our will from experience alone" (pp. 32, 48). Learning involves reasoning.

22. *Ibid.*, sec. VIII (I), pp. 64–65, emphasis in original.

23. Grossmann, *The Existence of the World*, pp. 73–74.

24. Quoted in Runciman, *Pluralism and the Personality of the State*, pp. 152–53.

25. Grossmann, *The Existence of the World*, p. 94. See also pp. 116–117.

26. *Ibid.*

27. W. V. O. Quine, "On what there is" [1948] in *From a Logical Point of View: Logico-Philosophical Essays* (Cambridge, Mass.: Harvard University Press, 1964), p. 8.

28. David Hume, *An Enquiry Concerning Human Understanding* [1748], sec. V, part II, in Millican (ed.), p. 34. Cf. the discussion in Ayer, *Language, Truth and Logic*, pp. 42–43.

6

Seeing All Relations Whole

If ontological Realism is right, then Nominalism is logically excluded. And if there is no middle way between them, it is only in versions of the former that we can work.

On an ontologically Realist view, we humans define the world, as our distinct domain in the all-encompassing universe. But while the idea of the world is abstract, the things of the world are no less concrete and real, insofar as they, like ourselves, are part of the material universe. There is no "unrelated" area of experience that we cannot potentially define—and defining, order—as *either* concrete *or* abstract. Moreover, though it may not be possible, even after centuries of sophisticated philosophical investigation, to acquire a single image of reality as a whole, there is no doubt that we all have a working image of this kind in, or at the back of, our minds. In this chapter I examine the implications for international theory.

6.1 Objects in International Theory

Realist ontologists set out to find universals—the common characteristics in things that enable their classification into categories, or most-general types of entity. Grossmann provisionally identifies seven such categories: individual (irreducibly single) things; their own properties or inherent characteristics; structures; sets; quantifiers (or numbers); facts; and relations.[1] Categories help us to define the constituent parts of reality, the "elements" of Empedocles's account; those things than which nothing simpler can be found. Take sets. A clutch of eggs, an album of songs, a team of footballers, and the citizens of Surinam are all *sets* of things (or persons)—plural entities bound together by some quality, yet remaining always separate in their parts; unlike a *structure*, where plural entities go together to make a single one. At the same time, sets are unlike—cannot be reduced to—anything else; a set of sets (say, a box of chess sets for export) is just another set. This irreducibility makes for a category within the reality we perceive.

Combining more of Grossmann's seven categories, we might say that a football team consists of a fixed *number* of players, each with the *property* of being human (and with it, having some knowledge of this human-invented game). Yet experience has many facets to it, and we can pick and choose our priorities. Seeing the team as a *set* highlights its oneness, its effectiveness through unity, while seeing it as a *structure* brings out the positional *relations* between the players on the field. And seeing the *individuals* in the team brings out the diversity of characters and personal aptitudes blending under the rules of the game. All these perspectives are possible; we can shuffle them in our minds at will. They also have equal value—when it comes to ordering them, only our preferences are involved.

No doubt this is why in general we use language flexibly—even, on occasion, allowing multiple definitions to be represented by the same word, as any dictionary will show. To take the one category of Grossmann's that I have not mentioned so far, a *fact* may be what we adjudge in no particular time or place to be the case (a fact as truth), or the specific present result of a past action. For example, I note casually at this moment that I am on page 101 of my writing as it appears on my computer screen. But I may also have in mind that I have reached this point by completing 100 pages of typing; my present position is a fact with a past. The same could be said of the fact that there is a British monarch. The incumbent of this institution today stands in front of a historical past—something on which monarchists and republicans, despite their differing political views, can agree.

When we appraise the world as a whole, again we can shuffle categories: to see the states system, or parts of it, as a structure or set of individual things (states) each having the property of a legal-formal entity. Take the European Union, a set of some thirty such entities in the second decade of the twenty-first century: the latest version of a political organization founded, in the 1950s, with six such parts and under a different name (European Economic Communities)[2]; whose administrative structure has been expanded by stages and through other names (European Economic Community, European Community) to the present. During this time the various economic, political, and legal functions making up the organization have been adapted and expanded, as has the "society" of human relations defined by its administrative boundaries—notably to include, after 1989, the peoples of Eastern Europe. The EU is another fact with a past.

The EU, then, can be variously studied: in historical perspective, referring to different stages of institutional development or the activities carried out in its name, based on the interconnections (conventionally, *relations*) between its member-states; as an individual thing, like a constituted state, with central institutions (the Commission, Parliament and Council of Ministers), an external policy enshrined in law, and a single diplomatic representation; or as a structure, an organization of such states which is comparable with others in the world (OAS, ECOWAS, ASEAN) across their historical, functional, legal, or political dimensions. Similar approaches could be adopted toward the universal state organization, the UN—and so toward the states system itself. (Comparative politics is part of international theory, and the EU is a paradigm, a microcosm, of a settled world—meaning both *inhabited*, and *at peace*.) We can impose priorities within and between these approaches at will, because they all refer to facets of the same complex notion of an ordered world.

The theory of international relations, with all human relations as its object, is likewise naturally plural and complex, which absolutely requires us to think multidimensionally. My friend Annie is a Frenchwoman *and* a Marseillaise *and*, like me, a citizen of the European Union. At different times, in different contexts, and to each of us, these identities will apply in our micro-international relations of two.

The World as a Fact

Facts may be simple, Grossmann tells us, or complex.[3] A simple fact is one which does not contain another fact. For instance, Annie is from Marseille; Annie is a teacher. A complex fact is built up from simple facts—so, Annie is a teacher from Marseille. We divide reality into categories and join it together again, to build an integrated vision, as a Rubik's Cube is a cube of cubes, and Annie's various identities make up Annie.

More is involved, however, than this. Facts are naturally normative, because for humans a thing can be at once (subjectively) important and (objectively) unimportant, just as being from Marseille is unlikely to carry weight if Annie seeks a visa to enter Mongolia on her travels. Similarly, the republican and the monarchist would not dispute the fact that monarchs have a historical origin, but they will diverge profoundly as to whether this makes for political legitimacy. The issue then becomes one of adjudicating between competing normative claims.

The world itself, Grossmann says, is a complex fact—or rather, the sum of all facts;[4] both the creation of all humans who have ever lived and an "objective reality caught in words" being lived today.[5] The world is a fact *about* human relations: that they can be conceptually isolated from the all-encompassing universe, on the one hand, and from relations between us and non-human things, on the other. But what justifies this particular normative claim; or rather, why do we so rarely think that the existence of the world has to be justified?

For justify it we do. The thought, for example, that the universe would continue to exist even if humans destroyed all living things on earth might be true, but it is a useless thought; while the thought that humans could destroy all living things on earth, including you, is one you would want to act on. In the world/universe distinction, the supreme normative act of our species is at stake, the one which validates everything else. Necessity comes into play.[6]

Necessity and Contingency

Let us compare in this light the European Union, the states system, and the world.

The EU is a complex political and historical fact in the lives of Europeans, an entity built up over time through legal acts conjoining constituted states. Its union-ness stands for things like the promise of economic benefits from cross-border trade (in the EU and its affiliated European Economic Area); or personal freedom of movement, residence, and employment between jurisdictions; or less tangible things, involving shared moral values, such as a belief in liberal democracy. At the same time, people can differ profoundly about how to interpret all this complexity. The proof is, the Union could theoretically be dissolved into its component states, and Europeans would still find cross-European cooperation useful on a less formal or institutionalized level; an underlying European identity would undoubtedly survive.[7] By this logic, some citizens of the present EU want to redefine the organization practically, into a "Europe of nation-states" with fewer and weaker joint decision-making institutions. Quite happy to define themselves as Europeans historically, geographically, and ethnically (and often gastronomically and oenologically too), they openly question the necessity for, and utility of, a political Union. Some of them have even deliberately, if rather paradoxically, sought election to one of its institutions, the European Parliament, with the intention of forcing its dissolution. For all such people, the European Union is certainly a fact, but also a contingent and contestable, not a necessary one—not constitutive of reality as such.

Then consider, by analogy, the states system. We can perceive it, to begin with, on the same general level as the EU, as a part of the world created by human society—something which would not exist if we did not exist; something defined, and open to redefinition, by human beings. At the same time, this is more than a local, partial organization of constituted states, and there is no election to its institutions for individuals; it is *the* institution of organized human relations worldwide. None of us stands outside the states system. As such, it is tied up with our relations with—our dominance over—other living creatures: a structure of order and division imposed on the earth's human population, the more easily to organize our relations, both human-human and with non-human beings. Even so, the universal states system is still basically the same kind of thing as the EU. The proof is, it is not fanciful to see in the EU the model for a more democratic and co-operative universal states system, or for the world as a single representative state.

The states system, then, is *not* the world in the existential sense that philosophers specify. It is just the beginning of a discussion about what matters in human society. States, multistate institutions, and the states system are human creations: abolishable, revocable *arte*facts within the fact of the world. To be sure, as Realist international theorists point out, preserving the states system is bound up with important considerations of order and security. But strictly speaking this reflects a mere historical conjuncture for humankind. In practice, lack of change on this level is desirable for some, a provocation for others. Take the constant debates on protectionism in the World Trade Organization, which turn on the value of differently owned commodities across the states system; or the debates on intervention against state sovereignty in the UN Security Council, which spring from differing conceptions of human rights.

This raises the most basic definitional issue in International Relations, which has varied in salience over time but will not go away: relations between whom (or what)? States, I have suggested, are not people as such. There are no "inter-state relations," except as the relations of abstract objects—mutable conceptions of social order. Nothing in human relations *under the states system* should be seen as partaking of necessity. Why especially does this argument need to be made in ontological terms? First, because the EU, states, and the states system are abstractions—not real in the way that material things, like the EU's Berlaymont building in Brussels, or the UN headquarters in New York or Geneva, or the people ruled by these institutions, are real. Abstractions stand in particular need of definition. Second, because people make mistakes, and on occasion deceive themselves and each other, in their evocations of the world. They reify things unhelpfully, sometimes perversely—things like state agents. Then we get into questions of moral truth, where competing normative claims have to be resolved. And here I would argue that if we treat the universal states system as intrinsically of the world, instead of something which merely replicates human society and identity, we shall never make progress as a species. The world itself, the domain we have made our own in the all-encompassing, anonymous universe, and in which all man-made things reside, is a necessity—not something that we could bear to see called into question. But all else can.

6.2 Subjects in International Theory

Relations, Grossmann says, as we first perceive them in our discovery of the world, are either spatial, temporal, or familial.[8] Now this instrumental approach will take us as far as a modern Empedocles might go, but we shall soon find it inadequate. It tells us, for example, that my neighbors' house is larger and set lower down the hill than mine. The Eiffel Tower is on the left bank of the River Seine. Lunchtime trains are less crowded than morning and evening ones. The Second World War lasted longer than the First. I have a female cousin of my own age in Australia. My father's cousin John looked very like his own father, also called John. And so on. These are not strictly speaking relations of minds, but relations as between insensate things. There is no choosing subject here. Even kinship relations (of blood, or of resemblance) have an impersonal element of chance. These are all relations of fact before being relations of conscious beings.

Relations of fact also govern how some writers describe the relations of states, as part of the positivist approach in social science. So some states are seen larger than others, some more populous; some are grouped together by topography, or by location. Some, as legal-formal entities, are traceable further back in time. But again, these are merely descriptions of states as objects. They explain nothing of human motives or sensibility.

By contrast, when we think of human relations in full, to include subjective perceptions, we think of something far more meaningful, dynamic, and precious than I have just suggested, yet which still include the relations in time, space, or kinship that Grossmann identifies. Suppose that my cousin, my childhood playmate with whom I was once childishly in love, grew into a beautiful woman who went to live on the other side of the earth, is now of a different nationality from myself, and holds completely opposite views to mine on important questions of human life. Or suppose that in the very last days of the Second World War—when the war was effectively over and had begun to be history— my great-uncle John, a villager sent to fight in that conflict of peoples far from home, died a death even more pointless and tragic than most in war, at the hands of a beaten enemy who had not heard the order to lay down arms; so that his wife received the news of his death on the day that she heard the war was over, expecting his return; and his son grew up fatherless to be the image of him and to carry on, quite literally, his name. By the intricacy and poignancy of such stories, extending from the personal to the familial, and the familial to the international, we can see the potential for human relations to ramify endlessly in, and against the grain of, inherited states. Clearly, international theory will be worthless, indeed meaningless, if not written in these terms.

Which brings me to moral concerns—the practical starting point, I have said, for normative international theory. What is *their* ontological status (since it is usual for international Realists and moral sceptics to deny them any)? At first, things specific to us as humans, unlike rocks or trees or even houses, may seem hard to define, because we are reflecting on our own reasoning processes at the same time. But a moral concern is more than that: it is a form of individual anxiety (what we are concerned about, after all, we are anxious about). Insofar as it involves intuitions, anxiety might be said to be abstract, but it is also a feeling here and now, physical and undeniable, part of existence itself and inseparable from it, regarding other humans along with ourselves.

Nor is it any less real because shared with people whom we might consider strangers. Many people demonstrate this directly and in full, by extending their imaginative sympathy to other, unknown people in distant countries, including by concrete actions. In so doing they assume from the outset that the very concept of stranger, as of someone potentially less deserving of their care and attention, is questionable, even in the vast and complex domain of the world as a whole. For the millions of people who routinely donate charitable aid to the victims of natural disasters in remote places—people they are unlikely ever to meet, still less be thanked by, in their lifetimes—the reality of shared human experience is not in doubt.

Then take a more general idea, like justice. This too can be seen as both an abstract idea and (better) a relation between people: a sense of right and wrong awoken in us, even on the scale of the world as a whole. Moral concerns begin with a sense of justice or order violated: a sense that it is *wrong* that life-threatening poverty persists for some, but not others, in an organized world; *wrong* that some people have weapons so powerful they are able to kill distant strangers with no possibility of self-defense, even without provocation, on the latter's part; *wrong* that some people can use superior force to subjugate others in the name of an idiosyncratic version of social order; and *wrong* that human beings are able to destroy all living things on earth—all others, that is, along with themselves. I have deliberately chosen the weaker term of moral concerns here, rather than judgments (as I said earlier, there may be some virtue in being reluctant to reach moral conclusions in international theory), but these are nonetheless shared social considerations about political power and its use.

Moreover, we can simultaneously feel concerned *about* some situation ("corrective action should be taken") and concerned *by* it ("it is my duty/right to engage in, or instigate, corrective action"). Our concerns may encompass perceived wrongs that we feel a responsibility to redress even if we bear no specific guilt for having caused them, or find their dimensions intrinsically difficult to define. One could cite here, in addition to people's concerns for the victims of natural disasters, a concern for the perceived effects of colonialism even on the part of societies with no notable colonial history. The citizens of Nordic countries since 1960, for instance, have not pleaded, as well they might, that they have no collective historical guilt to expiate in respect of European imperialism, and therefore no duty to accept the official, UN-brokered commitment to pass a proportion of their annual GNP to poor, mainly former-colonial societies in Africa, Asia, and Latin America. Rather, on the evidence of the past half-century the very opposite is the case: the official Nordic (and Dutch) record in fulfilling, even exceeding, this commitment is exemplary and enjoys unreserved public support.[9] On another level, one could cite the twenty-year campaign across international borders (including the award of the Nobel Peace Prize) in support of the democratic Burmese leader, Aung San Suu Kyi, after the military junta ignored her party's victory in free elections and put her under house arrest: a campaign, in effect, to help Burmese people gain something that they could not achieve by themselves.

It should be obvious from these examples that we rely on intuitions about the lives of unknown others to form a theory of international relations, and on ontologically Realist assumptions in doing so: on the one hand that the intuitions themselves are real, and on the other that what they refer to in the world beyond our immediate experience is real. So in this sense we can feel a relationship with people in other countries without having been there or met them. Multiplying this awareness to the world as a whole, seen in terms of peoples and societies, rather than individuals, we are able to form something like a theory of relations between them all, including our own society and ourselves within it, with the implication that societies themselves are potentially conscious and judging agents. We are able, in short, through moral thinking to form a conception of all human relations as a concrete thing of which we are part, and to make judgments in the light of it.

These arguments weigh against any approach in international theory which would exclude moral concerns, postpone or avoid them or banish them to a branch of theory of their own. On the contrary, in the instances I have referred to it is moral concerns that actually *explain* human behavior. They express a uniquely unifying relation: between human beings and each other, and between human beings and the universe, in which material and non-material things are together included. Moral concerns are supremely relevant—not existing as thoughts in our minds only, but directly connected to our sensibilities and our needs. They show us our true nature as special beings able to see all relations whole.

Strangers in Time and Space

Hobbes, arch-Realist, enemy of abstract emotion and advocate of brutal honesty in human affairs, would seem to be at the origin of all opposing views to these. And yet Hobbes himself, in his search for a holistic conception of human nature, discloses the imaginative sympathy at the heart of normative international theory.

As I pointed out in chapter 2, in a precursor-work to *Leviathan* he remarked that

> it must be extreme hard to find out the opinions and meanings of those men that are gone from us long ago, and have left us no other signification thereof but their books; which cannot possibly be understood without history enough to discover those afore-mentioned circumstances, and also without great prudence to observe them.

Then in *Leviathan* Hobbes turned to the problem of understanding people in countries distant and different from his own, to declare that "the savage people in many places of *America* . . . have no government at all; and live at this day in that brutish manner, as I said before"; like all people in a "time of Warre," who depend on "their own strength, and their own invention" in a situation of "continuall feare, and danger of violent death."

When we put these reflections together, we see Hobbes implicitly drawing an analogy between strangers in time ("those men that are gone from us long ago") and strangers in space—those contemporaries he had never met, and whom he knew he would never meet. But the analogy is false—at least if it depends, as his political doctrine seems to do, on the incontrovertible facts of experience. We can never meet the people of the past in person, while the same is not true for the people of our age.

What is more, in the latter judgment (regarding those "savage people" in "America"), Hobbes is relying not on his own experience of civil war but, as with the people of the past, on speculation and secondhand, incomplete, hard-to-interpret evidence. And having once admitted the hazards of such an approach, he becomes open to the charge that his whole sceptical generalization on human nature, in *Leviathan*, is unfounded. To put it another way, "savage people" are savage to Hobbes at least in part because they are backward *in time*, in relation to his way of thinking and his own society's development; yet he not only lacks firsthand evidence to prove this, he has already once suggested that speculative judgments of times past, and peoples past, may be wrong (or at least require "great prudence"). And in fact, at this point in his argument Hobbes hesitates—nagged by the thought that all human beings might not be as wayward, unfathomable, and prone to violence as his political doctrine requires; and he loses the thread.[10] The great logician stumbles here. But ingenuously: following the natural inclination of someone prepared to give strangers the benefit of the doubt; giving rein almost despite himself to imaginative sympathy.

What Hobbes ran up against is the problem of all Realist international theory, that the case for moral scepticism, though often strong, can never be conclusive. The defenders of human beings cannot quite be closed down, or doctrine will become dogma. No one today would deny the twentieth century's terrible events—to mention only two world wars and the Holocaust of European Jews - but to argue on that basis that human nature is essentially or radically evil is always to risk a charge of bad faith, and seeing one's judgment of others turned on oneself. A moderate realism, by contrast, is unobjectionable, if all it means is prudence in the light of a human capacity for wrongdoing; but that does not make for a systematic, forward-looking, predictive doctrine.

Turning the argument round, in our time even the propaganda of progress is vulnerable to reservations about the reliability of moral generalization. In the West, in modern societies, we are taught to believe that our lives are exceptionally, even unprecedentedly peaceful, secure, healthy, enlightened, and opportunity-filled. Well, it is also exceptionally, even unprecedentedly true that we in the West, in modern societies, are in a position to verify this assessment, by visiting our contemporaries elsewhere, as Kant once suggested. That, I suggest, is the first task of Western international theorists—to go out and know the world in practice, in all its diversity of human culture and language; to become part of it, and learn from its impact on ourselves, within the reasonable limits of our lifetimes. That is necessary in order to keep to the first rule of moral conduct, which is to be consistent with oneself. And the rule applies especially because, like Hobbes, we all rely unavoidably on suppositions about strangers, in the present as in the past, for our conception of human nature. We cannot know everyone in the world, but we do inescapably need to know ourselves.

In the meantime, one of the most illustrious and exciting aspects of civilization—in the West, in modern societies—seems to me the search for both certainty and balance in our understanding of the human past. Nowadays, historical records and vestiges are routinely subjected to new technology like carbon dating, DNA sequencing and mass spectroscopy, and consequently to new and profound interpretations. Competition in historical analysis, in the popular and academic media alike, has become both literate and standard. Historians are able to engage in a mass sociology of the human past, with new information and social support at their back; and history and international theory, in their search for a holistic conception of human nature, are seen to converge.

Now we can learn the daily habits and thoughts, as of facts of life like our own, of people in bygone ages—people both high- and low-born. We can relate to them in their foibles, their hopes and their pains. Take the Paston family of fifteenth-century Norfolk, whose letters have come down to us from another time of civil war—the menfolk in and out of favor at court, while the widows and grass widows, left alone at home, battle the depredations of armed men, yet still yearn after pretty hats and gloves.[11]

Or consider the obscure, illiterate, destitute Cathars in their rural corner of medieval France—a people caught in a naive amalgam of mysticism and sexual licence, and in the end persecuted, like outsiders in eras closer to ours, for their failure to conform to conventional society.[12]

Hear Joan of Arc on trial—on *show* trial—for her life, snapping at her prurient clerical inquisitors for their obsession with her trousers.[13]

Picture ill-fated, Shakespeare-diabolized Richard III of England: more plausibly, the loyal defender of his brother's realm, a king who married for love, and reformed the law to allow justice to the poor and arbitrarily accused; who, racked with disease, fought rebellion to the last at Bosworth Field—and refused a horse for his kingdom.[14]

Read Mary, Queen of Scots, writing calmly to the King of France at two o'clock in the morning of her execution, to ask for his help "in paying my unfortunate servants the wages due them—this is a burden on my conscience that only you can relieve." Only two teardrops blur the ink on the page.[15]

These people of that other world, the one that has gone before, need not be strangers to us. We know they lived. We can feel their humanity; we can pity them. We see in them the proof of the mortality all humans share. Only a failure of imagination, or a lack of experience, stands between us and a deeper understanding of their lives.

Notes

1. Grossmann, *The Existence of the World*, part III.
2. In this sentence "thirty," "second," "decade," "twenty-first century," "1950s," and "six" are quantifiers.
3. Cf. Grossmann, *The Existence of the World*, pp. 74–75.
4. *Ibid.*, p. 84.
5. David Wootton, "Traffic of the mind," *Times Literary Supplement* 21 October 2011, p. 5. Wittgenstein's famous formula, "The world is all that is the case," rather underplays the lived-in nature of reality. Ludwig Wittgenstein, *Tractatus Logico-Philosophicus* [1921] tr. D. F. Pears and B. F. McGuinness (London: Routledge, 2001), §1, p. 5.
6. The fact that the world is *not* all there is is the source of antinomies ("contradictory conclusions apparently deduced correctly": Godfrey Vesey and Paul Foulkes, *Collins Dictionary of Philosophy*, London/Glasgow, 1990, p. 16). This is because what is true of the world is not necessarily true of the universe, and vice versa, yet they are inextricably linked.
7. During the 1999 NATO action over Kosovo, which led to the bombing of the Serbian capital Belgrade, I recall a radio interview with an English rose-grower who lamented the interruption of relations with her Serbian

counterparts. Clearly to some people a common identity even across state frontiers is more important than contemporary political events.

8. Grossmann, *The Existence of the World*, pp. 9–10.
9. Net overseas development assistance, as a share of GNP, from Norway, Sweden, Denmark, and the Netherlands to developing countries and multilateral organizations rose well above the UN–agreed level of 0.7 percent in the early 1970s and has been maintained since, often reaching a level of 4–5 percent. See the annual reports of the Development Assistance Committee of the OECD (Paris: OECD) and below, Conclusion.
10. See Hobbes, *Leviathan*, ed. Tuck, pp. 89–90, and above, chapter 2 section 2.4. I would paraphrase Hobbes's argument (starting from "It may peradventure") as follows. "1. Some would say that war has never been endemic in the world as a whole. 2. This assumption is probably correct. 3. But there are many societies today, especially backward ones, in a permanent state of war. 4. Moreover, the frequency with which civil wars break out in advanced societies shows what happens when there is no strong ruler. 5. In any case, strong rulers' necessary independence inclines them to war." Now 3) and 4) together do not make the case for war as endemic worldwide, a possibility which 2) shows Hobbes partially doubting anyway. 5) is a non-sequitur, and in itself a tautology, as I pointed out in chapter 2.
11. Helen Castor, *Blood and Roses: The Paston Family in the Fifteenth Century* (London: Faber and Faber, 2004). See also for this time and place Ian Mortimer, *The Time Traveller's Guide to Medieval England* (London: The Bodley Head, 2008).
12. Emmanuel Le Roy Ladurie, *Montaillou: Village Occitan de 1294 à 1324* (Paris: Gallimard, 1975), in English tr. Barbara Bray, *Cathars and Catholics in a French Village, 1294–1324* (London: Scolar Press, 1978).
13. See the transcript of her trial for witchcraft in Régine Pernoud, *Jeanne d'Arc par elle-même et par ses témoins* (Paris: Editions du Seuil, 1962), in English tr. Edward Hyams, *Joan of Arc by Herself and by Her Witnesses* (Geneva: Edito-Service, 1968).
14. Most historians now agree that Richard, Duke of Gloucester did not kill his nephews held in the Tower of London, though it is unclear who did. The king's skeleton was found in an unmarked grave in Leicester in 2012, bearing wounds like those described by eyewitnesses to his death in battle on August 22, 1485—who also told of seeing Richard refusing to escape on horseback.
15. *The Last Letter of Mary Queen of Scots* (8 February 1587). National Library of Scotland Adv.Ms.54.1.1.

III

State, Nation, Agent

7

Struggling with States

I have made a case for forceful and coherent moral thinking about the relations of all humankind in the contemporary world, against the discouragements of mainstream academic theory. But what kind of human agency is conceivable in the states system, especially to favor historic change over the wars and confusions of the past? That is the question I try to answer in this section.

The ubiquity and the permanence of states mean that for practical purposes, no human beings exist outside the system, now or for the foreseeable future. Meanwhile inside it, new separate peoples have been delineated everywhere since 1945, but always implicitly with a common will of their own. States have been mounted as *nation*-states: as ideal communities transcending the family and the village, yet with a shared identity and a right and capacity to act in expression of it. This is implied in the language, structure, and norms of diplomacy and international law. But how far is it true in reality? We are talking, after all, of captive peoples here—de facto nations, defined almost without exception by state borders since 1945, rather than self-defining. Can these be considered real and effective communities—able to act together on their own behalf, in defense of their interests, as well as cooperatively, toward other groups so conceived? Can human agency ever be given meaning in this way?

This is an a priori normative question, concerning how willingly people act and see themselves in the plural. If you act in conformity with your will, you act freely. You carry into effect the person you are or seek to be. Whereas if you do something against your will, you are not an effective person. And if for some reason one cannot refer to a people acting willingly *together*, then one cannot speak of their acting at all.

How far de facto nations can be real nations will depend significantly, I suggest, on what people everywhere think of the state forms imposed on them at birth. In a contemporary sense, they will compare their conditions with what they know, or believe, about the conditions of people inscribed under other states. In a historical or inward-looking sense, they will compare their present conditions with what they know, or believe, about the conditions of their predecessor communities in the same, or approximately the same, place. And in either case they will think normatively—they will be influenced by an ideal of what their conditions *might* be. Not a political-theory conception from the books of Hobbes or Locke, Kant or Gierke, but a pragmatic one, interactive and homemade. In this chapter I shall speculate on the idea of a state which is likely to emerge. In the next chapter I shall assess prevailing theories of the nation; and in the next chapter again, I shall consider what collective (i.e., state) agency, in a world of mainly de facto nations, looks like to a critical eye.

I can imagine two objections to my procedure. One, that it is purely speculative, even subjective. My answer is that to some extent all judgments about international relations are speculative and subjective. We have only circumstantial evidence to go on about human relations in the world as a whole. There is no such thing as reliable world opinion about states or anything else. On the same grounds, I am inclined to be sceptical of Huntington's thesis on the "clash of civilizations."[1] His book has been criticized for stoking anti-Islamic feeling. But to me it seems most flawed by Huntington's working assumption that public opinion is an objective phenomenon, uniformly reliable everywhere, when in fact access to information and freedom of expression vary widely, even in the age of the Internet. Above all, fear of governments' power to cause injustice and do harm influences people's thinking in many, if not all societies and makes the ascertaining of their "true" opinions much more complicated than Huntington suggests.

Certainly it seems fair to suppose that there exists a common contemporary opinion of *the human condition* in some form or other; the mere fact that we all live under the auspices of the same kind of formal social organization must prompt us to comparisons of life in society, in the world as a whole. But equally, such opinion is likely to be uncertain, fragmented, conflicted and confused. When people talk, for example, of "the international community" being on the side of, or potentially disapproving toward, a public situation or event, then that, I think, is what is meant—some tentative engagement with a shared but generally intractable status quo.

The second possible objection to my approach relates to Martin Wight's classic criticism that there is no (i.e., no distinctive) international theory—a view I might seem to be endorsing by evoking a homemade, interactive conception of states worldwide. Roy Jones, indirectly agreeing with Wight, responded that all we need is political theory, because states are just the latest stage in the perennial human search for social order. This seems to me a true response but an incomplete one. It is certainly true in the sense I would want to hold on to—ruling out state agents absolutely; for if states amount to the end, or an end, in the search for social order, then they are obviously not the instigators of this or any other process.

Yet is there not something like a polity of the human race—overarching, underlying, or emerging from, the multiple created polities of today? This is an age-old question, given a new slant with the universalization of states in 1945. Most of the time since then has been taken up with the Cold War, perhaps the most obfuscatory period in human history. Reflection on the human race in such complex and contradictory circumstances seems at least to call for a new approach to political theory.

In any case, insofar as Roy Jones's approach is humanistic, conceiving political theory as normative, and embracing the whole of human striving, it comes very close to the one I have adopted. I have suggested that in the contemporary world, international theory and moral philosophy so far overlap that they should not be conceived as separate activities. Jones's own opinion implies an overlap between moral philosophy and political theory. What we call any of these speculations is surely less important than the concrete concerns that inspire them.

7.1 Essences of States

Borrowing the language of ontology, Wendt has argued that constituted states, as we find them in the world today, have five "essential properties":

> (1) an institutional-legal order, (2) an organization claiming a monopoly on the legitimate use of organized violence, (3) an organization with sovereignty, (4) a society, and (5) territory.[2]

But surely this is wrong: the essence of individual things must be single, if it is to be fundamental and irreducible, as an essence is. An essence must also be intrinsic to a thing, not attributed to it from the outside, as with man-made things. Otherwise we are dealing with a tautology: something is what it is because we say it is.

Certainly one can describe houses, for example, as "essentially" private buildings, while railway stations are essentially public ones; these material things have a single characteristic—their purpose or use, attributed to them by human beings. But as for states, those other man-made things, they are neither unambiguously material nor characterized by a single purpose. States' purposes certainly include the physical containment of societies; but a moment's reflection shows the containment to be ambiguous—serving social control, as well as organization. And if the "matter" of states—territory—combines with this purpose, it is for contradictory ends: to situate societies on earth, but also to divide up that in-principle indivisible thing, humankind, and deny the common essence of human beings.

Further, if we try to salvage Wendt's generalization by singling out items on his list, it becomes obvious that they have no essence of their own. Take territory. Without the legal sovereignty claim, territory is just mountains, plains, rivers, lakes, coasts. As for the society associated under the contemporary system with each state, if it holds together at all it does so because its members have some essential property of humanity, before identifying themselves collectively as Angolan, Belgian, Cambodian, or anything else down to Zimbabwean.

There are fundamental problems, then, with these "essential properties" of states: they should not in the first place be plural, and their individual validity can be challenged. These attributes would need to combine in one irreducible thing in order to answer the question: "What (essentially) is a state?" In practice, only the populations of states themselves can do this, and, I suggest, only according to some higher organizing principle than existing states; because in the system as constituted, difference and disparity are the only rules when territory, society, institutions, and their claims are taken together. But since Wendt's definition of states is an orthodox one, reproducing the formal characteristics of the modern system, the point is worth demonstrating in detail.

7.2 The Randomness of Diversity

Territory

Let us begin with territory. Some contemporary states are grafted onto a particular kind of territory—naturally distinct, like islands or, more contestably, archipelagos (Iceland, Madagascar, the Philippines). Some territories, by contrast, harbor more than one state despite being islands (Haiti/Dominican Republic, New Guinea). Some states are coastal, their physical margins partly defined by the sea, but giving access to its free area of movement for people and goods, and legal entitlement to a two-hundred-mile-wide exclusive economic zone. Where states are insular (Australia, New Zealand), or marked by a long coast (Chile, Namibia), these are great unearned advantages. Other states, by contrast, are landlocked, their unlucky peoples stranded far from the oceans' liberties and wealth (central Asia, the Sahel). Even in coastal states, there are low-lying parts where people's lives are actually threatened by the sea (Maldives, Bangladesh, the Netherlands). Better, you might think, in this case to have no coast at all. But where in all this diversity is the essential "territorial" state?

Society

Some contemporary states are territorially vast, occupying an overweeningly large part of the earth's surface and housing great populations (China, India), some are tiny by comparison (Luxembourg, Rwanda, Burundi). Clearly, social self-sufficiency is going to be a variable value over the states system (and self-sufficiency is the mark of a free agent). If one pushes the point further, to insist that the self-sufficiency be absolute, how is it to be measured? Perhaps in terms of human resources: say, if all major infrastructural posts, or key specialist ones, like air-traffic control or pediatric surgery, were able to be filled by a state's own citizens. But on this condition many, if not most existing states would fail to qualify.

Sovereignty

Some contemporary states, meanwhile, exhibit blatant *over*population in terms of their material heritage (Rwanda, Burundi, Bangladesh again), while others are markedly *under*populated (Mongolia, Australia, Argentina). In some, the demographic effect is allayed by industrial and technological skills, which afford the populace a head start in economic competition (the United States, all northwest Europe). But even here, raw materials have often to be imported; and there are many more peoples for whom comparative advantage is a fleeting dream. The essential "sovereign" state, implying a society in balance with its territory and making no demands on others, seems nowhere to be found.

Given the diversity of natural conditions like soil and climate, material resources themselves are significantly determined by a state's place on earth, as well as its territorial span. Some states are large and desert (Chad, Sudan), some large and abundantly fertile (Brazil). The potential simply to feed the people will therefore vary widely. Some states offer material resources that everyone wants to buy, like minerals (Congo/Zaïre), or oil (the OPEC states); while for others, more intangible possibilities must be conjured up, to be turned into assets, like location itself (Panama, Malta, Djibouti), the services of a factory-floor society (Taiwan, Singapore), or the wealth and indulgence of foreigners (Bahamas, Liechtenstein). Location, meanwhile, can cut both ways—placing some people at the center of world economic and political activity (Atlantic Europe), while crippling the prospects of others when the price of fuel is a factor in diplomacy and trade (many Pacific island-states).[3]

The result is inherently different and unequal benefits from statehood, despite the uniform attribution of rights to each society with its state. Sovereignty turns the universal states system into a closed system of competitive ownership, in which governments are tempted to view their citizens instrumentally, in terms of assets and liabilities, regardless of their own performance on the people's behalf. The "institutional-legal order" of the system is complicated accordingly.

Institutional-Legal Order

Here again we find no single model among the exemplars of constituted statehood in force today. Some show concessions to size, or democratic aspirations, through federative arrangements (Nigeria, Canada, Australia), most do not; in some places, people seem unable to decide the issue, and want to have things both ways (USA, UK). Some states are monarchies, some republics (there are many ex-monarchies, like Greece, but few ex-republics); some, like the so-called constitutional monarchies of Europe (the Netherlands, Spain, Sweden, UK), are at an uneasy point in between. A few are theocracies, where political accountability can be ultimately—and controversially—assigned to God (Saudi Arabia, or certain Islamic Republics). Or theocracy leads, under the pressures of modern constitutionalism, to the interpretation of political accountability in eccentric and unworldly ways (as in the daring Gross National Happiness index of Bhutan). But the great majority of states are by definition secular, at least in terms of public culture. Some undoubtedly are democracies in both form and practice, in a long and valuable tradition combining social welfare with political freedom. Here life is safe, pleasant, and promising of progress in individual opportunity and social equality; here governments work to turn the people's talents *fairly* into assets (Scandinavia). In large parts of the system, however, including those with a developed economy, states are democratic on paper only (Russia, China). Some have yet to display any democratic institutions at all (Saudi Arabia again, Brunei). Which brings us to the relation between political legitimacy and social peace.

Legitimate Monopoly of Organized Violence

Now this particular "right" of governments is often barbarically usurped for private ends, in places where armed gangsters in power make a mockery of institutions, law and order, and a misery of their compatriots' lives. These are places where many people, given the choice, would choose not to live; where you, if you read this freely, are glad you do not live; where even honest people—perhaps *only* honest people—fear the police. Sovereignty as terrorism: that is what the legalized monopoly of organized violence, under the universal states system, has often meant in practice. The record is long and checkered, from the countless dictatorships in superpower spheres of influence during the Cold War to the sinister freak-shows which survived it (the Gaddafi regime in Libya, the Kims of North Korea).

Then there is raw military capacity—often interpreted as an unconditional right to defend states' "territorial integrity" (not the same, of course, as the people living there). Here we find a minority of so-called nuclear-weapon states, in terms either of putative entitlement (UN Security Council permanent members) or brute reality (India, Pakistan)—but in any case, an attribute of questionable legitimacy when not everyone in the world is so endowed. In most places people seem able to live without donning deterrence's cynical mask of Janus, though they might also fairly feel aggrieved at the weapons of mass destruction in the hands of the few. In some places nuclear defense has been consciously, if not entirely willingly, given up (South Africa, Argentina, Brazil). Elsewhere, we find raw military capacity in the mobilization of large populations, even alongside a nuclear arsenal (China). Such incidences reek of mass chauvinism, even mass racism. But since this policy is exercised in the name of a state, in a competitive states system, with secure paid work hard to come by, we should view mass citizen-soldiers as victims of circumstance, or cannon fodder in the hands of elites. For all these reasons, deterrence need not be nuclear but is always controversial; and the military power assembled ostensibly for the defense of populations has little to do with equality, justice, or original rights.

7.3 The impact of inequality

In the light of this farrago of controversial and often-conflicting elements of statehood, agreement among the various peoples of the world on the "essential" state seems unlikely indeed. What we learn in any case from empirical international studies is a lesson already widely drawn in philosophy: that the search for human essences is reductive and misleading.[4] When we say something is essential, we merely mean it is indispensable *for us*, for our subjective human purposes. But on this level too there is the potential for people to differ widely in their conception of a state.

It is of course easy to point to the diversity of environments in which human beings have made their home down the ages, in order to argue that Africans and Inuits, for example, have nothing in common culturally, and perhaps institutionally as well. But that is not the issue, nor, I think, is such pessimism widely felt. More often, human diversity has been actively celebrated in the modern, post-colonial era, through television, tourism, and other forms of popular anthropology and cultural exchange. What *is* the issue arises from the ubiquity and the permanence of states. All those natural and culturally inherited differences and distances between peoples have now become formalized as a property of the system itself.

Much of what passes for international politics since 1945, in fact, could be seen as a reaction to institutionalized, but arbitrary, diversity, especially since the dissolution of the European empires in Africa and Asia; as expressions of dissatisfaction with the failure of the system to realize its promise. This is seen at the macroeconomic level, in the all-pervasive, much-fought-over goal of "development," where some societies' gain (in "the North") is seen as other societies' loss (in "the South"). It is seen at the intra-societal level, in peoples' efforts to achieve "their" human rights, whether libertarian (in UN parlance, "civil and political") or material ("economic, social, and cultural")—at times against their own leaders, at times against people elsewhere. All this must undermine a shared normative conception of what states, those man-made creations, have bestowed on humankind. From such dissatisfaction, moreover, action is destined to follow thought as night follows day. So it should be no surprise either to see people making international politics informally, by taking matters into their own hands.

Migration and Competition

Take the phenomenon of migration. If I, a Naguayan, see you, a Merovian, as different from myself, not only in some inherited cultural sense, but also richer, happier, freer, then I am bound to ask the reason why. And if, all other things being equal, I find that reason in the fact that you were born under the sign of a larger, or more democratic, or more resource-rich state, then I will very likely conclude that what makes our present and our prospects unequal is an accident of history, nothing more. This may well lead me to want to become a Merovian myself (perhaps together with my family, and so not out of simple envy or greed). But not all Naguayans can become Merovians, though many may try. Merovian society cannot absorb all Naguayan aspirants, especially in view of the many aspirants from other similar places—at least, cannot do so and remain as secure, wealthy, and stable as before.

Let us further suppose that Merovians' right to reject the entry of some, and allow the entry of others, into their number is absolute. Some would-be migrant Naguayans will be turned back, frustrated in their desire to alter their destinies. Meanwhile, not all Naguayans will want to pull up their roots. Some will think themselves too weak or poor to leave their homeland, or find the culture and climate of other places unappealing; many will fight shy of abandoning their native inheritance—even, on occasion, while finding fault with it. But since it is merely by accident that Naguayans in general start life poorer, weaker, and less free than Merovians (and than lucky others elsewhere), they will all equally be inclined to consider their native situation arbitrary, if not unjust. And those left behind by the emigrants—which in practice means most of Naguayan society—may be tempted to view their own state and its servants, and perhaps their society as a whole, as tainted with the same unlucky fate.

Transform my fictitious Naguayans into a hundred existing peoples, and the states system begins to look like an obstacle to peace and progress. A social situation of arbitrary unfairness is a natural spur to resentment. Even an individual situation of some comfort and security, in a system governed by competitive aspirations, is going to look unfair by comparison with one in which these advantages are enjoyed to the full. From this perspective, contemporary migration looks like blind attempts to iron out faults in the system, against inbuilt resistance, and only forbearance or ignorance enables human relations to remain peaceful at all.

Anne Hammerstad, in her analysis of migration, is in no doubt that "the world has never before seen so many people on the move." From such diverse causes as wars, terrorism, and financial uncertainty, she says, "the distinction between different categories of migrants (forced/

voluntary, legal/illegal, regular/irregular, economic/political, internal/ external) has become increasingly blurred." She adds that

> the combination of youthful and fast-growing populations in many parts of the global South, and an ageing population in many parts of the North, will ensure that a relatively high level of migration remains desirable for both sending and host countries for the foreseeable future.[5]

But this perspective itself may be too rosy, as regards the real short lives and destinies of people. We are all obliged to live in and under the auspices of states, yet none of us has chosen to be born into this or that state; moreover, most people will encounter a certain difficulty in acquiring, if they are so inclined, the citizenship of another state, or at least the right to reside under it at will. Eventually, in a global economy, formal rights become marketable objects like any other, with the aid of corruption and criminality among the officials and lawyers who make their living from the system. After the market in goods comes the market in people, a market of rich buyers and poor sellers and their predators and hangers-on. Human relations become infected with venality, in a domain of arbitrary borders where security is populistically elevated to the highest level of public discourse.

One can hardly take a poll on it, but I suggest that under such circumstances no created state is going to receive the definitive allegiance of any individual, with the exception of those, like politicians and diplomats, who earn their living by defending the current version of one, or some purblind beneficiaries of the luckiest windfalls of sovereignty; and no society, quite independently of its own political arrangements, can be said to be entirely at ease with itself. By the same token, there will be very little agreement among existing state populations on what a state is (though a quite forceful consensus on what it is not); and in consequence nothing anywhere resembling a consensual, voluntary, effective nation-state.

7.4 The Myth of State Continuity

Concluding this argument, we should note that all five elements in Wendt's definition of states—sovereignty, territory, society, institutional-legal order, and legitimate monopoly of the use of organized violence—are stated ahistorically. This is because his definition is an orthodox one, derived from diplomacy and conventional international theory. Yet if these five components do not make much sense singly, as properties of states, and do not hang together politically, as I have just argued, can we find some historical commonality in them, from before 1945, to help the definition?

Here again, however, the evidence is negative. The contemporary British state is not the same state as before the First World War, when women had no vote to choose their political leaders. The monarchical, absolutist French state of the Sun King was not that of revolutionary France, or of subsequent French republics, including the present one, from which the institution of monarchy seems to have been definitively uprooted. The Persian imperial state destroyed by the army of Alexander the Great is unrecognizable in the Islamic Republic of Iran, just as the Chinese Empire is unrecognizable in its Communist or quasi-capitalist modern successors. All history's lost empires, now officially discredited, had states of one sort or other at their cores; yet the perceived need for these to be incarnated by real persons (kings, emperors, hereditary rulers of all kinds) merely emphasizes their unstable identity for the people born under their sway.

Then again, all those variations of material wealth and geographical extent to which I have pointed among contemporary states apply over the course of history, but with added complications. Territorial borders, and the peoples and resources they enclosed, seem from our contemporary perspective to be disconcertingly shifting and difficult to define. We can say with some precision today who is an Iraqi, but who precisely was a Chaldean? Even where social continuity in one place can be perceived with certainty—for example, in Egypt, because of natural limits—political culture has varied radically: compare the muddle and instability of modern Egyptian society, under the ferment of religious and political ideas, with the inertia and gnomic despair of the Pharaonic god-kings. If difference and disparity are the only rules that govern the conception of contemporary states, it is discontinuity and disruption that govern historical ones.

This argument is not entirely damning, insofar as the putative uniformity of states today implies that each is to be conceived as ahistorical and secular anyway (using "secular" in both its senses, to refer to nonreligious, mutable institutions and to something perennial, not bound by time). We should also recall that the continuity of state institutions everywhere, throughout history, has been disrupted by colonialism, including in the period before the creation of the present system—which was intended, in a real historical innovation, to put an end to colonialism once and for all. So it is not necessarily

139

fatal for contemporary human relations to argue that there are no historical *states*.

It would, however, be fatal, in the light of the foregoing, if there were no historical *nations*. Nations ideally conceived are effective communities—the groups who in history are adjudged to have defined states, and who must give life to them today. And in this regard it is striking how little agreement one can find, among contemporary theorists of nationhood, on what a nation is. I shall explore this question in the next chapter.

Notes

1.   Samuel P. Huntington, *The Clash of Civilizations and the Remaking of World Order* (London: Simon & Schuster, 1997).
2.   Alexander Wendt, *Social Theory of International Politics* (Cambridge: Cambridge University Press, 1999), p. 202.
3.   The classic study here is Edward E. Leamer, *Sources of International Comparative Advantage: Theory and Evidence* (Cambridge, MA: MIT Press, 1984). See also Wood, *North-South Trade, Employment and Inequality*.
4.   For Grossmann, "the essence of a thing is the same as its essential property" (*The Existence of the World*, p. 23). He uses the term only to recount the early development of ontological theory, and to refute Nominalism (pp. 21–23).
5.   Anne Hammerstad, "Population movement and its impact on world politics" in Mark Beeson and Nick Bisley (eds.), *Issues in 21st Century World Politics* (Basingstoke: Palgrave Macmillan, 2010), pp. 238, 242, and 250.

8

Tracing Nations

What is a nation in the modern sense of the word, such that we can envisage it as a group of people in close identity with a territorial/institutional state, according to the principles of the contemporary universal system, and for it to have life and force within that system? First and foremost, I have argued, it must be an effective community. For a community to be a community, let alone to conceive of acting *as one*, there must be a sense of fellowship and mutual trust between its members. Second, because of the fixed territorial basis of the states system, it must have an association with a particular place, long enough for the association to be considered *historic* (in the word's twin senses of "long lasting" and "momentous"). Finally, the community must be large enough to be more than merely local or genealogical. These three conditions must, I suggest, be fulfilled, to give life to the image of territorially settled, putatively distinct, and autonomous social units which figures in diplomacy and international law. Nations must really exist, before we can begin to think of states as agents.

The main theories of nationhood are modernism, ethno-symbolism, and primordialism.[1] The first two I group together as critical—allowing significant scepticism about the concept of a nation. The third I define as idealist: strongly supportive of nations as cohesive historic communities, but problematic as regards their relationship with modern states. Later I shall come on to the experimental approach of Benedict Anderson in his celebrated *Imagined Communities*.

8.1 Modernism

For the modernists, the nation is a product of the recent past. This approach involves, in fact, two rather contradictory claims: that nations can be formed by design (as in Europe from the Renaissance on, culminating in the French and American Revolutions and European colonialism on other continents); and that nationhood itself is a contestable concept.

In this spirit of scepticism, Eric Hobsbawm argues that people tend to read the past backward from the present, interpreting it inadequately in the process.[2] John Breuilly thinks it almost impossible to know how people thought and felt about their institutions even in cultures as literate, and as close to us in time, as the European Middle Ages.[3] Atsuko Ichijo and Gordana Uzelac question whether anyone can "certify the existence of a pre-modern nation beyond doubt."[4]

Other thinkers of this tendency emphasize governments' willingness to manipulate the self-understandings, both contemporary and historical, of their citizens. For Anna Triandafyllidou, "the nation as any type of collective identity is constituted in interaction, by reference to inspiring or threatening Significant Others"; it is "not a static social object but a dynamic process."[5] Her critique is aimed at the idea, once ancient and now modern, of a Greek nation—but above all, one only recently emergent from Ottoman and Soviet hegemony in southeastern Europe. Stephanie Lawson mounts a similar case for an archipelago thousands of miles away. "Fijian national/ethnic identity is situational, relational and instrumental," she says. "In the case of Fiji . . . both 'nation' and 'nationalism' are very much part of the modern state-making process."[6] For these authors, modern Greek and Fijian nationhood has arisen as a relatively recent reaction to colonialism. Triandafyllidou's case is particularly striking. If a people with an identity as venerable as "the Greeks" lack substantial nationhood, how can anyone lay claim to it?

In fact there is ample evidence in recent historical times for negative or reactive motives for nation-formation—perhaps especially after 1945, when the settling of peoples on territorial states became an automatic and bureaucratized process. Singaporeans' secession from the Federation of Malaysia provided a refuge for Chinese persecuted under the Malaysian regime. Pakistan was founded as a kind of not-India, from people in the subcontinent who did not wish, or who feared, to live under a state dominated by Hinduism. Bangladesh was founded by East Pakistanis dissatisfied with the central Pakistan government's treatment of them in their enclave.

One can, moreover, turn this argument round, to look at nation-formation from the perspective of victorious colonials, and still see populations whose claim to nationhood is reactive and unhistorical. This would include the populist nationalism of Latin America, and even the liberal-democratic "civic nation"[7] of North America or Australasia—both rather recent historical products, developed by people of European origin. With the possible exception of the United States, none of the cases I have cited seems based on a long-term plan for the populations so constituted. Social solidarity based on reaction to others is ambiguous, and under free conditions likely to evaporate. So, arguably, is attachment to one place as a reaction to another. Nation-formation along these lines, whether by people perceiving themselves as victims, or as victors, of an original situation seems destined to run into the sands of history.

Modernist Methodology . . .

Not surprisingly, the self-criticism implicit in modernist approaches makes for a rather uncertain methodology. Ichijo and Uzelac begin by firmly answering their own question ("When is the nation?"). "There is," they inform us, "a consensus that nationalism itself is a modern product." Thus, "any study on nationalism should deal with the nature of modern society in which we live." But who is "we" in this context, since not all societies in the world have been modernized in the same way, at the same rate, from the same beginnings, or with the same results?

Then these authors openly undermine their own thesis. It can, they say, answer broader, timeless questions about modernity and "what society is. After all, nations and nationalism are social phenomena, not an article of faith."[8] But what is their object of study: a phenomenon, or the theory of a phenomenon; and is the modernity of the "modern society in which we live" equally "not an article of faith"? There is much room for confusion here. For his part, Umut Özkırımlı notes:

> The modernists share little in common apart from a general belief in the importance of modern processes such as capitalism, industri-alization, urbanization, secularism, and the rise of the bureaucratic state in the growth of nations and nationalism. Stressing different, at times sharply conflicting, factors in their explanations, they remain the keenest critics of each other's work.[9]

Modernist theories, therefore, from the claim that nations are defin-able only against other nations, to the claim that all chronologies and terminologies are suspect, seem to cast doubt on the very idea of a nation. Perhaps understandably so, since our conception of the modern is itself unstable—referring, in a fixed sense, to the recent past, and more elusively to what is emerging now. In fact these scep-tical assertions are aspects of the same problem, if one relies on the assumption in conventional international theory that nations and states are synonymous.

... and Tautology

A passage by Breuilly illustrates this point precisely. Contemplating the idea of nationhood against the claims of "globalization," the UN organization, cultural diversity, and democracy, he asserts:

> I shall treat as nation-states states that claim to be national (however nation is defined), are not confronted internally by powerful state-subverting nationalist movements, and are accepted by the international community.

If you think this sentence is hard to understand or even meaningless, you are right. "States that claim to be national" are nation-states by definition, since who can do the claiming but the inhabitants of states? "[H]owever nation is defined" is a red herring here. As for those "state-subverting nationalist movements," surely if they succeed in subverting a state "internally" they have an equal claim to be the nation of the "nation-state" in question, or a separate but equivalent one—but again, by their own claiming and self-defining. And who is the "international community" based on, in a world of universal states, but the inhabitants, on significant occasions, of putative "nation-states"? To that extent their presumed "acceptance" of a given "nation-state" into the "international community" is self-serving—amounting to recognition of their own (equally subjective) status in constituting that community.

Breuilly is doing here the opposite of what he claims to be doing—being a theorist of nations and nation-formation, which entails calling into question the concept of a nation. He is asserting, in effect, that in the modern world a nation is a state and a state is a nation. He says as much: "The term 'Nations' [in United Nations] actually means 'States.'" So why not just talk about states (United States Organization, interstate relations, etc.) and forget about nations? But surely the whole point about the latter term is that it stands for groups of people who are *not* identical with anyone or anything else; they exist insofar as their members collectively choose their *own* political, cultural, religious, or linguistic identity, in relation—cooperatively or otherwise—to other groups; and from that distinctness derives all the value that nations possess. This conception, however, is clearly not the one that Breuilly has in mind here. (As for "civic nationalism," a phenomenon he defines as "commitment to a state and its values," this is an equally

groundless approach, since he nowhere gives an independent definition of a state.)[10]

Next Breuilly reviews historical developments "from around 1750"—
conflating, in effect, "nationalism and nation-states"; focusing, in an
alternative and I think controversial conception of globalis/zation, on
"the processes producing the nation-state as the dominant form of state
power and nationalism as the dominant ideology," while deliberately
omitting "non-state elements such as communications, transportation,
economic and social interactions." Like other modernist theorists,
Breuilly considers the "processes" in question to be fundamentally
European-inspired. But now, disregarding Hobsbawm's warning, he
is merely reading the past of nations and states—together!—in terms
of the present—which is to say, in terms of nation-state *agents*. This is
clear from his language ("Britain attributed its success to Christianity,
parliamentary institutions, and free trade." "Powerful nation-states
challenged British hegemony. Britain responded in like fashion.")[11]
In order, however, to have some concept of inter*nation*al relations as
actual human relations, one must have some independent concept of
the nation. Breuilly does not even ask what that is.

Finally, it is notable that in what purports to be a general introduction
to nationalism, this author relegates to a separate table, on "Debates,"
alternative approaches to his own: a tacit admission that the whole
question is likely to be more complicated than he has argued.[12]

8.2 Ethno-symbolism

Let us turn then to ethno-symbolism, an approach refined, through suc-
ceeding versions and over decades, by the doyen of nationhood studies,
Anthony Smith. In his view, a range of traditional factors making for
community evolves over time into complex political institutions and
territorial attachments, with the direct help of the community's own
rulers, till something like the nation (-state) of modern discussions
emerges. For Smith, culture is vital in the formation of this hybrid—part
natural, part artificial—entity. A nation, he says, is

> a named and *self-defined* community whose members *cultivate* com-
> mon *myths*, memories, *symbols* and values, possess and *disseminate* a
> distinctive public culture, reside in and *identify with* a historic home-
> land, and *create* and *disseminate* common laws and shared customs.

This approach enables him to trace nations further back in time, and
more widely in location, than the recent European past—evoking

remote origins in, for example, "ancient Egypt, Second Temple Judaea and . . . early Christian Armenia." But equally, his stress on subjective factors (seen in the words I have italicized in the quotation) suggests that people's sense of community may be self-deluding, open to manipulation by unscrupulous rulers and mountebanks. He writes further of the "*discovery* and *appropriation* of ethnic history" (his emphasis), and of "golden ages . . . visions of an idealised ethnic past" manifesting people's need for "antiquity, continuity, authenticity, dignity and national destiny."[13] These are phenomena about which modernists are sceptical too.

Common Ground

The difference between modernists and ethno-symbolists on the question of nation-formation may be reduced to one of emphasis or discipline—say, a politics/sociology divide, in which the former focus on the dynamics of change and take common culture for granted, while the latter examine the appurtenances and continuity of culture itself. More significantly, the two approaches are alike in being critical, even ironic, about their object of study. Compare Triandafyllidou's assertion that the nation "is constituted in interaction, by reference to inspiring or threatening Significant Others" with Smith's noting of the timeless "differentiation of 'us' from 'them.'"[14]

This theoretical common ground is also controversial ground, which is why both groups may be called critical theorists; they both suggest, in differing ways, that there is no such thing as a (historical) nation. Take again the case of colonialism, in which they share an interest. Colonialism, defined as the imposition of others' culture, is the antithesis of free community-formation. Historically, this was both an active and a reactive phenomenon, whereby a people's sense of identity was manipulated simultaneously by outsiders and by "insider" collaborators, so that new influences were absorbed even as they were resisted. From this ironic, contesting viewpoint, Europeans can be seen filling up Africa, Asia, and Latin America from the sixteenth century onward with mere de facto nations: functional, but not deeply believed in; institutional, but not willing communities. As Adrian Hastings put it: "The political map of Africa, decided in the 1880s and 1890s by non-Africans for their own purposes, has remained almost unaltered ever since."[15] The peoples so "mapped" either lacked an original unity or found such rigid human divisions incomprehensible as against their older communities of allegiance.[16] Equally, in a longer-term perspective colonialism is itself an archetypal human practice; as Marx pointed out, not something invented by Europeans or "Caucasians."[17]

Considering, then, the subversiveness and the pervasiveness of colonialism together, nation-formation in history must appear a complex, highly politicized, and controversial process—on which modernists and ethno-symbolists agree. For Smith,

> there was, and there is, nothing inexorable about nation-formation; nothing like a general or a specific evolution of nations, not even . . . a single social model or ideal-type of the "nation-in-general."[18]

Or as Breuilly puts it: "I have not tried to write about 'nationalism in general': I do not think there is such a thing."[19]

That said, neither modernists nor ethno-symbolists explain fully why contemporary peoples' struggles to define their identity might be complicated by their inherited institutions' failure to express their culture and, in its train, their differences. This issue is raised directly in a third, more positive approach.

8.3 Primordialism

Primordialism is both anthropological and historical. It rests on a fundamental supposition that nations derive from traditional, and implicitly authentic, forms of social organization. In primordialism the nation is postulated as a *community of descent*: a people claiming distinctiveness, and the right to rule themselves, on grounds of their common origin.

This matter of origins should not be taken too literally. Van der Berghe, for instance, overstates his case when he comments that "the primordialism of ethnicity is rooted in the biology of nepotism. We have a biological predisposition to favour others to the extent that they are, or at least that we perceive them as, related to us by common descent."[20] Nepotism, however, usually refers to a cultural/normative concept of *un*acceptable behaviour, violating a *non*deterministic vision of social relations, while the idea of the nation seems part of a more positive moral vision; it implies human solidarity in a wider human group than one merely determined by biology. Also, in any society, the longer the passage of time the more memories weaken, the more records become suspect, and the harder it is for anyone to claim direct descent from anyone else. Even "biological" claims of commonality become subjective. They weaken, in fact, into the far fuzzier domain of ethnicity. Van der Berghe muddies an essentially normative issue.

147

Leaving his approach aside, commonality in the "common origins" element of primordialism seems to refer to one of two related claims: either of a people who have "always" (uninterruptedly) existed somewhere as a distinct, self-conceived group, or of one who have been displaced from their "historic" territory but still claim to be a distinct group in their own right. Longevity and attachment to place are important for nationhood, in the primordialist view. The putative community of descent is historical, rather than simply biological.

Take Armenians, whose claims to nationhood rest on there having been for centuries a people called by that name, associated with a specific place. Armenia is said to be the first place in which Christianity was adopted as a state religion, and an Armenian Christian Church has existed ever since, alongside the idea of an Armenian state.[21] Territorially, notwithstanding a substantial diaspora, Armenians have a historic association with an area in the south of what is now called the Caucasian isthmus. (Again, the twin senses of "historic" apply: "long-lasting" and "momentous.") In both ancient and modern times the people of the area were subjugated by outsiders. In the early twentieth century there was briefly an independent Armenian state, later absorbed by force into the Soviet-Communist empire. Since the Soviet dissolution there has been an independent state of Armenia within the former-Soviet borders.

All this is to say, if the current population of Armenia are a nation, it is not, or not merely, because like everyone else they are members of a modern state, but because they are descended directly from definable ancient Armenians—defined primarily by religion and a putative common origin in the "same" geographical place. This gives them confidence, we may presume, in their identity—it makes them an effective community, with or without the diaspora. Thus primordialism defines a successful and distinctive human group beyond local groups: in such cases as "the Armenians", the ideal type of the nation is realized.

At the other end of the conceptual spectrum we find the current inhabitants of the United States: for the most part an immigrant people, who have come from elsewhere—in fact, many elsewheres; rather recently, and not always willingly; bringing their culture with them, and leaving their community of descent behind. In these respects they are to be contrasted with the shrunken population of "Native" Americans, the former "Red Indians" whose ties with the North American subcontinent go back many centuries. All this explains why, for example, Alex Haley's *Roots*,[22] tracing a particular black American's origins to West Africa and the transatlantic slave trade, received so much publicity in the United

States, and why so many white Americans go east across the Atlantic to (re)visit Europe. These are manifestations of a common perception that most modern Americans' origins are not in America—that they are, in a sense, a people on the move. As a result, while modern Armenians may be expected to be (and on all the evidence are) confident of their historical identity despite the vicissitudes to which it has been subject, modern Americans may be expected to be confused, uncertain or— more positively—curious about theirs.

Real and Ideal

Primordialism is a powerful approach, owing to the depth of the human connections, cultural and historical, that are evoked. It gives political force to the belief that blood is thicker than water, and to the idea of human roots, by articulating people's attachment to that physical thing, the land. In the era of globalis/zation, and the individualism and anonymity of modern industrial society, it gives continuing life to the ideas of family and home, and even immortality, through the possibility for contemporary communities to be linked with a past and future place on earth. Arguably it sustains morality too, through the force of beliefs tied to long-tested social practice, and in this sense it supports expressions of collective will better than any bureaucratic institutions of state.

In many respects, then, primordialism is the approach against which other theories of the nation are to be judged. It is also of deep interest for the theory of international relations: in the modern system based on formal independence and territoriality, it postulates an authentic nation-state agent: authentic because indigenous ("native of, belonging naturally to" a given place—OED), but also able to transcend, through social unity, the rootedness of territorial associations and to act on its own behalf in the world.

Naturally enough, this is also the approach which most severely tests the impartiality of analysts. Nowadays we are all members of some formal political community or other, and so called upon to make our personal loyalties clear—whether to the status quo, or to some transcendent conception of human relations. In this connection, an essay on national identity in the United States by Susan-Mary Grant is revealing—first, because she describes the American national identity as uncertain and confused; and second because, in her efforts to define some authentic version of it, she herself appears uncertain and confused—muddling her interpretations of the various theories of nationhood in a manner which strongly suggests that personal

149

feeling has interfered with her judgment. In an all-too-human way, her American patriotism appears at odds with her loyalty to her vocation as critical theorist of the nation.[23]

8.4 Problems of Primordialism

On the negative side of the scales, the primordialist approach, in a world of fixed borders, is a potential source of conflict over both land and human identity. If for no other reason than the disparate histori-cal development, between regions, of records and communications, some groups' claim to have "always" been a distinct people is bound to be based on stronger evidence than others'. Also, efforts to fulfil any such claim come hard up against the norms of the contemporary states system, with its powerful presumption against all forms of political activity which threaten change in the territorial outlines and settled populations of states. All nations, in the UN doctrine, are real (because embodied by states). Primordialism threatens this doctrine directly, by suggesting that some nations are more real than others.

The classic problem case is the modern Israel/Palestine imbroglio, a conflict so potent because it draws on competing primordialist theses, romantic-ancestral claims to be an original nation favored by God in ownership of the same historic territory. A copycat process, in fact, has been at work in this dispute, involving assertions contradictory in them-selves of collective superiority and victimhood.[24] International relations in general since 1945 have been characterized by myriad irredentist, secessionist, and hegemonic challenges to the imposed order of states. As the violence erupting from the Israel/Palestine conflict has shown, moreover, competing claims based on indigeneity are liable to lapse into atavism. This is because indigeneity, simplistically asserted, really is no more than biological determinism. The very expression "blood is thicker than water" is ambiguous: potentially approving ("when it came to a crisis, he looked after his own") or disapproving ("some people are liable to sacrifice others as the price of looking after their own").

Steven Grosby develops a version of primordialism at once sub-tler and, in the light of the historical record, more down to earth, in which he points to breaks in the cultural and physical continuity of certain peoples whom we might, today, call ancient—breaks that he accounts for by acts of deliberate and symbolic choice. Yet even this more nuanced version of the thesis relies on tracing modern nations directly back to traditional society—what Grosby calls "situating the nation within the continuum of forms of kinship."[25]

Territorial Attachment ...

Traditional society, because of its roots in the land, is also the only kind of society with a claim to be associated with a particular place, and in so doing to secure a territorial state. One of the first assumptions, for example, that we make today about prehistoric human groups is that they were people without states. In part we do so because at this distance in time, and with no written records, their social organization is hard to pin down. But equally, it is because we think of them as rootless: defined, like hunter-gatherers or flint-tool workers, by accident or occupation, dependent on the local availability of food and materials, and for that reason lacking evolved social structures.[26] Similarly, nomadic peoples today—kinship communities associated with no specific place—are often stateless, or at least not primarily defined by adherence to existing territorial states. They are likely to have contested identity papers, or none at all, and to find that their nomadism puts the authorities ill at ease. It is the *being settled* that matters, in the modern system, for national authentication. In two senses: a) psychological, so that mutual trust brings society's members together in peaceful community; and b) physical or geographical, so that the members are content to occupy their current location and not have designs on another which would inevitably, in a closed system of ownership, be "someone else's."

... and Dislocation

The problem, however, is that society defined in these terms does not fit into the confines of the modern states system, or perhaps any permanent system of political divisions. The widespread phenomenon of migration, transgressing modern boundaries between states as well as historic boundaries between and within them, is living proof of this. Colonialism may once again be invoked here. Colonialism was itself a diaspora for many peoples, like the Iberian colonists in Latin America, or the Arab tribes who left the landlocked Nejd for the coast and continents beyond.[27] Colonialism in turn has caused long-lived diasporas of refugees, as well as local miscegenation—subverting, respectively, ties of settlement and of kinship. In this way it confounds in advance our search for real communities in history—even in Europe, following the divisive Roman expansion.[28] More recently, the phenomenon of economic migration could be seen as a kind of reverse colonialism—a reaction, in the modern states system, to inequalities sown by Europeans between the "North" and "South" of the world. All these factors dent the ideal image of a states system neatly and consensually populated, in primordialist fashion, by indigenous nations, whether we think of such a system as having existed in the past, or possible now.

Even without the worldwide phenomenon of colonialism, one could point out that dislocation, rather than territorial stability, has for many peoples been the norm. Where migration does not subvert social stability, war will take its place, as the many conflicts over the frontiers of states show—even in Europe, in relatively recent times. The historical Polish nation, for example—if there is such a thing—has been divided at least twice since 1750, and has twice occupied a different location from that of the present Polish state. During this time a state called Poland has gone out of existence on the map of Europe and come back into existence again, while "Germans," "Russians," "Ukrainians," and "Lithuanians" claimed that "Poles" as such did not exist, or at least not as a distinct people with the same patrimony as they themselves laid claim to.

Most of humanity, in fact, shares a history resembling the Polish case, if one is prepared to go back far enough: either some people claiming continuity with their state's historical past are no longer in the same geographical location as that state was in the past, or different people and their institutions have occupied the same location at different times.[29] Genealogical continuity, or continuity of territorial attachment, may be invoked in favor of a people's claim to be distinctive, but rarely both at once. "All forms of the modern state," says Michael Freeman, are "vulnerable to the charge of internal colonialism."[30] Or rival colonialism.[31]

Exceptionalism

There are further problems with the primordialist approach which cannot be brushed aside. One of its key components is a core religious institution, related to a messianic sense of destiny. "Ancient" nations so defined can be identified today (Israel, Armenia, Ethiopia, Iran, India, Greece). But as pure examples they are few and far between, and not above question in themselves.[32] In modern Greece, for example, one might see an ancient polytheistic nation reinvented as a monotheistic one, with one national orthodoxy replacing another. And then even among peoples with the strongest primordial claims, there are members who do not conform. One could mention the secular, diasporic Jews and Armenians settled elsewhere than in modern Israel or Armenia: people who apparently feel no need to live in a confessional community or exemplary group, yet still claim their place within a classical Jewish or Armenian identity.

The historically strong Armenian attachment to a homeland in the south Caucasus could itself be seen as the product of resistance to powerful invaders, from the Romans, Byzantines, and Persians to the Ottoman Turks and Russians. In turn, the long-lived Armenian diaspora could be seen as a historic reaction against enclavature. Or persecution. The slaughter of Armenians by Turkish forces early in the twentieth century, at a time when there was no recognized Armenian state, has doubtless strengthened through martyrdom the Armenians' sense of themselves as a people, like that of Jews after the Nazi Holocaust, so present to contemporary minds.[33]

In short, we can fairly imagine the religious affinities that give such peoples a strong sense of togetherness as having been artificially strengthened, as the sceptical modernists argue, "by reference to inspiring or threatening Significant Others"—and therefore perhaps not deeply or durably so. The diaspora phenomenon itself may be seen as opportunistic—now expanding, now concentrating national identity, as governments in the "home" state allow the acknowledged membership to wax and wane, perhaps claiming the wealthy or famous as their own while ignoring their political critics abroad. It is also striking how many "ancient" nations are diaspora-dependent in a way which defines, rather than precedes, our modern globalis/zation; one need only think of the worldwide dispersal of Jews, or Armenians, or Greeks. Diasporas today, in the more open political climate after the Cold War, make it possible to have things both ways in the system of formal nation-states. Their members can retain both a historic cultural identity and a modern one, or more banally, enjoy the benefits of dual citizenship, while the "home" governments can avoid problems of overpopulation.[34]

Things could not be otherwise. It is contradictory, as well as oppressive, to claim membership of a society which is both unique and archetypal of humanity as a whole. Primordialism on this view is either purely mythopoeic—symbolic, like the Book of Genesis or the Upanishads, of the whole history of human community—or irrelevant to a system of secular states. Which returns the debate about nations to the fundamental, subversive question posed by critical theorists, as to whether the object of discussion is a phenomenon, or the theory of a phenomenon.

In the world we live in today, in any case, it seems more realistic to argue that all societies, to varying degrees, share traditional and modern features. The existing states whose uniform politico-legal exostructures constitute the international system are peopled by societies who retain a traditional core—in its own right a source of social strength, but in some places more than others. The tension, moreover, between traditional social values and the rapid-change processes of modernization makes for conflicted societies. The European values of the Industrial Revolution, and the mass society organized to serve it, have been diffused along with this tension all over the world. The result is a contest in which neither modernity nor tradition wins out, and the mythopoeic temptations of tradition are for most people indefinitely, if reluctantly, shelved.[35] Some primordialists, against this background, may have their hearts in the right place, in the sense that community is a good thing for its own sake; but there is an inherent, destabilising ambiguity in the idea of ancient nations set among modern territorial states.

Ethnicity

Finally, ethnicity is a common thread in primordialist arguments, but again, one which becomes increasingly contentious. A minority of modern states have populations defined by a strong claim to ethnic homogeneity, but this is easily attributable to historic isolation, closed polities, or an ideology of racial conquest (Japan is an extreme case in point).

Increasingly, ethnicity is treated as a spectrum nowadays, with racial identity at the "hard" end and culture and shared values at the "soft" end. It is increasingly vague and subjective—a potential source of social confusion and division, rather than cohesion. So claims of ethnic unity as the basis of nationhood may provide a pretext for a new state to be set up preemptively, as a response to "threatening Significant Others"—as happened to destructive effect in the Balkans, at the end of the twentieth century.

What the sliding-scale interpretation of ethnicity permits is a blurring of the distinction between the genealogical and the cultural in a people's conception of themselves. This happens over time, as members of physically related, face-to-face communities leave them and intermarry with outsiders until original blood ties cease to be meaningful. Then the question of how to situate a larger group, historically, ramifies into other questions—such as how large the group may be while still remaining an effective community; and who decides, on what basis, who should be "in" and who "out." Grosby, having suggested that there is a case for primordial nations, fudges the issue of their definition.

"The proper understanding of the nation must tolerate ambiguity," he says, before remarking, unhelpfully, that "ambiguity is the norm of all social relations." He also chooses to answer "obliquely" (his word) the important question of whether there is a Jewish nation.[36]

Even Anthony Smith, who stresses the importance of ethnicity to mark himself off from the modernists, combines in his definition of it the abstract factors of culture and symbolism and the concrete one of race. He also writes, tellingly, of the instability of such a mixture. "Ethnocultural attributes," he argues, are "attributes of groups regarded as (presumptively) ancestrally related. (We are dealing here with *myths* of descent, imputed rather than biological ancestry.)"[37] Similarly, for Grosby kinship is "a pattern of real and presumed biological connectedness."[38] For Hastings, the presumed genetic unity underlying ethnicity is "partly real, partly mythical."[39]

Primordialist claims for common origins look very isolated, against this conception of ethnicity as a modern invention in which race and culture are arbitrarily thrown together. That, after all, is how state citizenry today can be tallied in hundreds of thousands (Malta, Montenegro) or hundreds of millions (China, India, Russia, the United States, Nigeria, Brazil), and include both people with a strong claim to be indigenous and people with none. A nation, says Reynolds, "must of course be sufficiently large for the use of the word not to be absurd"; but he adds, rather contradictorily, "it is not possible precisely to say what 'sufficiently large' means."[40]

National size alongside national composition is obviously a major factor in international relations; it has everything to do with the legitimacy and authenticity of a given "national" group in the eyes of others. The vagueness of ethnicity as a marker of shared identity, however, provides us with little guidance in this area. Before the twentieth century it was not strange to refer to organized groups of greatly varying size, including the very smallest, as nations. The concept of a nation was both more fluid and more kinship-dependent, borders were less formal, and there was no comprehensive states system. Now territory counts decisively, making competition between populations a factor, having a levelling effect on numbers and militating against the identity claims of the smallest "national" groups. That is why we do not (at least, I do not) think of Monégasques, or Liechtensteiners, or Sammarinesi, or Andorrans, as members of independent nations, but rather as citizens of microstates which are curious historical survivals. And in fact many of the people in question find it convenient to acquire a second citizenship from, and concede key administrative functions to, the people of a larger neighboring jurisdiction (France, Switzerland, Austria, Italy, or Spain), which rather negates their claim to a distinct political identity, no matter how ancient. Also, while pressures on all smaller political communities in Europe are eased by the pooling of sovereignty in the European Union, outside the EU the claims of micronation(-state)s have proved harder to assert, precisely because ethnicity has not, as in Europe, lost its force as a marker of shared identity.

Clearly, the stereotypical ideas of race and destiny in primordialist theory fail to fit in with the often arbitrary affiliations between people and place we find in the world today. In the modern states system, even established colonial language ends up being overturned. About the time that migrants from the Indian subcontinent began arriving in the United States on a socially significant scale, North America's older immigrants from Asia—the traditional tribes of the Europeans' "frontier"—were rather hurriedly reclassified as "First Nations." This prompts the question of what number of nation the modern American nation is—though no doubt real Indians are better than fake red ones.

DNA analysis introduces further complications, by showing the lack of a general correlation between social and cultural divisions and the populations of contemporary states.[41] The expression "ethnic cleansing" was, after all, coined by Serb supremacists for their campaigns of forced exile, in a region long isolated from historic change and population movements, and so from modern social understandings.[42] "Ethnic" for those demagogues simply meant anyone who disagreed with them on the future of former Yugoslavia. In most cases, however, ethnicity has become so broad a concept, and so reducible to race, precisely because of the mobility (or dislocation) of people in historical times. Seen in the light of DNA, the human race itself is a diaspora.[43]

For all these reasons, primordialism is highly vulnerable to criticism from those who would demystify the subjective attachments at the heart of the approach. Eller and Coughlan dismiss it out of hand as "unsociological, unanalytical and vacuous." Ethnicity in particular, they say,

> is surely an affect issue, making it distinct from strictly material or instrumental issues, but this by no means makes it primordial, since emotion is not necessarily or ordinarily primordial but has a clear and analysable sociogenesis. In fact, in the end primordialism belies the same faulty approach which has already come under fire in the realms of culture and affect—taking phenomena that are simply "already existing" and "persistent" and reifying and mystifying them

into things that are "natural," "spiritual," and "have always existed and always will."[44]

Similarly, Özkırımlı argues that primordialism "is not useful as an analytical category precisely because it lacks an analytical component."[45] We may also surmise that the ahistorical character of the current states system, its blurring of the distinction between nations and states, and its pressures for conformity have made some embattled champions of "primordial" values more intransigent than they would otherwise have been.

In any event, the British historian Linda Colley feels able to confidently assert:

> There has never been a substantial politically defined population anywhere on the globe that has been natural or primordial. All countries are synthetic and imperfect creations and subject to change, and most have been the result of violent conflict at some stage.[46]

Elsewhere, she describes nations as "culturally and ethnically diverse, problematic, protean and artificial constructs that take shape very quickly and come apart just as fast." Even in her own venerable polity, Colley sees "an invented nation superimposed . . . onto much older alignments and loyalties."[47] Compare Anthony Smith's formula: "we may liken the nation to a kind of palimpsest, on whose parchment many different texts and messages from various epochs have been collated and written down, and which go on being written down to our day and into the foreseeable future."[48] Much of this inventing and rewriting, moreover, has been sustained by domination over others; and we can expect new "national" challenges to arise, even within venerable polities, now that the colonial option has been formally outlawed in international relations.[49]

8.5 Theories Compared[50]

All things considered, primordialism is no better and no worse than other theories of nationhood. It has the virtue of evoking real human experiences, values, and hopes, but the vice of being poorly accommodated by the boundaries of modern states. There may be "true" nations in a deep historical sense, but they are likely to be in the extreme minority, and seen as a provocation by people with no claim to membership of them or a share in their benefits.

In fact, all three theories, set against the reality from which they extrapolate, reveal the strengths and weaknesses of the ideal type.

On a spectrum of positivity toward the nation-state, modernism and ethno-symbolism gather toward the sceptical end. The implication of these two approaches is that people will fail to "go into" modern states because they *have not chosen* to be nations in the first place (and never may); not, that is, as communities of identity transcending local or face-to-face attachments. Nations so conceived will fail to fit in with the automaticity of the universal states system and will merely reflect its weakness.

Primordialism lodges at the opposite, affirmative end of the spectrum, highlighting people's real shared needs and concerns, and attachments to place, over centuries. But equally, these could be described as fundamental, timeless. Primordial consciousness is of, and not of, this world, and so not necessarily linked to modernity or the exclusive institution of the "national" state. Self-defining primordial peoples have no doubts about their identity, but choose not to be *modern* nations, the kind now defined by (and confined to) states. Their claims to nationhood transcend the automaticity of the states system, but by the same token complicate life for anyone whose claims are weaker or just different—which may mean the majority of humankind. In a world, moreover, whose institutions imply an ironing-out of traditional differences and disparities, primordialism looks obsolete—or even offensive, like the Jewish American from the Bronx who reinvents himself as a claimant to historic Judaea and Samaria in order to evict Arabs with a more recent, and passably more legal, claim to live there.

Implications for International Theory

What of the broader implications? Well, first, if the modernists are right, then "international relations" is something of a charade, for there are no real nations to begin with. Ethno-symbolists would tend to agree or disagree with this view, depending on how far they consider cultural symbols to be authentic. But in the light of colonialism—a process which has seen both the imposition and the appropriation of cultural symbols—ethno-symbolist ambivalence is not much of an advance on modernist scepticism.

Second, some people (primordialists) clearly believe absolutely and passionately in nations—prize them, it would seem, above all else—but they also think that human beings qualify unequally for membership of them. On this view, some nations are definitely more real than others, while many if not most national claims are bogus. "International relations" so conceived is a recipe for permanent conflict.

Meanwhile, this is a debate in which everyone must take sides (or convincingly show that all sides are wrong), because we are all nowadays members of one kind of nation or other (old/young; changing/ unchangeable; large/small)—a society yoked, as a millstone around one's neck is a yoke, to a formally-constituted state.

Finally, the academic debate about nationhood is marked by a profound intellectual and even moral confusion, leading Peter Willetts to remark that "no such entities [as nation-states] exist."[51]

Or to be precise—since I believe in the sincerity and, as far as they go, the insights of the nation-theorists—the present world of formal nation-states is itself a source of confusion. That is why the nation-theorists disagree. It is inter*national* theorists—those for whom nations must exist, or they have nothing to talk about—who are left to pick up the pieces.

8.6 Imagined Communities

In the light of these arguments, it is interesting to go back to one of the most influential books to have appeared since the Second World War, Benedict Anderson's emblematically titled *Imagined Communities: Reflections on the Origin and Spread of Nationalism*.[52]

For Anderson, modern state-formation in Europe and European-colonial areas was the product of successful contrivances by ruling elites—notably their seizure of elements of culture for the sake of political control. This view, stressing intellectual rather than economic "hegemony," applies Gramsci's variant of Marxist conspiracy theory to history and society. In his first edition Anderson described elites' efforts to monopolize the print media and standardize vernacular languages; in the second, he added their use of the census, map and museum in their own propaganda. Thus, he argues, dynastic leaders secularized their status and invented language-based myths of discrete, territorially based populations coming under their rule. Disparate groups of people were brought together under a more complex and abstract model of social organization than in their older forms of community. This was nevertheless a paradoxical and even tragic development, because it meant they would eventually fight and die for a set of "national" myths against other people equally myth-driven. Nationalism and colonialism, in Anderson's account, are two sides of the same coin, like physical oppression and subjugation of the mind.[53]

Certain aspects of *Imagined Communities* detract somewhat from the force of the author's polemic. One is his nostalgia for exotic forms of "folk" nationalism linked, in Southeast Asia, to myths of common origin. Another is the Marxist schadenfreude which leads him to overstate his case, admiring the efficiency of modern methods of social organization while condemning their repressiveness. (It was Hobbes who argued that, as long as there is some element of imaginative identification between society and its rulers, no political system can be wholly unjust.) In the end, Anderson is too dazzled by the successful techniques of national mythmaking that he describes to deal with their troubled twentieth-century consequences; his story effectively stops in 1945. These weaknesses do not, however, alter the normative burden of his thesis: that people were everywhere gulled into accepting a social arrangement (formal nations) which limited their rights and travestied their traditional allegiances. Imagined communities, as described by Anderson, are not real communities.

Anderson's Ambivalence

Which "national" communities, then, are real? What light is shed by his thesis on the various non-Marxist theories of nationhood that I have outlined?

On an optimistic view, primordialism (assisted by ethno-symbolism) would be *right* as a theory of primitive community formation, but *wrong*—because outdated—as a basis for modern nation-status. That is to say, traditional territorial/genealogical communities were (and are) the only real communities, although people reimagine and adapt them creatively as local identities become eroded. Nations can in this sense "grow up," as children become adults, developing wholly different sensibilities, values, and relationships. This anthropological account of nation-formation connects with paternalistic views of the world after colonialism, like that expounded by Robert Jackson in his book *Quasi-States*.[54]

Alternatively (and pessimistically), primordialism would be *wrong*—in fact, always was wrong—and modernism *right* because, as Anderson himself asserts,

> all communities larger than primordial villages of face-to-face contact (and perhaps even these) are imagined. Communities are to be distinguished, not by their falsity/genuineness, but by the style in which they are imagined.[55]

The aside in parentheses implies not only that imagined communities fail to be real communities, but that real communities are not possible at all—at least, not as groups to which we might wish to belong because they give us meaning and moral support in the present and prospectively for the future. That is the anomic post-modern view, which Anderson seems by his own "style" to endorse.

Either way, however, he evades the normative implications of his own thesis. If there are no genuine communities to be had—if all society is at bottom an imagin*ary*, fictitious, self-deluding fantasy—then there is no real basis for culture, or human advancement through solidarity and cooperation between individuals; no workable politics; no inter*national* relations that are recognizable or even meaningfully human. And if traditional, genealogical communities cannot be successfully "modernized" into nations, there is no hope for them to be mapped onto the contemporary system of territorially fixed, self-sufficient states—a conclusion avoided by Anderson only by the truncation of his narrative at 1945, and which he has avoided ever since.[56]

In fact it is not hard to update his Gramscian thesis by reference to the Internet, that most comprehensive and advanced control system for the diffusion of culture and the exercise of influence. The Internet as electronic globalis/zation is the ultimate expression of deterritorialized human social identity. Anderson's own mannered evocation/dismissal of community hints at a deeper moral unease about modernity itself, like McLuhan's confused premonition of the Internet, the world as "global village"[57]—but again, to avoid rather than redefine reality. A virtual community is also an imagined community. A global village is not a real village. These expressions are all metaphors, half-definitions. They take whatever life they have from more concrete forms of society that the universal states system has blurred beyond recognition—a development with which neither Anderson nor McLuhan really comes to terms.[58]

Imagined Communities, therefore, though a brilliantly suggestive tract, is of interest more for what it asks about human social relations than for what it explains. Anderson's own indirectness is symptomatic of a general modern inability to conceive of any community without ambivalence.

8.7 Nations vs. States

Toni Erskine, in seeking to build a model of collective moral agency, proposes this formula:

> A collectivity is a candidate for moral agency if it has the following: an identity that is more than the sum of the identities of its constitutive parts and, therefore, does not rely on a determinate membership; a

decision-making structure; an identity over time; and a conception of itself as a unit.

On this basis she concludes that states are candidates for moral agency, while nations are not, because "they lack decision-making structures," the counterpart of the individual capacity for self-aware deliberation which, she says, precedes and determines moral action.[59]

Note the firm normative distinction between states and nations, as if the author's mental figuring of social action required a state freed of real people. Such a distinction, moreover, is not one that the modern system of independent (state) agents accommodates. But in any case I think Toni Erskine has things the wrong way round. Only nations can be moral agents; states never can.

First, it is arguable that self-aware deliberation is a capacity never lost to individual human beings, even in dysfunctional social situations (say, a riot), or personal self-preservation would not be possible. Second, as I would claim, even de facto nations have access to—at least have occasion to think about—the decision-making structures of constituted states. Everyone on earth, after all, has to live under them. Some shared, simultaneous thinking on this topic, then, and on the human condition in the light of it, must go on in the world, in everyone's mind—producing many cases of what I have called an interactive, homemade conception of a state.[60] Still, these will vary, and fail to match up with each other. The ad hoc thinking involved will struggle to attain "the capacity to . . . act in such a way as to conform to [moral] requirements," or "the *freedom* [to exercise moral agency]" on which Erskine insists.[61] For that, collective thinking must become corporate thinking, as David Runciman puts it. Individuals must think and act as one, in order to satisfy Erskine's demand for "an identity that is more than the sum of the identities of its constitutive parts." But that, says Runciman, never happens in the modern world.[62]

It never happens, I say, because people in general understand that they do not live in a fair world, since there is neither perfect material equality in the states system nor—what would make up for this lack—a profound capacity for institutional and material change. Which only strengthens the likelihood that the system will appear, to most people, dysfunctional and unreal.

In this situation even the most perceptive and articulate of international theorists will struggle to define their terms. Philip Reynolds, for example, firmly asserts that "a nation cannot simply be defined as the inhabitants of a state." Yet that is far from the end of the story, as Reynolds's own faltering argument shows:

> Nations can only be defined subjectively: a nation consists of those people who feel themselves to be members of it . . . the only way to define a nation is tautologically . . . a nation is a group of humans who have a sense of nationhood, who feel mutual affinities, who believe themselves to be members of that nation.[63]

But a tautological definition, of course, is no definition of anyone or anything at all.

So much for Conceptualism, the philosophical thesis that common elements of reality can exist for everyone, albeit "all in the mind."[64] If my argument is right, this is true only insofar as Conceptualism is emblematic of a common disappointment with the world. The source of this disappointment, moreover, is likely precisely to be the modern state—

> a complex normative idea, shared by a group of people, of how they should or might order their affairs. When it is *perfectly* shared, it is arguably not simply an idea, but embodied in a series of willed actions: for example, through instruments, like governments, which in that instance receive the voluntary and collective—the whole—support of "their" people; and also as implied acceptance by them of their particular inheritance among the common properties of all states, such as formally-established territorial limits. The problem is that the idea is rarely, if ever, perfectly shared in practice, and perhaps decreasingly so today.
>
> [. . .]
>
> I may be an Amazonian forest-dweller—indifferent to, unwilling even to be seen as partaking of the modern Brazilian state, in the name of which more powerful people than myself claim me and make my life difficult. Or I may be a Sahelian nomad, driven by my livelihood, or by blood ties, or both, to reject the territorial division of the desert which makes foreigners of my relatives and other people's property my only available means of sustenance. Or I may be a more complex secessionist or irredentist—say a believer in Scottish political independence within a European Union, rejecting the historical development and perhaps some of the values of the "United Kingdom" state. Or I may be simply a believer in the community of all humankind, above and beyond other things. Not one of these individuals is represented with any satisfaction (let alone perfectly) by the institutions which concretise, in apparent perpetuity, someone else's idea of "his" or "her" state. . . . Examples of this kind could be multiplied; and of course multiple reservations held about a state's legitimacy will end up undermining its effectiveness as well.[65]

The modern states system has made it controversial to define a nation as a community of worth. And as for "state," in the end the alternative dictionary definition may be best: referring to a temporary psychological or emotional condition—a *state of mind*, like righteous anger, moral uncertainty, or readiness for change.

Notes

1. This tripartite typology is largely based on Atsuko Ichijo and Gordana Uzelac (eds.), *When is the Nation? Towards an Understanding of Theories of Nationalism* (London: Routledge, 2005), and Umut Özkırımlı, *Theories of Nationalism: A Critical Introduction* (2nd ed. Basingstoke: Palgrave Macmillan, 2010).
2. Eric Hobsbawm, "Comment on Steven Grosby: the primordial, kinship and nationality" in Ichijo and Uzelac (eds.), p. 79.
3. John Breuilly, "Dating the nation: how old is an old nation?" in *ibid.*, pp. 15–39.
4. Ichijo and Uzelac, "Introduction" in *ibid.*, p. 4.
5. Anna Triandafyllidou, "When, what and how is the nation? Lessons from Greece" in *ibid.*, p. 178 and 181.
6. Stephanie Lawson, "Nationalism and the politics of ethnicity in Fiji: critical perspectives on primordialism, modernism and ethno-symbolism" in *ibid.*, pp. 200 and 210.
7. Susan-Mary Grant, "When was the first new nation? Locating America in a national context" in *ibid.*, p. 159.
8. Ichijo and Uzelac, "Introduction" in *ibid.*, pp. 3–4.
9. Özkırımlı, *Theories of Nationalism*, p. 201.
10. John Breuilly, "Nationalism" in Baylis, Smith and Owens (eds.), *The Globalization of World Politics* (6th ed. 2014), p. 389. He defines states as "sovereign, territorial (the "Westphalian system")"; and asserts—undiscriminatingly, from a "values" point of view—that the "dominant form of [European] nationalism was state-strengthening, civic, and elite" (pp. 388 and 390). He also skates over traditional factors like culture and ethnicity, asserting, with all the privilege of modernity: "Cultural diversity can be so great as to render implausible any claim that [UN members] are ethno-national states" (p. 389).
11. *Ibid.*, pp. 390–391.
12. On p. 389, table 25.1, mentioning, with their key advocates, primordialism, perennialism (see note 50 below), ethno-symbolism, and other versions of modernism than Breuilly's own.
13. Anthony D. Smith, "The genealogy of nations: an ethno-symbolic approach" in Ichijo and Uzelac (eds.), p. 98, emphasis added; pp. 100, 102, 103, 104, original emphasis. See also his *Myths and Memories of the Nation* (Oxford: Oxford University Press, 1999); Breuilly, "Dating the nation," p. 16; Lawson, "Nationalism and the politics of ethnicity in Fiji," p. 200.
14. Smith, "The genealogy of nations," p. 97.
15. Adrian Hastings, *The Construction of Nationhood: Ethnicity, Religion and Nationalism* (Cambridge: Cambridge University Press, 1997), p. 160.
16. See Leenco Lata, *The Horn of Africa as Common Homeland* (Waterloo, Ontario: Wilfrid Laurier University Press, 2004), and David Turton, "Mursi political identity and warfare: the survival of an idea" in Katsuyoshi Fukui and

John Markakis (eds.), *Ethnicity and Conflict in the Horn of Africa* (London: James Currey, 1994), pp. 20–21.

17. Marx, "The future results of British rule in India" [*New York Daily Tribune*, 8 August 1853], reprinted in David McLellan (ed.), *Karl Marx: Selected Writings* (Oxford: Oxford University Press, 1977), p. 332.

18. Smith, "The genealogy of nations," p. 106.

19. Breuilly, "Nationalism," p. 395.

20. See Pierre L. van der Berghe, "Ethnies and nations: genealogy indeed" in Ichijo and Uzelac (eds.), pp. 113–118; the quotation comes from a later remark to a discussion panel (p. 122).

21. See Diarmaid MacCulloch, *A History of Christianity: The First Three Thousand Years* (London: Penguin, 2010).

22. (New York: Doubleday, 1976).

23. Susan-Mary Grant, "When was the first new nation?." While arguing that US nationalism is a product of eighteenth-century European democratic ideas, Grant asserts that a common language is a "modernist" criterion for nationhood (p. 161). But this criterion is claimed by almost all theorists of the nation. She also asserts that America displays the primordialist criterion of "a sense of common ancestry" (p. 163). But this is clearly factually untrue, except in the restrictive context of her preceding reference (pp. 159–163) to European immigrants. It excludes, for example, the people now significantly termed Native Americans. Further, Grant suggests (p. 173) that the inapplicability to America of the three main "paradigms" of national identity formation is on a par with their inapplicability to other peoples in the world. But this assertion is contradicted by her own claim of American immigrants' special difficulties in forging a new national identity for themselves. At the same time, she displays critical acumen in condemning the long exclusion of Native Americans and African-Americans from the process of US nation-formation, and we can agree with her on the importance of the United States as "the first experiment in republican government" (p. 168).

24. First, in modern times and in order of prominence, came the orthodox Jewish claim, based on the Torah, to an ancestral homeland from which Jews had been exiled and dispersed into slavery, only to be providentially returned: a claim ostensibly fulfilled in 1948 by the creation of the state of Israel after the persecution of Jews in Europe. Next came the Arab/Islamic claim that modern Israelis, aided and abetted by Westerners, were usurpers of Arab/Islamic lands, to be opposed by the reconstruction of a mythical "Arab nation" under Islam—a project focused on historic Palestine, to be begun by the destruction of the state of Israel. This imitation of Jewish exceptionalism is visible in the speeches of the Islamist leader Osama bin Laden, with his practice of referring to modern states by their Arab/Islamic imperial names (e.g., Spain as *Al-Andalus*). But equally, bin Laden arguably did no more than articulate for the modern world a messianic project immanent in the ethno-cultural origins of Islam. Arab political leaders for decades before him referred to the peoples of Middle East and North Africa as *al watan al-arabi*, "the Arab nation"—an expression bearing the older colonial meaning of "country of settlement." Arabic is the vehicular language of Islam as Hebrew is of Judaism. The terms "Arab" and "Muslim" are routinely interchanged in Arabic-speaking societies, though these societies include

people who are identifiably neither Arab nor Muslim; and bloodline descent from the Prophet Mohammed is a badge of aristocracy.

25. Steven Grosby, "The primordial, kinship and nationality" in Ichijo and Uzelac (eds.), p. 74. Cf. perennialism (note 50 below), though I think Grosby's attachment to kinship origins makes him a primordialist rather than a perennialist.

26. See Marshall Sahlins, *Stone Age Economics* [1972] (London: Routledge, 2004). These are assumptions only. Sites like Göbekli Tepe in Anatolia suggest a more complex picture.

27. See Philip K. Hitti, *History of the Arabs*, parts I and II (10th ed. Basingstoke: Palgrave Macmillan, 2002).

28. See Christiane Eluère, *The Celts: First Masters of Europe* (London: Thames & Hudson, 1993) and Paul-Marie Duval and Christiane Eluère, *Les Celtes* (Paris: Gallimard, 2009).

29. See further Norman Davies, *God's Playground: A History of Poland* (Oxford: Clarendon Press, 1981), and *Vanished Kingdoms: The History of Half-Forgotten Europe* (London: Allen Lane, 2011).

30. Michael Freeman, "Democracy and dynamite: the peoples' right to self-determination," *Political Studies* XLIV (1996), p. 749.

31. Rival Spanish and Portuguese colonialism, for example, determined the territorial state structure of South America, and consequently the modern nationality of South America's older, pre-colonial peoples.

32. For interesting reflections see Philip Marsden, *The Crossing-Place: A Journey among the Armenians* (London: HarperCollins, 1993) and *The Chains of Heaven: An Ethiopian Romance* (London: HarperCollins, 2005); Michael Axworthy, *Iran: Empire of the Mind: A History from Zoroaster to the Present Day* (London: Penguin, 2008); and William Dalrymple, *Nine Lives: In Search of the Sacred in Modern India* (London: Bloomsbury, 2009).

33. Even then, there are complications. Take the irredentist Armenian claim to Nagorno-Karabakh, an enclave still formally part of neighboring Azerbaijan. Or the large minority of Armenians in Iran with strong local attachments, despite being descended from Armenians kidnapped from Nakhichevan in the seventeenth century. What is involved in both these cases is a historical claim to an "Armenian" identity outside modern Armenia that is nevertheless not one of simple exile ("prolonged voluntary absence from one's native land," Shorter Oxford English Dictionary).

34. Greek Americans, perhaps because of the Greek maritime heritage, seem to me among the most successful of people in maintaining an "international" dual identity. In turn the popular interest, in modern society, in archaeology and genealogy testifies to people's desire to have a dual historical identity as well.

35. An Iranian friend once complained to me about Israeli oppression in Palestine, saying, "We helped the Jews! Now look at all the trouble they're making." It took me a moment to realize that she meant not Iranian military cooperation with Israel under the late twentieth-century shah's regime, but the actions in Babylon of the Persian King Cyrus the Great (sixth century BCE) as recounted in Herodotus and the Old Testament Bible.

36. Grosby, "Question and Answer II" in Ichijo and Uzelac (eds.), p. 88.

37. Smith, "The genealogy of nations," p. 98, emphasis in original.

38. Steven Grosby, "The verdict of history: the inexpungeable tie of primordiality—a response to Eller and Coughlan" [1994], repr. in John Hutchinson and Anthony D. Smith (eds.), *Nationalism: Critical Concepts in Political Science* vol. I (London: Routledge, 2000), p. 184.

39. Hastings, *The Construction of Nationhood*, p. 169.

40. Reynolds, *An Introduction to International Relations* (1st. ed. 1971), p. 21.

41. "It is the unjustified assumption that physical differences are invariably accompanied by evolved behavioural ones that turns race from a biological reality [based on shared genetic inheritance] into a flawed social construct." Jerry A. Coyne, "Legends of Linnaeus," *Times Literary Supplement* 5317, 25 February 2005, p. 4, review of Vincent Sarich and Frank Miele, *Race: The Reality of Human Differences* (New York: Basic Books, 2005).

42. In the mountainous topography of the Balkans, scattered populations came under the dead hand of Ottoman rule. For five centuries this meant economic stagnation, localized taxation and corruption, and a near total exclusion from the events (the Renaissance and Reformation, the Enlightenment, and liberal-democratic nationalism) that elsewhere in Europe were serving to break down ancestral ties. The brief Communist rule of the late twentieth century was theoretically internationalist and progressive but in practice inward-looking because of disputes with other more powerful Communist parties in the Cold War. Only with the end of the Cold War and the death of Tito did long-lasting constraints on political freedom and population mobility begin to break down, giving rein to deeply ingrained local prejudices and grievances. For an insight into Balkan society between the Ottoman and Communist hegemonies, see Rebecca West, *Black Lamb and Grey Falcon: A Journey through Yugoslavia* [1940–41] (Edinburgh: Canongate, 2006).

43. "There is a farmer on the Hebridean island of Islay," writes Alistair Moffat, "who was astounded to be told that his DNA was linked in a direct line with an ancient lineage in Mesopotamia, modern Iraq. In the genes of the farmer and his sons, the story of an immense journey still lives." Alistair Moffat and James F. Wilson, *The Scots: A Genetic Journey* (Edinburgh: Birlinn, 2012), p. 23. Still, it is hardly earth-shattering to discover that one is not descended from Adam and Eve; and "having Viking blood" does not make one a Viking. It remains to be seen how far modern conceptions of national identity will be affected by microbiological discoveries. On the human race as a diaspora, see Stephen Oppenheimer, *Out of Eden: The Peopling of the World* (London: Constable, 2003).

44. Jack David Eller and Reed M. Coughlan, "The poverty of primordialism: the demystification of ethnic attachments" [1993] in Hutchinson and Smith (eds.), *Nationalism: Critical Concepts in Political Science*, pp. 161 and 177.

45. Özkırımlı, *Theories of Nationalism*, p. 202.

46. Linda Colley, *Acts of Union and Disunion* (London: Profile Books, 2014), p. 9.

47. Quoted in Susan-Mary Grant, "When was the first new nation?" in Ichijo and Uzelac (eds.), *When is the Nation?*, p. 158.

48. Smith, "The genealogy of nations" in *ibid.*, p. 109. For his (earlier) verdict on other schools of thought, see Anthony D. Smith, *Nations and Nationalism in a Global Era* (Cambridge: Polity Press, 1995).

49. Which explains, perhaps, why separatist movements (Catalan, Basque, Breton, Scottish) have arisen in the older former-colonial nations of Spain,

France, and Britain. See also Tom Nairn, *The Break-Up of Britain: Crisis and Neo-Nationalism* (London: New Left Books, 1977).

50. Here brief mention may be made of "perennialism," whereby *latent* nations, as it were, may be traced throughout history—disappearing and reappearing, but with an underlying continuity in culture or kinship. This approach seems to take elements from the two main sets of nationhood theories—critical/modernist and primordialist. Anthony Smith ("The genealogy of nations," p. 108) condemns "the sweeping claims of perennialists and modernists alike, as well as the organic naturalism and cultural or biological determinism of the primordialists"—but not with total clarity either (how can culture be deterministic?). Other writers refer to primordialism and perennialism indistinguishably (Grant, "When was the first new nation?" p. 159; Breuilly, "Dating the nation," pp. 15, 31). Elsewhere Breuilly defines perennialism without comment as "Culture (beliefs as creeds)," naming Hastings as its key exponent ("Nationalism," table 25.1, p. 389)—a judgment echoed by Özkırımlı. But Hastings's argument in his main work, *The Construction of Nationhood*, seems to me overdependent on his "prototype," England. There is also a subject/object problem in perennialism: if nations can disappear and reappear, surely this happens as much in the eye of the observer as in objective reality? Further, even a nation defined only by recurrent evidence of a common culture or kinship might be supposed not to have come out of nowhere, but to have an original historical—a primordial—beginning; otherwise those criteria could be contested, and seen as merely symbolic. So is a perennial nation an interrupted primordial one, or an ethno-symbolist one whose manifestations have been only intermittently present (or observed?) The case for perennialism as an approach in own right seems unconvincing, or beset by the same conceptual problems as its rivals but to a higher degree.

51. Willetts, "Transnational actors and international organizations in global politics."

52. (2nd rev. ed. London: Verso, 1991; with afterword, 2006).

53. *Ibid.*, ch. 8, "Patriotism and Racism."

54. See next chapter for an account of this book.

55. *Imagined Communities* (2006 edition), p. 6.

56. In the Preface to the second (1991) edition, Anderson gives his reasons for leaving his book "largely as an 'unrestored' period piece," whose "idiosyncratic method and preoccupations . . . seem to me still on the margins of the newer scholarship on nationalism"—naming Breuilly, Smith, and Hobsbawm, among others. *Ibid.*, p. xii.

57. Marshall McLuhan, *The Gutenberg Galaxy: The Making of Typographic Man* (Toronto: University of Toronto Press, 1962).

58. In his 2006 afterword, Anderson reflects on the variegated publishing history of *Imagined Communities* "in thirty-three countries and in twenty-nine languages." Though anecdotally interesting, this does nothing to update his thesis. Anderson merely treats his own book as a historical artefact in the ongoing debate about nations and nationhood, as I am doing here.

59. Toni Erskine, "Assigning responsibilities to institutional moral agents: the case of states and 'quasi-states'" in Erskine (ed.), *Can Institutions Have Responsibilities?*, pp. 21, 24, and 25.

60. With the exception of "uncontacted" tribal peoples, of whom I have more to say in my concluding chapter.
61. Erskine, "Assigning responsibilities to institutional moral agents," p. 21, emphasis in original.
62. Runciman, "Moral responsibility and the problem of representing the state" in Erskine (ed.). See below, chapter 9.
63. Reynolds, *An Introduction to International Relations* (1st. ed.), pp. 20–21. Further on peoples who do not "go into" contemporary states see James Crawford (ed.), *The Rights of Peoples* (Oxford: Clarendon Press, 1988).
64. See above, chapter 5 section 5.2.
65. Lomas, "Anthropomorphism, personification and ethics," p. 352, emphasis in original.

9

Contriving Agents

State, nation, agent: these three concepts combine to give the universal states system its characteristic rationale. Its formal populations are held to act like cohesive communities—like nation-states—within inherited borders and the resources they enclose. But this assumption, I have argued, does not work, because the borders and resources are arbitrary and unequal, and the peoples themselves are not as cohesive as the system requires. These reasons, moreover, are linked: nations and states cannot be considered synonymous when the human inheritance is not the same and cannot easily be changed. Which explains why we have only ideal, negative, or unsatisfactory accounts of states (as I argued in chapter 7), and why theorists of the nation disagree (as I argued in chapter 8).

So what of the third component, agency, which resides in the attributive independence of states? Can this by itself give the states system meaning and worth? One approach, proposed by Alexander Wendt, is to see state agency in terms of "state persons": distinguishing, in an analogical or reductive approach to group behavior, three formal types of such "persons": psychological, legal, and moral.[1] Now I argued earlier, in the light of Hobbes's doctrine and its modern reception, that the idea of imaginary persons as political agents is a complete nonstarter. Real persons, moreover—individuals—cannot (the word itself tells us) be split into types of person. As for group behavior, I have just given reasons why under the modern states system this must be problematic and not susceptible to being precisely rendered, even abstractly.

My own use of "agents" and "agency" is in the mainstream sense used by philosophers, for literal doers of actions, holders of a will. These may be individuals, or groups of individuals acting with a shared or collective will: with something like, but also unlike, the will of a person (and again, for that reason *not* a person). A philosopher might also ask, for example, if a rat is an agent—has a will, has volition. But again, a rat is not a person, and the philosopher's inquiry never rises to a personal analogy. It is human agency, the capacity for independent conscious action, that is at stake.

What is more, this seems implicitly to be acknowledged in the way in which action in the states system is commonly imagined. In conventional international theory, state agents are conjured up roughly, generically, inchoately—as both like, and unlike, persons; sometimes semi-normatively, in a context of moral assumptions (again like, and unlike real persons, who make such assumptions fully). Certain of the stereotypes which result are more persuasive or more worthy than others. But since I deny the reality of state agency altogether, I need to dispose of them too. I can think of five such forms. Let me take them in turn.

9.1 The Mandarin State

What is involved here is the most caricatural practice of all, the conflation of states and their governments of the day, often by governments themselves. Naturally, in this practice the legitimacy of particular states, or the institutional status quo under which their independence is licensed, is never called into question.

Now governments are real agents, a group of people with volition and autonomy and constituted precisely for the purpose of acting together. To that extent real group actions are involved, on the part (at least in democracies) of officials who are true proxies for society at large. But governments are not states. Arguably, in order to be counted as such, they would have to be monolithic in their personnel and their policies over long periods of time, and in the age of secular states that would quite properly give rise to suspicion. When political leaders are repeatedly declared reelected, as Alfredo Stroessner was (eight times!) in Paraguay—or drawn for decades from the same family, like the Kims in North Korea—their legitimacy is apt to be questioned outright.

The Uses of Detachment

Despite Chris Brown's strictures on "higher journalism," it is often from this source that the lesson comes. Foreign correspondents especially, with long residence abroad, can develop a formidable political sophistication through their knowledge of local people and languages. They are able to point out to a general audience the significance of changes of personnel in governments and the factions within them. In so doing they render everyone a service, by making it impossible to depict international relations as the sphere of activity of monolithic governments, indistinguishable from "their" states. In this respect we should all acknowledge a debt to high-class political journalism, whose influence has never ceased to grow since the invention of the wireless telegraph.

Three specific types of insight seem to me available from this direction. The first concerns peoples who have an especially problematic relationship with their institutions. Take Lebanese society, that patchwork of tribes, cultures, languages, and religions, riven for decades by civil war, and often paralyzed by the politics of the Israel/Palestine dispute. We need the insider view to explain the behavior of any part of this society in recognizably human terms.

We need this view, too, to understand the wellsprings of change, and imagine possible futures in societies that are strange or closed to us. Take the Islamic Revolution of 1979 in Iran, in which a modernizing, wealth-promoting, Western-backed regime was overthrown not by anti-Western Communists, as happened elsewhere during the Cold War, but by a group of religious traditionalists led, implausibly enough, by one of their members in exile in the West. Why this group succeeded, and went on to foment change in other Muslim-majority countries, was intelligently analysed from the start by overseas journalists, often at considerable personal risk.

Finally, well-informed insiders can tell us truths about societies that their members are unable to tell, owing to censorship, oppression, or the fog of war. Increasingly, such obstacles have been eroded by the Internet and various social media, but even these may break down or fall victim to local control.

High-class journalists, therefore, remain important as specialist interpreters of events and as witnesses to suffering and injustice which might otherwise go unreported. They are the allies of those who work to promote deeper international understanding. As for those other intelligent explainers, the diplomats, they serve first and foremost their government of the day, in their own relations with other governments of the day. Diplomats are professional proxies for governments, so the relationship between governments and states is not strictly their concern. On the other hand, diplomats have a certain duty to be truthful, and those who represent democracies must have some personal pride and sense of accountability to their societies of origin, which includes ideals of impartiality and independence of mind. Not all diplomats are mandarins, though I have observed that it is usually only on retirement that they shake off the habit of conflating governments with states.

"China" and the Rest

To illustrate the general argument, I will quote two examples from a single context—as it happens, from interviews reported on the same day. In the first the EU Commissioner for External Trade, a diplomat in his own right, chose to stigmatize what he saw as unfair trading practices by the Chinese government.

> Mr Mandelson told the BBC that pressure from the public and politicians for a level playing-field of trade was growing. "If we want to sustain a policy of openness towards China politically, we have to make sure that the public is satisfied that that trading relationship is being conducted on full and fair trade, otherwise we are going to be in trouble." China was "shifting the economic and diplomatic scenery so fast that it is almost impossible for policy makers to keep up let alone be ahead of the game," he added. "Because of China's extraordinary economic growth as well as its political and diplomatic reach, and the effect it can have on global security, we are seeing China changing the whole global landscape in so many different ways."[2]

Here we see multiple conflation at work, reifying "China" as both subject and object of actions. "Openness towards China politically" conflates the current population of (the People's Republic of) China, as objects of EU policy, with their government. A China, on the other hand, which can shift "the economic and diplomatic scenery" and voluntarily affect "the whole global landscape" is a putative agent in its own right.

Since the EU is an organization of democracies, standing for the democratic principle and openness of political discussion, perhaps we should not worry too much about the simplifications in such interviews (conducted for, routinely filtered and sometimes actually rephrased by, journalists). As a general rule, however, this is too complacent an attitude. The point is underlined by my second example, concerning the award of the US Congressional Gold Medal (Congress's highest honor) to the fourteenth Dalai Lama, the customary ruler of Tibet.

> Beijing described it as a "gross interference in China's internal affairs." "China is strongly resentful of this and resolutely opposes it," foreign ministry spokesman Liu Jianchao was quoted by the official Xinhua news agency as saying on Wednesday.[3]

The BBC report-writer uses "Beijing" here as shorthand for the Chinese government, while signalling his own independence—designating Xinhua as "official," naming the source of the comment individually, and describing him as a "spokesman" merely "quoted" by the agency. This is in direct contrast to the projection of "China" as a person-like entity by the Chinese spokesman himself—a completely demagogic practice.

Behind the Person "China"

First, this practice crowds out any consultation of the people of China (here, the PRC) on the honoring of the Dalai Lama, despite the fact that for the many Buddhists among them, the individual holding this title is an inspirational spiritual leader, perhaps even the direct leader of the tradition to which they adhere. For this reason many citizens of the PRC might fairly be expected to be appreciative in their own right, and not in the least "resentful," of the US Congress's action.

Second, the spokesman's remarks ride roughshod over the views of non-Chinese generally on the status of Tibet and the condition of the Tibetan people (symbolized by the honored Dalai Lama), in asserting that these are "internal" (i.e., Chinese government) concerns. This is wrong in principle, because political questions should be open to general discussion; and wrong in practice, because of the forcible occupation of Tibet, instigated in 1950 by the political ancestor of the current PRC regime, leading to the Dalai Lama's exile and to justifiable concern for the well-being of people in Tibet.

Finally, we need to observe that the attitudes of the PRC government quoted here compare unfavorably with the pacific introspection and tolerance characteristic of Buddhism. Had the territory of Tibet been ruled in 1950 by a military-fascistic clique from which liberal-minded Chinese rescued a suffering Tibetan people, we would be thinking from different premises altogether and the entire controversy would arguably not have arisen.

In all these respects, it is important to distinguish between the government of the day and "its" state (and the word "government" attached to "China" appears nowhere in the spokesman's remarks). That government may be illegitimate; that state itself may, by a different set of criteria, be illegitimate. Certainly a state purportedly representing a single society with a huge numerical superiority over any other, and protected by weapons of mass destruction, like the modern PRC, seems to me intrinsically threatening and misconceived. Implicitly, too, the shorthand identification of the PRC as "China" projects it as the authentic homeland of "Chinese" people, masking the diversity in that territory, along with the fact that people calling themselves Chinese are citizens of almost every state in the world.[4] But most obviously, it is wrong in principle for a government to pose, through its mouthpiece, as society at large.

Strictly speaking, all that can be said in this context is that successive governments of the People's Republic of China have made sovereign claims over the territory of Tibet and Tibetan people—claims implicitly contested by the US Congress's public commendation of the Tibetan leader in exile. This is simply the only assertion that is both objectively true and about identifiable agents. Beyond it, I am inclined to believe in this particular case the many and well-attested reports that successive PRC governments have forcibly occupied and run Tibetan society since 1950, and compounded this wrongdoing by sponsoring Chinese migration into Tibet. In the process they have illegitimately opposed the Dalai Lama, the most important Tibetan traditional leader. Failing, moreover, to curb his political activities in exile, they have even taken over, in China proper, the traditional Tibetan procedures for choosing spiritual leaders, in order to invent legitimacy for their own rule in Tibet. These judgments I base in part on my own reading of works of high-class journalism.[5]

One counterargument, voiced by the occupying PRC regime, is that Chinese rule in Tibet has served to modernize Tibetan society, formerly an antique theocracy. But this is easily dismissed. In the first place, it is a separate issue from whether Tibet and the PRC are historically, territorially, one. Second, owing to the forcible occupation, generations of people living in Tibet have been unable to choose what form of modernization, if any, they would have wanted. There is undoubtedly some advantage for people in developing a modern society in order to defend their interests in the contemporary states system. But it is precisely the *self*-interest of Tibetans in being agents in their own right in this regard which has been obliterated by the Chinese occupation. To compound the irony, the Dalai Lama forced into exile by the occupation showed himself from an early age to be a modernizer (as was to some extent his predecessor). In 2010 he renounced his temporal title in favor of an elected Tibetan parliament in exile.[6]

There has, in short, been a clear pattern of wrongdoing toward whole generations of people in Tibet by successive Chinese governments. At the same time, this is not in any sense a wrong to be explained as the "behavior" of the Chinese state—or by analogy the people of the PRC in general. It is being justified after the event, as we see in the quotation above, by deception: by means of a fictitious Chinese state agent, a mysterious quasi-person regally sensitive to insult on behalf of unspecified others. One might in fact surmise that many citizens of the PRC themselves are not taken in by this bullying pretence, and were they not afraid of their own government would openly oppose it, along with the wrong done to Tibetans in their name.

This is how the states system fosters demagogy, and injustice to foreigners and "domestic" citizens alike, by those who hold power within it. Sometime-governments are real agents, but they are not states or synonymous with the people confined in them. Of course, exposing this lie lays us open to others' scrutiny of our own societies and political systems; but that is fair enough, if their intentions are honorable, and directed at sincere concern for us. International theorists, moreover, with their global vision, have a special duty to keep truth and freedom everywhere alive. That is what Philip Reynolds meant when he wrote courageously in the middle of the Cold War:

> [in international relations] the "national interest" which is at stake is that of people, not of the state, which is an abstraction. Service of the ends and values of people may require the submergence of the state. The state is not a person. It has no innate moral attributes. It has no honour. It has no inherent right to survive.[7]

9.2 The Lawyer State

The assumption here is that states can be "corporate" or person-like unitary agents in international law. This status is derivative of sovereignty as a general attribute of states, which ostensibly enables state governments to determine outcomes binding on all their citizens. A double fiction, then, is involved: first the state as agent (as opposed to government as agent), then the convention of international law itself, which, like all law, relies on a normative presupposition of responsible—obedient—agents. But the "rule of law" is not to be confused with justice as such; it is merely the phenomenon of collective obedience in society at large. This is the problem that confronts us. Corporate legal agents, especially corporate state agents, are neither normatively justified nor socially explained—at least, with nothing like adequacy.

Bend the Law/Break the Law

David Runciman elucidates the problem well. He distinguishes two conceptions. First, the "collective" or "partnership" state, whereby all individuals join together in shared—and equal—responsibility for actions. This conception, stressing political accountability rather than state unity, Runciman traces to Rousseau; its modern equivalent, he says, is the legal partnership, as in a firm of solicitors. But this is not, says Runciman, the version that obtains today. Instead, it is the "corporate" state, involving

> an entity that is understood to exist apart from the individuals who have brought it into existence (in the most familiar setting of the business corporation, its founders), apart from the individuals through whom it acts (its board of directors), and apart from the individuals who may have claims over its property (its shareholders). Corporations exist in order to allow notions of agency to hold even when there are no readily identifiable individuals to whom responsibility can attach: corporations may be said to act, to assume responsibilities, to sue and to be sued, but this is only because the individuals or groups of individuals who actually perform the actions in question are distinct from the corporation itself, and are merely representing it. . . . The modern state is an association of this kind.

Such an entity, however, which "cannot be identified with any individuals or groups of individuals in particular" cannot, Runciman stresses, be a moral agent.

> International law may recognize states, but it does so by recognizing their sovereignty, and thus repudiating responsibility for the relation that holds between the government and the state. . . . Modern political life seems to depend upon our assuming that what states do is the responsibility of states rather than of named individuals, yet the highly individualistic, legalistic, and sceptical slant of much modern thinking means that we lack the ability to make sense of this assumption, or indeed to do anything more than merely assume it.[8]

In short, in the domain of international law, state governments are judge and jury in their own cause. The prevailing conception of agency itself, therefore, is likely to be very narrow or very cynical. *Either* one takes the existing law of states at face value, assuming minimal morality at best, *or* one takes legalized (state) agency at face value without any pretence of morality. To most of us, the first means: bend the law rather than break it. The second means: if you must break the law, do so from a position of strength, by taking it into your own hands. In recent times one can find examples of both practices.

Bending the Law of States: Legal Fictions

Colin Wight, in his treatise on international theory, finds the "notion of the state as a legal person" "unobjectionable"—and this despite his own scepticism, voiced elsewhere in his book, about state agency itself.

Here, he says that the conventional legal fiction of a single entity representing a collectivity provides "a necessary corrective to any form of legal individualism"; and if we accept that "complex social collectives" can change their composition over time and yet retain a consistent purpose and identity (as a state purportedly does), then we have the essential continuity which underpins a system of law. In such an environment, he argues, it is normal and legitimate to think of "structures," like states, as "causally implicated in outcomes." While this involvement falls short of imputed "intentionality," legal corporateness in the sense of joint responsibility can still be envisaged for football clubs, business groups, and states alike.[9]

The usual practice among international theorists—the practice condemned by Runciman—is to extrapolate state agency from the model of the international system. Colin Wight, by contrast, wants to reverse-engineer it from the model of domestic sovereignty, bound by specific rules and conventions. In a gesture to political pluralism, his business group/state analogy posits a context in which the norms governing states are conflated with those of commercial and other self-interested groups, all in competition for power.[10] But to begin with, this positing is obviously questionable, because a state can hardly compete with itself.

Wight's analogy is put forward in contradistinction to Alexander Wendt's literalist "state person" approach, in the course of Wight's own discussion of the "agent-structure" debate in international theory. This aspect of his proposal, however, is a red herring. Wight wants to make the case for corporate agency in law, as against the agency of individuals, so that is how his analogy is framed. But for political agency to be demonstrated, surely the need is for proof of life in the acts of conscious, willing people, rather than in their plurality or singularity. Wendt's own case was derived from social, rather than legal, theory.

Either way, Wight's case relies on legal fictions, and it is hard to see how any kind of fiction can be any kind of agent. Sensing this, perhaps, he seeks to bolster his case with moral considerations—citing the Nuremberg trials in 1946–1947 of surviving members of the Nazi regime, and legal moves to attribute responsibility for the chemical poisoning of people in Bhopal, India, following the accident at the Union Carbide factory there. "Structural responsibility," he observes, "cannot deflect individual responsibility. It seems clear that we would wish to hold on to the notion of certain forms of collectivity being held to account. If structures are a necessary component for any social act then those same structures must, in part, be held causally responsible for some element of outcomes."[11]

"Causal responsibility," however, is not the same as "being held to account"; structures are not people. An unsafe building that collapses on passers-by may be the cause of their death, but we do not put buildings on trial; it is the human agents who designed or failed to maintain the unsafe building who are morally responsible and should be held to account. In fact, Wight has already given away his case with his admission that "intentionality" is not causality. Only real human beings have intentions in the light of causes.[12]

On the Bhopal case, he remarks: "it is a fact of social life that human agents must have played some role in the unfortunate outcome."[13] But again, this is too loose. What certain individuals were guilty of at Bhopal was knowingly to participate in the operation of a dangerous factory. Even the accused Nazis at Nuremberg did not, for the most part, try to hide behind the regime as the "real" cause of the crimes alleged. Rather, they argued in their defense that they were not personally involved, or that the acts themselves were not criminal.[14]

The Civic Domain and the Rule of Law

The assumption that Wight seems to be relying on here is that of a kind of civic domain provided by states as legally constituted entities, on which level these two cases would go together. What else connects Nazi sadism with the negligence of American chemical engineers in India half a century later? Not the fact that they both crossed international borders. The Bhopal case was beset by jurisdictional disputes over how far the American directors of Union Carbide could be held responsible for the actions of their overseas employees, and the victims of Nazi crimes included the Nazis' own compatriots. And whereas Bhopal was an accident, the Nazi atrocities were not. The common ground between these two cases is that in both instances the accused denied their "duty of care" for others, a liability incurred by dint of holding positions in the legal apparatus of their own established states.

Still, this assumed civic domain is of rather limited moral value. It gains whatever force it has from the impartiality in principle of law, which gives contemporary states a certain bureaucratic and impersonal character. But this principle can be abused and obscured; states, like the law, can be turned into a facade for private interests. The leaders of the racist apartheid regime in South Africa, in promoting the interests of one-sixth of the country's population, erected a facade of the rule of law, enforcing it with a well-armed civilian police. That regime was also aggressively pro-capitalist—protective of wealth in the hands of its chosen few. Similarly the expansionist Nazi and Fascist regimes who provoked the Second World War relied on a facade of public law for their acts, as they did on the rules of diplomacy when it suited them.

The ultimate test of moral responsibility is obedience not to established law but to one's own conscience. Now conscience is private insofar as it is for the individual to consult, but for the rest is by definition other-regarding, whether the other is God or one's fellow human beings. Its scope, moreover, is potentially infinite—not defined by ties to artificial entities like modern states. In this regard, the scientist who first identified methyl isocyanate can hardly be blamed for the deaths and injuries at Bhopal, but this is not the case for individuals knowingly negligent of the poisonous gas's release there in 1984.

Corporate Standards, Double Standards

With regard to the exercise of conscience, in a group of workers with varying official responsibilities the precise level of individual knowledge of, and participation in, a given joint action will vary but is unlikely ever to be nil. Normal corporate activity, whether in business or public administration, is the product of shared efforts under agreed operating standards. This is especially the case in a large body like a corporation or state government, where information and the power to affect the lives of others are concentrated. Guilt by association, therefore, though potentially controversial, has real, including real legal, significance for such contexts, especially when a clear and grave mishap has occurred. Leaving the scene of an accident, for example, is a criminal offence in modern societies—leaving, that is, before the nature and extent of individual liability has been impartially established or remedies have been sought, including help to any injured. (This is made clearer in the French version of the offence: "non-assistance à personnes en danger.")[15]

Daniela Kroslak, in an insightful review of French government actions in and around Rwanda at the time of the 1994 genocide, pinpoints official knowledge of the background to events, participation in their unfolding, and the capability to alter their course, as criteria for assessing moral responsibility even on the part of "collective external bystanders." In the end she settles on a French government sin of omission, rather than commission, in the Rwanda genocide.[16] But even omission in the face of such an enormity carries an irrefutable degree of culpability; and certainly in my view, subsequent French governments have failed adequately to scrutinise the historical involvement of French advisers and trainers attached to the Rwandan armed forces, in terms of their ability and their duty to avert the genocide.[17]

Meanwhile in civil cases like Bhopal, or the 1987 sinking of the passenger vessel *Herald of Free Enterprise* (both accidents, rather than voluntary acts), the courts' inability to convict anyone on grounds of corporate manslaughter merely demonstrates the limits of the law of corporateness, when the associated members decide to hang together in order not to hang separately. So under commercial confidentiality, highly placed executives may seek to frustrate investigators from above, while shareholders deny that they ever knowingly sought to profit from a culpable enterprise. The same venality and disingenuousness then operates as within corrupt governments ("I acted in the company/country's best interests"; "I was not aware of that policy or its implications"; or merely "I didn't vote for that"). Black boxes of firms are parasitic on black boxes of states, and it is the law of corporate agency that makes the black box in the first place.

Bending the Law of States: Diplomatic Fictions

Some liberal-democratic governments live explicitly by such legal double standards, as Swiss governments did for decades through the national banking sector with its closed private accounts. This opened the way for international financial corruption on a vast scale, when outsiders began to place money whose provenance Swiss governments were prevented from scrutinizing. Swiss officials' hands were tied in this instance not only by conventions of business confidentiality but by the fact that central governments themselves had technically limited powers in the Swiss Confederation.

Business confidentiality serves in liberal-democratic states because it enables economic competition, which governments perceive a patriotic interest in promoting. It becomes normal for the government to have limited legal oversight of private funds in banks. This public/private separation is heightened when the form of state is federal and there are several, perhaps different, social settings in which legalized confidentiality applies. In Switzerland, in an earlier diplomatic era, the weakness of the central government was turned into an advantage in conjunction with the external policy of neutrality, adopted as a permanent legal status rather than an ad hoc stance. Neutrality and federation together made for a different kind of polity, only half-integrated into the modern states system (and in fact for decades after 1945 the Swiss state was outside the United Nations framework). The Swiss banking sector became a haven for safe financial deposits from abroad, which helped to allay the disadvantages of a country poor in natural resources. In reality, however, "Swiss bank accounts" were a byword for official kleptocracy in the states system.

Swiss neutrality itself was parasitic on the Western sphere of influence in the Cold War, since a nuclear war could not be confined to state borders, Swiss or any other. Swiss economic prosperity, and even national security, benefited from restrictions on parts of that sphere which governments in other Western countries felt obliged, in their own interests, to impose. Until those others' disapproval had effect, high officials in Swiss private firms and the federal government could collaborate freely in actions which, if they thought twice about the matter, must appear hypocritical on their part and potentially harmful to anyone not Swiss. When, for example, sections of the Argentine armed forces, within the dictatorship of the late 1970s, pursued a clandestine nuclear-weapon program, they did so with the help of Swiss technology. This help was winked at by the Swiss government (which had binding international obligations under the Nuclear Non-Proliferation Treaty), by means of a federal law which made it impossible for Swiss firms to be prosecuted for the actions of their overseas subsidiaries, one of which operated in Argentina. This absolved the government from enquiring too closely into whether Swiss firms' overseas left hands knew what their overseas right hands were doing. It was only after three planeloads of equipment had been shipped from Switzerland to the uranium-enrichment plant at Kahuta in Pakistan that other Western governments brought pressure to bear, forcing the Swiss authorities to align their commercial and export legislation with their global non-proliferation commitments. And if this pressure succeeded, it was only because no one in Berne could ignore any longer the fact that a subsidiary of the same Swiss firm as in Argentina had been engaged in similar industrial work in Pakistan.[18]

In a world of universal states, even legalized state exceptionalism is an anomaly that will eventually be exposed. Swiss neutrality gradually lost all its meaning through the flattening of hierarchies of power in the states system—a trend heightened by the end of the Cold War. But the policy had been possible in the first place only through the claim that Switzerland was a federal, not a centralized, state and therefore not like other states or bound by their rules.

Another instance of legal federation serving double standards internationally is the practice of United States governments refusing, at will, the jurisdiction of other states over US citizens, while engaging in extrajudicial kidnapping of non-US citizens to try them under US law. Notoriously, this included the constitution of a prison at Guantánamo Bay in Cuba to house indicted foreign terrorists after the attacks of "9/11" (2001) in the United States. The international judicial status of the Guantánamo enclave—a Cuban concession to the United States from a bygone era—provided the legal rationale for setting up the prison. For this purpose, US governments adhered to the traditional diplomatic practice of recognizing states, rather than governments. This is ironic, because the convention of states as legal persons in international law depends on *pacta sunt servanda*, that treaties signed should be kept, just as a real person manifests his or her honesty by keeping his or her word; and established US policy toward the Cuban Communist regime from its inception was one of non-recognition rising to hostility. Surely the "honesty" of the United States, even as a fictitious person, toward Cuban people in general required the surrender of legal advantages over them dating from before the institution of the "outlaw" Communist regime.

That above all is why the use of the Guantánamo Bay enclave was wrongful. The official argument of the US Bush administration that terrorists could be tried there extraterritorially, under US military law, was amoral but not illogical; amorality after all is what terrorists engage in. What was both amoral *and* illogical was the use of the fact that the US government and the US state, in international law, were unrelated entities, to enable US officials to use the territory of a regime they called criminal for criminal trials of their own. And this deceitful practice, wilfully casting doubt on the representativeness of the government in Washington, was the more easily maintained under the fiction of federacy, that the United States both was, and was not, a united state.

Bending the Law of States: Sovereign Liability

Tomohisa Hattori's study of the "sovereign debt" crisis of the 1980s is also of interest here.[19] On that occasion, some exceptional remedy had to be found to protect the international financial system, already under strain from multiple oil-price rises and the vast quantities of "petro-dollars" in circulation. Hitherto "sovereign debt" had been an oxymoron: states were the very source of finance and currency, the domestic lenders of last resort; and their sovereignty was technically inviolable. However, the private foreign banks from which successive Mexican (and later other) governments had overborrowed were now threatened with bankruptcy themselves; and they called in their loans. Since these banks were also supported by Northern governments with a direct, powerful, and unignorable influence, but "Mexico" was in no position to help out, there was a crisis of the system. As the last sentence suggests, the situation is understandable in terms of corporate state agency: "Mexico" imagined as a person who is a defaulting debtor. And the situation was a crisis of agency, because the defaulting debtor was not a real person whose rights could be taken away to enforce a solution.

As Hattori points out, under medieval monarchies where the king was the effective owner of all state assets, sovereign liability was as straightforward as sovereignty itself, since they were both concentrated, as that particular form of state was incarnated, in the person of the king. But as capitalism developed and monarchical polities weakened,

> it became necessary to institutionalise a new kind of depersonalised debt liability. The institutionalisation of juridical norms and rules governing sovereign loan transactions, in short, was a necessary step in the formation of a depersonalised capitalist state.

Still, overborrowing by state governments raised a dilemma, as they were the mere transient individual representatatives of states, and it was state assets (and future assets) that were now being demanded (and found to be lacking). So it became necessary, says Hattori, to visualize "depersonalised" modern states as "responsible and blameworthy juridical persons" as well.[20]

The eventual solution found was for the International Monetary Fund to arrange bridging loans on behalf of the banks and the defaulter-state governments, to enable the rescheduling of the debts. This paved the way for many further such arrangements down the years, which have turned the IMF into the world's most famous loss-adjuster. But as Hattori points out, the mechanism of third-party intervention has always come at a price for sovereignty, in the form of the imposition of "structural adjustments" on government economic policy:

> devaluation, trade liberalisation, free capital mobility, privatised state enterprises, etc., all designed to commit the state to the capitalist development path. It is a mechanism, in short, that cannot be understood in the context of traditional Westphalian sovereignty but must be conceived as constitutive of a new capitalist sovereignty. The rights and duties of this new sovereignty are constrained by the norms

that define what it is to be a juridically responsible and recognised member of a capitalist states system.

Hattori lays out his case study in the context of a general argument in favor of a Marxisant "critical" or "scientific" realism (of which I shall have more to say in the next chapter). But for the purpose of my argument here, he makes the point clearly enough:

> The institutionalisation of juridical norms and rules governing sovereign loans is evidence not of the moral agency of states and international organisations but rather of a misrecognition of social reality in two senses: (1) the false attribution of conscious intention to social *entities* (i.e., non-human entities); and (2) the failure to distinguish the institutionalisation of juridical norms from the moralisation of these norms as socially accepted conventional morality.[21]

It is also, however, important to note that this particular aberration came about in the universal states system, as part of the very nature of the system. The IMF itself is technically an organization of states. It is not unimaginable for the Fund, through the collective wills of its managers, to form, like a government, a "conscious intention" of its own. But in order to put this intention into action, the IMF would have to be a unified agent, a truly-corporate entity. Hattori is mistaken to conflate "states and international organisations (hence his muddled designation of 'social entities' as 'non-human'). But his mistake is understandable, because the conflation is precisely what certain influential governments did, when they used the IMF to impose their wills on the Mexican and, later, other governments in financial difficulties.

In my view the true origin of the debt crisis of the 1980s, insofar as it can be isolated as a particular event, lay not simply in overborrowing, but in the fact that corrupt elites in Mexico (and later other Latin American societies) systematically and at length embezzled public money, sending it to private accounts of their own abroad. From as sober a source as the United Nations Commission on Trade and Development came the comment: "Over the period 1974–1982 capital flight amounted to as much as 40 per cent of the total accumulated external debt of the Latin American countries."[22] These were societies of limited solidarity, limited traditions of public integrity, and limited public access to foreign currency (either through poverty or formal exchange controls), at a time of acute international currency instability—largely because *too much* money, in the shape of petrodollars, was in circulation and being proffered in international loans.

186

The corrupt elites, groups with privileged access to foreign currency, gave in to temptation, or overreacted to the instability. They acted in numbers, using the same diplomatic or extralegal channels, because they were either the same people (in government) or groups acting together in government and out, acknowledging shared interests. And the scale of their peculation was such that in the end it tipped their countries' sovereign indebtedness over the edge of international acceptability. Through corruption and deception, they stole not only their compatriots' money but even money being borrowed by the government from abroad; for clearly, if even a small proportion of the loans had been used for the public good, there would have been no crisis of default in the first place.[23]

From those individuals, therefore, the missing money should have been recovered. But in Northern governments' manipulation of the IMF to sort out the situation, states were blamed instead of real people, facilitating a cover-up for the culprits. Whole societies, in the end, had to pay for the wrongs of a corrupt minority, who already had their means of surviving the austerity to come (because the loans were rescheduled, rather than repaid). And the Northern governments were able to do this by pretending that they "were not"—not the same as—the IMF (a state-composed, intergovernmental organization). That is the point of Hattori's criticism. Governments put forward the IMF as a neutral broker, when in reality it was their proxy.

Breaking the Law of States: "Deregulation"

With the waning of the Cold War and the decline of the Soviet economic and political model, the idea of a civic domain in which the law of corporate agency differed between states and private firms was further weakened. Egged on by organizations like the IMF, governments began to take initiatives to refurbish their own activist credentials—notably in policies of "deregulation" or economic liberalization, leading eventually to the marketization of state functions themselves. The process was analysed in detail by Susan Strange.

Historically, she argued, "the necessity of the state as a public good . . . arose with the emergence of a developed market economy" and the need for secure private property ownership and exchange. But from the late Cold War on, property relations began to outgrow the aegis of states themselves—with disastrous consequences. At the same time as the authority of states was declining, the legal regulation of people's lives was increasing; but since this regulation involved trivial functions, legitimate authority exercised in the name of states was even further degraded. State authority was now

> less effective on those basic matters that the market, left to itself, has never been able to provide—security against violence, stable money for trade and investment, a clear system of law and the means to enforce it, and a sufficiency of public goods like drains, water supplies, infrastructures for transport and communications.

"State authority" correctly conceived, in Susan Strange's view, was dependent on governments taking the moral initiative in society, by providing key public goods, including "a clear system of law and the means to enforce it"—"in the interest of society as a whole and including the weak and poor." But this duty, she felt, had been comprehensively betrayed by governments themselves—intervening in the economy ideologically against the general good. None of which, for this specialist in markets, meant that markets themselves were at fault: rather, it was human decency and social solidarity that were undermined.[24]

Since Strange's critique, the public sector within states, in the world as a whole, has shrunk even more precipitately, to include areas where state monopoly was not previously challenged. In the next section I shall argue against the cardinal principle of the current system that states have a justified proprietary role in the division of the earth's inert resources. Even less may this be argued in respect of those valuable public "infrastructures for transport and communications," or energy and health, which Susan Strange evoked. These services are precisely dependent on states' human resources; they have traditionally been run by the people, for the people, to support core social expectations of secure and civilized life. Yet it is these same services that governments, from the late Cold War on, rushed to sell off to private individuals and firms, both from their own jurisdictions and from others.[25] Deregulation meant breaking the law of states as non-profit-making social enterprises set up for their inscribed peoples. Governments sold for gain what they did not own.

The result could only be chaos and confusion. In Northern countries, first came the series of uncontrolled mergers and acquisitions of the 1990s, putting into a spin the financial markets on which the very efficiency of transactions depended; then the recession of the early years of the new century, first detected in 2007–8. The recession itself, by general agreement, was triggered by excessive, unsupervised lending from the transatlantic banking and "securities" sectors to individuals and corporate agents—a development predicted by Susan Strange.[26] Under what she called the Westfailure system, very large fortunes were made by an increasing number of individuals, while state indebtedness grew exponentially. If states really were literal corporate agents, this lemming-like rush to "boom-and-bust" would have to be counted as their mass suicide.

Corporate Body, Body Corporate

To talk of a "legal person" or "corporate agent" is always to talk tendentiously. No authority can be derived from such talk to describe in agential terms either states or their alternatives and opposites, para- and anti-statal "bodies" (the "non-state actors" of conventional international theory). Corporateness in commercial contexts is not the same as societies legitimately actuating, giving life to, states through their own shared actions.

I think this is why, in common usage, when we talk about corporate agents in law, we almost always mean private agents, with private interests: set apart from, and potentially in opposition to, society at large. Since we generally think of our minds as, like our physical bodies, separate and individual, we do not normally speak of people having a "corporate" political will. In the twentieth century this was a fascist slogan. We mind these linguistic principles because we wish to preserve the idea of free will in general. And it is this idea that is corrupted by so-called democratic governments when they behave as if state functions can be bought and sold.

Once again it is international theory which gives us the intellectual lesson. To market or privatize assets of an essentially public nature held in the name of, or in association with, a state, contradicts the very principle of states as public *democratic* property. Vital services that uphold states, by providing an ordering framework for society, and so supplying the means of human independence, are not the government's to sell, whatever the governors' economic philosophy. This protective principle was instituted for people everywhere in 1945, with the creation of the universal system of independent states—largely as a reaction to the carving up of the territorial globe by imperial regimes.

That is why the Cold War is such a historic watershed. Formally, it was about the opposition between political belief systems—favoring, on the one hand, individual freedom and on the other social solidarity. These conceptions are not necessarily incompatible; human life involves compromises. What made conflict between them inevitable after 1945

189

was their entanglement with states as public property—a dilemma that the Cold War itself left unresolved. The end of the conflict in a short space of time exposed the exhaustion of all twentieth-century political principles—after socialism, liberalism—and the moral limitations of all law.

9.3 The Landlord State

The image here is that of a state as owner of a fixed territory and its resources—the image to which Berki drew attention.[27] Rules of secure property operate in almost all societies today. But to begin with, states themselves are not proprietary agents, because territory is inert, non-sapient—no kind of life-form. The presupposition of state agency fails completely to get past this fact. My argument here, however, is situated on a different—normative—level.

In the first place, within the closed system of state ownership the contemporary world is marked by a drastic inequality of territorial resources. Second, these are not owned in the sense of having been earned, but simply attach to the identity of states. Third, the distribution of the resources has come about largely arbitrarily—often as a result of colonialism, through frontiers established by outsiders who have since withdrawn, and whose descendants, as the citizens of independent states themselves, bear no effective liability for the past. In some cases, making property in land synonymous with any single group, even a "national" one, actually offends against some people's idea of themselves. This appears particularly to be so in sub-Saharan Africa, where historical populations tended to be scant and shifting and frontiers nebulous. The Organisation of African Unity and its successor, the African Union, made the unrevisability of colonial frontiers a founding principle, yet this is arguably the continent where such frontiers are the least meaningful.

Owing to all these factors, competition, controversy, and disaffection with the frontiers and resources of states are endemic in the states system, especially with regard to former-colonial areas. "North-South" conflict in the modern era, notably at the GATT and its successor, the World Trade Organization, has developed between governments adopting bloc policies on behalf of older-industrialized or former-colonial, "less-developed" states. These conflicts hinge on the trading prices of raw materials, finished goods, technological knowhow and services, due to incompatible or confused perceptions of the value of these things as historically inherited or socially earned; conflicts, in effect, between the perceived cost of colonialism and the perceived value of industrial development. For the purpose of these disputes all states are landlords, but some landlords think themselves more deserving than others.

Disputes over territory alone—at the International Court of Justice— are rarer, perhaps because governments in former-colonial countries attest to a certain solidarity in victimhood, or are readier than in older-established states to seek dispute settlement by war. All governments know in any case that the Court, as a UN organ, is entirely a court of their peers, in which any dispute is unlikely to be perfectly resolved.[28] Otherwise, the UN has no specific department for boundary disputes.[29] The system of universal states is arguably no freer of resource wars than when such wars were waged over the establishment of states themselves.

That said, there are some disputes, or potential disputes, over territorial resources that dramatically transcend the state division of them. Here are two examples.

Rain Forests

It is now a routine scientific tenet that tropical rain forests should be valued and protected for the sake of all living (and future) creatures, owing to the vast amounts of oxygen they exhale and of carbon dioxide they absorb from the burning of fossil fuels.[30] These considerations logically transcend the principle of the "ownership" of rain forests by the people of—say—Brazil, Indonesia, or the Congo, though not necessarily their right to be compensated for keeping such vital resources in pristine condition. Steps have already been taken, in fact, to facilitate voluntary payments for this purpose by governments and individuals in other countries. Yet this piecemeal movement has apparently not been enough to achieve its effect; the cutting-down of the rain forests has continued. The idea, therefore, of a Brazilian, Indonesian, or Congolese *nation's* "unlimited right to use and dispose of its . . . [state] natural resources'[31] should be rejected; it is an idea that humankind simply cannot afford.

Oil

Regarding the "ownership" of crude-oil reserves (including undersea ones), this is not a matter of human survival, but it is certainly a matter—until some comparable source of energy is found—of the realization everywhere of a minimum material quality of human life. Oil-driven technology is indispensable in all countries for industrial construction, manufacturing, transport, heating/cooling, and lighting. The international economy itself is dependent on volumes of cargo, carried in trucks and ships of steel, that could not be moved over land and sea without some such powerful fuel. In this way oil has become essential to a loose fellowship between the peoples of the earth, based on trade and travel, which nowadays gives the United Nations any effect it has. Even the Internet, which contributes so much to economy and efficiency in this regard, could not exist without the reliable generation of electricity, which in many places is still oil-dependent.

Should these core expectations of civilized life be subject to prices imposed by a minority cartel of (mainly undemocratic) governments (a question first asked when OPEC became politically active from 1973 on)? Fixed territorial resources after all, whether the rain forests or oil or anything else, are merely a windfall inheritance of statehood.

Meanwhile, important subsidiary questions arise. It is no accident that, for example, Saudi Arabia houses a pure *rentier* society, where democracy is nonexistent, and essential services have been largely provided—and actually run—by non-Saudis since the founding of the modern state; that Brazilian and Nigerian political institutions are regularly adjudged to be the most corrupt in the world, and their citizens the most unequal; or that the Nigerian oil industry has led to the extensive pollution of the Niger delta and the near destruction of life there. The economist Paul Collier, in his study of "failed states," includes some of the richest in the world. In his account, massive unearned income lends itself to a "politics of patronage" which subverts democratic initiative and over the long term institutionalizes mass poverty in an alienated, unskilled underclass.[32]

Collier's work, based on decades of data collection, provides concrete evidence of how the state "ownership" of marketable resources—especially those internationally perceived as scarce—can make everyone in society, from the government down, lazy and corrupt, when hiring or squeezing foreigners is seen easier than working.[33] The problem is compounded when neoliberal policies to untie the state "ownership" are introduced; the process, ostensibly instigated in the name of social equality, merely fertilizes the roots of graft. We must, I think, conclude that the moral dilemmas first created in Europe by the enclosure of property in land have now ramified through the states system over all the earth.[34]

9.4 The Heir-to-History State

Historical continuity between the periods before and after 1945 provides the main basis of sovereignty today—arguably the master value and attribute of states. It means the right of a people to act together on their own behalf, and in defense of their own interests, among other peoples doing the same. This idea, projected over time, is more real in human terms than the conventional fiction of states as corporate legal agents, and wider-ranging than states as proprietors of territorial resources, while remaining essential to both.

It is also rather new. The Roman Republic's centuries-long dominance, for instance, so influential in European history, rested on continuous overseas expansion and exploitation of others. The later personalization of Roman power shows the decline, rather than the strength, of these values. The Empire split, and the emperors themselves multiplied, becoming increasingly eccentric and anodyne and "sourced," like a commodity, from anywhere able to supply them.[35] The locus of sovereignty was vague, because the boundaries of empire were vague—which could be said of any empire in the thousand years since the end of Rome.

The form of international relations we recognize today is usually traced to the Peace of Westphalia (1648), which gave rise to the European-generated states system. But Westphalia itself was concluded by, and between, sovereigns as monarchs, conceiving themselves as personally synonymous with "their" states. These rulers sought to ratify, rather than reform, a religio-monarchical status quo of their own devising. Several more centuries were required for the evolution of secular polities in which individuated, territorially-based societies might collectively "own" their sovereign rights. This change did not, however, lead to an equal distribution of power.

The "Maturity Thesis"

In this connection Robert Jackson argues that the ahistorical dispensation of 1945 has given rise to a two-tier or two-class system, consisting of states and "quasi-states." The latter—roughly, the former-colonial "Third World" of his subtitle—allegedly possess all the rights and privileges of sovereignty without the practical ability to exercise them, yet without having to live up to the related obligations either.

> The ex-colonial states have been internationally enfranchised and possess the same external rights and responsibilities as all other states: juridical statehood. At the same time, however, many have not yet been authorized and empowered domestically and consequently lack the institutional features of sovereign states as also defined by classical international law. They disclose limited empirical statehood: their populations do not enjoy many of the advantages traditionally associated with independent statehood. Their governments are often deficient in the political will, institutional authority, and organized power to protect human rights or provide socioeconomic welfare. The concrete benefits which have historically justified the undeniable burdens of sovereign statehood are often limited to fairly narrow elites and not yet extended to the citizenry at large whose lives may be scarcely improved by independence or even adversely affected by it. These states are primarily juridical. They are still far from complete, so to speak, and empirical statehood in large measure still remains to be built.[36]

This thesis is a popular one: partly, no doubt, because Jackson's criticisms of post-colonial regimes as lacking, as a group, both legitimacy and effectiveness can be echoed alike by sympathetic proponents of human rights and unsympathetic Realists and reactionaries. His argument could be summed up as: these regimes have little real power, but in any case more than they should. The argument is often echoed, for good or ill, by the actual protagonists of the late-colonial world. Ex-colonial civil servants might grieve, after their departure, over disputes between people to whom they had become attached, while others might consider former-colonial peoples too "backward" to govern themselves. Hence Rob Walker's dismissal of Jackson's thesis as "a familiar form of liberal angst."[37]

Jackson's tone, by turns slapdash and patronizing, only encourages this impression. He describes the multiplication of state jurisdictions in the post-colonial era as a "lengthening list of specks on the map"; but those specks contain people. Still, insofar as the states system is an artificial creation in which political power in the shape of sovereignty comes as an unearned accompaniment of territory, there is some basis for his view that "the juridical cart is now before the empirical horse."[38] The same could be said of his observation that the North-South part of the system is a kind of international welfare state in which the handouts are of development aid. Neither of these opinions might be wholly fair, but neither is wholly untrue.

Quasi-States could be summed up as an account of how the builders of the modern international system got things wrong. It is both an extension and a critique of the English School conception of a law-governed "society of states." Along these lines, Jackson contrasts the current global conjuncture with the process by which power-balancing in historical Europe eventually led to the creation of a stable basis for political relations. He implies that the UN process was rushed, with no consideration being given to some intermediate, trusteeship stage between colonialism and independence in which proper institutions of representative democracy could be developed in former-colonial territories. His normative thrust also draws on the "significant individuals" approach to history, invoking Southern leaders who, had things been different, might have led their societies out of their presumed immaturity and into a liberal-democratic condition like that of contemporary Europe and North America.

This thesis, it should be stressed, is not aimed directly at the more recent phenomenon of "failed," or politically and socially collapsed, states. State failure in places such as Somalia, Liberia, and Sierra Leone arose in the late Cold War from a complex of climatic, demographic, and political factors, and then from the end of the Cold War itself, which altered for good a situation in which no post-colonial regime, no matter how despotic or ramshackle, could quite be allowed to go under for lack of aid. A country where a civil war is going on, and where there is no recognizable political authority, is by definition the site of a state failure. But "failed states" are not, for Jackson, the same as "quasi-states." His sights range wider, purportedly taking in the whole world since decolonization. The main problem of international relations, he implies, is North-South relations. His complaint is directed at the numerical majority of regimes in existence, effectively the Southern ones—but also, and not a little anachronistically, at people in the North for letting the current chaotic state of affairs happen.

His argument is nevertheless full of contradictions and loose ends. For one thing, it is too late now to reinstate protectorates for guided democracy in former-colonial regions. To do so would mean intervening on a massive scale, against a key international norm, and very likely against the wishes of the people directly involved—people determined to govern themselves, even badly. William Bain makes this point in the context of the same "society-of-states" approach as Jackson's—even for "failed states."[39] Conceivably, there are extreme instances where such reservations do not apply: desperate situations where years of natural disaster and political failure call for government to be placed temporarily in the hands of well-meaning, capable, and well-endowed outsiders.[40] But common sense suggests that such interventions should be exceptional and very strictly defined.

It is also contradictory to complain that large numbers of state governments in the South are at once too weak (internationally) and too strong (internally). Jackson gets out of this self-inflicted bind only by inventing a distinction between "positive sovereignty," which First World regimes allegedly possess, and the "negative sovereignty" of Third World regimes. But this merely confuses the issue. Sovereignty, as any diplomat will tell you, is indivisible, and for reasons in their own right normative. "In the traditional sovereignty system," says Benedict Kingsbury,

> even relatively fragile states play a potentially important function as a basis of identity and a focus of loyalty, balancing the pull of identities based on a clan or ethnic group or religious solidarity or city. The representativity of the state and the performance of its institutions condition its effectiveness in these functions, but it is almost impossible for externally based institutions to perform these functions.[41]

Robert Jackson's entire thesis, in fact, is, like his defining adjective, ambiguous. "Quasi" in the dictionary sense can mean either "seemingly" or "almost." So a quasi-state can be an *almost*-effective state, or misleadingly *appear* to be an effective one; but Jackson is too concerned with laying blame to consider the difference. Doing so, in any case, would mean him having to abandon state agency, the uncritical conflation of peoples with their inherited institutions on which he relies.

The truth is more complicated: the UN founders willed into existence a universal system which was intended to be both self-perpetuating and territorially stable. The paradox gestured at by Jackson, therefore, lies not in any particular conjuncture of the system, but in the legalistic conception of independent state agents taken as equal. His thesis is both an explanation and a symptom of this approach. If states really were person-like agents, and simultaneously equal and law-abiding, then it would be natural to argue for an evolutionary approach to sovereignty—and fair to complain about those who failed, or refused, to "grow up" under it.

The "Maturity Thesis" again

An approach taken by Sørensen is very like Jackson's. It is of interest here mainly because Sørensen sets out to refute both the Realist paradigm of the uniformity of states and what he calls the traditional "Westphalian" state with its ideal autonomy—while still retaining state agency.

Sørensen posits two types of state, the "pre-modern" and the "post-modern," as active in a different kind of anarchy to the absolute Realist version. For him the "pre-modern" are, as in Jackson's thesis, the "Third World" states—lacking strong political institutions (above all democracy), social cohesion, or economic self-sufficiency, with their "ideal type," or rather worst exemplars, to be found in sub-Saharan Africa—he gives examples from Mozambique to Somalia, from Uganda to Sudan. Again like Jackson, Sørensen sees these states as having "juridical statehood" without "substantial statehood." Meanwhile, "post-modern" states ("the industrialized countries of Western Europe, North America and, to a lesser extent, Japan") are seen as having strong economic and political institutions, but (contrary to the Realist paradigm of anarchy/ self-help) engaging in substantial cooperation with each other; they even "allow other states a measure of influence on activities within their own borders, in return for a measure of such influence on other states." Clearly, in Sørensen's view it is better to be post-modern than pre-.

This is the "maturity thesis" in slightly different garb. Sørensen argues that identifying states' degrees of un-likeness will help us understand "the nature of the conflict and cooperation which has characterized different historical periods of the international system."[42] The truth, however, is that in the Realist/liberal debate about uniformity and anarchy among states, there is a common assumption which alone makes the debate possible, and that is state agency. To my mind, moreover, there is a qualitative leap in aberration between describing states as acting in a human-like way—where actions of some political import are involved—and attributing to them individual personality traits like virtues and vices, in order to "judge" them, as Sørensen seems to want to do. In the relatively recent context of colonialism, out of which much of the current states system developed, this appears an especially contentious, even provocative practice. Sørensen calls for flexibility from theorists, but to my mind for an entirely bogus purpose: in favor of his right to make differential moral judgments of entire peoples. When these judgments take strong form, they show up the "maturity thesis" in its full, grotesque guise:

> The territories that had previously been regarded as unfit for self-government did not all of a sudden acquire the attributes of substantial statehood.

> Applying [neorealist] reasoning to much of the Third World around the time of decolonization would mean that the new states-to-be had learnt their lesson and acquired the necessary prerequisites for substantial statehood.

> ... "pre-modern" states want to have their cake and eat it too.[43]

Imagine telling a territory—all those mountains, lakes, and rivers: "you are unfit for self-government." Imagine informing a random Mozambican that expecting to enjoy formal sovereignty *and* to receive "development assistance and other preferential treatment" was wanting to have his cake and eat it. Imagine confronting an average Ugandan with the news that she had not learned the lessons of decolonization which entitled her to partake in substantial statehood. Conversely, imagine praising French people at large for sacrificing their sovereignty for the sake of international cooperation and declaring them fit for self-government solely by virtue of being French. Even children understand that the world is a more complicated place than that. And they do so because they instinctively grasp the experience of being talked down to, which is what the exponents of the "maturity thesis" engage in.

Sovereignty and Policy Continuity

Hobson's historiographical approach is far stricter, even tonic. He undertakes an imaginative development of English School doctrine, to focus on the model English School protagonist, the historical European state; and he presents this as a resolution of the "agent-structure" debate in international theory. His aim is to identify "international agential power" *favorably*, in foreign-policy actions over time. So in European trade policy from 1879 to 1913,

> the strong domestic governing capacity of the British state (derived principally from its highly embedded relations with domestic social forces) enabled the state to extract income taxation and cooperate with both the working and dominant classes, which meant that it could avoid raising indirect taxes and tariffs. It thus gained high

levels of international agential power and followed a cooperative free trade policy. Conversely, the low domestic governing capacity of the German and Russian states [in this period] meant that they could not raise income taxation, but instead chose to repress various social actors in society through increasing regressive indirect taxes and tariffs . . . In the process they gained only moderate levels of international agential power and thereby defected from international cooperation, pursuing tariff protectionism rather than free trade.[44]

Here, ostensibly, is a reasoned case for a state as historic agent—seen exercising useful power on behalf of "its" people through time, and drawing strength from them in return.

Power for Good

In this approach, moreover, explicit normative terms are involved. The emphases are Hobson's.

If the domestic agential power of the state refers to the ability of the state to make domestic or foreign policy, and shape the domestic realm, free of domestic social-structural requirements or the interests of non-state actors, so the international agential power of the state refers to the *ability of the state to make foreign policy and shape the international realm free of international structural requirements or the interests of international non-state actors*. And at the extreme, high agential power refers to the *ability of the state to mitigate the logic of inter-state competition and thereby create a cooperative or peaceful world*. This "international state power" must not be confused with the neorealist notion of "state power" or "state capability," which refers to the ability of states to effectively conform to international competition and the logic of what Waltz calls the "international political structure." In fact my definition of "international agential state power" precisely inverts neorealism's notion of state capability.

[. . .] High international agential state power enables the state to shape and reconstitute the international system as well as to solve the collective action problem and create a peaceful, cooperative world. Liberalism is the outstanding theory which accords such agential power to states. Classical liberalism stipulates that as states conform to individuals" social needs within domestic society, so they are able to create a peaceful world.[45] (Author's emphases).

The originality of Hobson's view, within the "agent-structure" debate and in international theory generally, seems to me to lie in the assertion that the rational assumption of state agency is not confined to Realism.

One need not, in other words, assume that states are "bad" in order to argue that they behave like persons. A state as historic agent in the exercise of its sovereignty can, on this view, also be "good."

Hobson's approach is still, to my mind, inadequate (states, I hold, should never be seen as person-like or agents as such), but it does elaborate a well-established normative element. The Kantian "democratic peace"—the idea that liberal-democratic states do not (or do not easily) "go to war" with each other—is based on the argument that such polities are inherently unaggressive. In line with this logic, Hobson's implication in the earlier quotation is that Russian and German autocracy actually contributed to causing the First World War. And clearly, the more states "conform to individuals' social needs in domestic society," the more they may be considered legitimate and therefore agent-like. On this level, international theory and foreign-policy analysis begin to converge.

There is a further interesting aspect, arising from Hobson's invocation of three case-studies by Martha Finnemore.[46] He takes up her argument that states are "normative-adaptive entities," able to "learn" valuable lessons from international organizations: for example, the value of having a science-policy bureaucracy (learned from UNESCO); of knowing rule-governed norms of warfare (learned from the International Red Cross); and, in the case of "third world states," of prioritizing poverty-alleviation in economic policy (learned through the guidance of the World Bank).[47] In this way states are seen building up their legitimacy by adopting a cultural heritage of, so to speak, best political practice. Hobson picks out Finnemore's approach as an example of an "international society-centric constructivist theory of the state." What both authors seek to portray is the "international agential power" of states as a beneficial exercise of sovereignty, manifested over time in foreign policy.

Now, it is possible to appreciate the originality and optimism of both these approaches while still arguing that they involve reification—of states as agents. In criticizing this practice from the outset, I have been conscious of the need not to fall into it negatively myself. So I have sought to avoid the crude stigmatization of "the state" for its own sake that conspiracy theorists engage in—erecting shadow enemies in bureaucracies, the police, or government—or which some feminists and pacifists engage in, when they vilify "the state" as inherently sexist or militaristic. Reification by demonization is commoner than reification for praise, but they are all forms of reification.

What we have in Hobson's own narratives of nearly half a century of positive state "behavior" (in the British people's economic interest) and of negative state "behavior" (to the detriment of the peoples of Germany and Russia) is retrospective foreign-policy interpretation. Just as it is possible, as I argued earlier, to isolate a pattern of wrongdoing in the policies of successive Chinese governments since 1950 toward the people of Tibet, it is possible to demonstrate that the pattern of foreign policy built up in Europe by successive British governments in the nineteenth century was virtuous. That is certainly Hobson's implication, in arguing that the British state was "strong" in its "governing capacity," which depended on the willing cooperation of the British people, in contrast to the "repressive" policies followed by governments in Germany and tsarist Russia.

However, governing capacity is a quality of governments, not of states. Here it means the cumulative actions of individuals making for a policy "good" enough (reflecting the people's wishes or interests), for long enough, to strengthen the legitimacy of states. The same applies to the case-studies of Finnemore that Hobson commends. And in fact, in the first exposition of his own theory Hobson refers alternately to states *and their governments* as agents of change;[48] his aim being to show the superiority of liberal democracy over autocracy, by implying, in a compromise typical of liberal political theory, that fair governments are also effective ones.

Judging History

Hobson's approach builds on a technique of historical writing, a high-level generalization by which the exercise of state power is depicted as intrinsic to—manifesting the "national character" of—certain societies, like the celebrated British diplomatic practice of "balancing" between continental rivals. Talk of trends in power and influence in the interrelations of states is the stuff of international history, as exemplified by works like Paul Kennedy's *The Rise and Fall of the Great Powers* or Immanuel Wallerstein's *The Modern World-System*.[49] A "power" in Kennedy's narrative, or a "hegemon" in Wallerstein's, is constituted by the accumulated actions over time of a *succession* of specific state governments and/or their peoples in manipulation of their political institutions. But, we should still insist, it is the historian him/herself who reifies, for praise or blame, the state agent of history; and such judgments work only when based on a fairly explicit normative stance. Otherwise writers will slip into an omniscient Macaulayesque afflatus, an empty grand theory, as in Philip Bobbitt's nonsensical assertion that "France pursued war to aggrandize the French state."[50]

Moreover, it is only with reference to a well-defined conception of democracy that one can speak at all of society's synonymy with a state, and then only for the duration of particular policies. This provisionally accommodates Hobson's and Finnemore's case-studies but excludes Wallerstein's Marxist, mechanistic identification of historical agency with the dynamics of capitalism. Equally, Anthony Brewer's conventional generalization that during the Industrial Revolution "Britain controlled the markets of the world" must be (and here is) accompanied by a critique of precisely how and why British governments and their helpers succeeded for so long in the manipulation of the British state, in the cause of imperialism.[51] This underlines the point that even historical international theory is political writing—which rules out unthinking reference to states as agents. Nor are we licensed to write of contemporary international relations that "the United States controls the markets of the world," even though the same grain of truth is contained in this as in Brewer's historical reference to Britain. The past we can only interpret; the present and future, by contrast, we can change, and this calls for a different set of terms. History and international theory are not the same.

Hobson's own approach is couched in the international Realist canon of power and its exercise, because in the Realist/neo-Realist view that he wants to refute, what matters is the concentration of power in central state institutions. So he can fairly speak of the putative "ability of the state to make domestic or foreign policy, and shape the domestic realm, free of domestic social-structural requirements or the interests of non-state actors." This is an elaborate way of saying that some writers argue that "the state" can conceivably make policy unaccountably, without the people, but what is the state, if not the people?

So far, so true. Hobson in his approach, however, merely replaces the Realist/neo-Realist state as reified amoral power with the liberal's reified power-for-good. His agent, in his own examples, is a state conflated with government in historical perspective, judged by the criterion of political accountability. But to assert accountability in the first place as one's criterion of approval opens up the whole question of political agency. Hobson's theory works retrospectively, but only retrospectively. There are no live people inside his state agent, only dead ones. His approach is in its own way unaccountable in respect of the past (which we can only interpret, not change). Its entire credibility depends on whether continuity can be demonstrated between the historical pattern of political actions observed and the actions of current agents, making those agents believably "the same" over the period in question.

In any case, if the period extends before and after 1945, I suggest his approach is unworkable, because of the altered conditions of states. A British government operating, with the best will in the world, as the foremost imperial power in a system of partial independent statehood, and subject to the votes of only a fraction of the population at home, is an essentially different agent from one open to recall by universal suffrage at home and operating among nominally independent and effectively more equal rivals abroad. The conjuncture of the nineteenth century, for better or worse, is not the one we live in. Nor is the practical relationship the same between foreign policy and domestic politics; nor, as a result, can the conception of states and political action be.

Or take the case of nuclear weapons. Since 1945, liberal-democratic governments in the UK, United States, and France have faced public decisions on the acquisition and modernization of nuclear arsenals. But these decisions, always involving a *prospective* succession of such governments (because of the widespread international implications, and the time lags of technological development), should be seen as a) exclusive to a minority of states, and so not a general principle of foreign policy; and b) only related to "good" government in a very narrow, security-orientated sense—predicated on sustained evil intent on the part of other governments and peoples, which may be a miscalculation and have little to do with foreign-trade relationships. Turn Hobson's eulogy of liberal-democratic policymaking to the real modern world and it loses much of its force.

"Good Government" and the Modern State

Hobson's extrapolation of a state agent from history reflects a particular characteristic of modern states: more than policy continuity, *consistency*—something closely related, under modern conditions, to democratic and secular institutions. In the past, empires and monarchies were ruled by personality and patronage, as opposed to ability and merit. Of empires and monarchies, it was normal to expect inconsistency—whether in the personalities of their rulers, or the nature of their institutions. By contrast, modern states (at least liberal-democratic ones) are characterized by a tradition of impersonal, objective public service (as in "civil service"). We expect consistency in the nature and the actions of their institutions. Fairness and consistency, moreover, are related. This is Hobson's point, when he argues that even relatively democratic British governments could foster peace and flexibility ("cooperative free trade") in international relations because they had the confidence to do so, built up from fair policies of "income taxation" at home. He works with an implicit (liberal-democratic) normative theory of international relations, based on a normative interpretation of history.

And yet, to derive actual state agency from this is still a reification too far. It is to assume, as the principles of the universal states system imply, that consistent or uniform political institutions "are" agents in their own right. But this is true only in the stories and metaphors that make up our history. A succession of good governments is a succession of good governments, not a replacement for human moral choice. To say that a state "behaves" in history is simply to encapsulate the behavior of (some of) its representatives over time; to define an observed phenomenon mechanistically, with a metaphor. When construction engineers describe the "behavior" over time of pre-stressed concrete in bridges, they do not think of bridges as people.

State agency remains a biologically incorrect and philosophically unreliable notion. Democracy, fairness, policy continuity and institutional consistency all make for good human experience; of that there can be no doubt. But we need to identify and praise the individuals in government who have made for that good experience, and not give in to the temptation (which politicians everywhere for their own ends promote) to reify and romanticise states as an inheritance from a past which, being past, can never be subjected to a complete critique. Empirical exactness in this regard is, after all, is part of the effort of sustaining democracy itself. I too would want to argue for positive government actions in the name of states, over long periods of time, in consistent ways, and with valuable, even momentous results—but without falling into the trap of describing states themselves as agents of, or in, history.

9.5 The Patriot State

Since the beginning of organized society, the primary interest of collectivities has been the physical security of their members, which leaders have on occasion been punished for failing to guarantee. In the dogma of Realist international theory, this commitment is the supreme justification for states, and for the Realist vision of international relations as a living struggle.

On one level there is an obvious aspect of self-fulfilling prophecy to this dogma, because insecurity could be seen as a natural human reaction to the formal division of the world, especially when the division is on an unequal basis. Moreover, common sense tells us that it is not states, but transient governments and their subservient armed forces, who are the true agents in this domain. What is sometimes referred to as "state behavior" can merely mean, as I have just been arguing, aggregate *government* behavior (or more persuasively, government-and-people behavior) retrospectively observed. So there is no general justification for state agents as guarantors of national security, above and apart from the people, any more than for the other reified images projected in the conventional wisdom.

Conceivably, however, there are situations perceived as critical by a whole society, and reflected in government opinion, in which government and society really do think and act as one, and in that sense "are" a state. Brent Steele, in a set of historical case-studies, addresses this question directly. From a reductive claim that one can interpret the "behavior of states" through the behavior of their leaders ("because [the leaders] have the moral burden of making policy choices *and* the capacity to implement those decisions"), Steele goes on to argue more ambitiously that this enables us to see, over time, states (by which he means whole societies) constructing a normative identity for themselves through "ontological security." This happens especially, in his view, when people wish to secure honor and avoid shame vis-à-vis their peers, even through self-sacrificial actions; his examples include the attempt in Belgium, in the First World War, to fight off German invasion against hopeless odds.

In addition, Steele sees his normative approach as consonant with the English School of international theory, with its society-of-states conception. He begins with some scepticism:

> It is the placement of the "self" of the state in international society that matters for the security interests of states, and this Self can be problematized.

"Problematizing" states, in this context, means "revealing the manner in which a targeted state's practices exclude or subjugate certain populations." In other words, security policy, as a call for sacrifices from society at large, can be abused for demagogic ends. Steele, however, is interested in the opposite case: the positive ways in which a collectivity, in harmonious conjunction with its leaders, can realize a national "Self."[52]

Against a National Self...

As mentioned previously, I also incline to a view of states that accentuates shared moral values. What I do not accept is that this sharing occurs, leading to effective joint action, very often—certainly not often enough to support a general argument for state agency. Steele's case-studies focus on crises as the occasion for the emergency formation of a national "Self," and by definition crises are untypical events. They are also of limited duration in the history of states. Nations are mortal; states are putatively timeless. By this logic, a national Self is either ephemeral or an anomaly.

More generally I have ruled out state "persons" as a complete fallacy, but would retain the hypothetical possibility, still normative, of a collectivity acting as one. Agents at this ideal level would have to incorporate a) the people, in conscious harmony with their leaders, and b) these two, in conscious acceptance of key attributes of their state (notably, its territorial borders and resources) over an extended period. Steele's call on the English School for support brings in a third condition, c) some complex appraisal of law, including international law. This is a demanding set of requirements, which outside of crises seems unlikely to be fulfilled.

There is a further point to be made. Steele relies on his Belgian example to support the idea of leadership-sponsored reification of a national "Self" for self-defense; but equally, in real wars there are no surrogates. If a people perceive strongly enough the need to defend themselves as a united group, they will do so whether or not they have been exhorted to it by their state leaders, and whether or not they see themselves acting in the name of a given state. There is the status quo, and there is survival. Certainly, the two world wars of the twentieth century were wars of mass mobilization which could not have been fought without initial mass conviction in the validity of those struggles. Yet the 1945 British general election, in which the wartime coalition, led by the people's hero Churchill, was defeated shows the limits of people's willingness to sacrifice themselves. That election also testifies to people's capacity to punish their representatives for involving them in avoidable wars—in other words, precisely to subvert anyone's totemic attachment to state institutions.

...and for a Patriotic Self

This point underlines both the narrowness and the depth of Steele's approach. His conception of the security needed to constitute a national

"Self" excludes, for example, economic security, even over extended periods of time—which rules out Hobson's conception. Steele focuses instead on the crystallization of collective belonging at times of absolute existential threat, which is his approach's source of moral depth. He also includes a less obvious source: the impulse of aid, in crisis, to other nations. His national "Self" is expansive.

Within limits, this is plausible. There is no obvious reason for a national Self to be only self-interested. The generosity of spirit involved in identifying a community worth fighting and even dying for, beyond local and family ties, may transcend even national boundaries. What Steele is really concerned with is patriotism; and patriotism as a moral idea can extend to the defense of other nations whose interest in security and identity preservation is seen as at least as worthy and threatened as one's own. Both the First and Second World Wars were presented, at the outset, as just wars in this sense. So Steele's idealized national-state agent can logically include the agent of humanitarian intervention as well (one of his case-studies even involves what one might call creative non-intervention). This aspect links his approach to the international "solidarism" of the English School, represented by writers such as Adam Roberts and Nick Wheeler.[53] All three acknowledge a debt to Hedley Bull, who sought to reconcile the opposing concepts, as he expressed them, of order and justice.[54]

The Good Samaritan State

The key "solidarist" claim is that a people's conception of national security can be stretched beyond their own direct defense to include intervention against someone else's sovereignty, for those other people's sake, yet without calling into question the norms of the states system itself. Wheeler's study of humanitarian intervention mentions three instances of unilateral invasion which in his view did not threaten "international society," whatever the climate of multilateral institutions at the time.[55]

Still, "solidarism" calls directly into question a more basic principle of the English School: *non*-intervention.[56] On this view, the states system is a rule-governed "society" of (nation-)states whose independence, like that of individual persons, strongly deserves respect. "Solidarism," to the extent that it works, can conceivably sustain that "society" in cases when the rules break down. Humanitarian action itself sustains social life, as respect for rules sustains law, including international law. But by the same token, instances when the rules break down, and intervention is justified, must be exceptional if contradictions are to be avoided. The preconditions of a socially accepted norm of law, a complete self-identification over time between the leaders and the people, their history, heritage, and borders, and finally a worthy foreign cause, must be present before we can begin to think of state agents as real agents, and agents for good. And it is this ideal concatenation of factors that I say does not often occur, desirable though it might otherwise be.

I do not argue that this can never occur, nor do I oppose it in principle. Surely there are instances in which it might be good for a given society to feel at ease with its political institutions, its government of the day, its history, and its territorial inheritance all at once. Exceptional circumstances can result in exceptional solidarity—among a people, between a people and its leaders, or between a people and another people. Moreover, in cases of humanitarian intervention, which go against the general international norm of non-intervention, but rely on governments acting in causes that they think most of their citizens support, surely it is possible to imagine a people-and-government in one, acting for good in the world? So, Steele argues, some societies in a position to influence events may act together, and in harmony with their governments, to go against a perceived negative trend, or right a salient wrong, to clear their consciences or burnish their pride, while believing that they have simultaneously been acting in the interests of their own security. And indeed, who would *not* have welcomed the Vietnamese and Tanzanian interventions that ended the genocidal regimes of Pol Pot (in Cambodia) and Idi Amin (in Uganda)? Who would not wish to see all tyrants overthrown? One can demur on the tactics, but that is all.

Or consider the 1999 NATO intervention in Kosova, the only contemporary case mentioned by Steele. On that occasion we might suppose that many people in neighboring or influential societies, especially in Europe, felt shame that there had been no UN rescuing intervention in the Rwanda genocide in 1994, and ineffective UN protection in Bosnia in 1993 against Serbian "ethnic cleansing"; and so they were only too willing to support the unilateral NATO action to prevent the massacre of Kosovars at the hands of the same Serbian leader (Milošević, who was subsequently indicted for genocide in the Balkans). Such cases testify to a consistent chain of conscience over time, between peoples and governments, even if one not always fully or perfectly exercised. Again, the US government's reluctance to intervene in Rwanda was directly traceable to its disastrous intervention in Somalia the previous year, which had led to deaths among the US military bringing aid. Yet in the light of the genocide President Clinton came to view his own earlier reticence as fainthearted, and went to Rwanda to apologize.

Without such right thinking which ordinary citizens will not allow to be buried by the inertia of the states system, no intervention against sovereignty would ever be imaginable, still less effective, even though legal provision for such intervention has arguably been in the Charter since the UN's inception. Ethnic Europeans in particular, whether resident in Europe or living at one or two generations' remove elsewhere, would hardly be human, in the light of the Holocaust of the European Jews, if they were not especially sensitive to the danger of genocide—a danger enhanced by the international norm of non-intervention, if slavishly observed.[57] Clearly, the growth of civilized society, accountability, and democracy within created states may require a helping hand to be given to causes which cross the system's boundaries. In this light the Good Samaritan state is an honorable aspiration.

The Limits of "Solidarism"

Laudable though such sentiment is, it has been scarce and rather ineffective for most of the duration of the universal states system. Pressures on the UN Security Council to support the proposed NATO intervention in Kosova had no effect—despite the danger, after the massacres in neighboring Bosnia and Croatia, of this fate befalling the Kosovars at the hands of Serbian forces.[58] In the event the intervention went ahead, to ultimate good effect, because Western leaders, taking those earlier massacres seriously, ignored the UN opposition, and the opposition chose not actively to oppose.

A positive humanitarian outcome may even occur in direct contradiction of the reasons given at the time, as I would argue of the Western-led overthrow of the Saddam Hussein regime in Iraq in 2003. In my view this action deserved to be supported for its own sake, owing to the extremely cruel, personal, and entrenched nature of the regime.[59] Yet Saddam's overthrow was not the first or even the main reason given for the intervention; it was, instead, "illegal" weapons of mass destruction in Iraq, which UN inspectors had not found (and were later shown not to exist). Moreover, the earlier military intervention of 1991, after the Saddam-sponsored invasion of Kuwait, had been halted short of an invasion of Iraq and the overthrow of the regime, precisely on grounds of respect for international law and Iraqi sovereignty, in conformity with the UN Security Council resolution authorizing the action.

For every case of a tyrant overthrown, there have been ten of a tyrant spared. Look how long it took to get rid of the weirdly despotic Gadhafi regime in Libya (a country, after all, of only a few million people), a step which had to wait for the loosening of political certainties in neighboring societies. All this is accountable to the UN Charter article[60] offering all state governments a sacrosanct right of "domestic jurisdiction," and the decades-long sphere-of-influence competitions of the Cold War, which allowed demagogues from central America to Africa and Southeast Asia to manipulate the nuclear balance of terror for their own ends. The whole paradoxical issue of humanitarian intervention vs. non-intervention, in fact, graphically illustrates the traditional distinction that Realists, not always sincerely, recur to between domestic and international politics in their systematic preference for policies of force. For in the former, when right is done, one can fairly claim that it was done for the right reasons, whereas in the latter, right things may occur for the "wrong," or at least unpredictable, reasons—but in either case, it will rarely be with unmixed results.[61]

From this, returning to my discussion, one can draw the following conclusions: 1) there are undoubted instances of whole societies uniting for moral purposes, going beyond social self-preservation to help others, 2) on occasion they are united too with their state governments, but 3) neither constitutes the norm in international relations, nor, perhaps, 4) need it be the norm for good to be done.

If there are instances where sincere humanitarian intervention against sovereignty have been successful (here I would cite Kosova in 1999, and Sierra Leone in 2000[62]), we may fairly say that the divisions of the states system were for that moment transcended. But far from supporting the idea of states as guarantors of national security, this tends to undermine it overall. Humanitarian intervention amounts to a policy of running repairs on the system, not the cohesive philosophy which would eliminate its deeper faults. "Solidarism" is a foreign policy, not a theory of international relations. Popular support for it in practice, moreover, is always likely to be predicated on limited casualties, whether among the interveners or those to be rescued from harm.[63] Ensuring this goal requires the projection of superior force, which underlines the traditional origins of the policy and its potential contradictions.

"Solidarism" also comes hard up against the rules of the system of independent states, that status quo which English School theorists traditionally support. As Nick Rengger points out, the "English school conception of international society . . . is—and must remain, if it is to be distinctive—a state-bound and state-centred conception, yet the move to [Kantian] cosmopolitanism would force it to abandon that."[64] This is perhaps why Steele's approach is hybrid—half theoretical speculation and half case-studies, of which he gives only three, and only one contemporary. He also, significantly, fails to offer any extended typology of patriotic national Selves in support of his approach.

"Solidarism" itself is not free of contradiction, implying as it does that national security is at once the right, and not the right, of putative nation-states. Wheeler's own attack on the "statist paradigm," as he calls it, employs what could only be called statist language. Of potential critics of humanitarian intervention, he remarks: "it is not only that statists are arguing that states *do* not behave in this way, they are also asserting that states *should* not behave in this way." We can readily agree that humanitarian intervention is an intrinsically valuable and underused practice. But I suggest that most people, faced with the rights and wrongs of real situations, would fail to get past the idea of *states* "behaving" in them, as opposed to governments.

This underlines the basic problem that Hobson, Steele, and the English School "solidarists" must all encounter, in seeking to persuade us of the possibility of a beneficent state agent. There is simply no logical commensurability between individuals as literal, willing, conscious agents (a straightforward, everyday assumption), societies as the same (much more difficult, but still plausible where government actions are widely supported), and *states* as agents in either sense. So it comes as no surprise to find Wheeler slipping from "the moral responsibilities or obligations" of "state leaders and citizens" to those of "state leaders— those men and women who think and act in the name of states."[65] All these are authentic agents, but they are not the same agent; and it is only when they are all acting together, over time, in conscious furtherance of the same difficult and subtle challenge to the status quo, that it is possible to imagine the embodied state as the guarantor of a national interest which potentially includes the interest of other nations. That is a lot to ask. By this stage of the argument, in any case, the need for radical reform of the states system itself begins to appear.

Responsibility to Protect

In the wake of the humanitarian crises in Rwanda and former Yugoslavia in the 1990s, important steps were taken at the highest diplomatic level. The UN commission of inquiry into events in Rwanda in 1994 declared that "the failure by the United Nations to prevent, and subsequently, to stop the genocide . . . was a failure by the United Nations system as a whole," and a post of special adviser to the UN secretary-general on the prevention of genocide was created.[66] The Canadian government sponsored independent research into pre-empting or resolving such crises in future.[67] This gave rise to a significant addition to international humanitarian law, known as "responsibility to protect," which was subsequently endorsed by the UN Security Council and General Assembly. Two paragraphs from the document issued at the World Summit of 2005 may be cited:

> 138. Each individual State has the responsibility to protect its populations from genocide, war crimes, ethnic cleansing and crimes against humanity. This responsibility entails the prevention of such crimes, including their incitement, through appropriate and necessary means. We accept that responsibility and will act in accordance with it. The international community should, as appropriate, encourage and help States to exercise this responsibility and support the United Nations in establishing an early warning capability.
>
> 139. The international community, through the United Nations, also has the responsibility to use appropriate diplomatic, humanitarian and other peaceful means, in accordance with Chapters VI and VIII of the Charter, to help protect populations from genocide, war crimes, ethnic cleansing and crimes against humanity. In this context, we are prepared to take collective action, in a timely and decisive manner, through the Security Council, in accordance with the Charter, including Chapter VII, on a case-by-case basis and in cooperation with relevant regional organizations as appropriate, should peaceful means be inadequate and national authorities manifestly fail to protect their populations from genocide, war crimes, ethnic cleansing and crimes against humanity.[68]

Note in the first paragraph the usual state-speak presenting states as entities apart from either "populations" or governments. What is novel, nonetheless, in this official declaration is the implied universal responsibility (of "the international community, through the United Nations") to protect people, if necessary, against their own governments. This amounts to a break with the classical UN tradition of Security Council intervention under chapter VII of the Charter in the cause of "international peace and security." In practice, this was action only where local state sovereignty had ceased to be effective, so that the intervention could ultimately be presented as restorative of sovereignty itself. "Responsibility to protect," on the other hand, definitely implies sovereignty-*breaking*.

Certainly, restricting the pretext for this action to prevention of the worst of crimes (the four listed above) amounts to a fairly small and logical addition to international humanitarian law; these crimes are precisely the ones that, according to the jurisprudence of that law (notably the Genocide Convention), outsiders have a duty to prevent. But the right of humanitarian intervention against sovereignty had not previously been linked explicitly, illogical though the omission may seem, with the cause of international peace and security. It took the end of the Cold War to remove that particular taboo. Making the link now was an admission that governments had previously been able to hide behind sovereignty to perpetrate the worst of crimes against their own people, as the UN secretary-general himself spelled out:

> The twentieth century was marred by the Holocaust, the killing fields of Cambodia, the genocide in Rwanda and the mass killings in Srebrenica [former Yugoslavia], the latter two under the watch of the Security Council and United Nations peacekeepers. Genocide, war crimes, ethnic cleansing and crimes against humanity: the brutal legacy of the twentieth century speaks bitterly and graphically of the profound failure of individual States to live up to their most basic and compelling responsibilities, as well as the collective inadequacies of international institutions. Those tragic events led my distinguished predecessor, Kofi Annan, and other world leaders to ask whether the United Nations and other international institutions should be exclusively focused on the security of States without regard to the safety of the people within them. Could sovereignty, the essential building block of the nation-State era and of the United Nations itself, they queried, be misused as a shield behind which mass violence could be inflicted on populations with impunity? How deeply and irreparably had the legitimacy and credibility of the United Nations and its partners been damaged by such revelations? Could we not find the will and the capacity in the new century to do better?

From now on, "sovereignty entailed enduring obligations towards one's people, as well as certain international privileges."[69]

A late admission, one might say, in the history of diplomacy; but better late than never. Even so, putting "responsibility to protect" into practice is likely to be difficult. For humanitarian intervention to become a norm of the *universal* states system would conflict with the older norm of non-intervention in the affairs of *particular* states ("the essential building block of the nation-State era"), and call into question the legitimacy of the system's institutions ("the United Nations itself"). UN delegations from conservative regimes, moreover, may still seek to block humanitarian intervention against sovereignty; and if they have real influence, a legitimacy crisis is inevitable at the apex of international power.

Even a laudable conception of state agency has the potential to throw the traditional ordering principles of international relations into disarray. The Good Samaritan state, like the original Good Samaritan, is a taboo-breaker. But one cannot have a system in which something is a norm and not a norm. International theory must be normative, to lead us out of such dilemmas.

Notes

1. Wendt, "The state as person in international theory," p. 294.
2. "Mandelson warns on China trade," BBC World News Online 17 October 2007.
3. "Tibet leader to get top US award," *ibid.*
4. I leave aside here the status of Taiwan.
5. For example, Isabel Hilton, *The Search for the Panchen Lama* (London: Viking, 1999). The Panchen Lama is second to the Dalai Lama in the hierarchy of Tibetan spiritual leaders.
6. On the young Dalai Lama see Heinrich Harrer, *Seven Years in Tibet* tr. Richard Graves [1952] (London: Harper Collins, 2005). I would add that this pious, humorous and humble man (who for many years confined himself to opposing the Chinese use of force in Tibet, rather than Chinese sovereignty-claims per se) soon became renowned worldwide for his dedication both to his suffering compatriots and to the cause of international peace; which proves the folly and guilt of successive PRC governments in criticising his regime and persecuting the Tibetan resistance.
7. Reynolds, *An Introduction to International Relations* (1st. ed. 1970), pp. 46–47.
8. Runciman, "Moral responsibility and the problem of representing the state," pp. 42–43, 45–46.
9. Wight, *Agents, Structures and International Relations*, pp. 195–197.
10. Cf. "state actions should . . . be understood as the emergent, often unintended and complex result of what rival agents within states have done and are doing on a complex strategic terrain." *Ibid.*, p. 223.
11. *Ibid.*, pp. 196–197.
12. Cf. Moya, *The Philosophy of Action*, p. 167.
13. Wight, *Agents, Structures and International Relations*, p. 197.
14. See John and Ann Tusa, *The Nuremberg Trial* (London: Macmillan, 1983).
15. This impersonal duty is characteristic only of modern societies. Before going to work in Saudi Arabia, I was instructed by my employers not to intervene to help the victims of a public (say, a road) accident in that country. This was because of the patriarchal Koranic law in force there, based on kinship communities. To intervene even constructively across its human boundaries

was to make oneself liable for consequences—and incur (or cause one's employers to incur) responsibility for any compensation that must be paid. In the lore of ancient Israel—governed by the same patriarchal Semitic tradition—this was the law that the Good Samaritan broke.

16. Daniela Kroslak, "The responsibility of collective external bystanders in cases of genocide: the French in Rwanda," in Toni Erskine (ed.), *Can Institutions Have Responsibilities?*, pp. 159–182.

17. Further on the 1994 Rwanda genocide see below, Conclusion.

18. The liability involved both direct shipments of Swiss products overseas and relabeled trans-shipments from Swiss airports of products from other countries. The Swiss civil servants whom I interviewed in connection with these cases affected to laugh off their implications, and made clear their regret that the authorities had been obliged to change the law. See Peter Lomas, "Switzerland" in Harald Müller (ed.), *How Western European Nuclear Policy is Made* (London: Macmillan, 1991), pp. 220–221 and notes.

19. Tomohisa Hattori, "Is it real? The question of juridical, actual and causal responsibility in sovereign debt settlements" in Joseph and Wight (eds.), *Scientific Realism and International Relations*, pp. 115–128.

20. *Ibid.*, pp. 122 and 123.

21. *Ibid.*, pp. 122–123, 124–125, emphasis in original.

22. Quoted in Singer and Ansari, *Rich and Poor Countries*, p. 223.

23. Susan George went further, alleging, with evidence, that the borrowing and the embezzlement were one and the same phenomenon, and there was never any real intention to use foreign loans for the purpose of domestic investment. See Susan George, *A Fate Worse Than Debt* (rev. ed. London: Penguin, 1989), ch. 8.

24. Susan Strange, *The Retreat of the State*, pp. xii, 4–5 and 108.

25. For US–oriented views see Paul R. Verkuil, *Outsourcing Sovereignty* (New York: Cambridge University Press, 2007), and Michael Sandel, *What Money Can't Buy: The Moral Limits of Markets* (New York: Farrar, Strauss and Giroux, 2012).

26. "If we do not find ways to safeguard the world economy before a succession of stock market collapses and bank failures eventually lands us all in a twenty–year economic recession . . . then no one is going to be in a mood to worry overmuch about the long-term problems of the environment." Susan Strange, "The Westfailure system, 1999" in Roger Tooze and Christopher May (eds.), *Authority and Markets: Susan Strange's Writings on International Political Economy* (Basingstoke: Palgrave Macmillan, 2002), p. 246.

27. Berki, "On Marxian thought and the problem of international relations."

28. Take the dispute over the Bakassi Peninsula between Nigeria and Cameroon, formally concluded by the ICJ judgment of October 10, 2002. To mention only two issues: the inhabitants of the peninsula, classed as Cameroonians by the judgment, mostly claimed to be Nigerians of long standing; and there was fishing and offshore drilling for oil within exclusive economic zones. Full details of the case are at www.icj-cij.org

29. Further on this problem see Arie M. Kakowicz, "The problem of peaceful territorial change," *International Studies Quarterly* 38 (2), June 1994, pp. 219–54, and Paul Gilbert, "Prolegomena to an ethics of secession' in

Moorhead Wright, *Morality and International Relations: Concepts and Issues* (Aldershot: Avebury, 1996), pp. 53–71.

30. The same is true of the *taiga* or boreal forest, which however grows at latitudes inhospitable to human habitation.

31. Berki, "On Marxian thought and the problem of international relations," p. 102.

32. Paul Collier, *The Bottom Billion: Why the Poorest Countries are Failing and What Can Be Done About It* (Oxford: Oxford University Press, 2008), ch. 3.

33. Or blaming them (here, Americans), as in the case of Venezuela.

34. An exception is the 1982 UN Convention on the Law of the Sea (UNCLOS), with its provisions for landlocked populations. But of course the sea is precisely the resource on earth that it is the most impractical to enclose.

35. See Robin Lane Fox, *The Classical World: An Epic History of Greece and Rome* (London: Allen Lane, 2005).

36. Robert H. Jackson, *Quasi-States: Sovereignty, International Relations and the Third World* (Cambridge: Cambridge University Press, 1990), p. 21.

37. Review of *Quasi-States* by R. B. J. Walker in *Canadian Journal of Political Science/Revue Canadienne de Science Politique* 25 (4), December 1992, p. 805.

38. Jackson, *Quasi-States*, pp. 24 and 23 respectively.

39. William Bain, "Saving failed states: trusteeship as an arrangement of security" in Bain (ed.), *The Empire of Security and the Safety of the People* (Abingdon/New York: Routledge, 2006), pp. 188–205.

40. Following the earthquake in Haiti of January 12, 2010, former US Senator Mel Martínez (Republican, Florida) proposed that Haiti become a United Nations mandate. In light of this and other natural disasters, and endemic corruption and political violence, Haiti was, he said, a failed state (BBC Radio 4, "The World at One," 17 January 2010).

41. Benedict Kingsbury, "Sovereignty and inequality" in Andrew Hurrell and Ngaire Woods (eds.), *Inequality, Globalization and World Politics* (Oxford: Oxford University Press, 1999), p. 88.

42. Georg Sørensen, "States are not 'like units': types of state and forms of anarchy in the present international system," *Journal of Political Philosophy* 6 (1), March 1998, pp. 86–88, 94, and 95.

43. Sørensen, "States are not 'like units,'" pp. 79, 86, 91.

44. Hobson, *The State and International Relations*, p. 226.

45. *Ibid.*, p. 7, original italics; cf. Ashley, "Untying the sovereign state," p. 245.

46. Martha Finnemore, *National Interests in International Society* (Ithaca, NY: Cornell University Press, 1996).

47. Cited in Hobson, *The State and International Relations*, pp. 152–154.

48. *Ibid.*, pp. 208–209.

49. Paul Kennedy, *The Rise and Fall of the Great Powers: Economic Change and Military Conflict from 1500 to 2000* (New York: Random House, 1988); Immanuel Wallerstein, *The Modern World-System* (San Diego: Academic Press, 1974, 1980 and 1989).

50. Philip Bobbitt, *The Shield of Achilles: War, Peace and the Course of History* (London: Penguin, 2003), p. 153.

51. Brewer, *Marxist Theories of Imperialism* (2nd ed.), p. 6.

52. Brent J. Steele, *Ontological Security in International Relations* (London/New York: Routledge, 2008), pp. 18, 64, 65.

53. E.g. Sir Adam Roberts, "Intervention: beyond 'dictatorial interference'" in Bain (ed.), *The Empire of Security and the Safety of the People*, pp. 158–87; Nicholas J. Wheeler, *Saving Strangers: Humanitarian Intervention in International Society* (Oxford: Oxford University Press, 2000).

54. See Hedley Bull, *Justice in International Relations: 1983–84 Hagey Lectures* (Waterloo, Ontario: University of Waterloo, 1984).

55. The Indian intervention in East Pakistan/Bangladesh in 1971, the Vietnamese invasion of Pol Pot–led Cambodia in 1978–79, and the Tanzanian invasion of Idi Amin–led Uganda, also in 1979. Wheeler, *Saving Strangers*.

56. R. J. Vincent, *Nonintervention and International Order* (Cambridge: Cambridge University Press, 1974).

57. See the emotive study of the Rwanda genocide by Philip Gourevitch, *We Wish To Inform You That Tomorrow We Will be Killed With Our Families* (New York: Farrar, Strauss and Giroux, 1998).

58. Kosova was then a province of Serbia.

59. See for example Samir Al-Khalil, *Republic of Fear* (London: Hutchinson, 1989).

60. Chapter I, article 2 (7).

61. The initial attempt to protect the Kosovars by a NATO air campaign in 1999 was ineffective, owing to the survival and self-concealment abilities of the Serbian ground forces, who were left free to continue their "ethnic cleansing" of Kosovar society. This setback was traceable to differences within the NATO alliance: the US government had opposed a ground invasion, and this policy of the most powerful alliance member prevailed. So the Kosovars' suffering was prolonged, both deliberately by abuses by the Serbian armed forces and accidentally by the ill-informed NATO bombing, in which local people also died. It took a NATO ground invasion from Macedonia, combined with bombing of Serbian territory proper, to effect a Serbian military withdrawal from Kosova, by which time many of the supposedly-protected inhabitants of the province had perished.

62. British armed forces on a UN peacekeeping mission in Sierra Leone in 2000 became embroiled in the country's civil war when some of their number were kidnapped by rebels and had to be forcefully rescued from the interior. The resultant defeat of the rebel forces (armed and remote-controlled from Liberia, and responsible for countless atrocities against civilians) helped to end the civil war and so arguably was of unqualified benefit for Sierra Leonean people in general.

63. Cf. Gordon Graham, "Morality, international relations and the domestic analogy" in Moorehead Wright (ed.), *Morality and International Relations*, pp. 5–16.

64. N. J. Rengger, *International Relations, Political Theory and the Problem of Order* (London/New York: Routledge, 2000), p. 91.

65. Nicholas J. Wheeler, "Agency, humanitarianism and intervention," *International Political Science Review/Revue internationale de science politique* 18 (1), January 1997, p. 10, emphasis in original.

66. *Independent Inquiry into the actions of the United Nations during the 1994 genocide in Rwanda*, UN Report S/1999/1257 in English, p. 1. UN secretary-general Kofi Annan was influential in this regard; he had been the head of UN peacekeeping during the Rwanda genocide. See also the testimony of

the UN peacekeeping force commander, Lt.-Gen. Roméo Dallaire, *Shake Hands with the Devil: The Failure of Humanity in Rwanda* (London: Arrow Books, 2004).

67. *Responsibility to Protect: Report of the International Commission on Intervention and State Sovereignty* (Ottawa: International Development Research Centre, 2001).

68. UN General Assembly Resolution A/60/L.1.

69. *Implementing the responsibility to protect: Report of the UN Secretary-General* [Ban Ki-Moon], UN General Assembly Resolution A/63/677, 12 January 2009, paragraphs 5 and 7.

IV

Debates in Theory

10

Meta-theory and Modernity

In this section I review some theoretical debates in the light of my general argument. In the following two chapters I consider Kantian theory. In this chapter I look at some recent alternatives to traditional empirical and Realist approaches. First comes constructivism, which has involved the importation of ideas from social theory. Later I look at scientific realism and post-modernism. Finally I include a brief note on a feminist approach.

10.1 Constructivism

Here an awkward problem crops up from the outset: constructivism, despite having been intensively promoted in international studies, is highly elusive of definition. The fact that it is often qualified as *social* constructivism points to the approach's origins in social theory. But this leads straight into ambiguity, as suggested by the following typical comments:

> Constructivism is a social theory and not a substantive theory of international politics.

> Constructivism is empty as far as assumptions, propositions, or hypotheses about international relations are concerned.

> Constructivism is not a theory. . . . not an "ism" to be added to the list dominated in the IR studies by neorealism and neoliberalism.

> Constructivism is not a theory of international politics but a meta-theoretical position that embodies normative claims about what "good" social science ought to be.

> [Constructivism is], if anything, not an approach to international relations but rather a "meta-theoretical stance."

> Constructivism is *not* a theory itself.[1]

Fair enough, you might argue, for an approach with a history of application across various disciplines from the arts to psychology, education, and science.[2] But we still need to know what contribution, if any, constructivists can make to international theory.

Key Tenets

The following list sums up the constructivist tenets that are most commonly invoked in the context of international theory.

First and most important, societies and individuals co-constitute each other. Individuals have no intrinsic identity, isolated from their social settings and relationships. "Human beings collectively produce their own social realities."[3] Historical acknowledgments here to Durkheim.

Second, the interpretation of human behavior is of key importance, as part of individuals' self-definition in society. Acknowledgments here to Weber.

Third, the rules, norms, and institutions of human society depend on communicative acts (both spoken and written). This tenet is attributed to two near-simultaneous works by Nicholas Onuf and Friedrich Kratochwil.[4] In turn, in different places, with different emphases, the older inspirations of Wittgenstein and Habermas are acknowledged.

Fourth, Naturalism (the view that human life can be studied in the same way as non-human life) is rejected, on the grounds that human mental communication cannot be reduced to a physical or material phenomenon.[5] At the same time, philosophical idealism (the view that phenomena are reducible to events in the human mind) is rejected, because social relations involve not only shared ideas but even shared actions.[6]

Fifth, ideas and material forces are mutually influencing (acknowledgments here to Marx). In social perspective, structures produce agents and vice versa. "Social action produces social identities."[7] This tenet is familiar in international theory from the "agent-structure" debate.

Sixth, constructivists place an important emphasis on social change. In particular, it is stressed that constructivism came to prominence in international theory at the end of the Cold War, an event that Realists and other IR traditionalists not only failed to predict but seemed incapable of imagining. "The dramatic changes with the end of the Cold War and in its aftermath revealed the importance of historical context and raised questions about the transition from conflict to cooperation or from peace to war."[8]

Problems of Constructivism

Two things are immediately clear from this list. One is a great generality of terms. The other is the banality of the terms themselves. There
is ample space here for constructivists to talk past each other and not
connect, or connect only to clash. Even a sympathetic commentator
like Steve Smith finds that "there is little agreement over what social
constructivism entails," while Patrick Thaddeus Jackson calls constructivism "a methodologically meaningless category." For the defense,
Kratochwil says "we should not be surprised that concrete phenomena
are susceptible to competing explanations"; but, he adds, this kind
of "pluralism cannot be of the type that argues 'anything goes.' . . .
Consideration of methods and meta-theoretical issues, important as
they are, are not substitutes for substantive discussions of the political problems we all face." Knud Erik Jørgensen rather unhelpfully but
perhaps typically observes that "almost every possible paradigm in IR
can be cast in a constructivist mode."[9]

This vagueness might be reinterpreted as unobjectionableness: the
terms of constructivism are individually true *because* they are banal.
Let us look at my list of key tenets in detail. Consider the first one that
societies and individuals are "co-constituted." Surely this has always
been the case in human life. No man is an island, et cetera. If methodological individualism has featured powerfully in the study of modern
society, then perhaps we should attribute this success to limitations in
that society and its intellectual support systems, nothing more.

Certainly the basic premises of methodological individualism and,
relatedly, positivism (as extreme empiricism) are easily exposed as
restrictive, even mistaken—the first, that individuals count overwhelmingly as the object of analysis; the second, that only individuals and their
sense-experiences are real. In a context of social theory, such starting
points are patently self-defeating. At the same time, they are no longer
so influential in our developed mass-communication societies, where
a range of theoretical approaches circulates, even within government.
In international studies, the stranglehold of positivism has been well
and truly broken.

Second and third on the list of tenets: the argument that our identities
as individuals, and as societies manifested in culture and institutions,
are established by a process of communication and mutual identification, seems an uncontroversial reflection on a world we like to consider
organized, and full of individuals aspiring to better their critical faculties

through education. But it is also a world from which pre-modern societies are fast disappearing, and where social anthropologists have given us cause to reflect on what might be lost to human culture in the process. Profounder insights seem likely from that direction.

Fourth, that a crude Naturalism is to be rejected seems, once again, a sound basic argument. That much, surely, is shown by the diversity of human culture and society that international studies and social anthropology together reveal. Yet even here there are dissenters enough to confuse matters. Karin Fierke asserts that "there are no significant methodological differences between (conservative) constructivists and rationalists"; while "many constructivist scholars seek to occupy the middle ground between positivism and post-positivism," according to Jennifer Sterling-Folker. But such middle ground must be very narrow, if post-positivism means refuting positivism; or very crowded, if constructivism is as various as its advocates claim.[10]

Fifth, dominant though we humans may be through our ingenuity, the constitution of our society is influenced by material restraints, reduced only by our efficient use of science and technology. That too is a fair point. But like other arguments from constructivism, it is a truism—true only as platitudes are true, and about as valuable. It is just one of the many insights attributed to Marx which on closer examination come down to common sense.

A close appraisal of constructivist tenets, then, confirms the impression of a great generality of argument with little substance or originality, and ample room for contradiction.

Hazards of Meta-theory

Even a friendly critic like Andrew Moravcsik finds this frustrating. His reaction is illustrative in a number of ways. First, reviewing a set of essays on European integration, he writes of constructivists' "characteristic unwillingness . . . to place their claims at any real risk of empirical disconfirmation. *Hardly a single claim in this volume is formulated or tested in such a way that it could, even in principle, be declared empirically invalid.*" (His emphasis.) He further laments "the near absence of two critical elements of social science, each designed to put conjectures at risk: (1) distinctive testable hypotheses, (2) methods to test such hypotheses against alternative theories or a null hypothesis of random state behavior."

The last seven words look very like my argument against state agency as such. But leaving this aside for a moment, Moravcsik's objections matter because he is clearly genuinely interested in constructivist (or "interpretivist") claims—here, that influential individuals in the EC/EU integration project have been guided down the years by an ordered set of ideas; that they knew what they were doing as they developed the institutions. In the event, he thinks this thesis would be "disconfirmed" by empirical evidence, properly adduced.[11] Yet he finds the constructivists' methodology unhelpful in deciding the matter one way or the other.

Elsewhere he has argued: "The primacy accorded by social science method to theory, method and empirics makes sense only if we assume that its distinctive purpose is to illuminate patterns of cause-and-effect relations in the concrete empirical world of politics." This echoes Kratochwil's warning to constructivists that meta-theory (the theory of theory itself) cannot replace "substantive discussions of the political problems we all face." Meanwhile, Moravcsik's own declared aim of synthesising theories suggests a rather flexible attitude.[12] So his denunciation of particular constructivists on a political question of importance *to them* is all the more damning.

There is a broader consideration here. The only really convincing argument for meta-theory—in international or any other studies—is that the world is too complex and unknowable for "distinctive testable hypotheses" to be made. Jørgensen's claim that constructivism is open to all paradigms of international relations, and the more common claim that constructivism is a social theory whose precise applications in international theory are not (or not yet) clear, express such a general uncertainty. But the argument would hardly apply to partial or *regional* studies of the world—least of all studies of Europe, a region about which, as Moravcsik points out, we have copious reliable information.[13] His complaint, therefore, that the constructivists whom he wishes to consult engage in too much meta-theory—instead of, as they claim, too little[14]—is very much to the point.

To this I would add an argument of my own: given the steady progress of EU integration toward something para-statal, studies of the EU by European citizens themselves are questionable as international studies and should be recast in terms of domestic politics or political theory. Moravscik's critique reveals a culpable vagueness among constructivists on one of the most interesting and important questions of our time. What exactly is the EU? A novel entity in the states system—something between a state and an intergovernmental organization; or a centralized state in the making? Can it subsist indefinitely as neither one nor the other? These questions have been around since the formation of the first "European Communities" but have noticeably been ducked by the politicians. Since the EU is a kind of permanent convention of democracies, these questions are of interest to non-Europeans as well. Europe as a center for democratic inspiration is an idea that goes back centuries. Kant praised political leaders who "thought of Europe as a single federated state, which they accepted as an arbiter in all their public disputes."[15]

It is also, I suggest, a matter of natural interest to Americans generally whether there will one day be a United States of Europe, as either a rival to American power or a cooperative partner—not least because people of European origin have predominated numerically, culturally, and politically in the United States of America since the foundation of that state. And it is of interest to people on both sides of the Atlantic, since the United States was founded as a transplanted European polity, on the grounds that freedoms tardy of realization in Europe could be realized elsewhere. African Americans had no choice but to become ex-Africans, but how should ex-Europeans in North America react now to the European Union project? Was the North American colonial experiment, in hindsight, worth it? In what terms? To whose gain, and whose loss? Is there a transatlantic political divide, or not? (Is Moravcsik himself, with his European name and his vocational focus on Europe, an ex-, or a would-be, European?) Given, moreover, the importance of Anglo-American writing in international theory, the political identity of the EU is surely a key question for all such theory in English, which is to say, effectively all of it. In all these respects it is highly ironic to find Moravcsik calling on European theorists to define the terms of their EU analysis better, while Steve Smith, the prime analyst on the EU side of the Atlantic, defends meta-theory in the form of constructivism.[16] Challenged, the navel-gazers opt for more navel-gazing. There are Swiftian ironies here.

To my mind the explanation for the long, but widely tolerated, confusion over the status of the European Union and its institutional antecedents is straightforward: this is an unstable but entirely unthreatening entity in a system already riddled with anomalies. The EU has the qualities both of a state (a parliament and, in the European Commission, a "government") and of an intergovernmental organization composed of sovereign states. Or rather, it has these qualities, but, since they might conflict, it has them incompletely. The EU is inchoate—unlike other intergovernmental organizations, which run on a very limited sacrifice of state sovereignty, and unlike states as such, where sovereignty is a key internal and external rationale. But there is no real pressure, either, for the EU to become definitively one thing or the other (despite this being an absolutely live political issue in EU society), because states, the main components of the world system, are themselves contested and inchoate in people's minds.

By the same token, large federated states with formally democratic institutions, like the United States, Canada, or Nigeria, may be seen to subsist indefinitely in a like ambiguous condition to the EU. That is, between externally orientated unity and internal devolution—a condition open to demagogic manipulation (concerning, say, American manifest destiny, Nigerian social cohesion, or, dare one mention it, Canadian national identity). At the same time, in all these places it is still possible for people to ask normal questions, like: what is a state, and what is it for?—unlike, say, in Russia or China.

What are we to make of a world with such fluid conceptual and moral boundaries? On all the evidence, however, constructivists merely mirror these dilemmas, instead of offering solutions.

Constructivism and the Cold War

As noted, constructivism is said to have come to prominence in international theory at the Cold War's end, because Realists and positivists failed to predict this historic development. Yet to value prediction at all suggests an attachment to one key principle of these discredited theorists of the past. Is this the "middle ground" Sterling-Volker speaks of? Again, some explanation seems missing here.

We might also ask, conversely, what is so special about international theorists that they should *not* have been as blind as the great mass of humankind subjugated by the Cold War. After all, the characteristic feature of the period, the means by which a climate of all-pervasive fear was maintained, was secrecy, in particular around nuclear arsenals. Secrecy is the absolute denial of the communicative act as the glue of human society. But here again, the lack of coherence in constructivists' claims is evident, because their own declared emphasis on communicative acts ought to have led them to attack Cold War secrecy before the conflict was over.

Clearly there are acts which are noncommunicative but also socially significant. This proves the triviality of Onuf's argument that all actions are reducible to communicative acts—culminating in his extraordinary suggestion that "ontological categories match functional categories of speech acts and rules," which is tantamount to saying that language defines the world.[17] Such assertions are contradicted in the most literal way by the practice of secrecy. An intending suicide bomber in your vicinity, or anyone who knows your life to be in danger but keeps the fact from you, is acting *un*-communicatively, but with potentially dramatic consequences, toward you. This kind of behavior, conducted on a global scale, was at the heart of the Cold War—its manipulation by deterrence theorists into an obfuscatory aura, the putative death wish of the human race; and in the end, because obfuscation and intimidation on this scale could not be indefinitely maintained, its sudden resolution, leading to the disappearance of the Soviet Union, the most secrecy-bound polity of all.

Secrecy also explains, on a less dramatic level, why constructivism had no effective currency in international theory before the Cold War's end, despite the claims made for it now. All academic observers of international relations were in a sense prisoners of deterrence, because they had to live in the world as it was—with the limits on information, and the biases on information, in public messages. But by the same token, the claim that, had we but known it, constructivism was there and in use all along (several authors have argued, for example, that the English School is constructivist[18]) is being wise after the event.

At this point, in any case, any special link between constructivism and historic change disappears. In respect of the Cold War it disappears because international theorists, like everyone else, were victims of the lack of real historic change that the Cold War represented. To that extent they could not help being useless, in the mass, as predictors of change. But more generally, a revisionist interpretation of an earlier school of thought, in any discipline, has the effect of blurring the stages in that discipline's development. And there is something dubious, is there not, in praising a school of thought on historic change which somehow got lost in the vicissitudes of intellectual fashion.

Semantic Ambiguity

The radical confusion over the meaning of constructivism and its applications in international studies seems to me traceable to a certain semantic ambiguity at the heart of this approach. Two variations on the word "construct" are in play, as follows.

One, construction in the sense of interpretation, or *construal*, as when we speak about "placing a certain construction" on someone's remark or action.

Two, construction in the specialized sense used in social theory, of *constituting* a practice or institution in society—that is, bringing it into force by collective action.

Confusing these two senses only weakens the meaning of both.[19] Take the constructivist tenet of "co-constitution." In social theory, it means that individual and collective identity are mutually established, through social interactions. But this will not get us very far in the complex domain of the world as a whole. To assert that an individual or a group's identity is established (constituted) through interpretation (construal) of others' actions is to place a rather low value on character, intelligence, and initiative as forces of social cohesion, or as talents enabling individuals to make life-changing choices. Lions and monkeys on the African savannah could be said to engage in construal/constitution of their species identities, and to build group solidarity by contradistinction from other groups. Is this all constructivism means? As social science, and particularly as international theory, it seems to me contemptibly superficial.

Similarly, with regard to international law Christian Reus-Smit has argued:

> The Constructivist account . . . is under-specified and underdeveloped. This is evident principally in Constructivist arguments about the difference between social and legal norms. Constructivists tend to speak of norms in general, and they often slide, almost unconsciously, between different categories of norms—social, legal, political, or moral. For many theoretical purposes this is relatively unproblematic, but it inhibits the development of a coherent Constructivist account of the nature and functioning of international law.[20]

As I mentioned earlier, constructivism can even appear to mean contradictory things—either to establish a valid social identity on the basis of agreed norms, or to impose an invented one, by dint of having greater power in society. This becomes clear the moment a normative element is introduced into the argument. Take J. Ann Tickner's warning against gender stereotyping in international theory. "In everyday usage," she writes, "gender denotes the biological sex of individuals. However, feminists define gender differently—as a set of socially and culturally constructed characteristics that vary across time and place."[21] "Socially and culturally constructed" in this context means *questionable*, against a background of arbitrary power exercised by some people (men) over others (women). It means precisely the opposite of Tickner's verb "define," as lies are the opposite of truth. Constructivism here is shown worse than vague—it is Janus-faced.

A Minimal Theory of International Relations

It is also interesting to note a reaction by Wendt to the work of Onuf, considered the founder of constructivist international theory (and since Wendt himself has been called a constructivist). The "proliferation," he writes, of

> first-order theorizing about the structure and dynamics of the international system . . . has helped open the door since the mid-1980s to a wave of second-order or meta-theorizing in the field. The objective of this type of theorizing is also to increase our understanding of world politics, but it does so indirectly by focusing on the ontological and epistemological issues of what constitutes important or legitimate questions and answers for IR scholarship, rather than on the structure and dynamics of the international system *per se.*[22]

What then *would* constitute a valid theory of "the structure and dynamics of the international system"? At a minimum, I suggest the following.

First, it must refer to some concrete event, or pattern of concrete events (historical or contemporary), in human relations. Otherwise it fails on empirical grounds and is mere naked meta-theory.

Second, it must refer to these phenomena in the context of humankind as a whole. Otherwise it fails as (for want of a better term) international theory.

Third, it must give a clear, logical and consistent account of the phenomena in question. Otherwise it fails simply as theory.

Onuf's *World of Our Making* falls down comprehensively on the first of these counts. As Wendt complains, "very little *happens* in the world [Onuf] describes."[23] Even as bare theory Onuf's book presents major difficulties of interpretation; as a collection of ideas from secondary sources with little attempt at integration, it does not so much fall down as crash and burn. This is best seen in his concluding "synoptic table," an assemblage of words that I find overpoweringly fanciful and confused. "Paradigms of Experience," including "assertive speech acts" and "instructions-rules," are set down there alongside an injunction ("tell the truth"), people ("priests and professors"), and vague abstractions ("global comparison," "standing"; "touching"). These "categories of existence and the constitution/regulation of its meaning in space and time" make little empirical sense. The same may be said of the categories listed under "Faculties of Experience." Yet without this final synopsis we would be at a loss to grasp any cohesive intention on the author's part at all.[24]

Onuf's intellectual thrust is also weakened by his concessions to post-modernism, with its fatal flaw of wordplay. He collapses "rules" and "rule" into one, with reactionary overtones (rule as institutional authority is not necessarily the same as rules of social behavior, and arguably should not be). The price of detachment here is not simply excessive abstraction, but the impression that no one need care very much if international theory left human relations unchanged. It comes as no surprise, either, to find Vendulka Kubálková, in a work part edited with Onuf, suggesting in one place that his approach typifies constructivism and in another that it is unique.[25] Such intellectual promiscuity is possible only around an approach which lacks clear definition or practical relevance.

Onuf himself seems to believe it is unimportant for observers of collective social behavior to have a theory of international relations at all.[26] But it is not the world that is "socially constructed." The world is a fact, the fact of human dominance. It is the states system that is socially constructed, with all the sceptical implications that that expression seems, more often than not, to carry. It is the states system that constitutes an artificial form of human organization, imposed on each and every one of us. Constructivists, then, must have a theory of international relations—of *social* relations under the *states* system—because everyone must.

In this connection Raymond Cohen has developed an interesting empirical approach showing rules of communication as essential to order in a domain of states that is itself *sui generis*. His account is not free of the reifications and intellectual shortcuts of state agency, but Cohen is refreshingly eclectic in applying a combination of game theory, diplomatic theory, and normative considerations to case-studies in international relations, based on a flexible concept of rules (after all, rules are always at bottom *ad hoc*; there are rules for games, and rules for dear life). The result is too modest to count as full-blown international theory, but it is more concretely intelligible, and of greater human interest, than the typical constructivist approach to rules through meta-theory.[27]

State Agency Again

One might also think that an approach based on analytical principles would make it impossible to treat states and societies as synonymous and agents in their own right. But examples of this questionable practice are not hard to find among constructivists.

> A social structure leaves more space for agency, that is, for the individual or state to influence their environment, as well as to be influenced by it. . . . The USA and Britain have evolved as friends, while other states are enemies. Many states within the European Union (EU) are former enemies who have learned to cooperate.
>
> States, including great powers, crave legitimacy . . . [states] value these new institutions not because they truly believe that they are superior, but rather because they are symbols that will attract resources. . . . Iran's nuclear ambitions might owe to its desire for regional dominance. . . .
>
> [S]ocial relationships that are contingent to a large extent on how nation-states think about and interact with one another. . . .
>
> States might behave alike because of a common situation that none of them can hope to escape . . . states need only respond rationally . . . the efforts of leading states to best their peers. . . .
>
> When an individual or a state seeks to justify their behaviour. . . .[28]

Here is more nonsense-talk. In one instance the reified state agent is an "it" ("Iran"), in others a quasi-person, indicated by "who" ("former enemies who . . ."). In another, the uncertainty over the exact subject of the actions in question is increased by the sloppy English usage of "their" to cover indiscriminately what must logically be either "his"/"her" or "its" ("for the individual *or state* to influence *their* environment"; "an individual or a state seeks [*sic*] to justify their [*sic*] behaviour"). Not to mention states craving, states believing, states hoping, states besting . . . has anyone producing such assertions ever stopped to consider what, concretely, is meant by them?

One can even find, in constructivist texts, the false "actions" of state agents being described immediately alongside those of real agents (governments, non-governmental organizations, societies):

> Although the structure of the cold war seemingly locked the USA and the Soviet Union into a fight to the death, leaders on both sides creatively transformed their relations and, with it, the very structure of global politics.
>
> . . . frequently states adopt particular models because of their symbolic standing. Many Third World governments have acquired

very expensive weapons systems that have very little military value because they convey to others that they are sophisticates and are a part of the "club."[29]

Personally I would resist the idea that people in the United States and the Soviet Union, during the Cold War, would ever have wanted to "fight to the death"—but not that their leaders subsequently "transformed their relations" (though again, it is not clear whether "their" refers to the leaders or the unmentioned peoples, and who is to get the credit for the transformation). Similarly, no one would deny that certain *governments* have on occasion wastefully acquired weapons for show, but it is not clear how *states* for this purpose can "adopt particular models"—a term Michael Barnett uses, in this essay, in the loosest possible way, both objectively for his own notation of others' behavior, and reflexively to denote agents' own perception of themselves.

The latter assertion, moreover, is followed by the even cruder one part-quoted earlier, which for its appalling tendentiousness I give in full: "Iran's nuclear ambitions [*sic*] might owe to its desire [*sic*] for regional dominance, but it could also be that it wants [*sic*] to own this ultimate status symbol." In this essay littered with the anthropomorphism of states, it is very important for us to know (but we are not told) whether the author thinks that Iranian people in general are guilty of the fanatical and merciless attitude to non-Iranians that could be assumed from his language.

As for the revisionist interpretation of the English School as constructivist, with its cardinal principle of a "society of states" (i.e., state agents), this claim must fail for a different reason from that which I have suggested above. The "society of states" expression by itself implies a normative approach; but the one thing that can be said for certain about the norms of nineteenth-century European diplomacy, so important for the English School, is that they never involved peoples at large consciously and democratically construing/constituting their ministers and delegations as "the state," because the institutions and freedoms required for this overt reification did not exist. Accountability for foreign policy came—when it came—top-down, as a concession by governments, discernible only in retrospect, as Hobson makes clear.[30] Once this is established, all that remains of the English School is a set of genteel, but of course wholly imaginary, state agents taking their own formal-legal system at face value. Constructivism by its very generality should lead us to call the bluff of assumed terms, and in respect of the English School this is one call which is likely to succeed.

Let's Be Constructive

I would advocate a third but more everyday variant on "construct." This is "constructive," in the ordinary usage of "well-intentioned'—said of a person—or "having the quality of contributing helpfully"—said of an action or intention (OED).

Constructive actions and proposals in this sense are explicitly normative, even prescriptive, whether on conflict resolution in the Middle East, or disarmament, or economic justice, or human rights. Onora O'Neill makes the case for a Kantian conception of cosmopolitan justice and virtue which would be both constructivist, in the framework-making sense, and constructive in the normative sense.[31] In support of her approach I would recall Kant's insistence, in the very first sentence of his *Groundwork*, on the importance of goodwill.[32] Having a sincere goodwill is the very definition of being constructive—well-intentioned, positive, hopeful, and benign, always seeking the best outcome in our actions, especially toward strangers.

Even so, O'Neill's approach has problems of its own, as Katrin Flikschuh points out. She argues that Kant produced a reduced version of metaphysics; then that Rawls, with his "Kantian constructivism," adopted this version, avoiding the question of metaphysical foundations altogether; and finally, that O'Neill thins out Rawls's approach, falling into difficulties in her account of agency. Eventually, Flikschuh argues, O'Neill's thesis can be rescued on condition of returning to the original Kantian source, while stopping short of the full defense of metaphysics that she (Flikschuh) prefers. All of which shows the hazards of meta-theory, and the inherently trivializing nature of the decision, in the face of moral dilemmas, to adopt "a constructivist approach, where no foundations are assumed as given."[33]

Meta-theory Is Not Metaphysics . . .

In order to satisfy at one go my minimal criteria for a theory of international relations, we clearly need an approach which is both fundamental and holistic. But in this context the remark, by three of its advocates, that constructivism is "an alternative ontology, a redescription of the world"[34] is to miss the point entirely. There can be no "alternative" ontology, or "ontologies" in the plural, only better or worse (I would say, only Realist) versions of that comprehensive undertaking: accounts of reality as a whole, going back to philosophical first principles and asking to be judged as such, before we can begin to determine what we mean by international relations.[35] As I have also argued, the best (most complete) account of reality is anchored in moral ideas. So there is a strong distinction to be made between metaphysics, which needs no special justification, and meta-theory, which continually requires one.

Think about it: a theory is a hypothetical description of phenomena which becomes an actual—a true—description when evidence is adduced to support it. But why would anyone want a hypothetical description of a hypothetical description? This brings me back to the question raised by Moravcsik's critique. What kind of theory is left, if we find the world too complex and unknowable for "distinctive testable hypotheses"? At first sight, something novel and unclassifiable, with elastic conceptual boundaries, as constructivism apparently is. But here again I am at one with the sceptical Moravcsik. Most people instinctively resist the idea of incommensurable complexity. In addition, there are already worked-out methods in philosophy for coping with complexity. As Hume argued, we can happily ignore (he said burn!) any text which is not open to either inductive or deductive analysis. So we can criticize a given theory, on any subject, for either its logical flaws or its apparent inadequacy in the light of experience. But there is no need to erect a novel theory from complexity itself. The kind of intellectual debate to which such an approach gives rise is not a real debate, but only a debate in theory. Unless, that is, the complexity of the world since Hume's clarification is found to be especially intractable. Of this view (post-modernism) I shall have more to say below. But otherwise, constructivism has no case.

... or Moral Either

At the opposite pole to Moravcsik, Ronen Palan argues that constructivism (never, he says, "a well-defined sociological approach") has been adopted by international theorists for their own ends, in an over-eclectic and confused way; he is critical of both Onuf and Wendt. He regards this experience as a lost opportunity to develop insights from some original social theory of the twentieth century, though he does not even hint at an alternative approach of his own.

Once again, behind these parallel but never-meeting critiques of the same object, it is possible to discern an uneasy transatlantic relationship. So Moravcsik wonders why analysts in the EU, faced with this novel political entity, choose the abstract methodology of constructivism instead of the traditional empiricism that theorists on both sides of the Atlantic have excelled in; while Palan argues that the Americans Onuf and Wendt, in their forays into International Relations, are seeking to reinvent the wheel of radical social theory (originally invented, he means, by the Europeans Cassirer, Wittgenstein and Lacan).[36]

The elephant in this rather large intellectual room, darkened by the shadow of the Cold War, is Marx, the father of all radical social theory. But if Marx himself had not been so tainted with determinism, a clearer vision might have emerged of the kind of society which could develop simultaneously, on both sides of the Atlantic, if principles of justice were to be applied. And if theorists on both sides were to focus on real human relations and concrete moral concerns, instead of tussling over ill-defined abstractions, they would find fewer reasons to disagree.

10.2 Scientific Realism and the Mechanics of Social Imagining

Scientific realism has entered international studies through the "agent-structure" debate. Colin Wight provides a critical account of the connection. Like many recent theorists, especially on the European side of the Atlantic, he begins by condemning out of hand the positivism which was dominant in international studies during the Cold War.[37] His proffered alternative is to deepen the thrust of ideas from social theory, drawing on Roy Bhaskar's pioneering effort to synthesize social and "natural" science.[38]

The main value, in my view, of Bhaskar's project is to have undermined positivism and methodological individualism from the inside, as it were, by showing the "scientific" principles of these well-worn approaches to be false, as well as inhumane. What is rejected above all is a simplistic emphasis on "the facts"—ostensibly, knowledge accumulated through the sensory experiences of individuals working alone. As both Bhaskar and Wight point out, this is not how modern scientists really work. Or, indeed, how they *could* work; for without some concept of an overarching whole to begin with, scientists would have nothing firm by which to order their observations. So biologists, for example, start with models of the whole field of nature in their minds, and find the best "depth explanation" of phenomena through serial tests of the models.[39]

Unobservables

Modern science is holistic in another sense too—in its social inclusion of scientists, primarily as members of teams of investigators.

Increasingly, theories of natural phenomena are formed nowadays by incorporating unobservable entities, on levels of experience unfamiliar to our senses or Newtonian values but established by social consensus. That quarks, for example, might exist despite the fact that we cannot see or touch them, is the product of agreement first between scientific practitioners, and subsequently between them and the rest of us, the lay-people who accept their methodology and trust their integrity. In this way, atoms and atomic structure have acquired their status as accepted knowledge. Unexamined notions of scientific objectivity become displaced by intersubjectivity. The once-only acquisition of immutable truths "out there," waiting for lone prospectors to discover them, gives way to socially established and -revisable science.

In this connection Rudolf Carnap argued that objectivity can be sought in two forms. One is "objectivity in contrast to arbitrariness: if a judgment is said to reflect knowledge, then this means that it does not depend on my whims."

> Secondly, by objectivity is sometimes meant independence from the judging subject, validity which holds also for other subjects. It is precisely this intersubjectivity which is an essential feature of "reality"; it serves to distinguish reality from dream and deception.[40]

Whether we employ whim-free judgment, therefore, or ask others to confirm our experience, we seek the same thing: dependable knowledge. Either way, the search for absolute objectivity is revealed as misguided. For any inquirer into reality to attempt to proceed alone, with no systematic guide to next steps, no other concept of the real than his own fragmentary, accident-prone, easily misdirected experience, is unlikely to lead to any higher understanding and may rule out integrated human thought altogether. It is much more true to life to think of scientists determining their findings by agreement with—or in competition with—other scientists, according to pre-established principles and in awareness of the social applications of their work. And it is unfair to expect any seekers after truth to leave their imaginations, their education, their culture, and their personal and social relations behind.

Social Facts

Intersubjective or socially established knowledge, then, makes even "natural" science into a social activity. Conversely, social theory gains from incorporating intangible things, as scientific models of the world are intangible. On this view society itself, though we cannot see or touch it, is real and has an independent existence. There are "social facts" (as Durkheim's *le fait social* is usually rendered), based on shared (including scientific) culture. Modern civilization, said Bhaskar, is built on "intransitive objects of knowledge . . . the laws of nature, the entities, structures and mechanisms which are often not empirically 'observable,'"[41] but no less real to us for that.

Now agreement among individual human beings that a given society exists is the original intersubjective step—a leap of faith in the collectivity. This premise would also, on the face of it, accommodate those intangible things, states. But more deeply, it suggests that the idea of states as person-like agents must logically give way to the analysis of human action, especially group action, on the basis of intersubjective understandings. This rules out any facile acceptance of state agency, and as I mentioned earlier, Colin Wight is one of the rare commentators to single out this conventional device for criticism.

So far, so good. Scientific realism provides arguments for the construal/constitution of society and social institutions "from the inside," in people's heads. It is the diametrical opposite of methodological individualism, which may be neither social nor reliable as a representation of reality. Agreement that quarks exist, or might exist, involves a collective leap of faith, not unlike the one we take when we acknowledge that social wholes exist in addition to, but encompassing, ourselves as individuals.[42]

Not unlike, but not the same as: because the first refers to our relations with non-human things, and the second to our relations with each other. In the form of ontology I propose, these are distinct domains, but hierarchically linked: our relations with each other subsume (include, with a secondary importance) our relations with non-human things—and it takes a normative, a moral-minded approach to see the difference. When we focus on human social practices, we understand our dominance in nature. Through this understanding our distinctness from, and responsibility to, other life-forms crystallizes as morality.

Wight refers only glancingly to normative theory. "What distinguishes scientific knowledge from other forms of knowledge," he says, "is its explanatory content."[43] This remark places him among those who wish to marginalize normative theory in international studies—an approach which I have argued is inadequate and misleading. Despite, then, the high level of generality on which he argues, and despite his own claims to the contrary, Wight comes very close to reducing international theory to questions of method; and though the Wight/Bhaskar thesis rests on a sophisticated form of Naturalism, it is still Naturalism, applying similar terms of analysis to human and non-human life.

Wight's approach is rooted, in my view, in an intellectual project, like Bhaskar's original one, of reforming social theory without entering critically into the metaphysical tie which binds the science of nature to the study of society. Bhaskar himself has moved away from this position, toward theosophy.[44] I support the Wight/Bhaskar view that shared ideas are real and important; I believe in the leap of faith we take in accepting the existence of atoms or of human society as such. But these are different things, and to equate the perception of them, however loosely, is to play down the distinctiveness of human beings, on whom the exact perception of all relations depends.

Agency/Structure

Wight's own approach helps to show how the concepts of agency and structure, from the "agent-structure" debate in international theory, are inseparable in practice. Yet he has no unified international theory of his own to replace the social theory–led versions he sees emerging from Wendt, Giddens, and the IR post-positivists, with whom he is in varying degrees of agreement. In part this is deliberate; he wants to show that a range of approaches is possible in international studies. His own thesis is copiously researched and informed. But it is still, like constructivism, meta-theory. It fails my test of a minimal international theory on the empirical level, as well as normatively. Despite the "international relations" in his title, he has no case-studies or extended examples of identified human interactions in the world.

Wight also fails to come to grips fully with the artificiality of created states and the falsity of state agency. On "the ontological status of the state, and more specifically, whether or not the state can legitimately be considered an agent," he remarks (quoting Jessop) that as a "structured organisational and institutional ensemble," it is not in itself an agent but may be the locus of agency/action.

> ... the state, as a complex institutional and organisational ensemble, can only exercise power insofar as its structural imperatives are realised in the practices and modes of thought of state officials. The state cannot exercise power independent of those agents that act on its behalf. How far and in what way such powers are realised will depend upon the action, reaction and interaction of specific social forces located within and beyond the complex ensemble. In short, the state does not exercise power, but constrains and/or enables embodied agents to act. It is these agents who activate the specific

powers and capacities of the state inscribed in particular institutions and organisations.[45]

Wight's own ontological explanations, however, are confusing. He urges us to see a state "as a structuratum, rather than as a real or fictive subject," by which he means a structure seen as a discrete but structured object, a structured structure. Insofar as this definition means anything at all (as opposed to what it looks like, a tautology), it indiscriminately straddles concrete and abstract things, states as ideas of social order and states as people and claimed territory.[46] Even then, it evokes more of a concrete object than I would agree to. Wight's approach depends on taking "institutions and organisations" as givens, whereas I would see institutions and organizations as ideas first and last. Like states, they may or may not outlast the people who populate them and believe in them.

Wight certainly distinguishes between the *forms* of agency likely to emerge under the auspices of democratic, as against undemocratic, institutions and organizations:

> the state can only be understood by examining the emergence of individual initiatives to develop and/or safeguard collective projects . . . state actions should not be attributed to the state as an originating subject, but rather should be understood as the emergent, often unintended and complex result of what rival agents within states have done and are doing on a complex strategic terrain.[47]

But this factually correct—to my way of thinking—assertion still lacks an explicit normative element (a quality suggested by those "collective projects"). When, for instance, there is a civil war or a revolution, effectively *no* state exists as a "result" of the actions of those "rival agents"; and under conditions of social inequality, many people will refuse to place their faith in state "institutions and organisations." States are then *normatively* invalidated.

Wight also expounds a tripartite conception of human agency, extending from the individual to the collective to the "social actor" (*sic*). But here again comes that lazy, ambiguous "actor" usage, adopted to depict public individuals ("diplomats, prime ministers, soldiers, generals and so on") indifferently as position-holders and role-players, mixing up subjects and objects in social and international theory.[48] My own emphasis, marked out against Hobbes, would be on the difference between literal/symbolic, and proxy/free, action—between *actors* and *agents*—and on the potential for ambiguity in simply all social actions in a world of states conceived as an end in itself. All questions of agency, moreover, given human dominance, lead to questions of responsibility. Real position-holders and role-players in public life must decide at some point where the dividing line falls between their objectively and subjectively determined actions—between when they are "being themselves," and when they are playing their official, impersonal roles; they must do this or risk losing their sanity, if not their humanity. Actors and agents, for good reason, are not the same.

The Scientific Realist as Frankenstein

Rejecting state agency in social action, but also weakening subjectivity as human moral choice, Wight gives us something which is neither one nor the other: the half-human monster of a state agent dissected and disassembled on the laboratory bench of his critique—functional, if assembled, and threatening, if it had life. He concludes that

> under a structural relational account, we should think not of international relations, but of global social relations. . . . The state system we currently exist within is, in many respects, a chimera. It is a powerful chimera, but it is nothing other than the result of a particular configuration of structural relationships that are constantly changing.[49]

But this is merely to blur the locus of willed human action. Is the state system, under "global *social* relations," a society, or a chimera? Wight's assertions sound like an indirect way of saying that a holistic theory of human relations is impossible. In any case, his language is far from precise. Something that is only "in many respects" a chimera is arguably not a chimera at all.

Surely it is more useful to point out that a putative system of state agents is an incoherent way of dealing with real, important human concerns—and then to focus on those concrete concerns. Even a dysfunctional society, battling with dysfunctional (state) agents misleadingly reified by some of its members—including leading ones—is still composed of real, breathing, thinking people attempting to make sense of their condition. That is the reality we all confront, every day. More than a social problem, moreover, on the scale of the world as a whole it amounts to a metaphysical dilemma. A de facto society of all human beings, or a states system of de facto nations, can still be made sense of in international-theory terms, but only when the theory is shaped by moral concerns and the situation is considered ripe for change.

241

Ontologically, states can be said to exist, as Frankenstein's monster can be said to exist, provisionally—in the human imagination, for some human purpose. But only human beings live and have awareness of everything, including the real and the unreal. Only human beings have a life and purpose of their own. That is the point about Frankenstein's monster in Mary Shelley's story. A laboratory creation electrified into a semblance of life, he/it is neither human nor machine, but an artificial entity with characteristics of both; in part, it is suggested, an object of pity, doomed to self-destruction because unable to reconcile them in a single will. But of course he/it is also a fiction, his story allegorical—intended by the novelist to make her contemporaries reflect on the relationship between human beings and objects, nature and technology, knowledge and creativity, and the legitimacy of science itself; just as the major political issue of modern times is the legitimacy of that half-human thing, the created state. Frankenstein's own appropriation of creation is portrayed as an act of hubris: the odious and enslaving, because needless, replication of the human self.

On attributive functions and non-existent lives, Runciman comments:

> Both [states and money] have a life of their own, yet when you strip away the accumulated garb in which that life is dressed up—all the documents and uniforms and contracts and commands, all the petty officials and imposing buildings, all the gold and all the government—it is hard to see anything still there. Both share a quality that is distinctive of those things we call fictions: they function by having attributed to them as inherent the one thing that they inherently lack. Emma Bovary only functions as a character in a novel by having attributed to her the one thing that she inherently lacks—a real life of her own. Money functions by having attributed to it its own inherent value, even though it has no inherent value, being a way of valuing other things. The state functions by having attributed to it its own inherent power, even though it has no inherent power, but depends always on the power that is attributed to it, and exercised on its behalf by its representatives.[50]

As we have seen, Wight at one point uses almost identical words—"The state cannot exercise power independent of those agents that act on its behalf." But even this is too loose a formulation. In reality, no state *exists* independently of the people ascribed to it, constituting it, or sharing it as a value; no state can be the subject of a causative verb (like "enable" or "constrain"). Again, Wight affirms that "the state . . . can only exercise power insofar as its imperatives are realised in the practices and modes of thought of state officials." Whose imperatives? I am inclined to ask. An "it" has no imperatives. An "it" can feel nothing, think nothing. Better to admit that state agency is the chimera.

Durkheim's Time

Another of Wight's inspirations, after Bhaskar, is Durkheim, the great idealist of social wholes. On one level, Durkheim saw in social institutions evidence for the collectivity's emergence as an entity in its own right. This particular *fait social* is a *fait accompli*, an experience that cannot be gone back on or denied. Hence his example of a church as a community of believers. (We are concerned here, he said, with "a group condition repeated in the individual because imposed on him.")

On another level, he saw in institutions what society as a whole had done—*fait*, achieved—over time: a historical advance in culture to be acknowledged and admired.

> This becomes conspicuously evident in those beliefs and practices which are transmitted to us ready-made by previous generations; we receive and adopt them because, being both collective and ancient, they are invested with a particular authority that education has taught us to recognize and respect.[51]

So *le fait social*, in Durkheim's phrase, includes both the objective idea of a *fait accompli* and the intersubjective one of a collective achievement: a *feat*, civilization's own proof.[52] Durkheim himself lived through the extraordinary high summer of confidence in French institutions and culture between the débâcle of 1870–1871 and the First World War.[53]

Yet the same principle which led him to value these achievements for their own sake implies that moral considerations mark social studies off qualitatively from natural science and ultimately decide the legitimacy of natural science itself. Even in Durkheim's lifetime, this challenge had begun to appear as a result of science's destructive applications in the Great War; and since his time natural science and the humanities, technology and society, have increasingly been judged as conflicting, as Mary Shelley foresaw; in fact as *two* cultures—which Snow, who coined the phrase, and after him Bhaskar sought to reconcile.[54] And now we have nuclear physics, the first science of unobservables. The very same discoveries which have led to the harnessing of the residual energy of the universe to light and heat our homes, and drive our useful machines, underlie the deadliest weapons invented. In the Cold War this led to a worldwide existential dilemma whose implications for the future of humankind are still being worked out.

Science as Meta-theory

Successful science also depends on a consistent, holistic point of view on the part of the investigator. That, after all, is the ideal of methodological individualism and positivism. The protagonist of these approaches is someone who is effective precisely because he is an individual—undivided in his assumptions and procedure. He is in no doubt about—is *positive of*—his own reality, both in advance of and throughout the inquiry. Rightly or wrongly, he does not query his ability to distinguish between himself—the subject—and the other—the object—of the inquiry. For Bhaskar, on the other hand, individual approaches are permissible only in the context of social objectives and an assumption of social unity.

At the fundamental level, however, it has now become an intrinsic feature of scientific investigation that the subject and the object of the investigation are inseparable. Since the theory of relativity, explanation itself depends on this inseparability. In the light of which, some writers have suggested that nothing grounds individual perceptions at all, and in the absence of some overriding instrumental guide, what we discern may merely be what we prefer.[55] A radical uncertainty pervades all scientific theory-formation.

Sooner or later this was bound to spill over into international theory. To offset the likely dissensions, Fred Chernoff proposed a "quasi-Duhemian" meta-theory based on "the conventionality of all science." Such a solution would, he argued, help international theorists to avoid the problem of "paradigm-incommensurability" posited by Kuhn in his study of the historical progression of science. This is the notion of multiple frameworks for analysis coexisting on different levels of a discipline and with different terms of description, so that theorists talk past each other and are never brought to agree, while the conventional wisdom goes unchallenged—a notion which at times has been highly influential in debates in international theory.[56]

Wight, however, has countered Chernoff's proposal by arguing that it entails "a depth ontology" of its own.[57] It is notable too that in his survey of scientific realism, Chernoff does not mention Bhaskar once; which suggests a political difference in Anglo-American perspectives on this approach. The "conventionality of all science," then, is not so easily established, even transatlantically. And yet a careful reading of Kuhn's key work suggests that he himself mixes up cause and effect, explanatory and normative, change as factual and change as progress. To put it more simply, he cannot decide whether there is a problem or not in the structure of scientific revolutions. Paradigm-incommensurability looks like a difference dressed up as an insoluble dilemma, like the constructivists' vision of the European Union criticised by Moravcsik.

Wendt, meanwhile, takes radical uncertainty in science at face value, to argue for an elision of the agent-structure dichotomy:

> the quantum revolution in general points towards a process ontology, in which events (practices?) are more fundamental than—and irreducible to—either the agents or the structures from which they are usually thought to ensue.

Wendt pursues this approach in an explicit dismantling of his own "state person" concept which on closer examination looks rather conventional, even reactionary: "there is no real reality beyond the individual to do any causing," he says, while for him only individuals with education, in state employment or actual political power count in the states system at all. He concludes that "states and other putative corporate actors are not really actors, but holographic projections by individuals."[58]

This is a clever application of the ambiguities of quantum mechanics, but on closer examination is dubious in its own right. By "holographic projections" Wendt may mean mere illusions of authority, but he does not say. His explorations of collective consciousness, though brilliantly eclectic, are crippled by his dogged physicalism. He is drawn into densely-mechanistic language (human beings are "monads" or "pixels" in the world-projection). He insists on "the physics constraint on social science". But surely this is normatively the wrong way round; we find here more examples of his strangely-inverted habit, which I have criticised in the past, of "comparing and approximating inanimate things to people, rather than the reverse".[59]

Wendt's new thesis is also purely and by his own admission speculative; in fact circular, since the gradations of virtual reality which he posits as variants of "the quantum mind" never come into contact with what he calls (eight times!) "real reality"—which begs the question of what he thinks is real in the first place. For most of us in any case, up is still up and down still down according to the principles which make heavy things heavy, far-off people far off, and bombs on your house a deliberate act. Turning empirical at the last, Wendt proposes a view of the "War in Iraq" as the activity of "warring ant colonies," or as seen by "aliens in space," but this strikes me as merely whimsical, or the product of too much television.[60]

My own view is that the complications of quantum mechanics can be explained only by supposing that genuinely new dimensions of human understanding are being opened up, whose full implications are as yet unclear—or that these are not new after all, and result from a philosophical confusion. An either/or at this level, however, turns science itself into meta-theory. The likely result, as in constructivism, is excessive abstraction. So Patrick Thaddeus Jackson promises to explain the "philosophy of science and its implications for the study of world politics," but again, in his book no events in "world politics," and no real people, apart from theorists, figure.[61]

When all on this subject is said and done, science in the broadest sense can only reflect the norms of society—especially in our age, in which, paradoxically, science's material gains are everywhere taken for granted while materiality itself can be thrown into doubt, but no one is proposing a return to alchemy.[62] A critical theory of human relations in the world as a whole begins by *challenging* social norms; by taking moral sides. Science conceived as part of a search for truth comes under that description; no other conceptions of science do.

10.3 Post-modernism and Rational Ordering

Next among recent radical approaches to international relations I would mention that cloud of ideas or intellectual positions labelled "post-modernism." There are some features here in common with constructivism. First, a subject-matter stretching beyond political and social theory into literary and aesthetic domains (there is, for example, post-modernist painting, architecture, and literary criticism). Second, post-modernists clearly want to reserve a right to comment in a detached way on international theory and its concrete concerns—one might say as cultural, rather than social or political, commentators; a penchant they share with constructivists. In turn, I am inclined to link post-modernism with those problems of meta-theory that constructivism seems to display. Post-modernists also share some of the sceptical attitudes—and self-contradictions—of Realist international theorists (as Hutchings points out[63])—in a gadfly, anti-theory stance playing down metaphysics on the grounds that its questions can never be resolved, while playing down morality out of an opposition to metaphysics. Der Derian, not entirely seriously, lists some thirty different uses of the prefix.[64]

All this adds up to an extremely narrow argumentative base. Post-modernists make abundantly, often repetitively, clear what they are against but rarely explain what they are (collectively) for. As a result, our established critical apparatuses tend to run up against a problem of intellectual commentators resistant, on principle, to generalization about themselves. If, however, it is possible to identify "typical" post-modern writing, we can say that this will come in a range of genres; marked by a combination of dynamism and flux discerned in the world as a whole; and often inspired by a modernist Marx—this *style* substituting for metaphysics or formal theory.[65]

Modernity as Inescapable . . .

In response, I do not deny that to treat the things of the world as always strange and new, and not to insist on firm categories of reality in an integrated whole, may appear a more open-minded, and aesthetically more attractive, approach than the doggedly rationalistic "chore" which ontological Realism, according to Grossmann, entails. But in the first place I object that we do not grow up and construct our lives on this basis, and secondly I think we could not properly do so. Contingent necessity always prompts us to an ordered vision of things, even if we no more than glimpse its limits. And although we make this ordering through our reason, we free ourselves for action through our moral imagination. This is because we assume human dominance, either conceptually (only humans are able to form a comprehensive vision of reality) or practically (only humans effectively dominate the world). Inevitable questions of hierarchy are opened up—between actions and objectives (as for example between producing reliable quantities of energy, and arresting climate change); between species; and between these considerations and traditional human concerns, like social equality, prosperity and peace. Hierarchical ordering and moral choice are forced on us by our dominant capacities as human beings, or what we assume them to be.

What is more, these challenges, and others like them, seem to me aspects of modernity itself, in a broader conception than post-modernists trouble themselves with. Climate change, or the unintended consequences of progress in medicine and technological invention (overpopulation, pollution, stress) are phenomena presaged by writers from Rousseau to Ruskin, and which a time traveller from the Europe of, say, 1850 would have no difficulty in recognizing. Equally, the general psychological uncertainties and paradoxes of the modern world to which post-modernists draw attention—sometimes to lament, sometimes to celebrate them—are symptomatic of a condition one could link to the Europe of the Renaissance, or the Greece of the Stoics. They reflect that sense of secular freedom and power perceived by individuals that existentialists have emphasized, along with its other side, the loneliness of human consciousness, whose forms today may be traced to the Romantics, to the fractured individuals of Freud's diagnoses or the novels of D. H. Lawrence. Modernity's philosophical essence seems to me this: the recognition of our freedom radically to question given accounts of reality—including all social norms and expectations—yet finding a strength in that freedom itself. But modernity in this sense could also be said to be as old as unified human consciousness. Certainly, it seems a condition that we in the older-industrialized countries have yet to leave behind, were it possible or desirable to do so. By the same token, to abandon the idea of a holistic vision of reality, or to ignore the responsibility immanent in human dominance in the world, amounts to a flight from consciousness altogether.

Alternatively one may see, in the fanciful, order-resistant premises of post-modern texts, a reflection of the indeterminacy of the most recent developments in natural science, to which I have referred earlier. But even that would amount to praising post-modernists for being modern.

... and Unstable

It seems to me above all that what post-modernists challenge, or claim to have superseded, is a rather narrow version of modernity, the one emerging from the European Enlightenment and the Industrial Revolution, whose concrete effects in technology and social organization are on view all round us today. David Campbell makes precisely this criticism of post-modernism, in order to elevate post-structuralism, with which he says it has been conflated.[66] Yet the modern surely also refers, in the more abstract and fluid sense of the word, to what is most recent, up to date, emergent, being continually discovered.[67] Modernity in this second, abstract sense may really be always new and surprising. But by definition we never get "post" that.

Inevitably, with such generous, self-awarded latitude, everything for post-modernists tends to have a quality of instability and ripeness for revolution, expressed through wordplay and neologism in a caricature of traditional argument—as seen, for example, in Lyotard's influential

The Postmodern Condition.[68] In the original, this tract seems to me a literary tour de force—no more and no less. As for the instability of knowledge (*le savoir*), which Lyotard asserts as his theme, emphasizing the dynamism of communication in the electronic age, this is not self-evidently a new phenomenon. Arguably if it were, it would not be definable as knowledge in the first place. Knowledge exists, and knowledge changes, according to the means of discovery and communication available, but also according to agreement on what it is. Like change itself, it is relative. On this level of argument one can accept the author's claims to originality only if one accepts his verbal sleights of hand.

The "post" in post-modern is something that Lyotard himself has felt the need to explain—but again, not without the logical errors, tricks, and shortcuts of the genre. He selects for criticism a rather rigid and dated notion of modernity/ism, relating to the plastic arts (even "the avant-garde" for him merits the past tense). Yet he can also adopt an expansive concept of modernity when it suits him, to avoid the charge of following fashion. So the "modern" in post-modernism for him can somehow be continuous, and discontinuous, with "Christianity, Cartesianism, and Jacobinism." He reifies and anthropomorphizes ("Postmodern architecture finds itself condemned to undertake a series of minor modifications"; "we can think of the work of [certain artists] as a working through performed by modernity on its own meaning"). And he indulges in the usual showy wordplay, which cannot but mislead, though perhaps he has not mastered English sufficiently for this risky purpose.[69] He leaves us no clearer on what post-modernism means, except that it is not "post" anything in a straightforward chronological sense. So why not adopt another term (un-modern, anti-modern, etc.), or just admit to being confused?

Uncertainty of grasp, masquerading as originality, seems to me a general weakness of such writing, born of an underlying ambivalence, rather than reasoned scepticism, toward modernity. By the same token we can understand the peculiar lack of commitment to international relations of anyone with such leanings, since a degree of certainty about the modern world is a prerequisite to theorizing about it. Özkırımlı, in his survey of theories of the nation, comes out firmly against approaches that he sees as insufficiently "grounded in (the study of) historical processes," that avoid all "truth claims," and promote "radical scepticism" toward the very idea of the nation. This most cautious of commentators feels the need to defend his own past work against a "charge" of post-modernism![70]

If, however, post-modernists have an excuse for their ambivalence about systematic political or international theory, it must be a factitious one. Were they not themselves products, in part beneficiaries, of the detachment toward all things which the free-thinking condition of modernity affords—in democracies, in the twenty-first century—they would not be in a position to exploit its exciting potential for their own self-advertising ends. Much of their writing, in fact, seems infected with the characteristic schadenfreude with which Marx sought to welcome modernity while remaining free to condemn it. The magnificent sweep of economic history in the *Communist Manifesto* is far too admiring of bourgeois economic achievements to convince as an indictment of the bourgeoisie or reliably predict their overthrow. Yet Marx, as co-author of the *Manifesto*, could not resist a jibe at those buried in "the idiocy of rural life"—far, presumably, from urban sophisticates like himself.[71]

Those of us, meanwhile, who are lucky enough to live in materially advanced societies should bear in mind that the combination of freedom and order which we associate with modernity, together with its material applications in science and technology, like reliable energy provision and health care, are commonly seen as unalloyed benefits in countries where they are much less attainable—and whose inhabitants, therefore, are unlikely to see a world "after" modernity as attractive to them. Both these lessons—the moral ambiguity of the Marxist heritage, and the unevenness of socioeconomic development across the world—tend to be avoided by those who see post-modernism as liberating, though it is precisely through international studies that such lessons are to be learned. All that this leaves of post-modernism is an escapist slogan, a word with no more meaning than Bananarama or the slithy toves (two can play at the gadfly game).

One could, on the other hand, argue that modernity and universal statehood together generate uncertainty. Such diverse phenomena as terrorism and mass migration across frontiers could be seen as rebellions against excessive social control. To that extent there really might be something destabilizing in the modern (post-1945) speed of change, especially technological change, which constitutes a revolution in its own right, as Der Derian, after Lyotard, has claimed.[72] Perhaps the world we live in really does make human relations fraught with difficulty, just as some suggested that after the industrial Holocaust of European Jews, art, morality, hope, and all expectations of settled social life must be fragile or even impossible. The same could be said of the world after the invention of nuclear weapons. In this sense the post-modernists might be onto something, with their general rejection of metaphysics and rationality. But then what do we do? What is to go in their place? It is not much of an answer to throw up one's hands and say that none of the usual solutions apply. Der Derian argues that the Cold War fostered terrorism by institutionalizing idealized violence.[73] I agree with this view, but there is nothing original or "post-structuralist" (his word) about it; all that is needed is a little imagination and common sense. In order, moreover, to justify the judgment fully one needs an extended normative argument, and by implication a prescription for concrete, problem-solving action, which is about as far from post-modernism as it is possible to go.

The Modern World as Tautology

Then again, underneath post-modernists' predilection for wordplay there is an interesting and provocative suggestion that language in general is inadequate for the challenges of the age. But if this is so, it is a graver problem than mere wordplay will resolve. As it happens, I can illustrate this from my own general criticism of the universal states system—developing a straightforward non-literary, non-experimental analysis of meaning in the word "property," and following only common English usage; which will undermine post-modernists' key claim to our attention (their originality), while showing how grave all our modern condition is.

In chapter 4 I mentioned how under the universal system everyone alive "belongs to" (has citizenship of) a state, while all inhabitable territory on earth, along with its resources, "belongs to" someone or other through the jurisdiction attributed to states. This is property as *possession*, owned things. Yet since the system is all-encompassing, do we humans own the system, or are we owned by it? That is the question then implied.

Later, in more general reasoning I referred to "property" in the sense of *inherent characteristic*. Sodium has the inherent characteristic—the chemical property—of reacting violently when brought into contact with water. This is one of the properties of things in general that we discern, enabling us to form an ordered picture of reality, and so define the world.

But what about the property, in this sense, of the world itself? What is *its* inherent characteristic? Well, under a universal states system, I have argued, the world is putatively coterminous with that system, insofar as the existing states in the system together comprise all humankind. Following this logic, we can say that the property (inherent characteristic) of the world itself is humankind as such. But is humankind in this sense a property of the world, or is the world a property of (owned by) humankind?

In this way, through the exploration of two senses of "property" (1, *possession*; 2, *inherent characteristic*) I have arrived at the same question/problem: do we own the world (seen as the states system) or does it own us? But please note that I have not reached this point post-modernistically, by wordplay on "property"; or by suggestive literary devices—exploiting the sounds of words, their accidental phonetic and orthographic coincidences; or by any neologizing or hyperbole. I have merely pointed to two significations of the same word in English common usage: "property." This modern abstract noun has at least two precise meanings, which I have related to the object of the world using the linking verb "to own." But how is this possible? How can "property" mean, with regard to the world, literally two things in one?

One possible explanation (leaving aside the general inadequacy of language, not really an excuse at this level of abstraction) is that the world itself, in the guise of the universal states system, is a tautology—in fact a deliberate, constructed conceit. And taken at face value—with, according to the conventional wisdom, states as agents—that is what the world, as the object of international theory, becomes. The universal states system considered as an end in itself objectifies what should never be objectified—ourselves. It divides the arguably indivisible (the human species), and it does so unaccountably, inhumanly—with an imperfect consideration of the reasons for the division, and no clear prospect of change. In this light, the question: "do we own the world (seen as the states system), or does it own us?" is really the question: "Are we free, under the modern, universal states system—freer than before—or not?." And that is the most important question of all.

Language and Ambiguity under Modernity

If we are not freer than before, then as the post-modernists half grasp, literally all the language of the modern world must be shot through with ambiguity. "Property" is but one example of this universal semantic challenge. By the same token, the deeper we go into international relations, the more we can expect to be pushing at the boundaries of language. The ambiguities of language, in that sense, would really be due to our having uncovered a metaphysical crisis in modern life, in the ubiquitous, permanent, unreformed states system—a crisis which temporarily defeats language itself.

In this regard, however, a sub-species of literary writing (which is how post-modern theses are typically presented) will lead us precisely in the wrong direction: frivolously, playfully, away from modernity, instead of to modernity's reform; whereas literature in the full sense, the imaginative exploration of new forms of language and conscious-ness, is of real worth in understanding ourselves and the immanent tragedy of mortal life. That has been the case in all times, as long as language has existed. That is what we mean when we praise *Hamlet* as modern, independently of Shakespeare's topical references. It is a play which, though written centuries ago, helps us to understand our world, our politics, our times, and how to act (take action) in them; how to be agents of our own destiny, not procrastinators or dissem-blers. But that kind of realism, as truth to life in all ages, is not what I associate with post-modernist writing, which seems to me trapped in an artificial, self-regarding mode of expression, somewhere below creative literature proper.

Runciman makes a similar case which touches on my main thesis about state agency. "The fiction of the state's moral agency," he says, does not call for "some more flexible and open-ended form of philosophical reasoning: the somewhat paradoxical thesis is not a post-modern one, if only because it makes sense within the terms of modern politics, and describes the institution on which modern politics depends." Rather, it is the pure fiction-making of imaginative literature which helps us to understand the allure—and the falsity—of state agency.[74]

Given post-modernists' verbal fetishism, their approach may also be seen, in part, as a kind of aesthetic disgust at the rationality reach-ing its apogee in twentieth-century logical positivism, or perhaps a comment on the later failure of that movement, which seems to have come about through the exhaustion of its linguistic resources. Steve Smith sees a reaction against logical positivism as a formative influ-ence in the development of radical or "post-positivist" international theory.[75] Analytical philosophy in English in general has been criti-cized for becoming tied up in linguistic analysis, to the detriment of concrete concerns.

Yet insofar as analytical philosophers, in the twentieth century, came to focus on meaning in ordinary language, they were bound to the respect of common usage like the rest of us.[76] This was the

253

strength of that movement, in English, in the twentieth century. Ayer's achievements stand for the work of both logical positivists and empiricists in the tradition of Hume. If, therefore, some of their efforts ran into the sand, one reason may be that meaning itself, in common usage, grew thin from the political causes I have outlined: from the social emptiness of states, and the general sense of futility introduced into modern society by the balance of nuclear terror. Logical positivists and linguistic philosophers together failed to foresee the cul-de-sac they were heading into, because they isolated themselves from mainstream (including moral) philosophy, on the one hand, and from international theory and its concrete concerns on the other. They ran out of words not because their analytical powers failed, but because they turned away from the world.

Rorty

The work of Richard Rorty has often been claimed by, or identified with, post-modernists. His humanism, however, and his preaching of irony as a response to modernity seem to me of a different order. His wholesale emphasis on the contingency of truth is a fruitful approach from which all can learn, even in the occasional contradictions to which it leads. Moreover, Rorty practiced what he preached. Having condemned the whole enterprise of enlightenment analytical philosophy, he gave it up in favor of the search for truth (or its absence) in imaginative literature. Even when he resiled, on occasion, from this decision, he did so with an overtly humanist political commitment.[77] If these actions taken together are emblematic of the fragility of Western civilization to which Rorty sought to draw attention, they are also emblematic of a resilience inherent in modernity that he demonstrated by personal example.

Kimberly Hutchings points out the similarities between Rorty's position and Hume's, similarities that Rorty himself acknowledged. But she also claims that Rorty's position is original: reliant on an "idea of moral sentiment" that is "a constructed feeling of connection rather than some kind of inbuilt faculty that connects the individual person to humanity in general."[78] I think this is a false argument. "Constructed" feelings are unlikely to be real feelings, except as revivals of buried, forgotten, or neglected ones. Rorty's appeal to our better natures is not fundamentally different from Hume's, and perhaps Rorty himself would not have insisted on the difference.

There is a wider lesson here, which I have already suggested. Post-modernists need to explain how their critiques are worth more than a conventionally-logical analysis of our society and the pre-modern culture out of which it developed. Short of such an explanation, we are still stuck with the problems of modernity; we do not get "past" them to a "post"-modern condition at all.

I have no wish to argue that nothing in philosophy or international theory, or in the world in general, really changes; I am merely unconvinced that post-modernism is a coherent or positive challenge to the status quo, especially the problematic status quo of ubiquitous and permanent states that we face today. Post-modernists might reply that coherence is itself a bogus requirement of modernity; but leaving aside the contradictions of such a position, I think it remains for them to prove that their approach is in any way *constructive*.

10.4 A Note on Feminism

Finally, I want to venture briefly into intellectual territory which for me (as a man) is strictly speaking off limits—feminist international theory.

Sometimes we encounter the state-agent convention when theorists actually want states to be agents, in some cause of which they explicitly approve. Consider Mona Harrington's feminist essay "What Exactly Is Wrong with the Liberal State as an Agent of Change?"

The gist of Harrington's argument is that radical feminists have gone too far in seeking to do away with, or to reform, the states system. The liberal state itself, she says, may serve as a political instrument of (positive) change. She is addressing here certain feminist international theorists who pressed after the Cold War for non-state instruments in aid of their cause—what she calls "complex networks of denationalized, depoliticized regimes rationally and efficiently organizing the world's business." And yet, she avers: "The very fact that the state creates, condenses, and focuses political power may make it the best friend, not the enemy, of feminists—because the availability of real *political* power is essential to real democratic control."

The cause of women and other oppressed minorities may, Harrington suggests, be advanced directly by means of the "liberal" state, just as welfare and labor concessions were won "in the nineteenth and twentieth centuries." True, this history "is not the whole story":

> The nation-states of this period have also perpetrated horrors of torture and war, have aided the development of elite-controlled industrial wealth, and have not sufficiently responded to the human needs of their less powerful constituents. But I believe it is better to try to restrain the horrors and abuses than to give up on the limits

that state organized political power can bring to bear on the forms of class-based, sex-based power that constitute the greatest sources of oppression we are likely to face.[79]

Now it is important to note that on either side of this argument, progressive or democratizing aims are involved. The author is appealing, in effect, to the radicals of her own persuasion to join her in taking political power, in *occupying* the liberal state—in order to evict from it the traditional sexists, racists, and national-chauvinists and bring about social change. Her normative image is ultimately that of society as a whole, persuaded by liberal political convictions and led by feminists, actually *becoming* the liberal state. Let us, she says, draw the battle lines clearly in this contest for freedom; let us establish who have been the historical subjects (wielders) of power, and who the objects (victims) of it—and how that might be reversed.

All the more surprising, then, that she should write in a way that shows her mixing up "us" and "them," society and the liberal state, subjects and objects. She does it, for example, in the first sentence in the quotation above. States cannot simultaneously be "perpetrators" of wrongs against society and "constituted" by it. The same applies normatively. The bad state-occupiers of the past—the sexists, racists, and national-chauvinists of Harrington's account—could not conceivably be usurpers of power, controllers of an oppressive state machine outside society, and at the same time part of society—except, perhaps, in some vague general sense (we all have to get on with each other, nobody is above the law, etc.), but this possibility is ruled out by Harrington's cleaving of society, in historical perspective, into oppressors and oppressed. In short, the first sentence in the quotation is a purely rhetorical assertion whose effect depends on the reader being already emotionally in sympathy with the author, or confused, and in any case not reading her words very closely.

The same fault is present, in more muted and subtle form, in the second sentence quoted, where Harrington appears to want organized power (here, state power) to be "limited" in ambidextrous ways: on the one hand to rule out abuses by the traditional sexists, racists, and national-chauvinists; but on the other, implicitly, to limit the power of her feminist opponents, who see the only way forward in a bypassing of the liberal state. Her expression "give up on the limits" is deeply, and I think designedly, ambiguous. In obvious terms, it refers to the restrictions that Harrington argues should be imposed on sexists, racists, and national-chauvinists by feminists in charge of the liberal state. Yet limits are also, in political theory, what the liberal-democratic state itself is bound by (liberals speak of the "limited state")—another desirable meaning, from the author's point of view. So the overt message, for the sisters she is addressing, is that to reject the possibility of exercising certain "limited" forms of (liberal state) power is to miss a political opportunity; but subliminally, that to do so is to be some kind of extremist. In this way the radical feminists are indirectly slurred, coming under the same kind of criticism as the abhorred sexists, racists, and national-chauvinists. Mona Harrington's approach is faintly duplicitous. It leaves her in the right, independently of all other views in the debate.

Why then is her tract not an obvious caricature? Because present throughout it, underlying the two *open* conceptions of agency (feminists vs. sexists, liberal vs. radical feminists), is a third, covert one, the conventional conception of states as agents in their own right, independently of any social or cultural reference. This empty vessel can be filled at will, enabling Harrington to portray state power as *bad* in the hands of her adversaries and rivals (who are thereby surreptitiously conflated), but *good* in the hands of persons like herself—while still maintaining an appearance of detachment. Her style is politician-speak: I want the power of the state, but on condition you share it with me.

Clearly, none of these criticisms need be damaging to feminist international theory as such. I support the principle of equality between men and women; I agree with Ken Booth that "feminist theorizing is particularly helpful in breaking down essentializing tendencies" in various cultures.[80] My point is to show, in a further non-traditional context in international theory, the abuses which surround state agency, artfully deployed. Even those who have the weight of justice and history on their side (by which I mean the cause of equality for women) have no excuse for engaging in such deception. In this regard the flaw in Mona Harrington's argument is in her motive: she is concerned with means rather than ends. Feminist principles are taken for granted, rather than justified, in her approach, and states are treated as ends in themselves.

But that one can never do, without putting all human freedom at risk. In contexts like these, the language of human agency should be seen as the language of morality itself—the canary in civilization's mine.

Notes

1. Michael Barnett, "Social constructivism" in Baylis, Smith, and Owens (eds.), *The Globalization of World Politics* (6th ed. 2014), p. 157; Knud Erik Jørgensen, "Four levels and a discipline" in Karin M. Fierke and Knud Erik Jørgensen (eds.), *Constructing International Relations: The Next Generation* (Armonk, NY: M. E. Sharpe, 2001), p. 41; "Preface" in Vendulka Kubálková, Nicholas Onuf, and Paul Kowert (eds.), *International Relations in a Constructed World* (Armonk, NY: M. E. Sharpe, 1998), p. xii; Colin Wight, *Agents, Structures and International Relations*, p. 163; Friedrich Kratochwil, "The monologue of 'science'," *International Studies Review* 5 (1), March 2003, p. 126; Nicholas Greenwood Onuf, "Worlds of our making" [2002] in his *Making Sense, Making Worlds: Constructivism in Social Theory and International Relations* (Abingdon/New York: Routledge, 2013), p. 39.

2. E.g., Ernst von Glasersfeld (ed.), *Radical Constructivism in Mathematics Education* (New York: Kluwer Academic, 2002); Maria Gough, *The Artist as Producer: Russian Constructivism in Revolution* (Berkeley: University of California Press, 2005); Paul B. Baltes, Patricia A. Reuter-Lorenz, and Frank Rösler (eds.), *Lifespan Development and the Brain: the Perspective of Biocultural Co-Constructivism* (Cambridge/New York: Cambridge University Press, 2006); Paul Artin Boghossian, *Fear of Knowledge: Against Relativism and Constructivism* (Oxford: Clarendon Press, 2006); André Kukla, *Social Constructivism and the Philosophy of Science* (New York: Routledge, 2000).

3. Jennifer Sterling-Folker, "Constructivist approaches" in Sterling-Folker (ed.), *Making Sense of International Relations Theory* (Boulder, Colo./London: Lynne Rienner, 2006), p. 116.

4. Nicholas Greenwood Onuf, *World of Our Making: Rules and Rule in Social Theory and International Relations* (Columbia, SC: University of South Carolina Press, 1989); Friedrich V. Kratochwil, *Rules, Norms and Decisions: On the Conditions of Practical and Legal Reasoning in International Relations and Domestic Affairs* (Cambridge: Cambridge University Press, 1989).

5. Sterling-Folker, "Constructivist approaches," p. 118; Barnett, "Social constructivism," p. 162; Andrew Bradley-Phillips, "Constructivism" in Martin Griffiths (ed.), *International Relations Theory for the Twenty-First Century: An Introduction* (London/New York: Routledge, 2007), p. 60.

6. Philosophical idealism is related to Conceptualism, with the difference that the latter is more specifically directed at the question of universals. See above, chapter 5.

7. Sterling-Folker, "Constructivist approaches," p. 116. See also Fierke, "Constructivism" in Dunne, Kurki and Smith (eds.), *International Relations Theories*, pp. 168, 177–183; Bradley-Phillips, "Constructivism," p. 73.

8. Fierke, "Constructivism," p. 168. See also Sterling-Folker, "Constructivist approaches," pp. 115–116; Kubálková, Onuf, and Kowert, "Preface," p. x; Fierke and Jørgensen, "Introduction" in Fierke and Jørgensen (eds.), pp. 5–6.

9. Smith, "Foreign policy is what states make of it" in Kubálková (ed.), *Foreign Policy in a Constructed World*, p. 40; Patrick Thaddeus Jackson, *The Conduct of Inquiry in International Relations: Philosophy of Science and its Implications for the Study of World Politics* (London/New York: Routledge, 2011), p. 204; Kratochwil, "The monologue of 'science'" pp. 126, 127, 128; Jørgensen, "Four levels and a discipline," p. 45.

10. Sterling-Folker, "Constructivist approaches," p. 118; Fierke, "Bringing the social and cultural back in," review of Ralph Pettman, *Commonsense Constructivism*, in *International Studies Review* 3 (3), autumn 2001, p. 161. Steve Smith distinguishes between constructivism and post-positivism in defending both ("Epistemology, post-modernism and international relations theory: a reply to Østerud"). He foresees constructivism splitting "into two main camps, one broadly rationalist, the other more reflectivist"—his term for "more radical accounts such as critical theory, post-modernism and many forms of contemporary feminist work': Smith, "Social constructivism and European Studies" in *Journal of European Policy* 6:4, Special Issue 1999, p. 690.

11. Andrew Moravcsik, "Is something rotten in the state of Denmark? Constructivism and European integration," *ibid.*, pp. 670 and 677.

12. Andrew Moravcsik, "Theory synthesis in International Relations: real not metaphysical," *International Studies Review* 5 (1), March 2003, pp. 131–136, especially p. 133.

13. "In few areas of interstate politics are ideals so often invoked, identities so clearly at stake, and interests so complex, challenging, and uncertain. In few areas is so much detailed primary data, historical scholarship, and social scientific theory available to assist analysts in tracing the role of ideas and the process of socialization." Moravcsik, "Is something rotten in the state of Denmark?" p. 669.

14. *Ibid.*, p. 678.

15. Kant, *The Metaphysics of Morals* [1797] §61, in Hans Reiss (ed.), *Kant: Political Writings* tr. H. B. Nisbet (2nd ed. Cambridge: Cambridge University Press, 1991), p. 171.

16. On interdisciplinarity in international theory, at least, these authors agree: Moravcsik, "Theory synthesis in International Relations"; Smith, "Dialogue and the reinforcement of orthodoxy in International Relations," *International Studies Review* 5 (1), March 2003, pp. 131–136 and 141–43 respectively.

17. Onuf, *World of Our Making*, pp. 90–94. Cf. "Deeds done, acts taken, words spoken—These are all that facts are." *Ibid.*, p. 36; and "saying *is* doing," "Rules in practice" [2010] in Onuf, *Making Sense, Making Worlds*, p. 135, original emphasis.

18. Chris Brown links the "norm-governed relationship" of the English School's "society of states" with Wendt's view that "anarchy is what states make of it": Brown, *Understanding International Relations* (2nd ed. London: Palgrave, 2001), p. 54. See also Christian Reus-Smit, "Constructivism" in Andrew Linklater and Scott Burchill (eds.), *Theories of International Relations* (4th ed. Basingstoke: Palgrave Macmillan, 2009), pp. 230, 235; Sterling-Folker, "Constructivist approaches," p. 120; Rengger, *International Relations, Political Theory and the Problem of Order*, pp. 80–92. Following this line, Hedley Bull's *Anarchical Society* may conceivably be seen as constructivist/interpretivist, but I think Bull would have dissented. That book's elegance and intellectual power to my mind make it one of the most brilliant and stimulating works on international relations or indeed any subject, while its inconsistencies, such as they are, arise from Bull's own resistance to holistic theory making. His late work *Justice in International Relations* clearly shows him gravitating towards normative international theory.

19. These terms, along with constructivism and "constructionism," are tossed around to little clear effect in Gary K. Browning, *Global Theory from Kant to Hardt and Negri* (Basingstoke: Palgrave Macmillan, 2011).

20. Christian Reus-Smit, "International law" in Baylis, Smith, and Owens (eds.) (4th. ed. 2008), 290. Later Reus-Smit muted this criticism, saying "constructivists have found considerable common ground with legal theorists" and "offer resources for understanding the politics of international law lacking in realist and neo-liberal thought." Reus-Smit, "International law" in Baylis, Smith, and Owens (eds.) (5th ed. 2011), p. 290, a view reiterated in his "International Law" in Baylis, Smith, and Owens (eds.), *The Globalization of World Politics* (6th ed. 2014), p. 285.

21. J. Ann Tickner, "Gender in world politics" in Baylis, Smith, and Owens (eds.) (6th ed. 2014), p. 260.

22. Alexander Wendt, "Bridging the theory/meta-theory gap in international relations," p. 383.

23. *Ibid.*, p. 390, original emphasis.

24. Onuf, *World of Our Making*, p. 291.

25. "Since Onuf introduced "constructivism" in 1989 it has generated growing interest, and many scholars have adopted the name for their approaches. There are, in fact, not one but several "constructivisms" in the literature': Kubálková, Onuf, and Kowert, "Preface." "Onuf's constructivism is totally different from the other varieties and it is his approach alone which should continue using that designation": Kubálková, "The twenty years' catharsis" in *ibid.*, p. 52.

26. Onuf, "Worlds of our making" [2002].

27. Raymond Cohen, *International Politics: The Rules of The Game* (Harlow: Longman, 1981). See also Cohen, *Negotiating Across Cultures: International Communication in an Interdependent World* (rev. ed. Washington, DC: United States Institute of Peace Press, 1997).

28. Fierke, "Constructivism," p. 170; Barnett, "Social constructivism," pp. 161, 163, 164; Sterling-Folker, "Constructivist approaches," p. 118; Kubálková, Onuf, and Kowert, "Constructing constructivism" in Kubálková, Onuf, and Kowert (eds.), p. 10; Reus-Smit, "Constructivism" in Linklater and Burchill (eds.), p. 222. Onuf generally distinguishes between "states and their agents" but also writes, confusingly: "States are societies that have exceptionally clear boundaries as well as highly developed institutions for conducting relations with other states": *Making Sense, Making Worlds*, pp. 123 and 17.

29. Barnett, "Social constructivism," pp. 158 and 164.

30. See above, chapter 9, section 9.4.

31. Onora O'Neill, *Towards Justice and Virtue: A Constructive Account of Practical Reasoning* (Cambridge: Cambridge University Press, 1996).

32. "It is impossible to conceive anything at all in the world, or even out of it, which can be taken as good without qualification, except a *good will*." Immanuel Kant, *Grundlegung zur Metaphysik der Sitten* [*Groundwork of the Metaphysics of Morals*] [1785] tr. H. J. Paton as *The Moral Law* (London: Hutchinson, 1948), p. 59, Kant's emphasis.

33. Katrin Flikschuh, "Metaphysics and the boundaries of justice," *Global Society* 14 (4), October 2000, p. 498.

34. Kubálková, Onuf, and Kowert, "Preface," p. xii.

35. In *Agents, Structures and International Relations* Colin Wight writes of "ontologies" (e.g., pp. 2, 4, 5, 7). But ontology by definition cannot be plural, or all-encompassing, compete with itself. A philosophical level-of-analysis error is involved here. It lies in Wight's taking the object of ontology as *the world*, rather than the *whole of reality*. The latter includes the universe and is therefore greater than the world. We humans define the world, as a distinct domain in the concrete spatio-temporal whole of the universe that alone is real beyond dubiety. Ontology starts from both these premises. There can conceivably be "worlds" (humans can alter their domain within the universe), but there cannot be "wholes of reality." Later Wight asserts that only Realist ontology is worth the name (*ibid.*, p. 26). This is in line with the view I have adopted from Grossmann: everything we stably perceive is in some sense real; any other approach is not, properly speaking, ontology. But it is incompatible with the plural, qualified, and debased approach that Wight elsewhere deploys ("political and social worlds," "worldviews," "social ontology," *ibid.*, pp. 2, 3, 5).

36. Ronen Palan, "A world of their making: an evaluation of the constructivist critique in International Relations," *Review of International Studies* 26 (4), October 2000, pp. 575–598. Palan's own essay is sloppily drafted. He devotes a section to an author (Prus, p. 592) for whom he gives no reference. Bhaskar's name is repeatedly misspelled (p. 596). And "the Republican Legacy" which he cites as emblematic of Onuf's approach is a hidden book title (the book is Nicholas Greenwood Onuf, *The Republican Legacy in International Thought* [Cambridge: Cambridge University Press, 1998]).

37. See especially Steve Smith, Ken Booth, and Marysia Zalewski (eds.), *International Theory: Positivism and Beyond* (Cambridge: Cambridge University Press, 1996).

38. See Roy Bhaskar, *A Realist Theory of Science* (Leeds: Leeds Books, 1975), and *The Possibility of Naturalism: A Philosophical Critique of the Contemporary Human Sciences* [1979] (3rd ed. London/New York: Routledge, 1998).

39. Wight, *Agents, Structures and International Relations*, pp. 24, 32, 52.

40. Rudolf Carnap, *The Logical Structure of the World* [1928] in *The Logical Structure of the World* and *Pseudoproblems in Philosophy* tr. Rolf A. George (Chicago/La Salle, IL: Open Court, 2003), §66, p. 106.

41. Bhaskar, *The Possibility of Naturalism* (1st ed.), p. 29.

42. Cf. Bhaskar, *The Possibility of Naturalism* (3rd ed.), pp. 44ff.

43. Wight, *Agents, Structures and International Relations*, pp. 193–97 and 61.

44. In his early work (if I understand correctly this mercurial thinker and terrible writer), Bhaskar sought to reconcile dialectical materialism and philosophical Idealism. His recent work has an overtly spiritual dimension.

45. Wight, *Agents, Structures and International Relations*, pp. 163, 218, 222. Cf., also in a discussion of scientific realism, Koivisto, "State theory in International Relations," p. 86.

46. Wight, *Agents, Structures and International Relations*, pp. 26, 218–219.

47. *Ibid.*, p. 223.

48. *Ibid.*, pp. 213, and 212–214 generally. Cf. Bhaskar, *The Possibility of Naturalism* (3rd ed.), ch. 2.

49. Wight, *Agents, Structures and International Relations*, p. 299.

50. Runciman, "The concept of the state," p. 35.

51. Émile Durkheim, *The Rules of Sociological Method* [1895] ed. G. Gatlin, Glencoe, IL: Free Press, 1950, pp. 12–13.
52. As in *fait d'armes*, a "feat of arms."
53. His contemporaries included the Impressionists; Fauré, Debussy, Ravel, and Satie; Bergson; Mallarmé, Zola, Gide, and Proust; and Pasteur, Eiffel, Becquerel, and the Curies.
54. See C. P. Snow, *The Two Cultures* [1959] (Cambridge: Cambridge University Press, 1993).
55. See Samir Okasha, *Philosophy of Science: A Very Short Introduction* (Oxford: Oxford University Press, 2002), chs. 2, 4.
56. Fred Chernoff, "Scientific realism as a meta-theory of international politics," *International Studies Quarterly* (2002) 46, pp. 202–205. Thomas S. Kuhn, *The Structure of Scientific Revolutions* (2nd ed. Chicago: Chicago University Press, 1970).
57. Wight, *Agents, Structures and International Relations*, p. 18.
58. Alexander Wendt, "Flatland: quantum mind and the international hologram" in Mathias Albert, Lars-Erik Cederman, and Alexander Wendt (eds.), *New Systems Theories of World Politics* (Basingstoke: Palgrave Macmillan, 2010), pp. 286–289, 301, 303, 304.
59. *Ibid.*, p. 303, and Lomas, "Anthropomorphism, personification and ethics," p. 350.
60. Wendt, "Flatland," p. 298.
61. Patrick Thaddeus Jackson, *The Conduct of Inquiry in International Relations*.
62. See Rowan Williams, "Such a thing," review of Conor Cunningham, *Darwin's Pious Idea* in Times Literary Supplement, 22 April 2011, pp. 8–9. On quantum mechanics generally, Simone Weil questioned an approach which did away with the concept of work as energy measured in terms of effort applied to matter. See her "Réflexions à propos de la théorie des quanta "[1942] in *Œuvres complètes*, Tome 1 ed. André A. Devaux and Florence de Lussy (Paris: Gallimard, 1988), in English as "Reflections on quantum theory" in Simone Weil, *On Science, Necessity, and the Love of God* tr. and ed. Richard Rees (London: Oxford University Press, 1968). Anthony O'Hear sees "the quantum descriptions as essentially incomplete descriptions of the real world': O'Hear, *Introduction to the Philosophy of Science* (Oxford: Clarendon Press, 1989), p. 140. See also John Brockman (ed.), *What We Believe But Cannot Prove: Today's Leading Thinkers on Science in the Age of Certainty* (London: Simon & Schuster 2006), pp. 224–226.
63. Kimberly Hutchings, "The possibility of judgement," pp. 61–62.
64. James Der Derian, "Post-theory: the eternal return of ethics in international relations" [1997] in his *Critical Practices in International Theory: Selected Essays* (London/New York: Routledge, 2009), p. 190.
65. E.g., Marshall Berman, *All that is Solid Melts into Air: The Experience of Modernity* (New York: Simon & Schuster, 1982). The title is a quotation from Karl Marx and Friedrich Engels, *The Communist Manifesto* tr. Samuel Moore [1888] (Harmondsworth: Penguin, 1967), p. 83. See also Thomas Docherty (ed.), *Post-modernism: A Reader* (Brighton: Harvester Wheatsheaf, 1993).
66. David Campbell, "Post-structuralism" in Dunne, Kurki and Smith, *International Relations Theories*, pp. 221–222.

67. Clearly, I am using the word "emergent" in the simple chronological sense, not with the special meaning that some theorists (scientific or critical realists) want to attach to it. See David Leon, "Reductionism, emergence and explanation in international relations theory" in Joseph and Wight (eds.), pp. 31–50.

68. Jean-François Lyotard, *La Condition Post-moderne: Rapport sur le Savoir* (Paris: Editions de Minuit, 1979); in English *The Post-modern Condition: A Report on Knowledge* tr. Geoff Bennington and Brian Massumi (Manchester/Minneapolis: University of Manchester Press/University of Minnesota Press, 1984).

69. E.g., *relever* in French does not mean "relieve"; "destiny" and "destination" are not the same thing. Jean-François Lyotard, "Note on the meaning of "Post-" in Docherty (ed.), *Post-modernism*, pp. 47–50.

70. Özkırımlı, *Theories of Nationalism*, pp. 216–217.

71. *Communist Manifesto*, Moore translation, p. 84.

72. James Der Derian, *Antidiplomacy: Spies, Terror, Speed and War* (Cambridge, Mass/Oxford: Blackwell, 1992).

73. *Ibid.*, pp. 114–116.

74. Runciman, "Moral responsibility and the problem of representing the state," p. 47. See also "The concept of the state," p. 35.

75. Steve Smith, "Positivism and beyond" in Smith, Booth, and Zalewski (eds.), *International Theory: Positivism and Beyond*, pp. 14–15.

76. E.g., "To say of [the propositions in this book] that they are, in some sense, about the usage of words is, I believe, correct, but also inadequate; for certainly not every statement about the usage of words is philosophical." Ayer, *Language, Truth and Logic*, introduction (2nd ed. 1946), p. 26.

77. See Richard Rorty, "Human rights, rationality and sentimentality" in Stephen Shute and Susan Hurley (eds.), *On Human Rights: The Oxford Amnesty Lectures 1993* (New York: Basic Books, 1993), pp. 112–34.

78. Kimberly Hutchings, *Global Ethics: An Introduction*, p. 72.

79. Mona Harrington, "What Exactly Is Wrong with the Liberal State as an Agent of Change?" in V. Spike Peterson (ed.), *Gendered States: Feminist (Re)Visions of International Relations Theory* (Boulder, Colo.: Lynne Rienner, 1992), p. 66, emphasis in original.

80. Booth, "Human wrongs and international relations," p. 116.

11

Cosmopolitan Kant

States in our time have been settled on everyone as sources of identity, means of communication, and tools of social survival or prosperity—often with mixed results. Some people go beyond them, to embrace the values and culture of people elsewhere as an alternative to, or combined with, their own. Francophiles, Russophiles, or Sinophiles admire and favor some imagined essence of France, Russia, or China. The same tendency may receive official expression, as in the Anglo-French *entente cordiale* at the turn of the twentieth century. Foreign policy, too, can be friendly toward chosen others.

Some people take the tendency all the way, to envisage a peace-loving community of humankind beyond all states, their cultures and divisions. Kant set himself this task as the logical extension of his moral philosophy, in works popularized as cosmopolitan international theory. "What is crucial to a cosmopolitan attitude," writes Chris Brown of Kant and Kant's influence, "is the refusal to regard existing political structures as the source of ultimate value."[1] For Thomas Donaldson, "Kantian cosmopolitanism affirms the existence of cross-cultural moral truth."[2] In these statements Kantian humanism is seen as a moral-political conception transcending time and space, leaving created states with only a secondary, contingent status.

Kant's writing under this inspiration is extraordinarily wide-ranging. And still topical: from his perspective in the late eighteenth century, it could be seen to cover an array of themes familiar to us today, such as the implications of cultural, religious, linguistic, and racial differences between peoples; economic underdevelopment and international inequality; interdependence and the interaction of domestic and foreign policy; human relations with the natural environment; the idea of globalis/zation; anticolonialism; the ideal state; European integration; the purpose and value of international law, including supranational political institutions; the balance of power; and most prominently, the problem of war. If, as Whitehead remarked, the European philosophical tradition is a series of footnotes to Plato, then modern international theory, especially normative theory, could be seen as footnotes to Kant.[3] In our age, moreover, some of the most ambitious commentaries have been written in the cosmopolitan tradition which he exemplifies.

Despite this, dichotomies and even contradictions have been seen running through his work, whether in general philosophy or international theory. To a certain extent this is an unavoidable hazard of idealism, especially moral idealism; human beings fall short of the perfect happiness they imagine, or the ideal conduct they prescribe for themselves. But given the scale of Kant's ambition, criticisms of his work are likely to amount to theoretical positions in their own right.

Broadly speaking, these have been of two kinds. One, which I shall examine in this chapter, consists of treating his writing in international theory as a form of political idealism, leading to critical judgments of contemporary international relations and prescriptions for reform. The other approach involves a critique of Kant's metaphysics, which in theory should include but also transcend political idealism. I shall leave that to the next chapter.

11.1 International Theory as Political Idealism

Observing developments in Europe in his time, Kant foresaw the spread of independent states over all the earth, alongside arrangements to group them together. About their long-term worth he was more cautious, even ambivalent. While envisaging continued human divisions for the foreseeable future, he focused on reducing their damaging effects. Perhaps unsurprisingly, then, Andrew Hurrell finds

> a divergence over the relationship between what might broadly be called the "statist" and the "cosmopolitan" sides of Kant's writings. On one side, there are those who argue that Kant is primarily concerned with order at the level of interstate relations. Kant, it is argued, did not want to transcend the states system but to improve it. He wanted to subject the international anarchy to law and to find a solution to the problem of war but in a way which would not sacrifice the essential autonomy and independence of states. . . . There are, however, others who view Kant in very different terms and who have taken Kant as the paradigm for the existence of a cosmopolitan or universalist tradition in international relations. . . . First, there is the belief that the interstate system is of only derivative significance and that international life should be viewed instead in terms of a global society of mankind and of the existence of transnational ties linking all human beings. . . . Second, there is the claim that there are no unresolvable

conflicts of interest between peoples and that conflict results either from a lack of enlightenment or from the malevolent actions of those with a vested interest in fostering conflict. Third, there is the stress on the importance of morality in international life and, above all, on the moral imperative to move towards a more peaceful world even if this involves the creation of a new form of international political organization.

Here we find an early version of the "level-of-analysis" question for international theorists—whether the best approach is at the level of states or that of the states system; and a deeper one, as to whether to be a pragmatist/empiricist, taking the world as one finds it, or an idealist, contemplating how the world might or perhaps ought to be. How are these divergences to be overcome? Where does Kant's own final view lie—if he had one? Especially as, over key works, his emphases shift, as Hurrell points out:

> In *Perpetual Peace* and *The Metaphysics of Morals* [1796, 1797] Kant does indeed reject both world government and a federation with the power to enforce the proscription of war. Yet in both *The Idea for a Universal History* and *Theory and Practice* [1784, 1793] Kant's universalism is much stronger and he embraces both the idea of some kind of universal political system and a federation with the power to enforce the law.[4]

Things have moved on, moreover, since Kant's time, and the choices he imagined lie before us today. There is already a "universal political system," but it consists of independent states; and the new "international political organization" most obviously responsible, after 1945, for finding "a solution to the problem of war" (the UN Security Council) was itself, for the first half-century of its existence, deeply embroiled in war.

Hurrell points out that the view, popularized by Hedley Bull and Martin Wight, of Kant as a "universalist" has been to the fore among modern (post-1945) international theorists, with the "Kantian paradigm" taken to favor the transcendence, rather than the defense, of states.[5] In this connection, Colin Wight has argued that international theorists tend to take positions that ring-fence their field—fencing out political theory and its statist traditions.[6] So for that reason too we might expect "universalist" or "cosmopolitan" readings of Kant to predominate. But self-servingly; a more balanced attitude, or a change of fashion, might at any time emerge. A third possibility, therefore, is continuing ambiguity. A definitive interpretation of Kant's purpose would in any case depend on knowing the factors which influenced him at different times of his writing, and certainty in this area is difficult to establish in retrospect. We can speculate, as I shall do, but some controversy must remain.

The Statist/Cosmopolitan Divide

Hurrell remarks that "whilst Kant did believe in the states system, he believed in more than the states system." What that "more" is Hurrell leaves unclear, beyond saying that Kant hoped for better results in future than his own reservations about human nature allowed him to believe; and that not to give up hope was a moral duty.[7] But Kant did argue, both moralistically and optimistically, that like-minded people, learning from history, might transcend their contemporary social attachments to make war less likely, as well as less destructive. As he wrote at the end of *Perpetual Peace*:

> If it is a duty to bring about in reality a state of public right (albeit by an infinite process of gradual approximation), and if there are also good grounds for hoping that we shall succeed, then it is not just an empty idea that *perpetual peace* will eventually replace what have hitherto been wrongly called peace treaties (which are actually only truces). On the contrary, it is a task which, as solutions are gradually found, constantly draws nearer fulfilment, for we may hope that the periods within which equal amounts of progress are made will become progressively shorter.[8]

This argument, moreover, is stated again and again, quite deliberately, toward the end of all Kant's political works, as his parting message.

> Although [a great political body of the future, without precedent in the past] exists for the present only in the roughest of outlines, it nonetheless seems as if a feeling is beginning to stir in all its members, each of which has an interest in maintaining the whole. And this encourages the hope that, after many revolutions, with all their transforming effects, the highest purpose of nature, a universal *cosmopolitan existence*, will at last be realised as the matrix within which all the original capacities of the human race may develop. (*Idea for a Universal History with a Cosmopolitan Purpose* [1784]).

> We should be content with providence and with the course of human affairs as a whole, which does not begin with good and then proceed to evil, but develops gradually from the worse to the better; and each individual is for his own part called upon by nature itself to contribute

towards this progress to the best of his ability. (*Conjectures on the Beginning of Human History* [1786]).

I . . . rely . . . upon the very nature of things to force men to do what they do not willingly choose. . . . This involves human nature, which is still animated by respect for right and duty. I therefore cannot and will not see it as so deeply immersed in evil that practical moral reason will not triumph in the end, after many unsuccessful attempts, thereby showing that it is worthy of admiration after all. (*Theory and Practice* [1793]).

. . . the after-pains of the present war will force the political prophet to admit that the human race must soon take a turn for the better, and this turn is now already in sight. (*The Contest of Faculties* [1798]).[9]

Now if, after this reiterated optimism, Kant's position is still not entirely clear, then one possible reason is that he was unwilling to make firmer predictions: his faith in the power of human self-improvement was tempered by a natural caution. Transformations of fortune, in his accounts of human history, are always gradual, coming "after many unsuccessful attempts." Arguably, he was also being faithful to himself in not trying to second-guess a future that he saw as the responsibility of humankind as a whole. And unlike Hobbes, who insisted that the human future depended on forceful and largely amoral political solutions, Kant preached directly against "dishonourable stratagems" in international relations.[10] For the rest, the prescriptive clauses in *Perpetual Peace*, containing recommendations for the moral improvement of politics and diplomacy, show that he was not loath to think through the implications of his own vision of the future. Hence his advocacy, in that essay, of such principles as non-intervention against sovereignty, the avoidance of national debt, and the elimination of standing armies, espionage, and political secrecy.

Of this list Andrew Linklater comments: "its antiquated, even idiosyncratic character, should not blind us to the subtle relationship between ethics and politics which it embodies."[11] This seems to me a grudging, even backhanded judgment. We are still far from the realization of these Kantian ideals today; their application would have averted the most disastrous features of the first half-century of the universal states system, such as military dictatorship, aggressive mercantilism, "boom-and-bust" economic cycles, and the global nightmare of the Cold War. Chris Brown, by contrast to Linklater, describes the Preliminary Articles of *Perpetual Peace* as "strikingly modern. Open diplomacy, non-aggression, self-determination, non-intervention, the delineation of lawful means of making war (*jus in bello*), disarmament—these are the principles that constitute the settled norms of the modern international system [. . .] They are the principles that are to be found in such programmatic statements of the modern system as the Charter of the United Nations."[12]

Nor is it antiquated or idiosyncratic to argue, as Kant did, that a secular state could come to represent a larger and more inclusive society (a nation) than traditional, genealogical or face-to-face communities, as a moral project in its own right. This is the *form* of human society, at least, which is standardized in the current states system; and Kant argued that with the help of morality, one form of higher social organization would lead logically to another. Humankind could discover its social soul, so to speak, by following the original purposes of "nature" or "providence," eventually to establish a universal peaceable community beyond those contained in separate states. Liberal-democratic republics in particular would give place to a higher "cosmopolitan" order beyond both nationalism and parochialism.[13] This is a direct reversal of the Hobbesian line that autocracy in a system of human divisions was needed for social control. At the same time, as Howard Williams points out, Kant followed Hobbes in arguing that the direction of historical change would be from the centralized state outward. It was the learning experience of state-building which would lead to organized international relations. "Domestic popular sovereignty of a republican form is a key staging post in the gradual creation of a worldwide civil society brought together through a pacific federation."[14] Cosmopolis does not spring fully-formed from the human brain.

All in all, then, it seems inaccurate, as well as unfair, to blame a "statist"/"cosmopolitan" divide on Kant, since the conceptions underlying these two terms are, in his approach, compatible and indeed complementary; the one form of social organization prefigures the other. Change was built into his vision. It explains his insistence on "reasoned hope."[15] In the *Idea for a Universal History*, moreover, he had gone further, asserting that no institution could be the be-all and end-all for human beings. The "highest purpose of nature," he wrote, was to realize "a universal *cosmopolitan existence*" (Kant's emphasis).[16] Seen in this light, the challenge facing international theorists is not either/or, between statist pragmatism and cosmopolitan idealism; it is both/and.

Kantian theory also offers a positive rationale for state agency. On the one hand, his evolutionary approach puts the emphasis on political action as the means to improving the human condition. On the other, his republicanism supplies a democratic basis for this action. States as social possessions can develop, learn, and grow as individuals in their lifetimes do. When Kant writes of states as agents, it is implicitly in this collective, normative, forward-looking sense—inquiring how individuals can agree, bond together, make laws and abide by them; have a common culture; form a true, consensual society foreshadowing a peace-loving community of all humankind.

If this approach leaves questions, they are detailed, such as how long it will be before this ideal is realized, and what shape it will take—should states disappear altogether, or just be reduced in significance? Is there more than one kind of republic? One could also ask whether Kant's gradualism was not too timid. Perhaps, as Onora O'Neill says, he finally hesitated about "the dispensability of institutional structures in this life."[17] But equally, these are questions that he could fairly expect people themselves, by their actions, to answer in future. All of them, moreover—notably the human differences and disagreements that a world of states can be expected to throw up—are before us today. And in this regard even Kant's admirers have not taken us much closer to the answers.

11.2 The Contribution of Kantian Philosophers

John Rawls, through his *Theory of Justice*, first published in 1971, is usually seen as the initiator of a return to Kant in twentieth-century political theory. But it was only much later that Rawls produced an international application of his own approach. It was Charles Beitz who pioneered the "cosmopolitan conception" of "the moral relations of members of a universal community in which state boundaries have a merely derivative significance." On this footing, Beitz called into question such modern political givens as self-determination, the state "ownership" of material resources, and even state sovereignty itself when it might become a cover for governments' abuse of their own citizens. This radical approach was not, however, followed up, as in Kant's work, by a program of political prescription; and Beitz limited his case further by presenting it as subservient to the theory of justice that Rawls had yet to adapt to the world as a whole.[18]

Distributive Justice

Subsequently Shue and Pogge developed arguments for "distributive justice" in international relations—the idea that by a combination of aid and preferential trade, the material inequalities between poor, post-colonial societies and older-industrialized ones could progressively (but quite quickly) be overcome.[19] In the same vein, Onora O'Neill argued that international economic reform should be aimed to benefit the world's poorest and women in particular.[20] Carefully researched and argued, Kantian in their assumptions and prescriptive in intent, these contributions were nevertheless economistic in their focus and partial in scope.

Liberalism and the Democratic Peace

Another aspect of Kantian theory is the so-called democratic peace, or pacific union: the idea that peoples enjoying liberal democracy, as a version of the just and open society (for Kant, a representative republic), are unlikely to go to war with each other, and will form a nucleus of peace from which a universal community of humankind can grow. Exploration of this idea began to be popular toward the end of the Cold War. The general approach taken, however, has been disappointingly narrow, if not complacent—defining liberal democracy in terms of its institutions, or of liberal-democratic societies' achievements in material welfare. During the Cold War this could not help being identified with anti-Communist propaganda. Crude abuses of liberalism have abounded since, from Fukuyama's jaded comment that the end of the Cold War would bring a peace of vapid consumerism (the so-called end of history) to implausible list-compiling of all the supposed liberal-democratic states since 1800.[21] As Nick Rengger has argued, in the popular advocacy of "liberal democratic peace" one finds only rather shallow conceptions of liberalism, democracy or peace— "understandings of democracy [which] work to defend a particular status quo" of American values and American overseas power.[22]

Liberal Economics and Free Trade

The basic economic assumptions, moreover, of liberal-democratic apologetics must be questioned in their own right, notably the value-neutral or even positive assessment of free trade. In Kant's Europe, with organized statehood proceeding apace, a conception of original social exchange through the search for basic commodities may have seemed a reasonable view of the development of international relations. "In this way," he wrote, "nations first entered into *peaceful relations* with one another, and thus achieved mutual understanding, community of interests and peaceful relations, even with the most distant of their fellows."[23] But just as he strongly opposed colonialism, Kant would surely have opposed the inbuilt injustices of the post-colonial world economy that the dependency theorists identified. In a world with a fixed but unequal allocation of resources, preaching free trade can be disingenuous, serving the self-interest of the strong against the interest of the weak in change.[24]

Migration and International Integration

When Rawls's version of international theory eventually appeared, it was more conservative and less Kantian than the work of Rawls's own followers had given reason to expect.[25] Rawls's legalism, accepting the states system and international law as givens, followed the institutionally orientated approach to reform that Kant favored; but two centuries after Kant, and with a universal states system already in place, more radical political proposals seem to be called for which would still be Kantian in spirit. As Seyla Benhabib has put it:

> The Rawlsian vision of peoples as self-enclosed moral universes is not only empirically but also normatively flawed. This vision cannot do justice to the dual identity of the people as an *ethnos*, as a community of shared fate, memories, and moral sympathies, on the one hand, and as a *demos*, as a democratically enfranchised totality of all citizens, who may or may not belong to the same ethnos, on the other. All liberal democracies that are modern nation-states exhibit these two dimensions.[26]

Benhabib goes on to investigate the idea, put forward by Kant in *Perpetual Peace*, that a universal norm of hospitality to foreigners could grow into broader shared values and peaceful international relations. She engages in an imaginative but ultimately inconclusive discussion of the resistance of liberal-democratic governments, and of other liberal-democratic writers, to the acceptance of the "dual identity" she defines. That is, "modern nation-states," in her phrase, should include citizens with a strong claim to be indigenous, and citizens with no such claim; and democracy will facilitate this goal in the present and, through immigration, for the future.

Now, as I have argued, all the formal nation-states of the current system are modern by design, in Benhabib's sense (like her own United States), but some are less modern in practice than others, and this is one of the factors limiting population-exchange between them.[27] Questions of migration and national integration are, as Benhabib rightly assumes, complementary on a Kantian view of the world as a potential single society. But how far is her approach Kantian? And how far is it right anyway?

Kant himself was pragmatic in his caution—insisting that "Cosmopolitan Right shall be limited to Conditions of Universal Hospitality"— but idealistic in his aspiration: hoping this would develop into a "universal right of humanity" beyond the borders, and presumed rights and interests, of individuated societies.[28] Still, hospitality is not openness to migration as such. The "world's citizens," Kant wrote elsewhere, should certainly be encouraged

> to enter into a community with everyone else and to *visit* all regions of the earth with this intention. This does not however, amount to a right to *settle* on another nation's territory, [. . .] for the latter would require a special contract.[29] (Kant's emphasis.)

On this view, tourism, the pursuit of curiosity, and sociability are desirable and even beneficial, but universal rights of migration are not. Separate states have an essential purpose in preserving human identity and human diversity. A forcible erasure of this purpose in a single world state would, Kant says, lead to "a soulless despotism" (and ultimately prove unworkable).[30]

In this light, it is interesting to consider what kind of material world Kant imagined outside Königsberg (itself a city of variegated culture in his lifetime). First, he insisted, the finiteness of the globe meant finite resources.

> Accordingly, the only conceivable way in which anyone can possess habitable land on earth is by possessing a part within a determinate whole in which everyone has an original right to share. Thus all nations are *originally* members of a community of the land. But this is not a *legal community* of possession [. . .] and utilisation of the land, nor a community of ownership. It is a community of reciprocal action . . . which is physically possible, and each member of it accordingly has constant relations with all the others. Each may *offer* to have commerce with the rest, and they all have the right to make such overtures without being treated by foreigners as enemies. This right . . . affords the prospect that all nations may unite for the purpose of creating certain universal laws to regulate the intercourse they may have with one another.

At the same time, Kant imagined different degrees of practical organization across the world. Some states, he argued, would necessarily be larger than others by virtue of their economies.

> . . . if the nations involved are pastoral or hunting peoples . . . who rely upon large tracts of wasteland for their sustenance, settlements should not be established by violence, but only by treaty; and even then, there must be no attempt to exploit the ignorance of the natives in persuading them to give up their territories.[31]

Nowadays, colonialism and the exploitation of pre-modern societies have been outlawed, and there are no universal rights of settlement. But these Kantian principles, in a world of finite resources but more efficient economic instruments, surely also point to greater material equality *between states* (within feasible physical limits), especially when set alongside the equal human dignity implied in a "community of reciprocal action."

Otherwise Kant appears rather un-prescient of the material development of states as the successful social enterprises he imagined, which has brought us population-pressures on resources. Those same forces underlie the North-South, have-versus-have-nots controversies of the international relations of our time. More important, these pressures must logically impact on spatial human relations, and loosen the rivets of a fixed-borders territorial system. To that extent Benhabib's instincts are accurate: migration emerges as an important international bone of contention, while on an idealized view of states as collective agents—the Kantian view—growing democracy must hold between states as well as within them. Even Benhabib's "modern nation-states," satisfied societies in terms of both *ethnos* and *demos*, are unlikely to stand still. But migration as we see it today—people taking the system into their own hands—is a blunt and probably inadequate instrument of change. Some redrawing of material boundaries above and beyond those of citizenship seems to be required. Even liberal-democratic "great powers" must be proscribed, if people everywhere are to feel secure both as organic communities and as political societies. Fraternity requires equality, as well as liberty.

At the same time, if states were to become more equal in territorial size and assets, we can imagine that they would become largely redundant as human divisions, and that the "universal cosmopolitan existence" imagined by Kant would be closer to realization. In that sense his cautious millenarianism may be seen as a fertile, not an irresolute, stance. Kant saw only too well that democracy implies a perpetual openness to change, and that a universal system of human divisions exemplifying universal democracy contains the seeds of its own demise.

So we can say Kant thought like both an idealistic moral philosopher and a pragmatic international theorist, whereas Seyla Benhabib in her critique of current policies thinks like a Kantian philosopher but not sufficiently like an international theorist. She conflates "liberal democracies" with "modern nation-states" without taking account of the illiberality of the distribution of fixed assets in the system. Inevitably, in a system of independent polities, governments charged with looking after wealthier nations' endowments will show the limited hospitality toward would-be immigrants which she condemns. Defending those endowments is after all one of the things they were elected to do. An institutional liberal democracy is not bound to be a welcoming society. To that extent Kant was right in his reservations about the prospects for population-mobility leading to a single society of all humankind—at least, in the short term.

There is in fact a latent conflict between Benhabib's *ethnos* and her *demos*: between a state as *home*—to a "natural" community, formed from traditional, genealogical, and local groups, where government merely reflects established rules and concepts of moral authority—and a state as *polity*, where government is a secular institution, separate from society and charged (at least in democracies) with encouraging the critique of those concepts and of the rules of its own perpetuation. That latent conflict becomes an actual one when states comprise the entire population of the earth, and some people's conception of the state-as-polity comes up against other people's conception of the state-as-home.

Human Rights

Onora O'Neill has explored what she calls "the dark side" of the "international human rights culture"—criticizing, in effect, some practical failings of Kantian cosmopolitanism as it has become enshrined in law. She points to the usefulness of distinguishing between categories of rights, but also the false dichotomies about human identity to which this can give rise; and the dangers of placing effective responsibility in the hands of state governments, who may find some internationally-decreed rights (especially material ones) difficult to implement, or may simply refuse to respect them. O'Neill argues that in the light of these dangers, human rights can appear "aspirational" rather than real, and their very promulgation cynical. "The assumption that states and states alone should hold all the relevant obligations," she muses, "may reflect the extraordinary dominance of state power in the late twentieth century, rather than a timeless solution to the problem of allocating obligations to provide goods and services effectively."[32]

And yet O'Neill herself goes on to write in the idiom of conventional international theory, which implies that states are agents in their own right.

> States party [to an international human-rights agreement] may (or may not) set out to secure positive rights for their citizens.... Many states violate rather than respect human rights.... Some states—not only those we think of as rogue states—disregard or override many of the Covenant rights ... even strong and willing states [*sic*] may find that they cannot "achieve progressively the full realisation of the rights recognized" in Declarations and Covenants....[33]

Here is another instance of the practice I have repeatedly criticized: the postulation of an agent who/which stands above and apart from society in the interactions evoked, *yet is not government either*. For a normative theorist especially, this kind of writing is thoughtless—the very definition of failure. In this instance blame is implied, but unattributed; a profound philosopher diagnoses the moral challenges of the age, without exercising the same moral rigor and analytical acumen in respect of the human capacity for transformative action. Onora O'Neill shows herself a victim, as well as a critic, of the universal states system, which by declaring human agency to be everywhere leaves it nowhere in particular.

11.3 Popular Cosmopolitanism

Kantian ideas have also been present in popular debates. After 1918, pacifists like Noel-Baker evoked the lessons of a "war to end all wars." In the same spirit US President Woodrow Wilson set out terms for an international settlement based on national "self-determination." This led eventually to the setting-up of the universal system of independent states under the aegis of the UN—a system which came through the Cold War intact but also, because of the Cold War, unreformed.

Pacifism

During that conflict it became quite common to argue that the threat posed by nuclear weapons must logically focus the minds of people everywhere on their common humanity and bring an end to war. In Europe, the case was made by the English historian E. P. Thompson and his allies in European Nuclear Disarmament, who arguably did more than any other organized popular movement to ensure that

277

Soviet tyranny was abolished along with the Cold War.[34] That tyranny had been imposed in Eastern Europe in the name of global security, and it was in Eastern Europe that the revival of Europe-wide democracy began.

Yet we should not forget that the argument for common human values, debased as universal self-preservation, was routinely used throughout the Cold War by deterrence theorists in the United States, pleading for the stabilizing effects of a global balance of terror. This enabled them, along with their Soviet rivals, to prolong the Cold War in the name of peace, by arguing that they and the pacifists ultimately sought the same thing. It was Hobbes, not Kant, who argued that the potential for violence in human nature could be controlled by institutionalizing threats.

The optimistic "globalizing" argument for nuclear deterrence has not survived the end of the US-Soviet conflict. By and large, only Americans promoted it—out of a belief in American economic and technological superiority, or the perceived need to give deterrence some wider philosophical justification, or despair at the moral stagnation which accompanied the US-Soviet condominium in practice.

Environmentalism

In the late twentieth and early twenty-first century, the threat of environmental degradation to the point of catastrophe—notably through irreversible climate-change—was frequently evoked, just as environmental scientists had earlier argued that a "nuclear winter" resulting from a US-Soviet nuclear war would damage for decades, perhaps centuries, the natural world and the prospects of human thriving. These ideas and opinions eventually came together in an environmentalism espoused by the UN organization itself.[35] But again, the obvious cosmopolitan echoes (Kant wrote of nature as a precious human inheritance) were offset by the utilitarianism of self-preservation. There is no necessary contradiction here: Kant himself argued that commonsense self-preservation may have morally beneficial results; but he did so in a clear context of seeking the positive long-term good of humankind. Since the end of the Cold War, UN-sponsored environmentalism has continued through the Kyoto process, but still restricted in practice by the putative interests of states—notably on the vexed question of carbon dioxide emissions, which is connected both to economic development within individuated societies and to the prospect of their shared prosperity.

Cultural Cosmopolitanism

The Kantian legacy, since 1945, has also found expression in cultural forms. Peter Van der Veer argued for cosmopolitanism as a human tradition in its own right, dating it back to "the European Enlightenment of the eighteenth century." For Van der Veer, West European "colonial cosmopolitanism" should be seen as transcending pre-modern culture in secular, intellectual terms, while Eastern-inspired spiritual values transcended Western capitalist-colonial ones. The resultant fusion would approximate to a universal religion—an idea traced by Van der Veer back to Kant. Hence, cosmopolitanism represents "the engagement with the other in the colonial context" through the syncretizing work of key individuals—theosophists, cultural fusionists and political modernizers.[36]

Numerous passages on human evolution, often of a prophetic nature, in Kant's work could be invoked in support of this view.[37] Moreover, we now have a states system founded by Europeans and other, European-influenced intellectuals, in the wake of the European nationalist expansion to other continents, but also a system aimed at universalism, through the abolition of colonialism and the creation of states-for-all. In the first years of the UN, the policy-makers of the European states and their allies predominated both politically and numerically, but from the 1960s on the situation changed irrevocably, with the emergence of new states in Africa and Asia. About the same time, cosmopolitan popular movements sprang up in, and across, the countries inhabited or founded by Europeans—movements in favor of world peace and integration, against the immobilism of the Cold War or against post-colonial wars like that in Vietnam; movements often incorporating Eastern mystical or theosophical doctrines and culturally syncretist in their aims. The contemporary concept of globalis/zation can be traced back to this era. Cultural syncretism and state-transcendent politics can themselves be seen as interchangeable philosophies, since both rest on the idea of the shared social values which make a peace-loving community of all humankind conceivable.

On the negative side, the UN system has allowed real material inequalities to persist, and political progress to be held up, in the name of the independence of states. A more truly Kantian result would have been the removal of inequality, the exposure of the fakery of state interests, and the elimination of the politically-inspired abuse of citizens. As for cosmopolitanism expressed as mere cultural syncretism, this is

279

liable to lapse into a diffuse activity of individuals opposed to simply *all* social institutions—seeking to escape, rather than solve, the problems of organized society. The idea of the Sage of Königsberg as the original hippie does no justice to Kant's moral seriousness and intellectual rigor.

A popular author has even suggested that "cosmopolitanism" has fallen out of use, after becoming "one of a handful of words used dismissively by opposing extremes of the political process."[38] Certainly, some early Marxists wielded "rootless cosmopolitanism" as a term of abuse for someone with an insufficient commitment to socialism (when what they really meant was insufficient loyalty to the Soviet Communist Party); and diaspora groups in early modern Europe could be perceived as threatening, precisely because of their apparent lack of "national" loyalties.[39] Today, however, with everyone in the world having at least nominal rights of citizenship, and the Cold War over, these extremes have lost their force. Now "cosmopolitan" seems to have largely positive, if rather superficial, connotations, to refer to someone well informed about human relations owing to his or her experience of multiple societies and cultures—"a person free from national limitations" (OED). But not necessarily enlightened or progressive: the worldly experience may result from necessity—as in migration out of poverty—or exceptional wealth.

Kant argued, more profoundly, that the processes of social evolution were complex and at times apparently contradictory; cultural fusion would take place with difficulty, over long periods, through a critical dialogue between peoples, as well as through individuals' recognition of their common basic values.[40] This implies that culture itself should be seen as provisional, and not morally equivalent worldwide—meaning more politics for the future rather than less.

11.4 Weak Kantianism

By contrast with popular cosmopolitanism, the work of the more dedicated Kantian philosophers still seems to me the most cogent and refined of writing in international theory. Why then has it not been more influential, in intellectual or practical terms? Why has it not swung the balance, once and for all, in favor of normative international theory?

One reason, I have suggested, is a self-limiting approach on the part of these theorists, in which they have shown themselves unwilling to explore the full implications of Kant's work. Shue, for example, argued in his *Basic Rights* that there was a universally acknowledged right to the prerequisites of survival (shelter, clean water, and an assured supply of food).[41] This idea was already in the air at the time (the late 1970s), and subsequently became part of United Nations doctrine. But Shue himself, seeking the ear of the US government of the day, merely argued that as a goal it was the duty of US foreign policy to fulfill—an absurd and bathetic conclusion to a valuable, even inspiring proposal. Either the cause of basic rights is universal—in which case it must be universally tackled, by all governments (at least in proportion to their means)—or it is not. Shue's proposal, like much American Kantian philosophy, is weakened by its concessions to the perceived provincialism of American society, its inability to distinguish between universal and American values.

Kantian philosophers writing on international relations also appear not to have cleared up the ambiguities in liberal values to which I referred earlier. What is right, we might ask: liberal democracy or liberal economics? Are they the same? Are they compatible? The "distributive justice" and "democratic peace" theses clash in their treatment of Kant, as I have shown. They clash directly, over such matters as aid to poor societies living under undemocratic regimes (unconditional in the first case, but not in the second). The phrase "distributive justice" itself suggests a rather clinical view of one's fellow human beings as an abstract object of concern, if not actually of charity. Justice as a moral ideal, by contrast, is something people debate, define, seek to win and enjoy for themselves, as part of their relationship with others; something they have always been prepared to fight and even die for, not an object to be doled out, as in the economistic language of "goods and services." Kantian philosophers who want to be international theorists should be more concrete, more particular, more sensitive and daring thinkers. In this respect I find the imaginative and generous-minded work of Michael Walzer, though deliberately framed as non-cosmopolitan, going deeper into questions of international security and social justice than would-be Kantians do.[42]

The main self-limitation, however, among Kantians is arguably one that Kant himself would have treated with scant respect. This is to have taken his moral arguments for granted without examining their philosophical basis in depth. Arguably Rawls did this from the first in his theory of justice.[43] "On the whole," says Katrin Flikschuh, "contemporary advocates of a liberal theory of global distributive justice concentrate their efforts on extending domestic liberal principles to the global context, be this in the form of an internationalized difference principle or by devising alternatives to it. It is the Rawlsian liberal conception of justice rather than Kant's that informs and shapes their endeavors in this regard."[44]

The Rawlsian "difference principle" itself rests on an "original position," the so-called veil of ignorance about the social identity of the potential distributors of distributive justice. But as Ronald Dworkin has written:

> The device of an original position . . . cannot plausibly be taken as the starting point for political philosophy. It requires a deeper theory beneath it, a theory that explains why the original position has the features that it does and why the fact that people would choose particular principles in that position, if they would, certifies those principles as principles of justice.[45]

These arguments serve as a reminder that the touchstone of authenticity in Kantian international theory is not Rawls but Kant himself. Even Onora O'Neill, a great Kantian scholar and partial critic of Rawls,[46] has yet to combine a full critique of Kantian metaphysics with an integrated treatment of international themes. We should look to her, I think, and to Beitz, Benhabib and Shue, to lay a train of intellectual fire through the dry tinder left behind by Rawls.

Notes

1. Brown, *International Relations Theory: New Normative Approaches*, p. 24.
2. Thomas Donaldson, "Kant's global rationalism" in Nardin and Mapel (eds.), *Traditions of International Ethics*, p. 143. See also Garrett Wallace Brown, *Grounding Cosmopolitanism: From Kant to the Idea of a Cosmopolitan Constitution* (Edinburgh: Edinburgh University Press, 2009); and Garrett Wallace Brown and David Held (eds.), *The Cosmopolitan Reader* (Cambridge/Malden, MA: Polity Press, 2010).
3. Alfred North Whitehead, *Process and Reality: An Essay in Cosmology* [1929] (New York: Free Press, 1978), p. 39.
4. Andrew Hurrell, "Kant and the Kantian paradigm in international relations," *Review of International Studies* 16 (3), July 1990, pp. 183–185, 194.
5. *Ibid.*, pp. 183–184. He names F. H. Hinsley and W. B. Gallie as taking the contrary view.
6. See above, chapter 1 section 1.6.
7. Hurrell, "Kant and the Kantian paradigm," pp. 185 (cf. p. 202), 199 and 204.
8. Kant, *Perpetual Peace: A Philosophical Sketch* [1795–1796] in Reiss (ed.), *Kant: Political Writings*, p. 130, Kant's emphasis.
9. *Ibid.*, pp. 51, 92, 190, 234, Kant's emphasis.
10. *Ibid.*, p. 96.
11. Andrew Linklater, *Men and Citizens in the Theory of International Relations* (2nd ed. London: Macmillan, 1990), p. 119.
12. Brown, *International Relations Theory*, p. 35. See also Kant, *The Metaphysics of Morals* [1797] in Reiss (ed.), pp. 131–175.

13. Kant, "First Definitive Article of a Perpetual Peace: The Civil Constitution of Every State Shall be Republican," *Perpetual Peace* in *ibid.*, pp. 99–102.

14. Howard Williams, "Kantian perspectives on intervention: transcending rather than rejecting Hobbes" in Prokovnik and Slomp (eds.), *International Political Theory after Hobbes*, p. 116.

15. Onora O'Neill, "Kant on reason and religion," lecture I: "Reasoned hope" in *The Tanner Lectures on Human Values* 18 (Salt Lake City: University of Utah Press, 1997), pp. 269–290.

16. Kant, Eighth Proposition, *Idea for a Universal History* in Reiss (ed.), p. 51.

17. O'Neill, "Kant on reason and religion," *Tanner Lectures* II: "Interpretation within the limits of reason," p. 307, note 13.

18. Beitz, *Political Theory and International Relations*, pp. 181–182 and part III *passim*.

19. Pogge, *Realizing Rawls* and *World Poverty and Human Rights*; Shue, *Basic Rights*. See also David Beetham, "What future for economic and social rights?," *Political Studies* Special Volume on Human Rights 43, 1995.

20. O'Neill, *Faces of Hunger*; see also her *Bounds of Justice* (Cambridge: Cambridge University Press, 2000).

21. Francis Fukuyama, "The end of history?" *National Enquirer* 16, summer 1989 and *The End of History and the Last Man* (New York: Free Press, 1992); Michael W. Doyle, "Kant, liberal legacies and foreign affairs," *Philosophy and Public Affairs* 12 (3), summer 1983, pp. 205–235, 12 (4), fall 1983, pp. 323–353, and "Liberalism and world politics," *American Political Science Review* 80 (4), December 1986, pp. 1151–1169; David E. Spiro, "The insignificance of the liberal peace," *International Security* 19 (2), fall 1994, pp. 50–86; John M. Owen, "How liberalism produced democratic peace" in *ibid.*, pp. 87–125; and Bruce Russett and John R. Oneal, *Triangulating Peace: Democracy, Interdependence and International Organizations* (New York: W. W. Norton, 2001).

22. Rengger, *International Relations, Political Theory and the Problem of Order*, p. 119 and ch. 3 generally.

23. Kant, *Perpetual Peace*, in Reiss (ed.), p. 111, Kant's emphasis.

24. Cf. Beate Jahn, "Classical smoke, classical mirror: Kant and Mill in liberal international relations theory" in Beate Jahn (ed.) *Classical Theory in International Relations* (Cambridge: Cambridge University Press, 2006), pp. 178–203.

25. Rawls, *The Law of Peoples*.

26. Seyla Benhabib, "Democratic iterations: the local, the national, and the global" in Seyla Benhabib, *Another Cosmopolitanism*, p. 68.

27. See above, chapters 7 and 8.

28. Kant, "Third Definitive Article of a Perpetual Peace: Cosmopolitan Right shall be limited to Conditions of Universal Hospitality" in Reiss (ed.), pp. 105–108.

29. Kant, *The Metaphysics of Morals* [1797] Section III, "Cosmopolitan Right," §62, in Reiss (ed.), p. 172.

30. Kant, *Perpetual Peace*, First Supplement, in Reiss (ed.), p. 113.

31. Kant, *The Metaphysics of Morals* Section III, §62, in Reiss (ed.), pp. 172–173, Kant's emphasis.

32. Onora O'Neill, "The dark side of human rights," *International Affairs* 81 (2), March 2005, p. 435.

33. *Ibid.*, pp. 434–5.
34. See especially E. P. Thompson, "Notes on exterminism, the last stage of civilisation" in his *Zero Option* (London: Merlin Press, 1982).
35. World Commission on Environment and Development, *Our Common Future* [The Brundtland Report] (Oxford: Oxford University Press, 1987). Also notable are Jonathan Schell, *The Fate of the Earth* (London: Picador, 1982) and *The Seventh Decade: The New Shape of Nuclear Danger* (New York: Henry Holt, 2007).
36. Peter Van der Veer, "Colonial cosmopolitanism" in Vertovec and Cohen (eds.), *Conceiving Cosmopolitanism*, pp. 165–179.
37. Kant, *Idea for a Universal History*; *Theory and Practice I–II*; *Metaphysics of Morals* §43ff; *Contest of Faculties*.
38. Chris Roberts, *Lost English: Words and Phrases That Have Vanished From Our Language* (London: Michael O'Mara Books, 2009), p. 53.
39. See Susanne Lachenicht and Kirsten Heinsohn (eds.), *Diaspora Identities: Exile, Nationalism and Cosmopolitanism in Past and Present* (Frankfurt am Main: Campus Verlag, 2009).
40. Kant, *Perpetual Peace*, First Supplement, in Reiss (ed.), pp. 108–114.
41. Shue, *Basic Rights*.
42. See especially Walzer, *Spheres of Justice*.
43. Cf. Flikschuh, "Metaphysics and the boundaries of justice"; and more favorably, O'Neill, *Bounds of Justice*.
44. Flikschuh, *Kant and Modern Political Philosophy*, p. 183.
45. Quoted in Raymond Plant, *Modern Political Thought* (Oxford: Blackwell, 1991), pp. 105–106 (text corrected from original).
46. See chapter 11, "Constructivisms in ethics" in Onora O'Neill, *Constructions of Reason: Explorations of Kant's Practical Philosophy* (Cambridge: Cambridge University Press, 1989), pp. 206–18.

12

The Kantian Search for Unity

Kant's social philosophy is all of a piece; his international theory is
an essential part of his political theory, which emerges out of his
moral philosophy, itself locked into his philosophy of science and
"pure reason."[1]

Kant's theory of international relations was meant by him to be the
culmination of his general moral theory.[2]

Works like the *Idea for a Universal History with a Cosmopolitan
Purpose* and *Perpetual Peace* mark the high points in Kant's struggle
to define a universal or cosmopolitan "moral law" for his time and the
foreseeable future; they concentrate a preoccupation which repeatedly
breaks through the surface of his more abstract or specialized treatises.
Implicit in this project is an assumption of the unity of all humankind,
and of our ability to judge others, even dead, distant and unborn, as
we judge ourselves.

With this concern goes naturally a concern for personal unity, of
harmony with oneself. For that purpose, in what he considered his
own greatest work, Kant deliberately set aside "a critique of books and
systems" in favor of

the critique of our power of reason as such, in regard to all cognitions
after which reason may strive *independently of all experience....* In
that activity, I have made comprehensiveness my major aim, and I
venture to say that there should not be a single metaphysical problem
that has not been solved here, or for whose solution the key has not
at least been provided. In fact, pure reason is so perfect a unity that,
if its principle were insufficient for the solution of even a single one
of all the questions assigned to reason by its own nature, then we
might just as well throw the principle away; for then we could not fully
rely on its being adequate to any of the remaining questions either.[3]

What Kant meant by pure reason, however, and how it could be applied
to "the remaining questions" of practical morality, have given rise to

controversy ever since. This has made him the main target of attacks on the Enlightenment and the modern society seen stemming from it. The attacks have come from post-modernists, alleging that Kantian rationalism involves an unreal detachment toward human society and life in general (the "view from nowhere," as it is sometimes derisively called); and from moral philosophers like Alasdair MacIntyre, arguing that it deforms morality as such. Since MacIntyre argued in the same place that post-modernists were the Enlightenment's logical extension, his critique had the handy advantage of denigrating them too.[4]

From this it is but a short step to argue that normative international theory, conceived as the "culmination" of Kant's moral philosophy, must be problematic, and that our established methods of analysis will result in what Kimberly Hutchings calls a "morality/politics divide." "International relations," she says,

> is one of the areas of social science which most clearly brings home the tensions involved in the dual relation of inquirer to object of inquiry, as both scientific observer and moral judge. . . . As social scientists, we are required to understand and explain our object, as moral beings, we are required to judge or evaluate it. Received wisdom in international relations premises the possibility of the former on its rigid separation from the latter, so that the understanding of, for example, war, is necessarily distinct from the question of the justice or injustice of war. The former is the task of the science of international relations, the latter task is within the province of the moral philosopher or the normative theorist . . . this separation of the realms of morality and politics, on which so much social science and moral philosophy is founded, can be traced back to Kant's critical philosophy, and . . . has problematic consequences for the possibility of both explanation and evaluation in the international sphere.[5]

To put it differently, Hutchings agrees with my claim that the "received wisdom" of international theory is an explanatory/normative "rigid separation." But she also thinks this is symptomatic of a wider cultural failing for which Kant is ultimately to blame. I shall take her critique as a model before moving on to some comments of my own.

12.1 Angles to Kant

Hutchings starts from a concrete example, a radical conflict of opinion reported between nuclear strategists and moral philosophers—the first ostensibly focusing on the practicalities of how deterrence will or will not work, the second on its "rationality and moral permissibility."

Only ostensibly, however; she finds that the philosophers in question fail to "challenge the morality/politics dichotomy by bringing moral arguments to bear on political policy," because they rely too much on hypothesis; and that in fact "much of the work in the field of applied ethics remains within Kantian terms of reference, in which the division between real and ideal is presumed." So she turns instead to scrutinize international theorists for their angles to Kant.

First examined is Hurrell, writing in the wake of the English School founder-members Hedley Bull and Martin Wight. It seems, says Hutchings, that Kant could be classed in their terms "as a realist, a rationalist, or a revolutionist." The first and last of these terms refer to the "statist" and "cosmopolitan" approaches I mentioned in the previous chapter, with the "rationalist" placed somewhere in between. "Revolutionist" is Martin Wight's ugly neologism; only such an extreme conservative could think of Kant as a radical. But Hutchings herself, in any case, concludes that the elements of the Wight/Bull typology "are premised equally on a Kantian presumption of the morality/politics divide."

Next considered are some of Linklater's writings, seen as exemplifying Habermasian or "critical" theory. "Central to critical theory," says Hutchings, "is a rejection of the morality/politics divide." But on further inspection this approach also fails, for her, to overcome original Kantian dichotomies. The "critical" international theorist, in her view, reads history as if it were progress, examining and ultimately endorsing the direction of international relations in state-transcendent terms—taking for granted the political processes of modernization, development, and integration that Kant singled out for praise. But in Hutchings's opinion this approach has no foundation other than its own assumptions on the direction of history and the analyst's role.

Finally, she considers "the challenge of the theorists variously labelled as postmodernist, post-structuralist or radical interpretivist" (themselves critics, of course, of all the rest). Here she cites Ashley's view that the post-structuralist international theorist "automatically inverts traditional hierarchies to reveal their arbitrariness, and theorize from the border lines, from the void or no place." And yet, she says, this stance

> threatens to develop into a celebration of the arbitrariness of the theorist's representation of the object and his/her judgment upon it. Rather than taking us into a new criticism, this seems to return us to one side of the coin of the Kantian dichotomy, in which the morality/

politics split leaves the real world in the hands of providence, and gives absolute freedom to the philosopher's judgment. If critical theory depends on an *as if* reading of history to enable judgment, and thus is allied with traditional revolutionism . . . then the question must also be raised as to whether post-structuralist theory, in its dependence on the concept of history as contingency, does not take us back to realism.[6]

Now the first thing to note about this survey of positions is its breadth—which paradoxically only bears out Kant's importance, by showing how many ideas in international theory can be found in his work. To that extent there is no reason for Hutchings or anyone else to blame the "morality/politics divide" on him; the divide exists, if it exists, for everyone. This brings us back to the question of his intentions. Is Kant's judgment of human relations fertilely ambiguous, or just ambiguous; is the glass of life half full or half empty for him? To this question I have already given my answer: Kant believed that all human ideals could one day be realized through human nature itself. And on a "morality/politics divide," toward the end of *Perpetual Peace* he pointedly remarked: "I can indeed imagine a *moral politician*, i.e. someone who conceives of the principles of political expediency in such a way that they can co-exist with morality, but I cannot imagine a *political moralist*, i.e. one who fashions his morality to suit his own advantage as a statesman."[7] No ambiguity there, at least.

Kimberly Hutchings herself thinks that a "morality/politics divide" is a bad idea, whatever its origin. She begins:

> Until we recognize the identity of the moral and political in the international realm, and collapse the distinction between science and ethics in our moralizing and theorizing about that realm, our comprehension of it will remain limited and distorted.

And she ends:

> I have no easy recipe for this re-thinking, but one thing it must involve is the recognition that even as morality and politics are kept apart in the thinking of moral philosophers and strategists, revolutionists and realists, they are also continually being brought together.[8]

12.2 Deeper Divides

On a more damning plane, however, for social science and moral philosophy in general, Hutchings finds Kant's own work problematic—

holistic in conception and aim, but in practice showing apparently unbridgeable divides. These can be reduced to four.

First, on the level of *experience*, between our perception of things and our ideas of them. For Kant, says Hutchings, "the noumenal realm of the thing in itself and the guiding ideas of the faculty of reason always remain inaccessible, in principle, to our faculties of intuition and understanding." (And yet, she adds, Kant's own "critical project," in his most ambitious theoretical work, "demands that these gaps be bridged").

Second, on the level of *action*, between the ideals of moral behavior we can conceive, and our common practices, where we follow our natural desires. "Goodness is possible," Hutchings paraphrases, "insofar as we are capable of being motivated by pure reason.... The rule of reason over us, however, is always contested by natural motivation and ... can never be secure." (And yet, she adds: "All of Kant's practical philosophy is governed by the project of reconciling nature with reason, of bringing desire under the sway of the categorical imperative and of turning *ought* into *is* through the subsumption of the real under the ideal.")

Third, on the level of *politics*, between social practices and institutions we value, and the reality of political, including international, life. "In practical terms, ironically, pure practical reason is practically impotent. Humanity is in the uncomfortable position of being obliged to pursue goals which it is not capable of realizing.... The world of law, politics and history is, for Kant, the realm of natural motivation, in which people are coerced into coexistence in spite of themselves." (And yet "Kant admits that the identification of real with ideal and is with ought in history is, and can only be, a matter of the philosopher's judgement").

Fourth, on the level of *ideas*, the Kantian philosopher, recognizing the other three divides, becomes a judge, but by the nature of things cannot derive any overriding authority for his/her views; and so is "equally justified in condemning or endorsing the status quo. This becomes obvious as we explore the way that Kantian presumptions are at work in the moral philosophy and political theory of international relations." Beyond morality and politics, this is a morality/metaphysics divide. (And yet, Hutchings argues, we must judge.)[9]

Now the first thing to say about this litany of profound ambiguities, and comments on them, is that Hutchings herself at times seems unsure whether she comes to bury Kant or to praise him. As I have mentioned, criticisms of his work, if they measure up at all, are likely to amount to theoretical positions in their own right. But let me take the issues concretely.

12.3 The Divided Self: Coping with States

The first is psychological and epistemological; it implies a divided, even conflicted self. Kant's approach here has famously aroused controversy—notably his distinction between appearances, on the one hand, and "things in themselves" on the other: the former being part of the "sensible" (physical) domain, and the latter part of the "intelligible" domain of reason or the mind. "Things in themselves" for Kant are definable only negatively, lying as they do in a "noumenal realm" beyond the limit of reason.[10] But this only provokes the unanswerable question of how he or anyone else could know what a thing-in-itself was. The "pure" reason *independently of all experience*" at which he aimed in his *Critique* is surely either impossible or pointless. It implies that we may never attain unity within ourselves, because we are continually striving after things that we can never fully know. Tantalizingly, we merely glimpse some ideal insight into experience which has the potential to illuminate our lives.

Kant's defenders, like Onora O'Neill, point to his qualifying remarks: "The noumenal world, [Kant] insists, is 'only a *point of view*, which reason finds itself constrained to adopt.'"[11] For Henry Allison, Kant's distinction "pertains to two ways of considering things: as they appear to us in the spatiotemporal form of our intuition, and as they may be in themselves independently of our manner of intuiting them." These conditions of "cognition" can be summed up, Allison adds, as "a propensity or mechanism of the mind, which governs belief and belief acquisition."[12] The trouble with these interpretations is that they reduce philosophy to epistemology or mere psychological technique. This was the direction taken by the American pragmatists in the century after Kant.[13]

Considered on a deeper level, however (and more traditionally), Kant's distinction takes on a tragic aura. This poignancy of human limits would still be somewhat obscured by his insistence on rational language—which is a general problem with his work, affecting core Kantian inventions, like "synthetic *a priori*" propositions, and making them appear merely technical, as well as hard to understand. Yet fill his language out with human emotions, and the whole apparatus of his thinking acquires a certain moral strength. That is what Allison seems to be arguing when he remarks that Kant's philosophical project is tied together by its "normative force."[14]

Ontology/Epistemology in International Theory

This insight should help with the problem of absent philosophical foundations which, for some analysts, has dogged international theory since Realism's grand simplicities first began to be discredited late in the Cold War. As the common argument runs, there is a Gordian knot binding ontology and epistemology; it is impossible to determine whether what we know is dependent on how we know it, or vice versa. Is there an objective reality of everything that we (at least partly) grasp, or is this simply a human invention? International theorists face this question with a peculiar nakedness, because our object of study is the world itself, based on a single organizing principle, the secular independent state.

In this connection Steve Smith has argued: "it is not possible to wish [epistemology] away, or undermine its importance, by arguing, as is fashionably the case amongst post-modernist philosophers and (philosophical) realists, that ontology is prior to epistemology . . . prioritizing one or the other . . . sets up a false distinction between the two and implies that one is separable from the other."[15] Yet elsewhere (and contradictorily), Smith has appeared to accept that "ontology is what counts in the end."[16] Meanwhile Colin Wight has taken a firm position that ontology is prior to epistemology.[17]

In chapter 5 I argued that ontology includes epistemology and is in that sense prior to it, whereas the reverse could not be true. We must have an original sense of the world from somewhere. Doubting oneself on this level is beside the point; only human beings, after all, conceive the world as such. That is the lesson of ontological Realism (though I think it mistaken to ascribe this view to post-modernists, as Smith suggests—they who above all others want to undermine certainty in human experience).

But more important, it is absurd to conduct debates in international theory—like the ontology/epistemology controversy—as an abstract discussion devoid of political events, social facts, or named human beings in their ordinary lives. Normative international theory avoids this hazard, by involving us in moral judgments about real human relations, with challenges that are always specific and concrete. To that extent the problem of "things-in-themselves" disappears, even for Kant. It is only by thinking of an object in complete isolation from ourselves and our fellow human beings that it is possible to imagine "things-in-themselves" at all; and to enter that condition is unnecessary, as well as artificial.

291

Modernity and Absurdity

In any case, the perfect example of such a thing is precisely the modern state. Ideally, it stands for the sense-making, knowledge-creating, hospitable community we would all like to belong to, amid the faceless mass of the human race. But only ideally. In practice, the states system consists of forced communities of strangers into which, under unequal and largely immutable circumstances, we all happen to be born. Here, between the social ideal we can imagine and the actuality we inhabit, there is indeed a divide—and one capable of destabilizing everything down to language itself. Yet the problem is in our institutions, not in our intuitions; it is states that are wrong, not human nature as such. It is the modern states system, as a set of permanent and ubiquitous human divisions, which is anomalous to minds conscious only of human uniqueness and therefore human unity; and in this regard Kant's perception of divides and contradictions between ideals conceived, and realities encountered, was prescient of our particular modern predicament.

In this regard it is surely no accident that the great range of post-Freudian, absurdist, and irrationalist movements in art and literature in the early twentieth century (Dadaism, Surrealism, the Theatre of Cruelty, the Theatre of the Absurd) developed alongside the growth of the states system, with its depersonalizing implications for human life. The spread of industrialization and cities, making for widespread social anonymity; the growing efficiency of government, extending a minority's capacity for legally sanctioned abuse; the growing force of technology, increasing the destructiveness and impersonality of war; the communications revolution, striking the death knell of face-to-face relationships—can all be portrayed as the nightmarish consequence of the worship of rationality, to which the only response is extreme individualism or escape into fantasy. The node of these developments, and the focus of collective anxiety, is the modern state, as intimated in the works of Kafka, Huxley, Koestler, and Orwell.

A vision of the human condition as the objectification of unease, leading to the individual divided against him/herself (even, under the totalitarian state, to the persecution of opponents by disappointed idealists), is the other face of the optimism and sense of purpose we are taught to associate with modernity. This may even be seen as an immature version of globalis/zation: individuals perceive the world as a unified whole for the first time, only to realize that they cannot have it; it means nothing concrete to them. Hence, perhaps, MacIntyre's depiction of Kant as the intellectual ancestor of existentialism, the individualized revolt against the perceived meaninglessness of modern life.[18]

One way to escape this situation is to reject modernity and rationality together, as post-modernists do. But this is a futile gesture. Deconstruction is just euphemistic destruction, providing no help for the divided self. Post-modernism, MacIntyre argued, is the last confused gasp of the Enlightenment. In making this connection MacIntyre was right. But as a moralist he overlooked the alternative, which is to interpret the modern state purposively, as Kant did, as the way-stage to something else, in the context of a reflection on human society; and MacIntyre missed this solution because he was unwilling to think like an international theorist and engage with the politics of his (and our) time. As international theorists we start with the advantage that our object of inquiry is human relations as a whole; we cannot but have a unity of purpose and a humanist dynamic, short of traducing ourselves. If there really is a modern "separation of the realms of morality and politics," then international theorists are in the front line of those whose task is to put this right, and heal humanity's wounds, including self-inflicted ones.

On all the evidence this was Kant's own aim. In *Perpetual Peace* he looked both back and forward, to make concrete prescriptions for the reform of politics and diplomacy in his own lifetime. That work could be seen as merely the most explicit and systematic attempt, in his writing, to express in political terms the relation between reason and morality. How is this *not* an integrative purpose? An all-important element, moreover, reiterated at the end of all his political treatises, is his insistence on the value of hope. As Onora O'Neill points out, he rejects many orthodoxies, including religious ones, in his penetrating search for what human beings might reasonably hope, but he does not reject hope itself.[19] There is logic, as well as modesty, in such a position. To despair of all possibility of change is hubris; and hubris means inaction, a political contradiction in terms.

12.4 Morality/politics: the duty of judgment

Kant's approach in the *Groundwork of the Metaphysics of Morals* foreshadows modern ontological Realism in key respects. For example, on human distinctiveness and dominance: "Man actually finds in himself a power which distinguishes him from all other things—and even from himself so far as he is affected by objects. This power is *reason* [. . .] it manifests its highest function in distinguishing the sensible and intelligible worlds from one another and so in marking out limits for understanding itself."[20] Equally, this capacity is the source of all morality. So as "earthly gods . . . we should proceed in our disputes in such a way that a universal federal state may be inaugurated."[21]

By the same token, the idea must be abandoned that some problems in international relations are sui generis and so can escape judgment. "Cosmopolitan" or "universalist" theory need not be conducted on such a high level of generality as to neglect existing political issues. As Onora O'Neill writes, paraphrasing Kant: "The point is to consider what we *can* consistently will be done, not only by ourselves but also by all others [. . .] the fact that not everyone can live in the same manner or place does not suggest that there cannot be moral principles."[22]

So international theorists can contribute to a resolution of, for example, the Israel/Palestine conflict over rights to statehood, by formulating, in consultation with specialists on the region, ideas for easier coexistence between the local peoples, and debating those already in the air (as Kant did in *Perpetual Peace*, where he drew on projects for democracy and integration in Europe[23]). Further, these ideas might be gradualist and pragmatic, while set against imagined ideal circumstances. So there is no necessary contradiction between a "two-state" solution in the short term to the Israeli/Palestinian conflict and the longer-term ideal of these two peoples living together under one state—cooperating, rather than clashing, as we have a right to expect of human beings anywhere in the world. (The original UN proposal was evolutionary and involved concessions on both sides.[24])

By the same token, there is no false impartiality to which Israelis or Palestinians, their factional supporters, or anyone else can appeal to avoid a resolution of the dispute. I refuse the idea that the Middle East conflict is insoluble or unique, and I do so in part for the sake of the people in that conflict themselves, and in part to defend the right of everyone else in the world not to have their lives blighted by it—either directly, by Islamic terrorists making random innocents the scapegoats for intransigent Israelis, or indirectly, by the neglect of pressing problems elsewhere. We *must* judge our fellow human beings, expecting to be judged by them in return; that is an essential part of our relationship with each other. International theorists are no more exempt from this principle than anyone else.

We must also judge, as individuals, because it is the only way to be a full moral person, especially in the problematic and morally compromising setting of the universal states system. It is only in judging our fellow human beings hastily, ignorantly, unfairly or ungenerously—

being *censorious*—that we are likely to go wrong. But that is a risk we have to take.

Kant the Professional Philosopher

Having said all this, even Kant was guilty at times of repeating himself, of rewriting the same thesis in different guise, of oversimplifying for effect or in order to popularize his work. He could even, on occasion, appear confusingly to backslide from positions he had previously taken. And he could overstress the need for consistency in human behaviour at the expense of instinct. For example, he argued in the *Groundwork* in favor of promise-keeping not because another person (here, a creditor) might suffer if we broke our promise to him/her, but because if everyone broke his or her promises no one would ever trust again, and promise-making would become universally ineffective as a result.[25] This example, strong in logic, could equally be interpreted as utilitarian in intent. So MacIntyre has rather facetiously argued that Kant's main principle of universalization can refer equally to banal and to uplifting contexts.[26]

Some say Kant was unimaginative, even unworldly, and chose terrible examples to back up his arguments.[27] Leaving aside this kindly but I think inadequate explanation, there were times when he bent over backward to answer his detractors, serving himself ill as a result. One notorious incident comes to mind, provoked by the Swiss-French writer Benjamin Constant, author of the lachrymose Romantic novel *Adolphe* and ambitious candidate for political office in his adopted France. In *Des Réactions Politiques* (1796–7) Constant declared: "The moral principle that it is one's duty to tell the truth, if taken absolutely and in isolation, would make all society impossible. . . . We have the proof of this in the very direct conclusions drawn from this principle by a German philosopher, who goes so far as to claim that it would be a crime to lie to murderers pursuing your friend who asked whether he was not hiding in your house."[28]

Constant's attack seems unanswerable—except that he was misquoting Kant, who had imagined a rather different situation ("For example, a householder has ordered his servant to say 'not at home' if a certain human being asks for him. The servant does this and, as a result, the master slips away and commits a serious crime, which would otherwise have been prevented by the guard sent to arrest him. Who (in accordance with ethical principles) is guilty in this case? Surely the servant, too, who violated a duty to himself by his lie, the results of which his own conscience imputes to him."[29])

Constant's cavalier first sentence in any case contains its own contradiction (if we assume all morality is social, any moral principle taken "absolutely and in isolation" would obviously make society impossible). In Kant's original text, the pursuer is a legitimate agent of society and the pursued a guilty man, while the person pressed to lie is not a free agent, but subservient. In Constant's version (assuming he ever read Kant's original), the roles are reversed—the pursuers are "murderers" implicitly pursuing an innocent, and the moral complication of the master/servant relationship is omitted. In Kant's parable, the guilt of the crime is shared (by "the servant, *too*")—but not, as Constant insinuates, to condone a betrayal of friendship; there is no friendship (at least, of equals) in the situation imagined by Kant. His point is different and finer: a guilt unequally shared is no less guilt. The point is also socially realistic: innocence and guilt are rarely neatly apportioned in human relations, especially close ones. In Constant's black-and-white account, by contrast, the guilt is all on one side (either the "murderers," or that of the liar who protects them), the easier to caricature his opponent.

Arguably, the only reaction needed to such a crude distortion was to point to the original misquotation. Yet having seen himself identified in public as the "German philosopher" so loftily dismissed, and overlooking Constant's carelessness toward sources, Kant dashed off a reply, "On a supposed right to lie from philanthropy."[30] In this essay extra generalizations are introduced which add little to the original argument, and his recourse to principle looks, in the end, like a concession of weakness in a debate where his initial position had been clear. This late work, according to one biographer, has been "often attacked because of the alleged absurdity of its conclusions . . . some have wanted to explain it away as a product of Kant's old age."[31] But it may also be put down simply to Kant's over-earnestness, leading him to seize the opportunity of a public debate with a critic, as on previous occasions in his career.

In the original example-situation, he steps aside from an easy condemnation of the master, whose guilt is clear (he "commits a serious crime"), to stress the less obvious guilt of the servant. Nothing, in other words, in our actions is without consequences. The servant's guilt may be partial and minor, as a measure of the shared guilt, but his guilt is still whole *for him*: in no part of his mind could he not have foreseen that his master might go on to commit a serious crime, effectively with his connivance. Kant's emphasis here is on the indivisibility of conscience, like that of consciousness itself. By extension, even the crimes which individuals in positions of power may get away with do not license wrongdoing by those who feel they have no power at all. Even servants are morally free to choose right and reject wrong. We are all responsible for our actions, all of the time.

Illustrations like these, when properly understood, give a favorable impression of Kant as both a subtle and a down-to-earth moralist. Readers with limited patience may well judge (as Constant obviously did, for his own self-publicizing ends) that Kant was neglectful of common sense or ordinary people's concerns, simply because he chose to focus on less-obvious moral arguments. Kant's own relegation of concrete illustrations to a final section on "Casuistical Questions" in his essay did not help his cause. Nonetheless, to complain that the powerful routinely disappoint us, and in so doing corrupt the weak, is very much a part of democratic political argument.

Kant's parable can, moreover, be extended to international theory, to counteract the "modesty" caveat I mentioned earlier—the assumption that we have a limited right to express value judgments of people and events in other countries, because our own accountability for the judgments is limited.[32] International theorists, as specialist observers and analysts, are like the servant in Kant's story—potentially "in the know" about everything, including crimes against strangers; on the face of it, uninvolved. But in justice, duty-bound to bear witness even at some cost to oneself.

12.5 Morality/Metaphysics: Beyond Abstraction and Convention

The most radical Kantian divide alleged by Kimberly Hutchings, between morality and metaphysics, arguably overarches all the others. And here indeed I would isolate as problematic Kant's teleology— history seen as the fulfilment of a final or grand design. As an at-least nominal Christian, he could not avoid this concern. The question arises as to what he saw as the ultimate form of human social organization. He also wrote of "the highest purpose of nature, a *universal cosmopolitan existence*." So what, in Kant's view, is in God's design for humankind? Ideal state as ideal polity, or ideal state as state of happiness? And how should we live now as members of humankind, to try to bring forward either of these ideals?

The Categorical Imperative

Kant's key principle for moral action is the categorical (or absolute moral) imperative: "Act only on that maxim through which you can at the same time will that it should become a universal law."[33] For Kant, the source of this judgment lies in our reason. Christine Korsgaard explains:

> According to Kant, as each impulse to action presents itself to us, we should subject it to the test of reflection, to see whether it really is a *reason* to act. Since a reason is supposed to be intrinsically normative, we test a motive to see whether it is a reason by determining whether we should allow it to be a *law* to us. And we do that by asking whether the maxim of acting on it can be willed as a law.[34]

Yet Kant also seemed to suggest that no independent support for the categorical imperative should be sought in the world as such. Here I part company with him. Why we should be moral must, in my view, be linked explicitly to our place in the world, just as a place for the world must be found in the universe. Our ontology (our total conception of reality) and our morality must be aligned. Then, and only then, can we be truly in harmony with each other and ourselves.

The way I express it is this. We must be integrated with the universe; that is the basis of reality. We must be integrated with each other; that is the basis of morality. And we must be integrated with ourselves; that is the basis of happiness. Truth resides in a simplicity only God and humans understand.

Kant's categorical imperative also seems perverse from a Christian point of view. In effect, he has isolated there one principle of Christian morality—Jesus's injunction: "Love thy neighbour as thyself." But in the original, this injunction comes on the heels of another: "Thou shalt love the Lord thy God with all thy heart, and with all thy soul, and with all thy mind." In context the two are linked,[35] as they are logically. We are enjoined to love each other because God loves us; and it is because God loves us that we are here. In the Christian version, the ontological and the moral justification are the same.

Nothing in life equals this ideal of integrity, once expressed. To see our perfect freedom reconciled with right action toward each other is the very definition of human happiness. Kant understood this as well as anyone, which is why he expended so much argument, in this and other places, on explaining the association between freedom and the categorical imperative (since any kind of imperative must appear freedom-limiting). But his central moral principle is still undermined by the withdrawal from it of either ontological support or its Christian associations.

The View from Nowhere

A related criticism, heard from professional philosophers, is that the categorical imperative taken at face value (that is, in secular terms) is an empty tautology, owing to Kant's attempt to formulate it as universal, impersonal, and objective. The criticism runs as follows. Naturally if we settle, even after rigorous self-examination, on a binding course of conduct it will conceivably be right for everyone else (and vice versa); but nothing has thereby been said, no specific guidance as to action given. At stake in morality, on the other hand, is not just what is universal in value, but what is fundamental: action which is right for its own sake whatever the circumstances, including unforeseen ones. Other people's opinions (even all other people's opinions) are not necessarily part of the judgment. In this regard it is also worth recalling that in the Preamble to the UN Charter (1944–45), a key goal of the organization is stated as the reaffirmation of faith in fundamental (not universal) human rights. In early debates of the UN's founding documents there was resistance to the use of "universal" as opposed to "fundamental" for international-normative assertions, because the former term was considered weaker.[36]

The categorical imperative works only by making an abstract principle of morality. Kant's stress on self-consistency led him to play down a truth of all morality: that a part of our self always belongs to other people. (In the case of marriage, potentially all of our self.) Thus, it is actually unnecessary for us to think of behaving in all circumstances in conformity with some idealized personal will. Though Kant may have believed this, his account of morality is damagingly hollowed out by his omission of an external ontological support for his central principle—a support conceived in explicit conjunction with other people, or with God.[37]

This abstractionism, moreover, or a misguided populism also led him to quote rather too often from the hackneyed teleology of his time. It took two forms, both of them unhelpful.

Nature, Providence, Chance

Kant's many references to "nature" and "providence" evoke an agency sometimes in conformity with human inclinations, sometimes as a corrective to them; sometimes as an expression of collective human will, sometimes in denial of it, albeit in a longer-term human interest. Sometimes "nature" for him is impersonal—what might, in an early version of ecologism, be called the balance of nature; sometimes it is related to *human* nature—a tendency working in our collective interest even in apparently paradoxical and hidden ways.

In *Perpetual Peace*, for example, a long and at times poetic passage is devoted to the way in which climate, the seasons, and ocean currents spread material resources over the earth, and different peoples are brought together pacifically through travel and trade. Kant calls this "mechanistic" nature; it is his anthropological explanation for the origin of civilization. Yet it is also "nature," he says in almost the same breath, which "wisely separates the nations" through linguistic and religious differences, thus avoiding "an amalgamation of the separate nations under a single power." As an apparent uncaused cause in human history, "nature" in the latter sense is partly contradictory of "nature" in the former, and bound to raise questions about Kant's conception of the relationship between morality and free will. A similar problem arises with his notorious remark that "the problem of setting up a state can even be solved by a nation of devils (so long as they possess understanding)." "Natural" self-interest, he maintains, will lead humans to live peaceably and in good order, though often "against their own inclinations"; "we may therefore say that nature *irresistibly wills* that right should eventually gain the upper hand."[38]

In these cases Kant is clearly deriving moral concepts from international theory—specifically, historical international theory—for the purpose of prediction. But the metaphysical basis of his claim is incoherent, at times radically so. In his text, a disembodied "nature" and "Providence" by turns provoke and enlighten human affairs; humankind, in the millennial course of history, is divided and united by them. The authorial stance shifts uneasily between a benign but banal futurology and stricter moral inclinations. Sometimes "nature" or "providence" is there to be used by human beings for their own good—effectively identical with humans themselves; sometimes it is an entirely separate force. Sometimes the philosopher's judgment of the course of human history, and his imaginings of the future, are the writer's own—Kant's own, potentially our own; sometimes the power and judiciousness of "nature" or "providence" annihilate this possibility. (For the latter term, I count no less than seven different meanings in his footnote to *Perpetual Peace*.)

Unsurprisingly, there are state agents at work in these reified struggles—at times doing the will of "nature," when they arrive at a condition of order in their "relations" by accident, through the exercise of self-interest—but "certainly not their internal moral attitudes" [*sic*]. At others, "the desire of every state (or its ruler) to achieve lasting peace by . . . dominating the whole world" is frustrated by wise "nature," who "wills it otherwise."[39] Here, it seems to me, Kant has a case to answer, as part of a wider problem of moral agency. In fact most of the time he lapses into the typical subject/object confusion of anthropomorphism, whether in relation to "nature" or the agency of states. (As Cohen elsewhere remarks, "the Kantian subject both is and is not the author of the [moral] law that binds it."[40]) Kant is capable of writing quite concretely and coherently on how morality (what he calls "cosmopolitan right") should apply in, for example, the distribution of land and resources in the states system. But abstraction creeps in when he begins to speculate on the direction history will take in practice, and how people will be guided in their sometimes-competing choices.[41]

Again, in his reproduction of eighteenth-century conventions, no place is given to chance, though much in his histories is unforeseen; everything that happens must be the product of some will, human or divine. Yet surely there are favorable occurrences in human history with aspects of pure accident (*good luck* being all the meaning left in the word today, when we speak of "providential" events). Take the discovery of penicillin: certainly a happy accident (leaving aside the research by which it was facilitated); but no divine or beneficent intervention is associated with the particular time when this happened—the fact that the discovery, with its life-saving potential, did not come, for example, ten or fifty years later.[42] That particular "providential" fact is truly a matter of pure chance; and without such a secular, neutral concept we can have no clear concept of our own wills or of reality in general.

Deism

Ambiguity also surrounds Kant's Deism—his recurrent references to an impersonal, beneficent God, again drawing on the common currency of eighteenth-century rationalism.[43] Deism's conventions enabled individuals to hint at their doubts about Christianity, or simply shelve their religious allegiances, at a time when the expansion of scientific knowledge in Europe was going hand in hand with that of secular political institutions; conflicts over religious practice were everywhere latent in society, but speculative philosophy was not entirely free (Kant himself came up against the problem of censorship.) In this connection Christine Korsgaard argues that essays like the *Idea for a Universal History* and *Perpetual Peace* represent Kant's exploration of "a more secular faith in the inevitable progress of history toward the realization of the good."[44] This attitude is compatible with the deistic view of a God who is absent from human affairs, while reason and free will subsist. Any attachment to Christian moral values is residual at best.

Kant's note to the First Supplement of *Perpetual Peace* is illustrative in this regard. First he sets out a typical rationalist vision, with nature as a great clock set going by the Creator; a beneficent design has been inlaid, through which the happy outcome of all nature's operations is ensured. Next he takes care to distinguish between the operations of nature and our will, and finally between our will and that of God. Yet our will and God's will, he stresses, may in fact come into harmony: "For example, we may say that we should never cease to strive toward goodness, for we believe that God, even by means which we cannot comprehend, will make up for our own lack of righteousness so long as our attitude is sincere."[45] The latter remark seems to me perfectly Christian in spirit;[46] the only problem is that it jars with a teleology in which human political development is on occasion determined by the will of "nature," "providence," or some impersonal God—the ontological equivalent of whistling in the dark.[47]

12.6 Cosmopolitanism as a Christian idea

The exact intimate synthesis of belief in Kant's mind seems, at this distance, irrecoverable.[48] No doubt it varied over his lifetime, as it does for all of us. Had he not set himself the impossible goal of making his secular philosophy consonant with his metaphysics at all points, our expectations of him would no doubt be lower. And yet his moral seriousness is as undeniable as his philosophical ambition, and perhaps this is the most important lesson to retain from his work.

In fact its most overtly political parts seem both wider and deeper than the philosophical problems of explanation that remain. In his political writings, the clearest and least programmatic of his works, he chooses deliberately to end on an optimistic note, even while stressing that hope is a human duty. Here, for Kant the practical moralist, the proof of moral ideas is in their demonstration, rather than in their faithfulness to received wisdom. Morality should apply in this world, rather than the next—should be political, as well as personal. As Michel Despland puts it, Kant "tolerated only those teleological beliefs which were required by and strengthened moral imperatives, namely those teleological affirmations which affirmed the destiny of the human race to cosmopolitanism."[49]

Certainly the supportive arguments for the categorical imperative (notably, the "kingdom of ends") make no sense unless one believes human beings to be sacred. Kant's language in this work progresses from praise of the "dignity of virtue" to asserting that "this ideal will which can be ours is the proper object of reverence."[50] Both the political philosopher Katrin Flikschuh and the historian of religion Diarmaid McCulloch see an underlying unity, in these terms, between his "critical" philosophy and his millenarian political theory.

McCulloch goes further, arguing that for Kant the noumenal and the numinous were the same. "Things-in-themselves," if they are insights at all, are mystical insights.

> There are vital "Ideas" which are beyond the possibility of experience, and therefore beyond any traditional proof derived by reasoning: Kant called them God, Freedom and Immortality. Although these are not accessible through reason, they can be reached by the conscience within the individual, a conscience which forces us to regulate our affairs according to its dictates. This is a new sort of faith to meet the battle between faith and reason: in a famous phrase, Kant said, "I had to deny knowledge in order to make room for faith." . . . [This step] is a solvent of Christian dogma, though it would present no problem for many Christian mystics throughout the history of the Church, who have ended up saying much the same thing.[51]

On this interpretation, Kantian ambiguity on the form of the political future—notably regarding the durability and worth of states—may be justified as a Christian anxiety over human divisions. Hobbes insisted on such divisions, to conjure up a future of endlessly warring, unstable nations, but Hobbes's doctrine was determinedly Judaic and tribal. Kant's political prophecies were more wisely moot: the reconciliation of peoples and the disappearance of political divisions would, he suggested, fulfil God's wishes for humankind, but sustaining this outcome would require effort and will on the part of human beings. Even divine help would have to be deserved. The international relations of the future could not be relied on to be better than in the present, and one could only hope for beneficent developments to come together in a strengthening chain of progress.

What philosophers and political thinkers alike, in this situation, should do was to formulate concrete measures for the progress of human society, starting with existing institutions. Hence *Perpetual Peace*. In this way international theory, as the theory of all human relations in the world, is seen to give the lesson to moral philosophers to involve themselves in politics. If Kant did not state this explicitly, it is perhaps because he saw himself as a philosopher, at the service of philosophy, first.

Moreover, even if his prescriptive message has been obscured, downplayed, or traduced in international studies ("antiquated, even idiosyncratic," says Linklater), no one can deny its farsightedness. Those developments of his time that he noted, like the spread of the secular, centralized state, are with us today. This points to an end to his political influence. And indeed, *universal* human rights have not been fully realized—have not perhaps even become clear—in a world of states conceived as an end in itself which obscures what *fundamental* rights might be.

As for his programmatic inclinations, which led him to compartmentalize religion and politics, ontology and morality, these may for him have been a source of strength, but they have also led to confusion among his interpreters. This points to the end of his influence as a philosopher too. In fact, despite his own claim to have achieved a Copernican revolution in the establishment of knowledge, the most meaningful judgment to my mind of Kant's life and work is of someone who was not an original philosopher—unlike, say, Descartes, Pascal, or Hume—but a celebrant, a great deepener and explainer, of the Western philosophical tradition that he inherited; and to say this is a proper reflection both of his personal modesty and of his intellectual ambition, which ranged from aesthetics to astronomy. His work in "pure" or critical philosophy represents the culmination of the rationalist-analytical tradition which has lost itself in dissensions ever since.[52]

Meanwhile, Kant's political writing has had to wait until the twentieth century and the creation of the universal states system for normative international theorists to discover. The holistic challenge that he set himself is there vividly exposed. It is the challenge of the theory of all human relations in the light of history and the future. This was also, whatever his conception of his own philosophical purpose, a religious vision of life. The same Kant who argued that religious differences between peoples had a positive value, insofar as this served to prevent oppressively large states, held those differences themselves to be fundamentally false.

> *Religious differences*—an odd expression! As if we were to speak of different *moralities*. There may certainly be different historical *confessions*, although these have nothing to do with religion itself

but only with changes in the means used to further religion, and are thus the province of historical research. And there may be just as many different religious *books* (the Zend-Avesta, the Vedas, the Koran, etc.). But there can only be *one religion* which is valid for all men and at all times.[53]

In the *Metaphysics of Morals* Kant turned the categorical imperative round, away from its focus on individual duty, toward a more social conception of morality:

> Right is ... the sum total of those conditions within which the will of one person can be reconciled with the will of another in accordance with a universal law of freedom ... "Every action which by itself or by its maxim enables the freedom of each individual's will to co-exist with the freedom of everyone else in accordance with a universal law is *right*."[54]

To say, then, that Kant was not an original philosopher is not to say that he was anything other than a noble one, or that philosophy in his conception was not guided by a purpose equally noble.

12.7 After Kant

Saints in any case make no distinction between religion and politics, metaphysics and morality. The twentieth-century philosopher Simone Weil (a scholar of Kant) held that to be a consistent person of conscience in modern society meant sharing the lives of the laboring poor who ground out the nuts and bolts of its machines, and joining its just international causes unto death.[55] The search for personal integrity and intellectual coherence might lead her, as in Kant's case, to a rejection of organized religion; but for Weil the touchstone of authenticity was not Kant, but Christianity itself. The search for truth must be unified, with inspiration sought in all culture, all humanity, in the present and the past; following Kant's ecumenism, Weil became a Greek scholar and Orientalist. Christians must abide by the principles of evidence which science and analytical philosophy demanded; but for Weil the source of evidence was in action, in the world as we find it. "Je puis, donc je suis," was her motto: "I can, therefore I am."[56]

Between thought and action so conceived, moreover, ontological Realism provides the logical link. First, though there may be no way of defining God, ontology itself teaches that if God exists, it is not as an abstraction. Abstractions are the product of human minds, for the purpose of ordering reality. They live only as long as that purpose subsists.

Second, the world, like the universe of which it is part, may have no motive or purpose of its own, yet still be evidence for Creation—God's "absence" being explained by His love for humankind, to whom all things are given. As Simone Weil put it: "On God's part creation is not an act of self-expansion but of restraint and renunciation. God and all his creatures are less than God alone. God accepted this diminution. He emptied a part of his being from himself."[57] This was apparently Kant's view too.[58]

In this conception freedom is absolute, as evidence of God's sacrifice and trust in human beings. "Love is proved in the letting go."[59] Proved, as in *put to the test*, and *shown to be true*. Kant's supreme test of his own personal reality was his imagination of the Second Coming[60]; and the moral act for him involved a singular self-assertion of freedom, as faith is sincere only in the presence of self-doubt.[61]

In this scheme of things the platitudes of Deism have no place. But chance does, in our modern impersonal sense, unconnected with luck or superstition—understandable in a precise and concrete way, for every event in the world that we cannot, and perhaps need not, explain. Such a conception preserves, rather than undermining, reality: ambiguous Providence abolished by science.

The Realist ontology for which I have argued is the first step along the road to these understandings. Through an ultimate inquiry into order we demonstrate our perfect freedom in the mind. Beyond, there is only action, which our free will and our dominance define. But experience binds the two together. "The love of the order and beauty of the world," said Simone Weil, is "the complement of the love of our neighbour."[62]

Notes

1. Brown, *International Relations Theory*, p. 47.
2. David Boucher, *Political Theories of International Relations* (Oxford: Oxford University Press, 1998), p. 269.
3. Immanuel Kant, *Critique of Pure Reason* [1781/1787], tr. Werner S. Pluhar (Indianapolis: Hackett, 1996), pp. 8 and 9, preface to first edition, Kant's emphasis.
4. Alasdair MacIntyre, *After Virtue: A Study in Moral Theory* (3rd ed. London: Duckworth, 2007). But for a more positive assessment see chapter 14, "Kant," in MacIntyre, *A Short History of Ethics: A History of Moral Philosophy from the Homeric Age to the Twentieth Century* (2nd ed. London: Routledge, 1995). Onora O'Neill has argued that the differences between the two philosophers' core views are not very great: O'Neill, *Constructions of Reason*, ch. 8.
5. Kimberly Hutchings, "The possibility of judgement," p. 51.
6. *Ibid.*, pp. 54 and 56–62, emphases in original.
7. Kant, *Perpetual Peace*, "Appendix" in Reiss (ed.), p. 118, Kant's emphasis.

8. Hutchings, "The possibility of judgement," pp. 51 and 62.
9. *Ibid.*, pp. 52–54 and 62, emphasis in original.
10. Kant, *The Moral Law* tr. Paton [*Groundwork of the Metaphysics of Morals*], pp. 111 and 112.
11. O'Neill, *Bounds of Justice*, p. 75, quoting from the *Groundwork* in *Immanuel Kant: Practical Philosophy* tr. and ed. Mary J. Gregor (Cambridge: Cambridge University Press, 1996), emphasis in original.
12. Henry E. Allison, "Kant's transcendental idealism" in Graham Bird (ed.), *A Companion to Kant* (Oxford/Malden, MA: Blackwell, 2006), pp. 114 and 116.
13. But see the absorbing biographical-critical study by Louis Menand, *The Metaphysical Club* (New York: Farrar, Straus & Giroux, 2001); also Molly Cochran, *Normative Theory in International Relations: A Pragmatic Approach* (Cambridge: Cambridge University Press, 1999).
14. Allison, "Kant's transcendental idealism," p. 122. See also Douglas Burnham with Harvey Young, *Kant's Critique of Pure Reason* (Edinburgh: Edinburgh University Press, 2007), esp. pp. 61–63. Cf. *The Metaphysics of Morals*, where Kant passes from a discussion of justice in international relations to an abstract, but quite clear, assertion of the need for a leap of faith in morality. Kant, *The Metaphysics of Morals* Section III, "Conclusion" in Reiss (ed.), pp. 173–174.
15. Smith, "Positivism and beyond" in Smith, Booth and Zalewski (eds.), *International Theory: Positivism and Beyond*, p. 18. See also Smith, "Epistemology, postmodernism and international relations theory."
16. Hollis and Smith, "Beware of gurus: structure and action in international relations," p. 410.
17. Wight, *Agents, Structures and International Relations*, see especially "Introduction."
18. MacIntyre, *After Virtue*, p. 43.
19. Onora O'Neill, "Kant on reason and religion," *Tanner Lectures* I: "Reasoned hope."
20. Kant, *The Moral Law* tr. Paton, p. 112, Kant's emphasis, and ch. III *passim*.
21. Kant, *Theory and Practice* in Reiss (ed.), p. 92.
22. O'Neill, *Constructions of Reason*, p. 156, emphasis in original.
23. In Hans Reiss's opinion, Kant's *Perpetual Peace* "was presumably inspired by the conclusion of the Treaty of Basle on 5 April 1795": Reiss (ed.), p. 276, n. 1. Elsewhere Kant wrote of "a *permanent congress of states*" "designed to preserve peace. . . . A congress of this very kind . . . found expression in the assembly of the States General at The Hague in the first half of this [eighteenth] century. To this assembly, the ministers of most European courts and even of the smallest republics brought their complaints about any aggression suffered by one of their number at the hands of another." *Metaphysics of Morals* in *ibid.*, p. 171, Kant's emphasis.
24. The plan of 1947, envisaging separate Jewish and Arab states in Palestine, provided for an economic and customs union between them and "joint economic development, especially in respect of irrigation, land reclamation and soil conservation; [and] access for both States and for the City of Jerusalem on a non-discriminatory basis to water and power facilities." UN General Assembly Resolution 181, 29 November 1947.

25. Kant, *The Moral Law* tr. Paton, p. 85.
26. "So 'Keep all your promises throughout your life except one,' 'Persecute all those who hold false religious beliefs,' and 'Always eat mussels on Mondays in March' will all pass Kant's test, for all can be consistently universalized." MacIntyre, *After Virtue*, p. 46.
27. Cf. Onora O'Neill, *Constructions of Reason*, p. 161.
28. Benjamin Constant, *Écrits et Discours Politiques* vol. I, ed. O. Pozzo di Borgo (Paris: Jean-Jacques Pauvert, 1964), p. 68, my translation.
29. Kant, "Casuistical questions" in "On Lying" in *The Metaphysics of Morals* [1797-], quoted here from *Immanuel Kant: Practical Philosophy* tr. and ed. Gregor, p. 554.
30. [1797] in *ibid.*
31. Manfred Kuehn, *Kant: A Biography* (Cambridge: Cambridge University Press, 2001), p. 403.
32. See above, chapter 3.
33. Kant, *The Moral Law* tr. Paton p. 84.
34. Christine M. Korsgaard, *The Sources of Normativity*, ed. Onora O'Neill (Cambridge: Cambridge University Press, 1996), p. 138, emphases in original.
35. "Thou shalt love the Lord thy God with all thy heart, and with all thy soul, and with all thy mind. This is the first and great commandment. *And the second is like unto it,* Thou shalt love thy neighbour as thyself. On these two commandments hang all the law and the prophets." Matthew 22:37–40, emphasis added.
36. See *Yearbook of the United Nations 1946–47* (Lake Success, New York: United Nations Office of Public Information, 1947), and Manouchehr Ganji, *International Protection of Human Rights* (Geneva/Paris: Droz/Minard, 1962).
37. "The Kantian grounding of reason, as of morality," says Onora O'Neill, "cannot be foundationalist. Anything that could count as foundations would have to be transcendent, and so alien." O'Neill, *Constructions of Reason*, p. 64, and 59–65 generally.
38. Kant, *Perpetual Peace*, First Supplement in Reiss (ed.), pp. 108ff., Kant's emphasis.
39. *Ibid.*, pp. 108–110, 113–114.
40. G. A. Cohen, "Reason, humanity and the moral law" in Korsgaard, *The Sources of Normativity*, p. 171. See also Raymond Geuss, "Morality and identity" in *ibid.*, pp. 189-199 and Korsgaard's replies, pp. 234–38.
41. See the discussion on Seyla Benhabib above, chapter 11 section 11.4.
42. The story is told in James Le Fanu, *The Rise and Fall of Modern Medicine* (2nd ed. London: Abacus, 2011), ch. 1.
43. "**deism,** a line of rationalistic religious thought that affirms that there is a god but denies that he should be understood in any mystical way. The antecedents of deism go back to Aristotle's first mover, who moved 'the first heaven' at the circumference of the universe but is otherwise unconcerned with human affairs. . . . It is not a school in any sense, but rather typifies a general approach to religion: individualistic, non-mystical, non-institutional and often anti-clerical." Vesey and Foulkes, *Collins Dictionary of Philosophy*, p. 76. The *Groundwork* has a single reference to "the absolute necessity of some supreme cause of the world": *The Moral Law* tr. Paton, p. 123.

44. Christine Korsgaard, "Introduction" to *Groundwork of the Metaphysics of Morals* tr. and ed. Mary J. Gregor (Cambridge: Cambridge University Press, 1998), p. xxxiv.

45. Kant, *Perpetual Peace,* First Supplement in Reiss (ed.), p. 109. Cf. O'Neill, "Kant on reason and religion," *Tanner Lectures* I, pp. 286–288.

46. "Blessed are the pure in heart: for they shall see God." Matthew 5:8.

47. Cf. Kant, *Theory and Practice* III in Reiss (ed.), p. 91.

48. Three interpretations seem possible. 1). Kant was for much, if not all, of his life an ecumenical religious thinker who played down his own association with Christianity for well-meaning but, to us, confusing reasons. He deliberately omitted a metaphysical justification for the categorical imperative, lest it be taken to express only one particular (Christian) view. His Pietistic upbringing, moreover, was influential in inclining him to stress practical morality rather than doctrine ("works" over faith) as a criterion of religious authenticity. Stephan Körner quotes personal testimony that "Kant, though deeply religious, abstained from all external customs. In his later years he certainly did not worship in church." Kant's anti-institutionalism in religious matters was public knowledge in his lifetime. Körner concludes: "Kant believed, and believed he had demonstrated, that one can be truly religious without sharing the creed of any organized religion. He himself led the life of such a man." Stephan Körner, *Kant* (Harmondsworth: Pelican, 1955), pp. 170–171. 2). Kant took it for granted that his readers would read Christianity into his writings, as he was publicly identified as a Christian through references in his work in the Protestant Christian tradition of his time and place. Philosophy and Christian morals were for him mutually justificatory projects. The *Metaphysics of Morals* is only half of the overall design, meant to be completed by such works as *Religion within the Bounds of Reason Alone*. It was for reasons of logic and intellectual economy that philosophical explanation, rather than Christian ontology or morality, formed the subject matter of the *Groundwork,* where we find the categorical imperative. 3). Kant was in reality an agnostic, or free thinker, who believed in the core altruistic principle of Christianity for its own sake, without believing, or feeling the need to believe, in its religious foundations. He refrained, however, from explicitly refuting any Christian associations in the categorical imperative for fear of the Prussian censor, who might ban him from teaching philosophy and thus deny him his livelihood. This particular interpretation may appear anachronistic, since it was only in respect of later writings that Kant came close to incurring such a fate; but not if we speculate that he was always aware of limitations in the political climate in Prussia and happened, after a change of regime, to be overtaken by events. We know for certain that he regarded censorship as potentially devastating for his career as a professional philosopher engaged in public debate, though also morally corrupting for those who bowed to the authorities' will. Onora O'Neill's reading of *Religion within the Bounds of Reason Alone* (the work that led him to partially, but unwillingly, comply with religious censorship, after the *Groundwork*), shows Kant unwilling to endorse orthodoxy in Scriptural or ecclesiastical terms. This position was more radical then than it is now. See Onora O'Neill, "Kant on reason and religion" *Tanner Lectures* II: "Interpretation within the limits of reason," pp. 290–308; and Kuehn, *Kant: A Biography,* ch. 8.

49. Michel Despland, *Kant on History and Religion* (Montreal: McGill-Queens University Press, 1973), p. 27.
50. Kant, *The Moral Law* tr. Paton, pp. 96 and 101.
51. McCulloch, *A History of Christianity*, pp. 803–804. See also Katrin Flikschuh, "Reason and nature: Kant's teleological argument in *Perpetual Peace*" in Bird (ed.), *A Companion to Kant*, p. 395.
52. The inspiration for epistemological challenge in the twentieth century, from Wittgenstein to the logical positivists, was not the academic philosopher Kant but the amateur philosopher Hume, who in his lifetime was considered far too radical to be let loose on university students.
53. Kant, *Perpetual Peace*, First Supplement in Reiss (ed.), note p. 114, Kant's emphasis.
54. Kant, "Introduction to the Theory of Right" in *Metaphysics of Morals*, Reiss (ed.), p. 133, Kant's emphasis.
55. The industrial experience is recounted in Simone Weil, *La Condition Ouvrière* (Paris: Gallimard, 1951). See also Simone Pétrement, *Simone Weil: A Life* tr. Raymond Rosenthal (London: Mowbrays, 1977).
56. Quoted in Peter Winch, *Simone Weil: "The Just Balance"* (Cambridge: Cambridge University Press, 1989), p. 9.
57. Quoted in English in André Comte-Sponville, *A Short Treatise on the Great Virtues: The Uses of Philosophy in Everyday Life* [1996] tr. Catherine Temerson (London: Vintage, 2003), p. 273.
58. "Such union with us may . . . be regarded as a state of humiliation of the Son of God." Kant, *Religion within the Bounds of Reason Alone*, quoted in O'Neill, "Kant on reason and religion," p. 301.
59. The line is from Cecil Day-Lewis, "Walking away" [1962] in *Selected Poems* (3rd ed. Harmondsworth: Penguin, 1969), p. 35.
60. "Even the Holy One of the gospel must first be compared with our ideal of moral perfection before we can recognise him to be such." *The Moral Law* tr. Paton, p. 73.
61. Kant, "On the failure of all attempted philosophical theodicies" [1791] tr. Michel Despland in Despland, *Kant on History and Religion*, p. 295, note 6.
62. Simone Weil, "Essays" in *Waiting for God* [*L'attente de Dieu*] tr. Emma Craufurd (New York: Putnam, 1951), p. 99.

Conclusion

Conclusion

A Double Prison

In this book I have put forward two main arguments. First, we cannot, without deception or pretence, use language of state agency in the modern world. But second, since this language remains pervasive—in the mouths of politicians, in books of academic analysis, and the texts of international law—our theory of international relations must be revolutionized, and take as its object the moral concerns of all humankind.

On the first count, whether a state is reified as a person or some kind of concrete thing, the reification is pointless and unhelpful. Clearly, a state is neither.

Certainly *nations* are concrete—made up of many real persons; and persons are what we generally understand as (free) agents. Some groping to combine these ideas in an effective political entity goes on in the postulation of a complete system of such agents, bound to—effectively coterminous with—territorial states. Hobbes sought to formalize this conception, with his doctrine of society at once ruled and symbolically embodied by absolute monarchy—drawing a parallel with dramatic creation for the constitution of a state. As we are all authors of our actions, so are we all potential authors of this entity set up to enact our collective wishes and reflect us to ourselves. In this way—the Hobbesian way—the state becomes agent and actor in one. Subjectivity and objectivity fuse in this projection, as when we lose ourselves in the theatre or cinema, in the imagination of a moment.

The analogy works insofar as life itself is felt to be dramatic, heightened. Hobbes argued that a general propensity to violence made a drama of human life in the mass. Among all humankind, he said, or between groups larger than "small Families," relationships were unstable, and unpleasant domineering tendencies would come to the fore. Some instrument of order had therefore to be invented—and imposed—to avert a war of all against all. In fact permanently installed, so as to preserve the human future. Hence the prescription, in *Leviathan*, of dynasties of absolute monarchs to govern the world indefinitely.

Two kinds of reservation arise about this view of things. One is practical: if human beings were ever shown *not* to be dangerous to each other on the scale and to the intensity that Hobbes supposed, then peace and order would be possible without such strict instruments, and such strict social divisions, as he demanded. The other is logical: if the fundamental origin of human violence is, as Hobbes claimed, "natural" equality between individuals, then this will never be completely overcome, least of all by instituting a hierarchical social order; such an arrangement is bound to appear despotic, and for that reason be unlikely to last (as Hobbes himself partly admitted). Three centuries on from *Leviathan*, the near-total disappearance of absolute monarchy, and the ephemerality of dictatorship in England in Hobbes's own long lifetime, bear these reservations out.

'The best we can get from Hobbes," says David Runciman,

> is a sense that the independent moral identity of the state is a kind of necessary fiction, something that we have to assume if the state is not to be reduced to a series of endless and fragmentary personal power relations, but which we can never establish. It is, in a sense, the one wishful element of Hobbes's theory, but it is also part of Hobbes's theory that comes closest to describing the conditions of state agency in the modern world. We assume that states can act in their own right, yet their actions always depend upon the actions of their representatives. So, we say that states are ultimately responsible for what is done in their name, but they cannot ultimately take responsibility for it, since whatever the state does is always the action of some or other representative . . . the moral agency of the state is a fiction.[1]

Still, the personalized state of Hobbes's conception retains some value through the social contract—the mutual, if minimal, accountability of rulers and ruled on which, to his credit, and not without paradox, he insisted. His imagined absolute rulers are not *practically* accountable, in that they can never justifiably be replaced; but they are morally, indirectly, accountable to their subjects, through the order they are beholden to provide, and their own accountability to God, as the father of all life. Morality is acknowledged as the world's core, even as its political working-out is seen to be difficult.

What subsists in our own time is the secular shell of Hobbes's prescription, a mere structure of divisions outlined on humankind. In its first phase, for half a century after 1945, the negative implications were obscured by the world civil war that the US-Soviet competition imposed. Since then we have been thrown back, amid the political rubble of the Cold War, on the original human equality that Hobbes discerned and the other, purely formal, equality of the system itself. This reopens the question of social order that he set himself to solve. What is the best form of government now? And though discrete populations of a sort exist in the system, is the fit between them and their assigned states exact (or at least, exact enough to work)? Can the divisions created in 1945 be trusted to serve future generations of human beings without some principle of change? Is universal inter-*national* relations not a tautology? Kant had his doubts even before the system was complete.

Runciman's last word is also moot:

> The fiction of the state's moral agency . . . is one of the conventional certainties of modern politics, and any attempt to get away from it, and to resolve the moral identity of the state into an entity that can be collectively, or even reductively, defined, is a move beyond the conditions of modern politics into something else, as yet unknown.[2]

Yet nothing stands still. Received ideas of states, or any other social arrangement, as necessary fictions are not simply extinct; they never lived. Hence my second argument. International theory must be normative: aimed to develop morality through norms, or accepted social practices, in the world as a whole—its purpose, to guide and to assist historic change. Faced with this challenge, international theorists must be social theorists, political analysts, and philosophers rolled into one.

A practical way to begin, I have suggested, is to confront persistent moral concerns in the world, to see what kind of society emerges from the attempt to resolve them in an integrated way. I have named four such concerns: weapons of mass destruction, human rights, North-South relations, and the future of human society in the natural environment. Here by way of conclusion are some remarks on this theme.

Weapons of Mass Destruction

On the first concern my position is very simple. Even leaving aside the humanitarian objections which weapons of mass destruction routinely, and to my mind conclusively, incur, they destabilize the states system as a set of independently functioning societies. For every imaginable reason, then—human decency, order, freedom, progress, maybe even survival—our aim must be a world in which such weapons are assuredly neither available nor being sought. I take nuclear weapons as my example, as the most destructive of all.

Lessons from Science

It is sometimes said that in the light of science (and science is an institution in the modern world), nuclear weapons cannot be disinvented—or, by implication, abolished. But whatever disinvention means, I say we must do it. The radiobiological case alone is unanswerable. There is no, and never can be any, defense against ionizing radiation, an original energy in matter which, concentrated, works to destroy the fundamental makeup of life, beginning with warm-blooded creatures like ourselves. Nuclear weapons are radiation weapons. Their renewed use on any scale would sow genetic deformity in the human race until the end of time.

Joseph Rotblat was the radiobiologist on the Manhattan Project to build the first nuclear weapons. He left the Project once it was clear that the Nazi nuclear program was embryonic and Germany would be overrun (for it was against German, not Japanese, militarism that the Project had been initiated), and subsequently became a tireless campaigner for nuclear disarmament. Following a nuclear war, he wrote, the effects of local fallout

> would be felt just as badly in some non-combatant countries, but global fall-out would result in long-term damage in *all* countries; it would be expressed in an increased incidence of cancers and of genetic defects in future generations. The property of fall-out to extend the injurious action both in space and time, is a novel and unique characteristic of nuclear warfare. Not only the inhabitants of the combatant countries, but virtually the whole population of the world, *and their descendants*, would be victims of a nuclear war.[3]

It is this prospect which makes nuclear deterrence, the systematic manipulation of the fear of nuclear weapons, so evil and corrupting. No moral defense for this policy can be found, even in the anonymity of the created state (and since we all live in such states, there is no real anonymity in them anyway). "Bluffing aside," say Finnis, Boyle and Grisez, "whoever chooses to make the deterrent threat intends . . . what is threatened. If what is threatened includes the killing of innocent persons, the threat includes an intention prohibited by common morality."[4] Political progress everywhere hangs on the renunciation of this threat. Moral progress hangs on it: who wants children to grow up—who can consider other human beings to be fellow members of society—in a world in which planned murder, let alone mass murder and the ruin of the human future, are normal features of public debate?

The very rationality of modern life is menaced by a weapon against which no science can protect.

Lessons from History: the Cold War

Now the entire conduct of the US-Soviet Cold War, and the underpinning of the highest human institutions today, somehow presuppose the opposite: the normalization of nuclear weapons, through historical explanation and the (relative) transparency of government, with international security ultimately assured by the guardianship of "declared nuclear-weapon states." The reasoning is that of leadership against a background of necessary evil in politics, especially international politics. International theory was for long completely bound up with this idea. But I accept neither the general nor the specific proposition. One cannot normalize evil. Even "declared" nuclear-weapon states to my mind are anomic, dangerous, and oppressive.

In this context it is interesting to refer to a perspective of social relations laid out by the military historian John Keegan. He argues that the earliest states crystallized round an "actor" role played by political leaders which was also that of the man of action. Democracy held when their display of courage in battle was noted, and replicated, at every level of society. All institutions in this way depended on inspiration by example in a theater of real life, with leadership itself defined by an authentic virtue, courage. "Acting," under such circumstances, could be both literal and symbolic. Encompassing visible heroism, it allowed for tragedy, and with tragedy the whole of human emotion; encompassing action, it allowed a conception of states as instances of social change.

This vision of original democracy, with the death of leaders as the ultimate proof of political accountability, may be seen characterizing societies as different as medieval Europe and ancient Greece. Though connected, like Hobbes's own vision, with the tension between violence and social order, and based on the same metaphor of the drama, it is as far removed as possible from Hobbesian absolute monarchy, where kings are to command armies but sedulously avoid the risk of their own lives. In Hobbes the principle of leadership is purely formal, part of the logic of social organization by obedience.

In societies under nuclear deterrence, in any case, Keegan sees the slide toward autocracy becoming complete. The abstraction of institutions and the anonymity of bureaucratic government, already basic features of modern life, are driven to extremes. In the end, all social values are threatened, including states themselves.

317

Let us briefly remind ourselves of the imperatives that have combined to define leadership in the past: they have comprised an element of *kinship*, by which the leader surrounded himself with intimates identifiable by his followers as common spirits with themselves, thus guaranteeing that their mutual humanity, in all its strength and weakness, will be constantly represented to each other; kinship has been bolstered by *sanction*, the reward—or punishment—of followers according to a jointly accepted value system; sanction has been reinforced by *example*, the demonstration of the personal acceptance of risk by the authority who requires others to bear it at his behest; example has been amplified by *prescription*, the explanation of the need for risk-taking by the leader, in direct speech, to his followers; and prescription has finally been made concrete . . . by *action*, the translation of leadership into effect, of which victory was the desired result.

Power over nuclear weapons has undermined or invalidated all these imperatives. The exclusivity of the nuclear community, burdened by secrets it is legally forbidden to communicate, and physically isolated from the community it is charged to protect, has sundered all *kinship* between it and society at large; *sanction* has lost its force, since the proper management of a nuclear system will generate no occasion for either punishment or reward, or none at any rate that can be readily revealed; the opportunity for *example* is . . . denied by nuclear logic, which requires the leader to be at least risk among all members of his or her society; *prescription*, in consequence, is self-defeating, if not downright destructive of authority, since all exhortation to courage and fortitude invites the riposte, And What of You?; and *action*, the test by which leadership has always ultimately been validated, is, of course, denied by the necessity to avoid all outcomes in nuclear confrontation whatsoever.[5]

"Power over nuclear weapons" amounts on this view to *self*-subjugation, the very opposite of power. Society drifts in an ahistorical, anomic milieu without effective politics or visible future; all the wells of legitimacy have been poisoned. Equally, a world system ruled in the name of such an arrangement is oppressive and unreal. Hence the "black-box," "billiard-ball" states of Realist international theory after 1945—uniform entities in continual conflict, but as mere objects reacting on their outer surfaces, with no detectable inner—no social—life. Hence too the popularity in 1950s America of versions of "political science" (game theory, systems theory, behavioralism) removing the human subject altogether from accounts of collective action—a syndrome that soon enough found its way into international theory.[6] And logically so: on the Cold-War view, there never was any point in differentiating between societies and the territories they happened to inhabit (nuclear weapons, if used, would not); between societies and their leaders (leaders could not afford to); between societies as such (immutably defined by states); or even between right and wrong, when a momentary misunderstanding could spell the end of civilization as we knew it. Culture, politics, difference, change, all those forces drawing individuals imaginatively into a life beyond themselves, vanish under deterrence into a vortex of generalized fear.

The Responsibility of Theorists

Ideas about states, then, though given new stimulus in 1945, were effectively subordinated over the next four decades to the nuclear arms race, even in democracies. So was International Relations as a discipline. Some theorists were complicit in this development—either directly, by engaging in strategic nuclear planning, or indirectly, by constructing a grand theory of evolving power in which world leadership passed from Britain and France to the United States.

Now the creation by fiat of a system of unaccountable state agents, as the institutional expression of distinct, implicitly competitive peoples, was itself a questionable development in 1945. Yet also an understandable one, as the outcome of centuries of European colonialism. The world war just ending had been fought over the lands of empire's subjects from North Africa to East Asia. Against this background, universal independent statehood could fairly be presented as reversing the whole history of armed encroachment on human society, while the new United Nations Organization would bring the peoples of the world together "in larger freedom," as its Charter proclaimed. The key complicating factor, soon to become apparent, was the invention of nuclear weapons: in the first all-embracing system of constituted states, the first extra-statal weapons of war. Their demonstration at Hiroshima and Nagasaki robbed all societies of security at the precise moment when, through political representation, it was being conferred. In this sense the UN's claim to legitimacy was strangled at birth.

For a brief period after 1945 there were efforts to avert this outcome, and to take nuclear weapons and their special fissile material into suprastatal, out of governmental, hands. But before long the competitive worship of the constituted state won out, and the nuclear arms race between "great powers"—the race *for* great power—in the reconstructed system began. From now on, though nuclear weapons made absolute invulnerability from attack impossible, national vulnerability could more easily be played down in large territories than in small ones. It is this which explains how societies in the small territorial jurisdictions of Europe, descendants of the recent protagonists of history, now became hostage to its power-struggles. The Cold War developed as a war over the European legacy of the secular state, waged, because of the new strategic givens, between a reified United States and a reified Soviet Union. And in this transformation, the reifiers-in-chief were ex-Europeans in the United States—fugitives from the battlefield of present ideas.

Among them, European historians like Morgenthau rationalized the new conjuncture; deterrence theorists like Schelling and Waltz, explaining the uses of nuclear weapons, formalized it. They and their kind exercised on "the world stage" the autocracy they claimed, in America, to have left behind; for the world civil war which developed over the next four decades was overwhelmingly fought by, and over, strangers distant from them. They wrote the global manual of blackmail. They infiltrated the language of diplomacy with their deceptive acronyms from MAD to MIRV; they guyed us all, with their technical fixes from throw-weight to silo hardening, from the neutron bomb to "strategic defense"—which always and only meant defense of themselves, beyond the Atlantic's span. Safe at home in America, they praised dog-eat-dog and called it pluralism; with the McCarthyite menace at their shoulder they alienated even their friends. They canonized the lubricious politics of suicide bombing: challenge me and I'll blow up the world. Placing themselves, in emulation of the Machiavellian leader, in the minds of their perceived opponents, they condoned the intent at the core of deterrence and were tainted with its wickedness. Consider the hypocrisy of North Americans with European names inventing ways to sacrifice the peoples of Europe while they themselves were spared![7]

Some might choose to view things differently—arguing, perhaps, that people in liberal democracies could hardly blame planners on their side, in the face of the tyranny of the Soviet regime. But that is not really an answer. Intellectuals in Western society always had access to the most open and influential of public media, and were freer than their Soviet counterparts to work unconnected with national policy or the Cold War. Freedom, for some of them, simply meant conspiring with another, supposedly-enemy set of intellectuals to preserve the status of "superpower." Nor is this an argument about the pros and cons of Marxism. The contribution of official Soviet writers to international theory was as nugatory as their contribution to human culture in general. Soviet ideologues purported to reject nuclear deterrence, and to reach out, radical-style, over the heads of governments to promote friendship between peoples; but when it came to the crunch their view of the world was close to the Western Realist one, when not actually lifted from Western publications.[8] They served the interests of Soviet power over post-colonial societies as the "interdependence" theorists in America served the policy of détente. In this way, the so-called convergence thinking between intellectual circles in East and West which some later claimed to detect was a consensus for US-Soviet condominium, not historic change like the end of the Cold War and the collapse of the Soviet polity which eventually occurred.

International theorists may not have invented the Cold War, but some of them made a profession of it; with their insensitivity to the global effects of the nuclear arms race, their studied ignorance of other societies and cultures, their conflation of theory and policy, socialism and communism, and their own careers and their governments', they made the conflict last and arguably made it worse. In the end their champion (the "cowboy President" put in the saddle, according to Kissinger, by Soviet inflexibility) had to be dragged from the scene by his closest political ally in Europe, an event which made nonsense of the Cold War as a struggle of ideas.[9]

The opponents, by contrast, of the conflict from its early stages, and who did the most to end it, were those who faced up to the long-term implications of nuclear weapons. Rotblat's example has already been mentioned. In the Soviet Union Andrei Sakharov, the key scientist of the Soviet fusion bomb, became to his own detriment the chief critic of government policy at home and abroad. His intellectual trajectory parallels that of the North American scientists, founders of the *Bulletin of the Atomic Scientists* and the Pugwash movement, who reneged on their own technical achievements to denounce the nuclear weapon as the worldwide instrument of oppression. In the field of diplomacy George Kennan, having been traduced as an extremist in 1947, spent the rest of his life in condemnation of the Cold War.[10] Carr, after pouring oil on the troubled waters of his own early writings, devoted himself to furthering institutions beyond states. Later the social historian Edward Thompson led the European disarmament movement on the frontline of the Cold War, reaching out to East Europeans under Soviet control— a control relinquished, finally, by the Soviet leader Mikhail Gorbachev at the cost of his own career. Together, these heroic individuals tore down the sinister political prison of their age, by resisting the fantasies of apocalypse that so many, in and out of government, had exploited for their own selfish aims.

Equally, that the Cold War ended not with a bang but a whimper testifies to the faith in human nature of the silent majority of the human race—disenfranchised by deterrence, but reluctant to join in the mass murder of innocents that deterrence implied. Only massive, buried dissent from decades-long propaganda explains how political leaders were able, swiftly and without incident, to dismantle Europe's divisions after 1989, and the movements for freedom springing up elsewhere ever since.

A Historic Vicious Circle

The Cold War, for most of humankind, was an overpowering muddle, to add to the nightmare scenarios of Armageddon and the maelstrom of proxy wars. This might lead some now to say (as some at the time did say), *plus ça change, plus c'est la même chose*: muddle is the historic character of human relations, which nuclear weapons merely qualitatively and temporarily (if excessively) increased; yet political Realism can accommodate muddle and still, by preaching order through a combination of firmness and prudence, be the orthodoxy by which all other views of human society are defined. On this interpretation, it was through political Realism that the Cold War was successfully brought to an end, and political Realism can and should remain the fallback position in international theory even today—especially since nuclear weapons can no more be disinvented than science can.

To my mind, this is the historic vicious circle which has bounded much human thinking ever since 1945, and long prevented outright nuclear disarmament. It is not what Einstein meant, when he asserted that with the release of the power of the split atom everything had changed except our thinking (and having done more than most to make this development possible, he was in a position to know). Here is an invention which symbolizes, on the one hand, the irreversible impact of technology on the society of human beings, and on the other humankind's self-destructive potential—a potential seen as having no limits, and so able to make meaningless even the rational activity of science.

Waltz's answer to the conundrum was universal deterrence—a controlled spread of nuclear weapons to avert the logical but worse alternative, as he saw it, of a single global state. Yet only someone without compassion, foresight, or knowledge of the world could seriously make such a suggestion. Most obviously, because the failure of universal nuclear deterrence would mean universal destruction (and one could never completely rule out failure). But also because individuated territories, in the states system as it is, are inherently and irreversibly unequal in their physical endowments, and different populations are unequal in their scientific and technological understandings. The equality of capability Waltz outlined was and perhaps always will be unachievable.

But also, in its own way, irrelevant: as any child can understand, the rough equality of nobody, in a situation of potential conflict, possessing a given weapon is not essentially different from—but much less costly than—everybody having one. The idea of abolishing weapons of mass destruction within a mass social organization is only common sense. It need not undermine the organization itself, or require the removal of its structure altogether. Universal nuclear disarmament can take place without abolishing the states system (assuming that the system itself is worth preserving). And indeed this insight may have crept over the states system with the passage of time and contributed to the Cold War's lifting. There were always alternatives to the "balance of terror."

Nuclear Double Standards: the Security Council and State Succession

Clearly, however, universal nuclear disarmament has far-reaching implications. Notably it would seem to rule out "great powers" as such. Nuclear weapons are instruments of great power; they acquire meaning only in association with large territorial states, based on the—largely illusory—notion of a hinterland of survivability; they require the deception, corruption, or intimidation of society into a vested interest in exorbitant forms of defense, which may, self-servingly, include more nuclear weapons. Their presence offsets the democratic impulse on a world scale, as the Cold War showed.[11] As Keegan explained, what goes for autocracy within states goes for states in general, because of the devices of political control which nuclear weapons by their nature—within, or against, us—impose. Since 1945 these facts have worked against the hope of some social scientists that the states system, alongside intergovernmental institutions, would evolve into practical units of more equal size and power.[12]

Nuclear weapons also induce rigidity at the highest institutional level of human affairs, where action for change by the UN Security Council, and the politics of the veto underlying it, devolve on deterrence between the permanent members—all "declared nuclear-weapon states." The result is a mechanistic system where all states are agents, but some are always more agents than others, and institutions set up a distorting mirror for human society at large.

Take the incident of the Soviet-Russian succession in 1991–1992, as the final diplomatic resolution of the Cold War. From one day to the next, the Soviet Union was supplanted at the United Nations by the Russian Federation in all its privileges and responsibilities, including the status of "declared nuclear-weapon state" and permanent UN Security-Council member. Yet by no stretch of the imagination could the Russian Federation be said to correspond, territorially, politically, ethnically, or demographically, to its state "predecessor," a multinational, multi-ethnic polity mapped onto the largest legal space in the world.[13] As it happens, the Vienna Convention on the Succession of States (1978) does not go into questions of substance, but operates on the concept of a state as a legal person "which has consented [*sic*] to be bound"—a fiction wrapped in a solecism, and entailing no consultation of actual people. But even this formal document clearly defines the succession process as "the replacement of one State by another in the responsibility for the international relations of territory"—implying some continuity in the changing government of human lives.[14]

Prior to the succession, moreover, the Russian (Soviet Federative Socialist) Republic had actually been extracted from the Soviet Union to constitute a separate state (what would become the Russian Federation)—implying another kind of relationship to the former Soviet populations than the formal embrace which eventually, with UN support, occurred. These diplomatic maneuvers, in fact, were driven from the outset by different aims: acquisition of the former-Soviet nuclear arsenal and permanent seat on the Security Council—the creation, in short, of a new Russian entity to take over the failing great power of the Soviet Union. This ambition in turn was perfectly consistent with the stability of the Security Council itself, over and above the well-being of the former-Soviet peoples or the opportunities for nuclear disarmament at the end of the Cold War. Acceptance of the Russian case for total post-Soviet subsumption would avert the disappearance of one of the institution's permanent members, and so the risk of institutional imbalance, leading to new pressures to reform the much-criticized UN hierarchy.

There was a precedent of sorts: in 1971 Taiwan had been supplanted on the Security Council by the People's Republic of China, representing mainland Chinese. Arguably this step redressed the decades-long anomaly of a state with a smithereen of the post-revolution population of "China" being formally assigned to the Council in that people's name. But in the event, the switch came about through political blackmail, in the shape of the first PRC atomic explosion in 1964. The subsequent co-opting of the PRC as an official "nuclear-weapon state" confirmed the unwritten rule that membership of one exclusive club was an entitlement to membership of the other institutional one of the permanent UN hierarchy. This could not but encourage the demagogic notion that nuclear weapons are synonymous with the legitimate exercise of great power.

All this, as the end of the Cold War beckoned, was understood by the demagogic Russian leader Yeltsin. He had been expelled from the Soviet Politburo after trying, and failing, to seize control of that body from the reformist leader Gorbachev. His response was to defect from the Soviet Union altogether, and arrange for his own election as president of the RSFSR—at the time, the largest constituent Soviet republic, on whose territory most Soviet nuclear weapons and their control mechanisms were situated. Next, he ordered the Russian secession from the Soviet Union, while negotiating the transfer to Russian territory, from Belarus and Ukraine, of the remaining Soviet weapons. Soon afterward he and the leaders of Belarus and Ukraine met to declare the Soviet Union dissolved and to establish the Commonwealth of Independent States as a home for other fugitive Soviet regimes and their peoples. This last maneuver was yet another ploy: the CIS was a device for Russian hegemony, a Potemkin Soviet Union. But by these means the plan of the real Soviet leader, Gorbachev, to recast the USSR as a free union of democratic societies alongside the European Union, in a "common house of Europe," was short-circuited.

Within a fortnight Yeltsin came before the Security Council, uttering vague threats of nuclear disorder and promising stability under his rule. In a secretive, rushed, and shambolic process the Russian Federation was awarded the Soviet permanent seat as a "declared nuclear-weapon state."[15] Yet the Security Council's ratification of Yeltsin's coup was disingenuous, because the disorder had been instigated by the Russian leader himself. He had manipulated, in the highest councils of human affairs, the threat inherent in weapons of mass destruction.[16]

Some might say (noting, perhaps, the lack of public protest at the time) that the nuclear issue was a side issue; or that Russians and their culture so dominated the Soviet Union as to make the Russian Federation the logical successor-state; or perhaps that any expedient was tolerable as the price of bringing the Cold War formally to an end. But apart from the facts of demography and Yeltsin's duplicity, strong arguments of principle were (and still are) at stake. For one thing, Russian dominance is precisely what was denied in the Communist internationalism which formed the USSR's ruling ideology, and retained some credibility within the multinational, multi-ethnic Soviet state. (Conversely, the claim that the Soviet Union was, in effect, a tool of Russian hegemony is precisely a reason *not* to have granted the seceding Russian government and its citizenry former-Soviet privileges.) One can also ask why a single successor-state was necessary at all: why not many separate successor-states, taking up the former-Soviet populations (including Russians, as actually happened in some cases), with the Soviet nuclear arsenal dismantled and abolished?

All the more so, because the transfer to the Russian government of this arsenal was, and still is, a prima facie violation of the Nuclear Non-Proliferation Treaty.

Nuclear Double Standards: Realpolitik and the NPT

Article I of the Treaty (signed 1968, in force 1970) reads:

> Each nuclear-weapon State Party to the Treaty undertakes not to transfer *to any recipient whatsoever* nuclear weapons or other nuclear explosive devices or control over such weapons or devices directly, or indirectly; and not in any way to assist, encourage or induce any non-nuclear-weapon State to manufacture or otherwise acquire nuclear weapons or other nuclear explosive devices, or control over such weapons or explosive devices.[17]

If this were not clear enough, Article IX (3) of the Treaty defines a nuclear-weapon state as "one which has manufactured and exploded a nuclear weapon or other explosive device prior to 1 January, 1967." The first Soviet nuclear explosion was conducted in September 1949.[18] No independent Russian state existed at that time, nor did it come (back?) into existence for another forty years. Anachronism defeats law, in theory and in precedent. There was, and is, no justification for a Russian "nuclear-weapon state," especially in the international law of these matters. All Soviet nuclear weapons should have been dismantled and destroyed after the Soviet state's abolition, and their fissile material taken out of weapons use, to be placed in supranational custody—for which purpose a sophisticated UN organization, the International Atomic Energy Agency, existed. Nuclear disarmament is explicitly urged in NPT article VI. With the end of the Soviet Union there should have been one fewer "nuclear-weapon state" in the world.

What happened instead casts a cynical retrospective shadow over the NPT, to give it the appearance of an instrument of elites. The Taiwan-PRC succession had taken place amid a barrage of criticism from Beijing of the Treaty as an instrument of great-power hegemony. But the criticisms were quickly dropped, once PRC accession to the Security Council was effected. The NPT also served to ratify the restrictions on atmospheric nuclear testing agreed in the Partial Test-Ban Treaty of 1963, in response to widespread malaise about the effects of radioactive fallout—restrictions which in their own right worked against the development of new nuclear arsenals. The later fiction of accommodating Russia as identical to the former Soviet Union fits in with this view of the NPT as a status-quo-reinforcing treaty. Still, one cannot have things both ways. The events of 1991–1992, in the light of NPT Article I, suggest that the leaders of the world's "great powers" made their own law, then broke it.

The true explanation of the Soviet-Russian succession is also the cynical one. Yeltsin's own intentions were cynical from the start. On the Security Council, state governments with permanent representation showed that they would rather rig the rules of the institution than allow a vacancy which would weaken their own exclusive rights. They would rather foster the idea of nuclear weapons as legitimate, by identifying the weapons' use with their official responsibility for international peace and security—and this despite the widespread acceptance, even in some versions of deterrence policy, that by the time a nuclear war broke out all forms of either peace or security would be irretrievably lost.[19] International law is, as Runciman says, a series of fictions; and fictions can be made more elaborate, or subjected to differing interpretations. It has now been demonstrated that changing from being a "non-nuclear-weapon" to a "declared nuclear-weapon" state is as easy, politically, as making the declaration.[20]

What this meant primarily, after 1991, is that great-power aspirations would continue, destructively, to predominate in international relations, even as the Cold War shrank to the portals of the Security Council. So while Chinese and Russian inaction allowed for Western humanitarian intervention in Kosova (1999) and Libya (2011), Chinese and Russian obstructionism meant that atrocities by Chinese and Russian client regimes elsewhere would go unchecked.

These events by themselves provide an argument for removing Russian and Chinese representation from the Security Council, and for the reform of the Council itself, along with the veto system (which would operate differently in the absence of weapons of mass destruction). But beyond this, there is a case for saying that all overweeningly large territorial states should be dissolved, both for the sake of natural justice and because nuclear weapons and great power, with all their evils, go together.

A Degree of Public Assurance

Abolishing weapons of mass destruction will require rules whose stringency transcends any conceivable advantages of the formal states system. Sovereignty must be subject for the foreseeable future to provisions for the elimination and (within reason) assured absence of these weapons.

The international nuclear non-proliferation regime still holds out a practical model for this process, if it is properly—impartially—applied. Its focus is on the fissile material which goes into nuclear reactors and weapons. The regime functions notionally to separate civil and military nuclear fuel and technology in societies where nuclear fissile activities are carried on (notionally, because the physical materials are often the same), and secondly to differentiate these societies from all others. At individual nuclear sites, a "material balance area" is drawn to quarantine and inventory the nuclear material within each; the sites themselves are quarantined; and both are laid open to impartial inspection under the auspices of the International Atomic Energy Agency (IAEA). Such inspection, under the safeguards arrangements of the Non-Proliferation Treaty, is routine and unrefusable and may come unannounced. These arrangements provide for the formal establishment of a "non-nuclear-weapon state"—a society in which nuclear weapons are assuredly being neither produced nor sought. Meanwhile, in declared "nuclear-weapon states" (a Treaty category implying no approval as such), a notional line is drawn between facilities given over to military use and those dedicated to civilian energy production and research. The intellectual basis of abolition, therefore, is already in place. All that is needed, formally speaking, to begin the process is that decision-makers in "nuclear-weapon states" (whether official or unofficial) agree to erase this notional line, and allow the IAEA to do the same work of accountancy and verification everywhere.

From late in the Cold War, the elimination of nuclear weapons has been brought closer by significant reductions in the US and Soviet/ Russian arsenals, beginning with the Intermediate Nuclear Forces in Europe treaty of 1987. The broad model has been the non-proliferation regime, extended to the weapons themselves: declaration of a quarantined area in which the objects slated for destruction (missiles and launchers) are concentrated; permanent surveillance of the area, including by sealed automatic instruments; and impartial (or at least mutual) inspection of the process. Actual physical destruction has then taken place by cutting, crushing, and burning of the missile systems, and the recycling of their nuclear material into national inventories. Each process has had a time frame, and so an end. "Intrusive" on-site inspections to ensure its conduct and eventual conclusion have been an integral part—demonstrating that sovereignty is not unlimited even for democratic societies. These inspections first became possible following Gorbachev's decision to allow, under the 1986 Stockholm Document, on-site monitoring of Soviet armed forces as a peace- and confidence-building measure. More than any single decision, this put paid to the US-Soviet Cold War, since it had been Soviet secrecy, combined with knowledge of Soviet internal tyranny and the unbreakable fact of sovereignty, which licensed deterrence in Western strategy. Intrusive inspections have since become a norm, institutionally reinforced by the CSCE and its successor organization, the OSCE.

In the late 1980s hitherto-unsuspected chemical weapons were used by the Iraqi regime of Saddam Hussein, first on a wide scale in the Iran-Iraq war, then against the regime's own opponents (even unarmed civilians) in Kurdistan. Following the international campaign in 1991 to liberate the people of Kuwait from Iraqi occupation, extensive Iraqi programs to build nuclear, chemical, and biological weapons were discovered and dismantled.[21] Chemical weapons were used again in the Syrian civil war in 2013. These events also underline the need for a stringent, comprehensive, and intrusive system of verification to underpin disarmament. The "precursors" of chemical and biological weapons—their basic product components—are socially more banal than for nuclear weapons, being present in pharmaceutical or industrial processes which are themselves benign and therefore likely to be in use in many modern, or modernizing, societies. The effects on human life of these weapons are also different from the effects of radiation weapons, but still massively and persistently harmful. To guard against this threat, the quarantine model focusing on key materials, technology, and facilities, supplemented by impartial on-site inspection, has been broadly copied in the international control organizations which parallel the IAEA.[22] What is required for the effective abolition of all three types of weapon of mass destruction is a process of verification that follows the reduction of stockpiles of readied weapons down to zero, and supervises related scientific and technical activities before and after that point.

This aim also presupposes a supranational civil service of highly qualified individuals whose official primary duty is to humankind, over and above their personal and national allegiances. But the IAEA/NPT model process itself is certainly capable of being extended to zero in terms of known weapons, and of providing a strong degree of public assurance against their remanufacture. It sets up a standard of scientifically informed transparency to which all governments may be expected to conform, on pain of seeing their own good faith and, indeed, their international legitimacy called into doubt.

Criminality, Legitimacy, and the Territorial State

In 1983 US President Reagan described his adversaries in the Soviet regime as "the focus of evil in the modern world." More precisely, he stigmatized those who "preach the supremacy of the state, declare its omnipotence over individual man, and predict its eventual domination of all peoples on the Earth."[23] Leaving aside Reagan's easy conflation of communism and totalitarianism, and his own culpable ambivalence in nuclear strategy, I think these remarks had a point. The states system, as a system of permanent human divisions, in a sense institutionalizes deterrence, by making territorial defense a right regardless of the justice of the divisions themselves or the character of state rulers. At its worst, this fosters dictatorship and criminality.

Leaders like Hitler and Stalin, with modern weapons in their hands, became criminally dangerous for their own citizens; through their violent, though often legalized, measures they established themselves as tyrants and liars in positions of power. Such individuals seem positively to invite their own overthrow. Yet through the rules of sovereignty and diplomacy, sheer callousness and fear, the brutal dictators of Europe and Japan ranged freely till only world war could countermand them. Despite this experience, after 1945 intervention against sovereignty was severely restricted in the rules of the new universal system, as part of the general proscription of colonialism. In practical international relations the problem was exacerbated by the invention of nuclear weapons, which made intervention against regimes wielding such weapons (like the Soviet one) dangerous in itself. The result today is a presumption in all societies that nuclear weapons are uniquely powerful (and by definition illegitimate when not all societies have them), but no one is able by force or persuasion to make the possessors give them up. Yet only the proof of a general rejection of violence lends any society dignity, and by definition the possessors of weapons of mass destruction are unable to give such an assurance.

Kant in his time held that standing armies should be abolished altogether, "for they constantly threaten other states with war by the fact that they are always prepared for it"; and "the hiring of men to kill or be killed seems to mean using them as mere machines and instruments in the hands of someone else (the state), which cannot easily be reconciled with the rights of man in one's own person."[24] Weapons of mass destruction are the modern equivalent of standing armies for Kant, but with far worse implications for physical harm and psychic and moral degradation. They make political change even more difficult than the artificial rights of states, under the present system, allow. They have a corrupting effect on all human relations through the impersonality of war that they have introduced. For they are of use to their possessors only if the possessors themselves believe they can remain immune from their effects while destroying other human beings en masse. This is a conception of war divorced from any kind of politics, negotiation, or society, and even from traditional grievance. Kant called it "dishonourable stratagems" ("For it must still remain possible, even in wartime, to have some sort of trust in the attitude of the enemy, otherwise peace could not be concluded and the hostilities would turn into a war of extermination").[25]

Only a new conception of the states system will enable future human beings to live free from fear. Even after weapons of mass destruction have been removed, societies with sophisticated scientific and technological activities must be willing to accept intrusive inspections against the risk of their clandestine remanufacture. This will not be a contingent or haphazard, but a systematic and indefinite, surrendering of sovereignty, as a moral criterion by which those societies (or at least their governments) can expect to be judged. By the same token, individuals who work deliberately for the concealment or remanufacture of weapons of mass destruction must themselves come to be considered as international outlaws, subject to arraignment by anyone for their actions.

In an earlier comment on Kantian universalism I argued that at stake in morality is not just what is universal in value to human beings, but what is fundamental—action which is right for its own sake whatever the circumstances, including unforeseen ones. The promulgation of universal independent statehood concurrently with the invention of weapons that threaten independent statehood itself seems to me an example of unforeseen historical circumstances giving rise to a fundamental moral dilemma. One way or another, that destructive nexus must be undone.[26]

Human Rights

International human rights, in the established sense that we know them today, are defined as either civil and political, or economic, social, and cultural. The first represent traditional liberal-democratic freedoms focused on the individual, like freedom of expression and freedom from arbitrary arrest—sometimes called "freedoms from." In the eighteenth and nineteenth centuries, these came to mean freedom from unelected monarchical or theocratic rule, and freedom to form in its place secular, democratic polities with governments directly accountable to the people. Political philosophers from Locke to Mill turned their attention to the nature of the ideal state. The twentieth century, however, saw the emergence of states-for-all, regardless of political culture—a movement crowned in 1945 by the UN system and its ruling institutions. Since that date, liberal-democratic rights have come, problematically, to mean rights both *for* and *against* states. But unsurprisingly too, because one cannot have freedom for all humankind and for all humankind's divisions—at least, not at the same time.

What is assumed in this particular tautology is that states as encapsulations of individual (civil and political) rights are synonymous with states as encapsulations of collective (economic, social and cultural) ones—the latter implying a conception of states as a kind of shared possession with products like institutionalized social welfare. Hence states themselves can have rights, without contradiction. But I as an individual am not the same as I as a member of a community am—not a secular community at least. Arguably only in the eye of God, and of all human beings in harmony with God, can the individual/collective distinction cease to matter. States' rights, then, are a right too far; "a right for sovereigns as opposed to a human right,"[27] quite independently of the fact, on which all could agree, that existing exemplars of statehood in the world today are imperfect in their own way whether as liberal democracies or as economic and social communities.

One way out of this dilemma is to take one set of rights as primary. In this section I shall focus on the mainly Western approach of favoring civil and political rights—of assuming individuals to be the irreducible members, and also the motors, of organized society. The alternative is to take collective rights, including the rights embodied in states, as primary, and envisage a "society of states"; but beyond the purely diplomatic conventions, to require that all recognized rights be fulfilled within that society, including the rights of states conceived as collective possessions. On this view, the evolution of human nature flows from social cooperation. I shall make a case for it in the next section, on "North-South" relations.

Still, either solution remains a compromise of sorts; and the confused identity of the modern state, caught between liberty and justice, individual self-assertion and social co-operation, is never far from the politics of our time.

Problems of UN Standard-Setting

Historically the international legal regime for the protection and promotion of human rights is one of "positive" (explicit) law, stressing specific, concrete, and effective measures of social restraint. The logical outcome of the permanent institutions established in 1945, it has largely evolved, and is popularly understood, as the correction of quantifiable, extreme rights-*violations*, above all crimes against the person, an understanding rooted in the wartime experience of fascism. This tradition runs from the Nuremberg trials of Nazi war criminals (1948) through the Special International Criminal Tribunals set up to investigate war crimes and genocide in the former Yugoslavia (ICTY, 1993) and Rwanda (ICTR, 1994), culminating in the International Criminal Court (ICC, 2003), "the first permanent, treaty-based, international criminal court established to help end impunity for the perpetrators of the most serious crimes of concern to the international community."[28]

As the key dates show, however, even this rather narrow and legalistic approach went effectively undefended for half a century—a testament to the cynicism and intellectual nullity of the Cold War. During this period "sphere-of-influence" competition enabled the most brutal regimes to flourish behind the double shield of sovereignty and the support, obtained at will in the form of arms and money, of some external patron. Some tyrants even exchanged Cold-War patrons, the better to carry on their personal feuds.[29] Human rights in such circumstances could mean little more than freedom from politics as such.

At the UN, a process was set in train to create legal instruments of human-rights protection for all, out of the 1948 Universal Declaration of Human Rights. But the official debate went on for eighteen years

333

and still ended in division, and the responsible institutions themselves were so polarized as to be ineffective. As a noted international lawyer laconically observed, "the role of the [UN] Human Rights Commission in respect of complaints of human rights violations was minimal prior to 1967."[30] That sentence gives an idea of the low regard in which UN institutions were held during the Cold War.

In the first phase of the Commission's negotiations, the debate about rights saw Western governments at loggerheads with the Soviet and former-colonial regimes. Delegates from the first stressed individual rights, like freedom of expression and representation, at the expense of state-enshrined power. This "liberal-democratic" approach was concrete, but unsocial. Delegates from the second stressed the rights of states as the embodiment of collectivities. This "socialist" approach was more abstract, often directed at central-government control—in practice, its advocates' own control. Hence the institutional impasse, which reflected the fact that no one on either the Western or the Soviet side could be sure of even wanting to win a nuclear war, while the Soviet/post-colonial consensus was a consensus of convenience. The formal division between categories of rights, moreover, had been there from the start. Early drafts of the Universal Declaration, reflecting the predominance of Western states in the early UN, included only liberal-democratic concepts; "socialist" rights were simply tacked on later, with no attempt to integrate the two.[31]

The result, when the UN Commission finally resolved on an outcome, was an agreement to disagree: not one instrument but two, the International Covenants of 1966, which have given us our versions of "civil and political" and "economic, social and cultural" rights but otherwise remained a dead letter—in part because of the Cold War, and in part because the Covenants themselves were hidebound by state sovereignty (only one made provision for individuals to challenge governments' record in fulfilling the rights decreed). In addition, twin international bones of contention—the *apartheid* regime in South Africa, and the status of the state of Israel—came to sharpen the opposing positions at the UN and seal its ineffectuality, not to say its corruption.

In the period between the International Covenants and the first former-Yugoslav tribunal, little progress was made in the further application of the Universal Declaration. It was a non-governmental organization with a citizens' membership, Amnesty International, which became the unofficial keeper of the world's conscience, by reducing human rights to the freedom to live honestly under a state without being subjected to violence in its name. At the core of Amnesty's practice were four articles from the Universal Declaration: 5, banning torture and "cruel, inhuman or degrading punishment"; 9, banning "arbitrary arrest, detention or exile"; 18, on freedom of conscience; and 19, on freedom of expression. Merely to read the organization's annual reports for the period gives a painful, but largely accurate, impression of the quality of social life under the great majority of regimes in the world. The very success of Amnesty, reporting with fearless impartiality on the record of all governments, testifies to the widespread violations of human dignity taking place in the states system, with the help of rapidly expanding techniques of repression.[32]

Following the end of the Cold War and the disappearance of the Soviet Union, the dead hand of compromise began to be lifted from UN deliberations. Special tribunals were created to investigate atrocities from the previous era (e.g., in Cambodia) and more recent past (former Yugoslavia, Rwanda, Sierra Leone). The need to bring all this activity together culminated in the creation of the International Criminal Court, based in The Hague. As Maurice Cranston wrote, "there is nothing essentially difficult about turning political and civil rights into positive rights. All that is needed is an international court with real powers of enforcement."[33] The international civil servants of the Court, however, will struggle to establish its practical effectiveness, as long as its membership is less than universal and state sovereignty cannot be overridden for the extradition of indicted criminals, except in the (unlikely) event of consensus on the UN Security Council. The ICC's power to extradite also implies a supranational military force that the Court does not have at its disposal and may, for a mixture of reasons, be undesirable in itself.

Universal Human Rights as Freedom

So much for human-rights *protection*. But can human identity be so objectified? Is that not merely a reflection of the ambiguous nature of human rights under states—constructs of social control, as well as order? The fundamental debate which never got off the ground at the UN, before being sabotaged by the Cold War, surely stands for something—notably the perennial question of the relationship between the individual and the collectivity, and the meaning and purpose of states as expressions of collective will. So we may fairly ask 1) where, in a universal, secular institution—even a decentralized, pluralized one like the states system—does the exact locus of legitimacy lie? 2)

335

from where, under such an institution, does political change and moral progress come; and 3) can one set of human rights lead another, to expand them all as it were dialectically?

The classical answer (and also the Western one, crystallized by the work of Amnesty International) is 3) yes, 2) liberal democracy, 1) in the individual, through the giving of priority to civil and political rights. For many, this led to the actual resolution of the Cold War, successfully demonstrated ever since through the encouragement to liberal democracy by forceful, if necessary sovereignty-*breaking* intervention: beginning with NATO intervention in former Yugoslavia in the 1990s, and on through the UN-promulgated principle of Responsibility to Protect, first invoked in the Anglo-French intervention in Libya in 2011. As I have argued, humanitarian intervention is morally justifiable on a case-by-case basis, though not without practical problems which imply changes in supranational institutions. Still, one can say that if the liberal-democratic conception of human rights were *not* widely supported in the world as a whole, the humanitarian interveners in its name would hardly have been welcomed in the first place, given that state sovereignty provides anyone, at any time, with a formal pretext for resisting the intervention of outsiders, and that this pretext has never ceased to be invoked since the creation of the universal system.

But leaving this issue aside, some of the interested parties themselves appear to have asserted the priority that they think should apply in matters of human rights, and sought to take liberal-democratic freedoms into their own hands. Two related shibboleths, it seems to me, about human nature and political capacity have been shattered in this way since the end of the Cold War. One is the paternalistic view that people in non-Western or "developing" countries cannot grasp liberal-democratic ideas by themselves and need help—in other words, political education—in these ideas and in running the institutions which embody them. I have called this the "maturity thesis."[34] The other concerns the relation between liberal democracy and secularism or individualism or both.

The "Maturity Thesis" Revisited

Paternalism in the name of liberal democracy, I have argued, is wrong-headed and overbearing. But it is also wrong because, even when well-meant, it is unnecessary. We need look no further than the outright electoral victory of the National League for Democracy in Burma in 1990, in an election that the Burmese military junta had, after a long period of rule, reluctantly allowed. The replacement of autocracy by liberal democracy is not an idea so complex as to be incomprehensible, even in a context which is culturally diverse (as the world itself is). The human will for such change is there; the capacity is there; only the sclerotic system of state sovereignty which gives rights and power to the holders of the status quo whatever their intentions or qualities can frustrate people's desire for political freedom (as when the Burmese junta went on to flout the electoral results which had proven the illegitimacy of their rule).

Liberal democracy is also institutional democracy, the democracy of "limited government," and therefore of emotional restraint. Kant argued that the world as a whole would be more peaceful if all societies were liberal democracies, because this form of polity demands self-restraint and the peaceful resolution of disputes. His optimism has been vindicated by people who have sought liberal-democratic government by adoption, especially in newly-created or post-colonial jurisdictions and since the end of the Cold War. Such people may need help and encouragement to get their way against conservatives in their own societies; but they do not, I think, need simple principles like self-restraint and fairness to others, the peaceful resolution of disputes, or the explicit social sharing of power, to be explained to them.

Secularism and Individualism

The second shibboleth to have been overturned since the end of the Cold War is the idea that some people, especially in non-Western or "developing" countries, are unable to grasp the secular values inherent in the liberal-democratic conception of human rights, including civil law; even unable to value themselves as individuals, because of some cultural predisposition of their own, or some historic damage to their identity and self-esteem; or conversely that they would be justified in rejecting, in liberal democracy, an extreme individualism which is destructive of social solidarity. In this matter, paternalists and anti-colonialists can find illiberal reasons to agree, strange bedfellows though they make.

To begin with the "historic damage" thesis, this is the source of the anti-colonialism which drove many regimes in newly independent Africa and Asia into the arms of the Soviet oligarchs during the Cold War. Given, however, the abuse that demagogues during that time (including in the Soviet Union) made of it, and given the end of the Cold War itself, this seems to be a diminishing source of inspiration.

"National" revolutions, after all, in the modern state system merely assert a fact of life in the system, the sovereignty of de facto nations. Nothing deeper in terms of human values is guaranteed. As the dependency theorists made clear, movements for justice and equality between *states* in the 1970s and '80s often held out false promises for justice and equality in the *societies* concerned. In fact, I would argue that it was the widespread violations of human dignity by governments in both post-colonial and Communist countries which long helped to give public validity to the work of Amnesty International. In time the UN secretary-general himself was moved to ask whether state sovereignty had not swung the balance of political morality completely against the interests of ordinary people.[35]

As for the "cultural" thesis around individualism and secularism, this refers largely to an upsurge of Islamic zealotry from the late Cold War on, especially after the 1979 revolution in Iran—a movement often manifested in terrorist actions against Western society and institutions, such as the attacks of September 11, 2001, aimed at the centers of political, economic, and military power in the United States.

The first thing to note, however, about Islamic zealotry is that it is not historically new; the reconciliation of secular and theological principles of government has arguably been controversial since the very inception of Islam.[36] Americans often view "9/11" as a rather unique event, but in fact this was merely the most dramatic and destructive of a series of terrorist attacks emanating from Muslim-majority countries, and which hitherto had been directed almost exclusively against society and institutions in Western Europe. This region was physically closer to the terrorists' focus of criticism, the state of Israel, and closer historically to imperialism—both of which, it was claimed by the zealots, came together to rob Arab or Muslim peoples of their rights. All of which helps to explain the impact of Huntington's explosively titled *Clash of Civilizations*.

But that is precisely why the pro-democracy uprisings in Muslim-majority countries, beginning a decade after "9/11," are significant, as the sociologist Olivier Roy was quick to point out:

> If we look at who launched the movement, it is obvious that this is a post-Islamic generation. The great revolutionary movements of the 1970's and 1980's are old history for them, their parents' history. This new generation is not interested in ideology—all its slogans are pragmatic and concrete ("dégage," "*erhal*" ["get out of the way!," first directed at Tunisian President Ben Ali]); they do not appeal to Islam

as their predecessors did in Algeria at the end of the 1980's. They express above all a rejection of corrupt dictatorships and a demand for democracy. Obviously that does not mean that the demonstrators are not religious, but simply that they do not see in Islam a political ideology able to establish a better social order; they are well and truly in a secular political space. The same goes for other ideologies. [The demonstrators] have national loyalties, and wave their national flags, but they do not advocate nationalism as such. More surprisingly, conspiracy theories are absent: the United States and Israel (or France in Tunisia, which supported Ben Ali to the last) are no longer marked out as the causes of the ills of the Arab world. Even the slogan of pan-Arabism has disappeared, precisely at a time when the copycat effect which brought Egyptians and Yemenis into the streets after the Tunis events has demonstrated a common Arab political reality.[37]

Regarding North Africa, in any case, where the uprisings began, and even large parts of the Middle East, one struggles to find any specifically-Western colonial presence from the Romans to Napoleon. In all that time the power, from the Atlas to the Zagros, was Arab or Islamic; and the Johnny-come-latelies who foisted the centralized, fiscal-extraction state onto illiterate pastoral peoples were the beys of the Ottoman Empire. Surely it is their oppressive rule, their institutionalized corruption, prorogued by their successors, the Nassers, Bourguibas, and Shahs, which undermined Islam as a belief system and source of social values, and explains the wave of personal conversions out of Islam that Roy also reports.[38]

European colonialism's main cultural impact was elsewhere—first in Latin America, then in sub-Saharan Africa and Southeast Asia. But again, I would argue, in the decolonization phase of the UN era it was corrupt, demagogic leaders who indulged in anti-Western, or simply anti-democratic, sloganizing. From Guinea to Somalia, from Nicaragua to the Philippines, populist dictators played the proxy game of the Cold War for all it was worth. They got the world's attention because they had the guns, not because they were readers of Fanon.[39]

Still, the fact that some of them retained power over lengths of time despite their brutal rule reflects, I think, sincere reservations in societies with traditional extended-family structures about individualism, materialism, and consumerism—phenomena which over the decades, through international advertising media, have become increasingly associated with Western society. To this one could add a confused idea of equality between men and women, associated with the liberating impact on women and sexual relations generally of reliable contraception, and a confused idea of social relations once traditional, kin-based authority has broken down. In time, and especially with the coming of the Internet, these influences spread to societies in the Middle East and North Africa where the culture of Islam was predominant.

But if the truth be told, these personal and social confusions, and related reservations about modernity, are a source of tensions between men and women, and between generations, in Western (or "Northern") countries too. The difference, if it exists, is one of degree; we are all, in different places, working out our individual responses to these challenges, especially as they connect with the impersonal, large-scale organization of society under the states system. Even in its heartlands of Europe and North America, liberal democracy has increasingly come under fire for its social limitations (such as an inability to build communities which would embrace their generational extremes, the hyperactive young and the inactive old). Such clashes of value are not between different civilizations, but within the same one—the civilization (if that is the right word) of the modern secular state.

To argue, then, that individualism and secularism are uniquely Western, neo-colonial, or inimical to "developing" societies, seems to me inaccurate, as well as patronizing. (It is also circular, if one defines development by the ability to grasp the values themselves.) All one can say for certain is that the libertarian part of liberal democracy has never ceased to gain popular support since the Second World War, irrespective of governments' attempts to refute or redefine it in favor of the blind worship of states. The Cold War in that regard merely delayed the inevitable in reform; for the "national," pro-state revolutions since disavowed were without exception illiberal and inhumane. Many—too many—people could echo the Iranian writer Azar Nafisi, when she declared, from her exile in America:

> I curse the totalitarian regimes for holding their citizens by their heartstrings. The [Iranian] revolution taught me not to be consoled by other people's miseries, not to feel thankful because so many others had suffered more. Pain and loss, like love and joy, are unique and personal; they cannot be modified by comparison to others.[40]

North-South Relations

Holding individual dignity sacred is perhaps not sufficient for a perfect conception of society, but is certainly necessary to it. The only serious reservation one could retain about the liberal-democratic conception of human rights is that in contemporary circumstances it seems absolutely to require fixed institutions, rather than the "universal cosmopolitan existence" that Kant considered the highest and most desirable condition for humankind. Liberal democracy is for states, rather than the soul; human rights require a complement in social, as opposed to political, morality. I take this to mean first and foremost the elimination of the life-threatening poverty that persists in parts of the modern world and is an emblem of its institutional failure. In a context of universal human rights, the abolition of "North" and "South" is what economic, social, and cultural rights imply.

It might seem that I am engaging in another form of reification here—erecting, after the "West" and the "rest," blocs of "Northern" and "Southern" societies. But provisionally I would defend the latter division as a moral reality. In material terms it already exists, ratified by the formal practice of foreign, mainly post-colonial aid. There are in this sense two groups of societies—one donors, the other recipients, of aid. Northern societies themselves have their "Souths," their divisions between haves and have-nots. We should all want to see such divisions permanently overcome. So what about another approach to human rights, based on the ideal of general equality, and beginning with the poorest of the poor?

On one level, a strong case can be made, as Shue did, that essentials of life like food, clean water, and shelter are the rightful expectation of everyone.[41] Besides, the most libertarian of political instincts must be dulled by homelessness, chronic illness, hunger, or thirst, so that it becomes invidious to preach freedom abstractly to the victims of these woes. But beyond basic rights, I think social equality is a real value, and its practice a real virtue. We can, in my view, open up this broader question without engaging in inconclusive debates about the colonial past. I have concrete proposals for the reform of North-to-South aid, as a way toward the elimination of international inequality and with it the North/South socioeconomic distinction as such.

Increase North-to-South Aid

To begin with, the level of foreign aid by Northern donors has surely always been too low. A figure of 1 percent per annum of gross national product for "overseas development assistance" was agreed under the UN Commission on Trade and Development in 1964. This was subsequently lowered to the nugatory figure of 0.7 percent. As an example of the practice of aid against this background, take the twenty-odd

341

societies represented on the Development Assistance Committee (DAC) of the chief Northern forum, the Organization for Economic Co-operation and Development. According to the DAC's own records, annual transfers from three-quarters of these donor societies, for the whole second half of the twentieth century, ran at *less than* 0.7 percent of GNP.[42]

Imagine an organized society in which the great majority of people were poorer than the minority, with large dispersed groups—perhaps a quarter of the population—permanently threatened with death from hunger and disease; and yet where taxation for general welfare was set at less than 1 percent of available public funds, indefinitely (and even then not properly collected). Imagine the divisions that must exist there, the inertia, the mutual ignorance and indifference that prevail, despite the best efforts of the poor to live honestly and of the well-disposed well-off to help them; and imagine such a society as *not* being allowed to be permanently at war with itself, owing to an assumption that everyone has his or her just deserts. Imagine, too, that as a result of this situation, large numbers of people are obliged to spend the greater part of the year working at an unwelcome distance from their homes and families. Everything in daily life, in such a society, becomes difficult—clear communication, firm information, even a balanced assessment of the condition of society as a whole. That, practically speaking, is the world we live in.

Obtaining a precise idea of the impact of public foreign aid, then, in the world since colonialism is already a complex and uncertain proposition. More to the point, such aid is unlikely to have a high profile in donor societies, because its level is too low to be perceptible to the donors themselves—the people at large, who nevertheless share with the recipients an interest in knowing its effect. *Aid is abstract.* The collection, moreover, of this public gift (leaving aside aid for emergencies such as natural disasters) takes place, when it takes place, invisibly and automatically, in the form of tax. *Aid is anonymous.* In this way, and especially at the existing low level of donation, foreign aid becomes scarcely felt, concretely, at all, whether as help to the unknown intended recipients, or as shared sacrifice by the donors. *Aid is insignificant.* On top of which, in functioning liberal-democratic societies (as most donors of truly multilateral aid are), there is much gathering of aid under the auspices of private or vocational charities; and these operations, like the constituencies they originate in, are particularized (food aid, housing aid, farm aid, water aid, eyesight aid, sport aid, Christian Aid, Islamic Aid). *Aid is fragmented.* This most obviously moral foreign policy of any society is hampered by the nature of the relationship involved. In practice, it scarcely figures in donor-society debates, except as governments' self-congratulatory propaganda, or when some gross abuse is alleged, like assistance to oppressive regimes, or white-elephant projects, or the embezzlement of donated funds.

Tomohisa Hattori would have us see public foreign aid as conscious munificence from the well-off to the poor, in a time-honored tradition.[43] But the "potlatch" paradigm he focuses on, with whole pre-modern peoples outdoing each other in ceremonies of extravagant generosity, seems to me the very opposite of the modern truth.[44] Nor does his other model, Victorian charity, seem relevant. To my mind, the record of a half-century of organized foreign aid in the wake of European colonialism is neither munificent, on the part of the donor societies, nor persuasive as a shared social action on their part.

There are exceptions to this picture, which I mentioned earlier, in the practices of Scandinavian societies, testifying to the existence of ordinary taxpaying people who sincerely wish to make a difference to unknown strangers' lives, and who actively work to do so—gaining a deserved satisfaction from their initiative, which takes high-level public form, and attains the highest recorded levels of Official Development Assistance.[45] These donations, coherently planned and enthusiastically maintained as a principle of democratic human exchange, seem to me most admirable, but they are the exception, not the rule.

So imagine instead that you lived in a wealthy society where the government asked you to support a policy of giving a significant, but still reasonable, proportion of the collective product to poor people in other countries, for a fixed period of time (say, 5 percent of GNP for 50 years, or 10 percent for 25). The higher level of fiscal extraction would still not greatly affect your general living conditions, but following such a transformation the political profile of foreign aid would certainly rise. The aid commitment would be high enough for recipient governments to budget properly for economic development, and for durable change to take place in their citizens' lives. A well-informed donor-recipient relationship between North and South would develop, making wastage and embezzlement of the public gift a thing of the past. A clear political constituency for aid would come into being among the donors, followed inevitably by pressures for progress in the day-to-day lives of the people in other countries to whom the donations go. At the same time, a prospective end to all external aid would focus the minds of the recipients themselves on the accountability of their leaders for its proper use.

So much for the level of aid. What about its form?

North-to-South Aid Should Be Technical Assistance

Technical assistance, in official aid parlance, refers to the transfer of skills, rather than finance, in the North-South public relationship. In this form of aid no money need be retained by recipient governments. Nor are they required to find the foreign currency to pay any expatriates employed on projects in their countries, or to finance the projects themselves. All monies are directed to specific objectives, commonly the training of local individuals and related infrastructural development.

This form of aid also answers, over the longer term, the difficulty faced by Southern societies in international economic competition, namely the generation from domestic sources of investment capital, especially in the hard currencies which circulate around the more highly industrialized and -organized sectors of the world economy. Mobilizing labor in such societies presents no problem, as most people are so poor that they will do any available work. It is the position of original disadvantage in infrastructure, skills, and technology, accompanied by weak currency positions, official corruption, and social unrest, which makes for a hapless, helpless "Third World." Escaping this condition depends acutely on the indigenous development of infrastructure and industry through applied knowledge and skills.

Now some of these skills are already being obtained, along with foreign currency, by Southern migrants working in Northern countries. But on a rather low level as regards the skills, and at the cost of international tensions too. Tensions of all kinds, in fact, as Northern governments squabble with Southern ones over the control of migration; with their own citizens over the level of immigration; and with each other, as they strive, in an international labor market of their own making and manipulation, to fulfil their domestic economic goals. In this situation one can fairly ask whether anything substantial is being done to reduce poverty and inequality in the world as a whole.

Anne Hammerstad, in her survey of migration, takes a surprisingly positive view of its economic aspects, including informal ones. She argues that the value of remittances to developing countries from their migrant citizens in the North, "even on conservative estimates," now "[dwarfs] that of official Development Aid . . . and [outpaces] Foreign Direct Investment (FDI) flows globally." She describes these remittances as "a capital flow unhampered by bureaucracy and corruption," with direct beneficial effects for Southern societies and, over the longer term, indirect benefits in the form of inward investment by returning migrants. Even "regular migrants," she adds, "may choose cheaper alternatives to official transfer channels" for their financial sendings home, so this is a more substantial phenomenon than is generally perceived.[46]

Against this, I would argue that the very nature of the phenomenon makes such precise calculations as Hammerstad offers impossible. On her specific arguments in favor of personal financial flows, I would reply that where bureaucracies, including banks, are corrupt (which one could say of most of the economic South) or bypassed (as in the case of those "cheaper" financial channels), a significant proportion of the hard currency flowing to Southern societies will be wasted on them *as societies*. This wastage may come about through currency controls (usually a corrupt prerogative of bank and government employees), or the bribes and favors required to evade them, or to facilitate migrants' travel in the first place (e.g., the purchase of passports, rarely an unqualified right); or in the course of investment in the home economy (e.g., through the obtaining of building permits, which invariably requires some form of covert favor). The gross economic value of North-South remittances may, as Hammerstad says, be higher than official figures suggest, but the net effect may be less than she supposes, and into the bargain unevenly, and perhaps unjustly, distributed. Meanwhile, one certain effect overall will be to reinforce the hardness of Northern currency, as the medium of reference in all North-South transactions, and to that extent preserve the division between North and South.

Besides, we should all want to see an end to economic migration, which in an unequal world will always have an element of compulsion, and encourage corruption among those in positions of power. (Even in Northern liberal-democracies we find a steady stream of ministers caught employing illegal migrants or exploiting legal ones). It creates jealousies between, and sometimes within, societies. It favors young men over older men and over women in general. And it causes great pain and hardship in its own right, when families are divided—sometimes for longer, in their shared lifetimes, than they spend together; sometimes forever. People of the Scottish island of Raasay, forced by poverty into exile in the nineteenth century, in tears snatched handfuls of soil from their ancestors' graves. Even today, in comparatively easier times, from Tajikistan to the Philippines, from the Corsican mountains to the Peloponnese, the homes of migrant workers—so much more luxurious and better equipped than those of previous generations, or of non-migrants—are for much of the year deserted, in villages peopled by children and the unproductive old. Diasporas have done much to define the ethnic structure of the modern world; yet what are diasporas themselves but making the best of a bad hand dealt by history? This is a syndrome which a world of true voluntary nations would as a priority avoid.

All these are arguments for bringing the reform of North-South relations officially within the ambit of the states system, and focusing on the creation of a safe and secure life for Southern citizens where they want to be, in their own homes. Southern people's energies in the North can then be spent, not in underclass occupations which Northern natives scorn to fill, but in skill-specific education and training of direct relevance to the development of Southern economies.

The simplest argument in favor of aid as technical assistance, however, is that it involves the building of mass human relations to counteract the anonymity and divisiveness of modern state arrangements. Foreign aid conceived as financial is invisible and impersonal; it involves no direct relationship between the donors and the recipients. Taxation is raised for the benefit of strangers who remain unvisited except by diplomats and tourists. Foreign aid as technical assistance, by contrast, is personal: it involves going there and doing the job yourself—and over time, under a consistent and properly supported national policy, seeing your family, friends, and compatriots doing the same. It means learning the reality of unknown others' lives, making new and unforeseen friendships, and taking account, at home, of the deeper implications of foreign policy. This is a relationship with the potential to change all human relations for the better.

The French Example

During the late- and post-colonial period, for nearly half a century, French aid policy was dominated by technical assistance. *La coopération* was implemented through the hands of French expatriate trainers, with the projects themselves, like the trainers, French-financed. It formed part of a wider global policy of voluntary expatriation which even today sees outposts of French society on every continent. At any one time since 1945, between 2 and 5 percent of French citizens have been in employment overseas, mainly on some form of government contract. This is the modern expression of Republican principles, forged in the 1789 Revolution, of spreading French values and institutions worldwide.

As French decolonization gained pace, voluntary expatriation in foreign aid was augmented by the use of compulsory national service. Under *co-opération civile*, young men (and later women) were given the option to fulfil overseas, in a civilian capacity, a slightly longer period of duty (sixteen to eighteen months) than the military one, but still on conscript wages. Since conscription is not socially selective, French *co-opérants* (teachers, doctors, agronomists, electricians, engineers, and craftsmen of all kinds) came from all sectors of French society. There was in effect an official French policy, funded by taxation, to send a cross-section of the nation abroad to work.[47]

The result was that by the millennium, when conscription was abolished, hundreds of thousands of French men and women had had the experience of living and working in Southern societies from New Caledonia to Cameroon, from Madagascar to the southern Mediterranean littoral. Today, in a French town of any size, there is still a large demographic group of individuals over the age of forty with this overseas past. Many continue to share their experiences through acquaintances at home, often in the same line of work as under *co-opération*; these people make up what sociologists call a communicating group, with a particular culture of their own. Others have gone on to further years, spent voluntarily abroad, to make new personal relationships or to renew those made during previous service. All this makes for an informed constituency in French society on foreign aid; it gives a special cosmopolitan character to French society at large.

French foreign aid has not been immune to criticism at home, not least because of its political saliency and its economic costs.[48] French society itself is not free of chauvinism (including a rather perplexing sense of injury that the world's *lingua* is no longer *franca*). And the presence of large numbers of French overseas has paved the way for military interventions, notably in sub-Saharan Africa (Congo/Katanga, Rwanda), having more to do with French prestige or the security of expatriates than the interests of local people.[49] It could also be argued that through *co-opération civile* and conscription generally, French governments avoided the problem of youth unemployment, until political pressures forced the abolition of conscription itself.

None of these criticisms, however, need apply to technical assistance as such. Revived as a publicly-financed, voluntary option for all DAC societies—that is, as aid from much of Europe, North America, and Australasia—it could significantly help to maintain constructive relations between Northern and Southern peoples, and in time the elimination of North and South in material terms.

The general trend in Western post-colonial policy has been away from government-to-government financial transfers and toward project-specific support—though, as I have pointed out, often under the auspices of non-governmental organizations and private charities and not, as in the French case, by drawing on the resources of society at large. Also, in the aftermath of the Cold War Western financial transfers became more thinly spread, as donor governments sought to secure former-Communist regimes' allegiance to liberal democracy. This was in fact an outright abuse of the established principles of aid: first because the newly directed funds were donated within Europe, and were therefore only marginally altruistic; and second because they were taken for what they were—bribes—and pocketed, by former Communist *apparatchiks* reinventing themselves as capitalist magnates (*apparatchiks* being generally, after 1989, the only members of Communist societies with experience both of public administration and of the uses of hard currency). Meanwhile, the former-colonial recipients of Northern aid in Africa, Asia, and Latin America were forced into competition with these new "clients" (since the gross financial outlay from DAC societies did not increase). All these are reasons why the need for public aid in the real South is still perceptible today, and the reform of aid so important.

Aid Donors: Who Does What?

My argument, then, is that North-to-South aid should be increased; it should be explicitly conditional; and it should mainly take the form of technical assistance—focused, in the poorest societies, on infrastructural projects and training.

Hitherto the DAC has served as a forum for the coordination of Northern aid policies and national quota-setting against a complex institutional background, including loans, "tied" aid (requiring purchases from donor societies in return), and financial aid, funnelled through the IMF and World Bank. DAC technical assistance itself, as public international aid, has consistently waned. The resulting vagueness, for the taxpayers of donor societies, concerning the level and impact of their gift reflects the vacuity of any intergovernmental negotiation conducted in purely financial terms. And the shared preference of donor and recipient authorities for financial transfers probably has less to do with post-colonial sensitivities than self-interested reasons like diplomatic bargaining and political control.

By contrast, a coordinated policy of technical assistance run solely by the DAC and drawing on DAC society directly, would provide the nearest thing to a precise accounting of North-South economic relations in an essentially contentious domain. It ought also, logically, to enable a clear division of labor among the societies giving public foreign aid. For example, one could envisage a recipient-society being formally "adopted" by one DAC donor society for all its aid needs; or several recipient-societies together, say in a geographical cluster; or clustered by donor-recipient historical ties, or a shared vehicular language. In this way the DAC can become, like the IAEA in different circumstances, an institutional force for good.[50]

Above all, we need these "special relationships" in which ordinary people are in direct touch with each other across the North-South divide—peacefully, daily, with public support at their back. Technical assistance means relationships forged in the rough democracy of the workplace; it implies reciprocity, and ultimately the elimination of "North" and "South" in the mind. It is a path to the ideal of international relations as voluntary social relations between equals.

Human Rights vs. the Law of States

A world of true nations, then—of real, effective communities united in themselves, and equal with each other—is the ideal suggested by the realization of economic, social, and cultural rights; as opposed to the world of individuals, and of individuated states, implied by the placing of liberal-democratic (or civil and political) rights at the forefront of reform.

That said, I would return to my point that the compartmentalization of rights, leading to their proliferation as separate entitlements, is in its own way misleading. It implies the dividing-up of human beings, perhaps against themselves, and the practical dividing of rights from duties, and to that extent the confounding of morality itself. This is one more consequence of the excessive formalization of human society resulting from the universal states system. Human rights attract our attention by pointing to a deeper conception of society; they are justifiable moral claims we would make on each other, in a putatively just world. But arguably the debates over their meaning and priority would have been less intense and wayward, had the general promulgation of states not retracted some original quality from our expectations. For "would you rather live in a free society, or a fair one?" is the question that a contest between liberal and social conceptions of human rights provokes.

The question was asked in extreme and threatening terms during the Cold War and has not been satisfactorily answered by events since the end of that conflict. And the reason is surely that it is a rather divisive question to begin with, in respect of beings who are ill-suited to choosing between the individual and the social. If there are any human rights, logically we should have all of them, all at once. Prioritizing one version to the exclusion of another is, like international law itself in the wake of the Universal Declaration, broken-backed—the result of an enterprise to decree universal human rights when they are nowhere fulfilled in their entirety and perhaps, with the best will in the world, under states could not be.

Here we need to remind ourselves that justice and law are separate things—a moral fact which is overridden by the establishment of permanent states with rights of their own. For governments, even in democracies, will seize on that right to make and unmake laws, and impose their version of social rules; and judges will not disobey them even when they deprecate the rules, because to do so would jeopardise the independence of the judiciary of which they are part. They will even, on occasion, enforce unjust laws while criticizing them; that is an aspect of the tame liberty which, in democracies, judges enjoy. But the judges themselves are part of the unjust greater system of states.

Moral right, therefore, is not guaranteed in our legalized world. For that, concrete changes are required to the nature and purpose of states - or their abolition.

Nature and Society

Finally in my list of moral concerns, we need to recall the operations of *non*-human nature that we cannot affect, like the tides of the sea or the lifespan of our sun. No matter how much we would want to embrace nature for its own sake, or for our own aesthetic and spiritual satisfaction, we shall succeed fully only in the mind. The Romantic poets discovered this lesson, from their attempts to escape from what they saw as an over-organized, over-enclosed world—the world of the Industrial Revolution—into a pristine environment of ideal natural beauty. Modern culture combines, not without contradiction, the romantic vision of the questing, free individual and the rational vision of social order shaped by science.

The negative results were described by Philip Reynolds in 1970, in an assessment which still rings true today.

It is a commonplace—the evidence is everywhere—that advances in the natural sciences have outstripped advances in the social sciences, that, in other words, the capacity to understand and fashion the social and political structures which can contain and exploit, not be mastered and destroyed by, the opportunities that science has created, simply does not exist. The threats are innumerable. Pollution or destruction of the human environment through poisonous effluents, through ecological disruption, through exhaustion of natural resources, through noise, through the creation of indestructible plastic or radioactive waste, through ugliness and the spoliation of natural beauty; uncontrolled and possibly uncontrollable demographic explosions because of new and widely disseminated health and hygiene methods; undermining of social patterns, values and beliefs because of the global circulation of cultural influences, the increasingly universal acceptance of the value of wealth maximization, and the soul-destroying employment in which large numbers of humans consequently spend large parts of their lives; the looming possibility of genetic manipulation and control; the already existing destructive capability of eliminating all life from the earth—these are but a few of the menaces contained in the material and intellectual affluence which the sciences have created. In face of them human behaviour in its political and social forms appears puny and helpless. Man's capacity to survive in competition with creatures larger, stronger, swifter and better armed than he derived from his mental capacity that enabled him to adapt, and adapt to, his environment. He can now mould his physical, chemical and biological environment far more effectively than before. But it is his social and political environment which he now must learn to understand and appropriately to control. If his adaptive capacity is unequal to this task then he will have lost the faculty that has enabled him hitherto to survive.[51]

To these specific threats one could add human-induced climate change—raising again the prospect of an end to all life on earth—and the loss of biodiversity—ultimately the reduction of all living things to those of direct use to human beings.

Taken together, these prospects give the modern world a paradoxical character which our education is only just beginning to define. Reynolds had begun his book by declaring: "Knowledge is a unity," which international theorists might hope to encompass with the help of the resources of modern science and technology. Yet against this background, the very idea of a universal social organization, the states system, which allows us, the dominant species, every imaginable freedom to express ourselves materially—separately and together, all at once!—amounts to conflating human self-interest with the interest of everything else.

In large part, then, our modern problems may be understood as a consequence of human "uncontrolled and possibly uncontrollable demographic explosions"—and by the same token, by some dismissed. On one level, too many people on earth makes it irrelevant to ask what to do about human dominance. If we humans are the problem, there *is* no solution. Or more optimistically (and anthropocentrically), there is no problem: as clever animals we have more or less got things right so far, and we shall probably continue to do so, though there will be times when life is less tolerable (for some). History, on this bland view, is a series of accidents showing human beings variably in control of themselves; the Cold War was one result, but we survived the Cold War.

But surely it is also possible, more creatively, to argue that human dominance over all other forms of life, though not complete, is now so secure that it can be relaxed. A successful species is precisely that: successful. Nothing threatens us. We can try to be less in control of "nature" as an object outside ourselves, and live more fully in nature instead.

In this regard there is particular value in "deep green" visions of the human future, like those of Arne Naess, in which the human footprint on the earth is seen lightened, and communities are conceived as more closely integrated with the natural environment than in the past, while more dispersed between themselves.[52] Some ecologists, following up this thinking, have suggested that if we take the most efficient modern societies, their ideal size in future would be one-tenth of what they are now. The same infrastructure could be maintained, and the same standard of living sustained, with far fewer people—with the help, principally, of energy from renewable sources and computerized systems of communication and control. The kind of society so imagined is not one in which human dominance is relinquished, but one where more space is left for living nature. In the human-occupied space, the same ordering, cleansing, recycling, and inventive activities which characterize modern technological society could be maintained; the same living standards could be expected (or better ones, notably in health protection), but the space for nature, especially nature left alone and wild, in all countries would be larger than it is today.

Relieving Competitive Pressures

There would also be significant political consequences if this kind of thinking were put into practice—notably, a relieving of competitive pressures in the world economy and in particular on the poorest societies.

Our Northern societies in fact are already so far ahead of all others in material terms (especially given our stable population-levels) that we may plausibly be said already to own the complete stock of common metals and building material that we require. We no longer need to extract or import most minerals; efficient recycling of what we have, from steel girders to tin cans, will supply our manufacturing and construction industries. And indeed, our governments have come increasingly, over time, to push firms in an ecological, economizing direction for their own sake: ecologically, in view of the growing consensus against carbon dioxide emissions, and toward frugality in response to rising prices in imported oil and oil-based products. By contrast, in Southern countries generally, people can avail themselves far less of finished products, ambitious construction schemes, or governmental initiatives on the use of natural resources or the protection of the natural environment. But this contrast cannot, I suggest, be simply attributed to these societies' being "behind" the North in terms of economic and industrial expertise, or burdened with an excessive birthrate; or unable, as neoliberal economists often claim, to "afford" democracy. Underdevelopment measured internationally actually means that some peoples in the world have less, in terms of bulk metals, stone, bricks, cement, and machines, with which to develop an infrastructure or industrial base, and less finance with which to acquire them from scratch. And this disadvantage cannot be accidental, in view of the historical dominance of extractive industries in North-South relations, both before and after 1945.

Basing themselves on research from the late 1970s, the expert writers of the Brandt Report suggested that such international disparities could be ironed out by managed North-South competition.[53] But the infeasibility of that proposal is clear today. First, because the petrodollars which very quickly, after 1980, became the most forceful factor in transnational financial flows did not receive—were never destined for—equitable distribution; and second because Northern societies have continuously been in a stronger position to limit either the price of other imported raw materials or the imports themselves. The same goes for ecology as for economy, as the history of the Kyoto Protocol shows: formal North-South relations now include the marketization of rights to pollute, on top of the marketization of production (in practice, meaning the export of pollution from North to South, rather than the reduction of pollution as such). It seems as if the world economy conceived as a competition for raw materials and their uses will always have the same winners—those whom the Northern consumer lifestyle favors.[54] Northern societies, therefore, have a moral duty to control their own expansion, as well as to give direct aid to peoples in the South.

For new generations in Northern societies, growing up after the formal repeal of colonialism, such thinking might seem difficult to accept. But part of Northern insensitivity, if that is the word, to Southern disadvantage is attributable to a misleading convention of economics, especially neoliberal economics, which suggests at one and the same time that the world economy is a zero-sum game and that it is not. How else can educated people argue, as neoliberal economists do, that the world's resources are unlimited *and* that the equitability of their distribution is not a matter of fundamental moral concern? Economists in general, I think, are as confused as the rest of us by the anthropocentrism of the universal states system, which divides the human race from the natural environment and in so doing divides us against ourselves.

A world which is materially more equal, as well as more unified, also implies taking back power from the paladins of the Internet, who batten on the inherited disparities of peoples everywhere by profiteering in—and hence perpetuating—the competition for electronic systems of communication and control. The result: life in general is not more single, or simple, but more confused than before, and "globalis/zation" becomes a tautology, a prison of multiple self-deception. A *universal* states system, on the other hand, calls for a basic and concrete organizational solution: a universal system of communication and understanding, one language for the machines by which its efficiency may be continually improved and our own dependence on machines diminished.

In a more ecological and less intensively occupied world, human diversity and creativity need not be lessened, but would be differently directed. Common sense tells us that fewer people may mean a better and more equal life for all people, and that with the help of material security and reliable contraception this can be realised. Meanwhile, modern technology opens the way to long-term schemes to reverse historic human damage to the earth's ecosystem and bring unnatural waste spaces like the Sahara to life again, where people may make their homes.[55]

Finally, the "deep green" vision relies on the intuition that kindness to creatures and organisms more vulnerable than ourselves is a genuine virtue. This is an original—yet still humanly-configured—vision, where the fact of human dominance is constructively and imaginatively, but also unselfishly, applied.

Omens for the Twenty-First Century

If this approach seems unconvincing, think of the alternative of an unrestrained development of the present human occupation of the earth. Leave aside, for the moment, weapons of mass destruction and their potential for a war of all against all which some would see as the ultimate Malthusian tool. Think of Amritsar in the Punjab, India: a city where it is impossible to buy a street map, though India is formally a democracy, and the city itself, with the shrine of a major national religion, is a magnet for year-round tourism; where for weeks during the monsoon, no maintenance work is done on the roads, and double-lane traffic moves, when it moves, at the pace of the slowest vehicle on all main streets; where the sky is invisible all day, owing to air pollution and the humidity rising from the intensive irrigation in the countryside around (without which it would nevertheless be impossible to feed the city's inhabitants). Consider that in this sprawling conurbation of two million people, one can hardly find an unbroken pavement or functioning street light, and that from nine o'clock in the evening, when the shops and cinemas close, until dawn there is no public or social life of any kind, only vagabonds and criminals in the pitch-dark empty streets, no doubt because most people are so dog-tired from the working day that they are at home fast asleep. In India as a whole, with a billion-plus inhabitants, a national space program, ambitious investment in computer software engineering, and an assemblage of domestic and imported nuclear technology, governments struggle to keep the electricity on at all.[56]

Unsurprisingly, the commonest public advertisement in India, from billboards to sandwich boards, is for organizations helping people to leave the country. (I have seen law firms in the Punjab whose entire business is in appeals against rejected migration applications from abroad). One can feel perfectly at home in India, as one can feel at home in a crowd (after all, there no rival species in view), but one can also feel perfectly helpless, as many Indians appear to do, or they would not flock to join the emigration racket which dominates all educational activity in the country.[57] Even Galbraith, one of the twentieth century's greatest economists, who asked to be sent as ambassador to India for his own instruction (when the population was a third of what it is today), had no solution to the problem of too many people for too little land.[58]

All this, despite the fact that historical India stands for an ancient and rich culture which includes great respect for nature, and a deep-rooted religious pluralism embracing the whole sub-continent.[59] The result, in modern India, is a democracy of sorts despite widespread corruption, illiteracy, disparities of wealth, and persistent caste-ism, where tolerance of diversity coexists with intense and occasionally violent movements for change, not always in the direction of modernity or social equality. But the intensity and the violence, I suggest, are themselves fuelled by overcrowding. And I have not even begun to speak of female infanticide—that age-old atavism which through abortion, sexual selection, and private medicine stains Indian society like original sin.

India is in all these senses an intimation of a human future in which the social organization of modernity has failed, and for most people only luck or supreme forbearance makes life tolerable at all. Consider, then, that this future might await generations of humankind, perhaps exacerbated by problems of extreme climate (and with no possibility of emigration)—and the "deep green" panaceas for the voluntary restriction of human dominance begin to make sense.

Amazonia: a Country Free of the Modern State

In one instance, ecologism, demography, politics and culture come very obviously together: on the fate of the Amazon rain forest, among the most important natural resources on earth—something vital to the well-being, perhaps even the survival, of humankind. No one, I have argued, can allow such a resource to be privately "owned," in the putative modern sense that territory is owned for one state population's exclusive use. At the same time, the uncontacted tribes of the Amazon rain forest—a few tens of thousands of people, whose impact on this resource is negligible—have a right to live free of the jurisdiction of local modern states, an abstraction which means little to them except as a threat to their way of life.

Ever since the creation of the universal states system, in fact, groups of people with a shared, pre-modern identity have adopted forms of political representation of their own, in state capitals or at the United Nations, to defend their right to live on the territory, but not in the style, of modern states (like, for example, the so-called First Nations of North America on their reservations).[60] Uncontacted peoples, however, constitute a special case of human beings in need of protection: not only from the norms of modern states, but even from other humans. Such peoples would lose their uniqueness, and perhaps perish, if they were forced to become part of a modern state—as the trend of all modern economic and political expansion suggests is inevitable unless halted by an act of deliberate international restraint.

What I am suggesting is a United Nations Protectorate to be set up around the core of the Amazon rain forest, solely to preserve the status quo there, both human and natural, from the encroachment of modern civilization—to keep the uncontacted peoples in, and the rest of us out. The preserve should be surrounded by a buffer zone of the semi-assimilated indigenous inhabitants of the Amazon region, those people who are already in touch with, counted by, and subject to, the governments of the several liminal states. Such a project could be financed by the citizens of all states in the world, in the way that other UN protectorates are, out of public taxation—but at minimal cost, since in the core zone no economic development whatsoever would be entailed. The official policy of the United Nations has always been to discourage UN mandates, to distinguish the organization from its predecessor, the League of Nations, which was criticized for over-deference in the face of colonial governments. But what I am proposing is something different: an arrangement instituted in the name of all humankind to protect people who do *not* seek self-determination in the form of a modern state.

The fact that such a protectorate would be geographically defined—but as generously as possible—by the rain forest means that territory would have to be taken from all the liminal states at once (notably Peru, Colombia, Venezuela, and Brazil). Still, given the position of the forest, by far the largest part of the territory would have to come from northwest Brazil. What would have to be sacrificed in the process is a certain idea of the historical or potential Brazilian nation-state.

Anticipating objections here, I would argue that most ideas of national destiny in the modern states system, even when sincerely held, are shallow and mutable. And then the physical size of Brazil as a single state (the fifth largest in the world) is problematic in its own right. Like other over-large countries, Brazil is a colonial creation—in this case, of Portuguese overseas expansion. Only under an imperial regime which ignored the rights of indigenous peoples could such occupancies ever have been claimed as single political entities (here, a claim to half the South American landmass). But in any case, everywhere one looks in the world, there is the potential for national-political claims to run up against the inheritance of colonial—and therefore artificial—boundaries. The well-attested desire of (some, perhaps all) uncontacted peoples in the region to be left alone to pursue their lives is an anti-colonial claim in its own right. And one may fairly contest the right of Brazilians in their modern state to own (and potentially wipe out) a natural resource which is vital to all humankind, along with its present inhabitants, a few tens of thousands of people whom they are unlikely ever to meet.

As for a "strategic" conception of Brazil—implying future national expansion—it derives some force from Brazilian Lusophone uniqueness in Latin America. From a modern Brazilian national point of view the geopolitical status quo on the subcontinent is rather balanced. But even so, the physical disparity with other Latin American states is so gigantic, and the Amazon area so demographically sparse, that to set up a protectorate there mainly from Brazilian land could scarcely impinge on the imagined future prospects of the Brazilian nation. It is also worth recalling that within living memory, "strategic" illusions of Brazilian grandeur were fostered by military regimes who denied their compatriots democracy, who imprisoned, killed, and tortured their opponents, and saw nuclear weapons as instruments of manifest destiny (for which read hegemony) among other military regimes on the subcontinent who thought the same way.[61] Brazilian society has yet to come together in a functioning democratic alternative to this recent experience.

It is also a society which is regularly assessed as one of the most corrupt and unequal in the world. On the country's territorial margins, the government's writ has never run, especially to prevent the persecution, by ranchers, loggers, and miners, of indigenous Amazon peoples who happened to be in their way. Survival International has called the European colonization of the Amazon region "the longest genocide."[62] Even FUNAI, modern Brazil's "National Indian Foundation," has not escaped the ineptness and corruption dogging the country's institutions. To my mind these flaws go together, in the confused self-image of a people with limitless inherited wealth but little national cohesion.

The donation of the Amazon rain forest, therefore, to those to whom in all its pristineness it truly belongs would be an unqualified good. Alongside the indigenous peoples who seek only to continue living in the forest as it is, we all would profit from the saving of the forest's oxygenating sources and its biodiversity. Brazilians and those in other neighboring countries would benefit from a lowering of their national political sights; and they would gain a positive unifying cause in championing the protection of the forest and its inhabitants, so much more vulnerable than themselves. They could turn to the good of all humankind a resource that fell to them by chance. Beyond Amazonia, such an initiative would encourage the sharing of the earth's natural resources, as against the venality of the market which the states system, by its divisions, institutionally promotes.

Finally, it would be a gesture of generosity and reflection by all of us modern human beings, as the inheritors of a civilization which we still only partly control, to leave uncontacted peoples alone with some part of wilderness in their hands. As José Carlos Meirelles of FUNAI has said:

> Their future does not depend on them. It depends on us—on our conscience. It is important for humanity that these people exist. They remind us that it is possible to live in a different way. They are the last free people on the planet.[63]

Reforming States, Restoring Society

A consciously ecological future requires a certain conception of how to live naturally, democratically, and self-sufficiently in the universal states system for as long as that system exists. But it also, I have suggested, requires a certain degree of equality in the system itself. This in its own right is an aspect of human self-restraint. Large concentrations of people living without self-restraint, whether politically—without democracy—or demographically—in very large territorial jurisdictions—threaten others in addition to themselves. This they do indirectly, because of their demands on the world's resources, ruling out the idea of a global commons, including wild nature, which belongs to everyone because it belongs to no one in particular.[64] And they do so directly, by virtue of the individuation principle of the autonomous state, which requires self-sufficiency even at others' expense. Any group of people claiming *by right* to have several times as much of anything as others is an offence against justice and an abuse of the heritage of nature.

Two further kinds of reform, therefore, are called for in the states system: the abolition of very large states, as a minimal moral expectation of all humankind, and the correction of the most flagrant mistakes of colonial boundary-drawing to redress the tenacious injustices that they can cause, especially in terms of poverty and overcrowding.

Large States, Hegemony, and Demagogy

Large states have always been characterized by imperialistic, or dema-gogic, politics or both. Rousseau argued in the *Contrat Social* that the larger a state in population terms, the more liberty is diminished. With increasing numbers of citizenry, popular sovereignty slackens and apathy grows, because individuals' perceived stake in political outcomes shrinks. In the end the government is obliged to become repressive merely to ensure the people's conformity to laws for which they themselves have voted.[65]

Under today's conditions of universal competitive statehood, large concentrations of apathetic people may easily be tempted into oppres-sive behavior toward others, provoking wars which numbers encourage them to believe they are certain to win. This tendency is likely to be heightened by the belief, illusory though it is, that they stand a better chance, through numbers and a national hinterland (effectively, a state within a state), of surviving a war with weapons of mass destruction against others so armed; or by some self-fulfilling prophecy of their destiny as "great powers." Atavistic demography and political excep-tionalism are two sides of the same coin, which does much to explain historical imperialism, the Cold War, and national chauvinism in large territorial states such as Russia, China, and even the United States.

Russian and Chinese influence on the rest of the world through Security Council membership has been, I have argued, mixed at best and destructive at worst. More generally these two states stand for a long-outdated ethnocultural hegemony, brassbound by modern sovereignty, which is inimical to their citizens' freedom as well as everyone else's. A cohesive Russian society, since the Cold War, has been artificially maintained, partly by military repression from the centre, and partly by the manipulation of access to internationally-marketable assets opened up in Soviet times. Weak institutions and the corrupt and unequal distribution of wealth have made for a poli-tics of faction-fighting and slanted elections, dominated by former Communists turned entrepreneurs (commonly, embezzlers), with successive Russian governments playing the fake-democratic role of power-broker between them. Under Putin, institutional leadership was transformed into a game of Russian dolls, as the president emerged, at the end of his first term, as "prime minister" before reappearing, only slightly diminished, as president again. Russians in general since the Cold War have experienced limited *glasnost* and no *perestroika*—a drastic regression from the promise of true socialism that Mikhail Gorbachev once held out.[66]

In "China" since 1949, largely under the influence of one man, the messianic image of a united, formerly imperial nation has been artificially preserved, to which all "overseas" Chinese are held to owe allegiance. Mao's Great Leap Forward was aimed, after the civil war, at the consolidation of the territorial state within antique geographical and conceptual boundaries. To this end, in a grotesque caricature of Marxism, an army of petty tyrants unleashed chaos in (or rather against) provincial society, ruining a largely rural economy and reducing millions to destitution.[67] Meanwhile, Chinese foreign policy consisted of supporting every political thug from Africa to Korea who would endorse the Maoist project, advance its mischief, or buy its arms.

The death of Mao and the end of the Cold War created an ideological vacuum which successive faceless oligarchs have sought to fill with state capitalism, drawing on the vast population at their disposal to create the workshop (or rather the sweatshop) of the world. The result, in the People's Republic today, is a brain-dead political culture: a society exhausted by repression, sunk in materialism, conformity, and the self-censorship of fear, and oblivious when not actually hostile to the part of the world that is not "China."[68]

Political learning in these two societies seems to me to have little prospect of success, least of all in institutional terms; a reduced international salience of nuclear weapons, if not their abolition, is the only hope for the dissolution of the existing state and the initiation of political reform.

In North America, following the end of the Cold War and the removal of overarching nuclear threats, it ought to be easier for smaller democratic countries, or at least a genuine federal process, to emerge. Meantime, there are strong arguments for the closer integration of the whole North Atlantic area, given the strong cultural roots in Europe of many Americans and Canadians. Putting our Northern house in order means, I have argued, a radical reform of Northern aid to Southern societies to enable them to acquire secure homes and livelihoods, and to end economic migration from South to North. But it also requires, in its own right, abolishing invented political differences, like that between North Americans and the citizens of Europe which structured the twentieth-century states system into economic factions, classes, and markets and opened up Southern societies to exploitation, both before and after 1945. The Leviathan built by Europeans across the

Atlantic has nowhere to go. The United States, if they stay united, ought to harbor a kinder, less ruthless, and less isolated society—one which will shed the dream of manifest destiny. There *is* no American exception, no unique transnational project there; that is the project of all of us, the human project.

On an enlightened view, socialism and public ownership can be retrieved as the common heritage of civilization in all older-industrial societies (a perception which prevailed even in the United States before 1945); which in turn would make less urgent a United States of Europe. Northern states could then authentically become what Sørensen calls "post-modern states," which really means societies open to change in themselves, and to give-and-take in respect of other societies perceived as distinct. That is the natural condition of a world at peace—the vanguard politics of humankind.

Redrawing Colonial Boundaries

On the question of colonial boundaries, I would propose correcting only the most flagrant anomalies (since almost everyone in the world can lay claim to ancient territorial grievances of some sort), and by a managed reclassification of populations in situ, within redrawn state frontiers. This is unobjectionable in principle if done in the cause of general equality, and can help to relieve inbuilt tensions in the system. I will illustrate my argument with a case from Africa.

In the Great Lakes region of central/east Africa, one territorial jurisdiction is excessively, impractically large, and two adjacent ones are unreasonably, inhumanly small. Yet their modern frontiers are creations of the same European empire. The Democratic Republic of Congo, formerly Zaïre, situated to the west of the Albertine Rift, is a territory almost as big as Western Europe. Population density there is actually lower than the average in Africa, already the most sparsely inhabited continent. Vast natural resources, especially in minerals, hold out the possibility of a higher per capita income than anywhere else in Africa, yet there is a negligible modern infrastructure amongst the equatorial forest, and a negligible sense of nationhood across a myriad of ethnic and tribal groups. By contrast, east of the lakeland rift, in Rwanda and Burundi, people have endured for decades the lowest incomes in the continent combined with the highest population density. In these two rural highland societies there are more persons living per square kilometer than anywhere else on earth except for city-state enclaves like Gaza or Macao.[69]

Competition over land, breaking out into violence, was endemic between the two main ethnic groups in historic Ruanda-Urundi, who marginalized the third, descendants of the pygmy peoples of the region. In the fertile, landlocked heart of Africa a complex, introverted society developed at a time when settled polities existed nowhere south of the Sahara. European anthropologists, coming upon this scene at the end of the nineteenth century, imagined an internecine conflict like that portrayed in the Old Testament Bible between Cain and Abel. They pictured the cattle-owning, nomadic, "Nilotic" Tutsi as a warrior race with a "culture of the spear," lording it over the peasant, "Bantu" Hutu with their "culture of the hoe." As in the Biblical story, these archetypes express the incompatibility of the pastoral and agricultural ways of life: animals provide food, but need unlimited space for grazing (and eat crops); nomads lack (or spurn) the values of settled society. But it would seem that oversimplification was in play in the European observers' accounts. As elsewhere in Africa, Hutu could acquire cattle and so earn wealth and status, while Tutsi kings were only locally powerful.[70] On all the evidence, ethnic rivalry in Ruanda-Urundi was sharpened, in the first half of twentieth century, by measures of social control associated with modern administration—in which, moreover, the European colonizers took sides, cultivating one group (the Tutsis) as the territory's natural leaders.

The separation of Rwanda and Burundi at independence did not help, as these became twin micro-states, mirrored in their ethnic composition and even weaker economically than when one. In Rwanda, powerful Hutu oligarchies took "revenge" for perceived historic (including colonial) disfavors.[71] Pogroms of Tutsis eliminated, or forced into exile, the best-educated and most outward-looking individuals, and the heady days of pan-Africanism passed the region by.[72] Even the fertile volcanic soil meant that economic development was concentrated on agriculture, which continued over-exploited and under-reformed. Over time and with the reduction of infant mortality, two states developed with the densest *and* the most rural populations, in the poorest continent on earth, in which everyone overlooked everyone else's property in shrinking, divided land, with a 4:1 ratio between the two main ethnic groups. Overcrowding within colonial frontiers does much to explain the genocide of almost a million mainly Tutsi people in Rwanda in 1994.

That cataclysm, after all, was one that Rwandans inflicted on themselves—countrywide, mainly at village level, at the behest of a faction in the Hutu-dominated government.[73] In the space of three months, almost one-tenth of the national population was wiped out, largely without the use of firearms, in this most intimate of civil wars. The fact that a similar disaster did not overwhelm the people of Burundi, trapped in an identical ethnic and territorial bottle, is owed solely to the fact that the Tutsi minority there had already seized power in the army and government (at the cost of one hundred thousand Hutu lives in 1972 alone).

A major share of blame, however, for all these events should be laid at the door of those Belgian colonial lawyers who, half a century earlier, had contrived borders to separate people with a common culture from each other and from any escape to the west, where a territory twenty times larger was preserved as the game-park of the Belgian king. The Rwanda genocide can be viewed simply—as an act of mass murder planned and instigated by a singularly evil group holding the levers of government power—or more completely and compassionately, as the Malthusian suicide of Rwandan society as a whole.[74]

A comparison with Sudan, at the other end of the territorial scale, is instructive. Over the Sudanese province of Darfur in 2003–4, as earlier over Rwanda, the UN Security Council preferred conflict to agreement when faced with humanitarian crisis; no saving interventions were mounted, and government-sponsored atrocities continued unimpeded.[75] Both in Rwanda in 1994 and in Sudan in 2003, the direct cause of the trouble was the exploitation of government powers to impose an oppressive concept of national community on the people at large—exaggerating, if not actually inventing, ethnic and racial stereotypes in a conflict related to resources in land. But in Sudan, the largest country in Africa, with a mere ten persons per square kilometer, overpopulation was never more than local.

For Darfuris, escape from government persecution was possible. Many fled into UN camps or across the porous border with Chad, where they had kinship ties. As one writer later put it, "the bloodshed in Darfur has declined primarily because the *janjaweed* militia and their government backers have succeeded in forcing the black population into exile."[76] In Rwanda, at the other end of the scale in territory and population density (250 persons per square kilometer), overcrowding was a countrywide problem, and emigration was not an option. In the villages, the mainly Tutsi victims fell easily into the assassins' hands. Neighbors killed neighbors, because neither had anywhere else to go.

The factor of space alone, the limits it allows or denies on population mobility in a system of fixed-border states, is all that is needed to explain why genocide might be feasible in one place and "only" crimes against humanity in the other[77] (which makes the difference, in international law, between mandatory UN intervention and no intervention). In Rwanda, in an unmistakable echo of Europe, sovereign immunity facilitated government by extermination. In Sudan, this was a less practical proposition simply because the country was a hundred times larger. But in either case, the space of the territorial state was a mere accident of colonial history—a factor likely to influence the calculations, rather than the motives, of would-be murderers with a preponderance of deadly weapons in their hands.

In Sudan, a redivision of the territorial state proved possible, in the wake of earlier atrocities sponsored by the government in Khartoum. Southern secessionists in 2011 obtained a separate state of South Sudan—an act enthusiastically endorsed in a UN-supervised referendum (and probably helped by the crisis in Darfur, which had seen the Sudanese president indicted for genocide by the International Criminal Court). Colonial Sudan was split and reduced, in the wake of *post*-colonial government actions, because the vast size of the country allowed it. But no such redivision is imaginable for Rwanda or Burundi; any glance at the map will show that the territory involved is far too small.

The solution, therefore, is to do the opposite of what was done in Sudan, and join together the two overcrowded, deprived, and similar societies of Rwanda and Burundi, but release them into a larger space, obtained by their merging with the neighboring populations of Kivu in the eastern Congo—to make a new Great Lakes state. Authorities in the DRC must be encouraged, by political pressure and aid, to cede the two eastern provinces of North and South Kivu for this purpose—bearing in mind that the DRC as a whole, territorially, is twenty times the size of Rwanda/Burundi, with one-twentieth of the population density, and the potential to develop one of the richest economies in the world.

This solution is above all necessary, I would argue, because of the history of ethnic violence to the east of the Kivu frontier. Without it, there will always be a danger either of further genocide in Rwanda/Burundi, or a spillover war, including a war of occupation, into Kivu from there (of which there have already been intimations since 1994). But the solution I propose is also realistic, because in Kivu itself the local ethnic composition of society is not dissimilar to that of

Rwanda/Burundi, including both Hutu-associated groups and the Banyamulenge Tutsi.

Moreover, the Democratic Republic of Congo is so large and underdeveloped, with such a long history of government corruption, that on the eastern fringes, people's attachment to a DRC identity is minimal. Since colonial times, the inhabitants of Kivu have resisted the "Congolese" identity patented by King Leopold, which in the early twentieth century emerged as one of the great disasters of deliberate state-making.[78] Like Afghanistan, like Sudan, the former Belgian Congo entered the era of universal states in an almost completely unmodernized condition in terms of infrastructure, industry, or literacy; but unlike those two territories, with a vast potential in terms of natural resources. Then, as many commentators have pointed out, inherited wealth became a curse. Only the capital and the mining province of Katanga developed, two pockets of extreme affluence linked to exploitative outsiders. Even the overthrow of the long Mobutu dictatorship, after the end of Cold War, did little to change the imbalance of wealth and power in the country. Over time, underdevelopment made the isolated people of Kivu, on the eastern margins, a prey to a host of destructive forces: fugitive Hutu militias from Rwanda, rival local Tutsi militias, the corrupt Congolese army, and rogue miners from all over the region.[79] Local society was turned into an extended protection racket, with gunslingers moving between the militias, the mining mafias and the official army, depending on who would pay for their services. These "soldiers" embarked on mass social disruption for their gain, along with the mass rape of women—activities against which successive UN forces have proved useless, when not corruptly participating themselves.[80] The Kivu provinces are no longer governed by anyone, let alone the hapless authorities in the capital of the Democratic Republic of Congo; and the regional status quo in the Great Lakes is untenable.

The solution I propose, then, would have the potential first to relieve pressures on land to the east of the lakeland rift, in Rwanda and Burundi, where agriculture is overwhelmingly the means of subsistence. Second, natural resources like fisheries and upland farming could be extended by combining the Kivu highlands and an undivided Lake Kivu in a territory open to East African markets and transport links. Third, society in a reduced DRC could benefit, in the shape of greater social cohesion and more even economic development over the country, with the eventual prospect of effective government. With careful planning and consultation, it should be possible to create a new territorial state which would remove the bases of conflict in the region, and fourth, improve the status of the weakest group of all, the pygmy peoples of the Congo and Great Lakes.[81] For this purpose Northern aid should, I suggest, go toward the purchase, under UN auspices, of the two Kivu provinces of the DRC and economic development and social cohesion in the newly formed society. The present populations of Kivu would, as I have explained, be reclassified in situ as citizens of the new state, alongside the populations of Rwanda and Burundi, on the grounds (and the fair practical assumption) that this is the best solution for them all together.

Kant argued, in a less crowded age, that pastoral, agricultural and nomadic peoples should be allowed as their right the greater territorial space that their way of life required.[82] Hardly anywhere in the world, however, is this feasible today, and the pressures of modernization make the challenge of fair human settlement more complicated still. The vagaries of colonial borders, hard-wired into law, sharpen existing social dissatisfactions—which highlights the need to intervene, where possible, to reform the negative legacy of the past.

Rather than see the events in Rwanda in early 1994 as uniquely barbaric, we should take them as an example of the extreme suffering that, with the help of historic mismanagement, human beings can inflict on themselves. The genocide also provides a warning of what could happen in future in the absence of action to curb population growth and competition over inherited material assets—problems which in a closed system of independent polities go hand in hand.

States as Provisional

Other historic reversals of colonial fortune which I think should be effected include a state of Kurdistan drawn from parts of Syria, Iraq, Turkey, and Iran;[83] and the reunification of Korea—a country divided first by the Cold War, then by a family of extreme dictators. It is also logical to promote the unification of island peoples for the sake of practical economic development, as in New Guinea or Hispaniola (Haiti/Dominican Republic); and, as I have argued, to promote a "one-state" solution as the ultimate goal in Israel/Palestine, with whatever external incentives and moral pressures the realization of that goal takes.

Reforming the system may even involve the temporary approximation of large territorial and demographic states; for example, I think that the Punjab is the key to undoing the sectarian partition of India which led disastrously to the creation of Pakistan.[84] But if society in Pakistan itself is close to ungovernable because of the unnatural division of Indian culture, contemporary India is close to ungovernable because of the size of the Indian territorial state. In the end, the shibboleth of territorial integrity will have to be broken in both countries in the name of smaller and more proximate government.

Having mentioned Pakistan and Israel, I will add that confessional states are a bad idea on two levels. First, because populations are not naturally homogeneous (and should not be forced to be); and second because faith is not faith unless it is evolutionary, and confessional states are an excuse to lock individuals into a prison of fixed ideas. In practice some deeper grievance or abuse underlies such situations, whether this be historical, as in the case of Israel and Pakistan, or racial, as in Malaysia.

Reforming the states system in future may mean the creation of new independent states, in places where colonial withdrawal-arrangements continue radically to impair the prospects of local peoples: for example, in enclaved Kashmir, where political leaders should have the courage to assert an identity which is neither Pakistani nor Indian, but a democratic one of their own. Or in the Falklands/Malvinas Islands, where British governments should help create, through economic and demographic expansion, a truly self-sufficient society. (The case for historic association with British society, at 8000 miles' distance, may be sustainable, but the case for dependence is not; whereas the Argentine claim over the islands is in its own right weak).[85] Within the European Union, the peaceful secession of democratic societies (Scotland, Catalonia) from larger territorial jurisdictions may be positive, if aimed at democratic renewal and innovation in the heartland of the modern state.

At present the United Nations has no department to deal with the partition and repartition of states or the agreed alteration of frontiers. The International Court of Justice is the body usually charged to deal with such questions—but on a basis which takes existing, constituted states as givens and their governments as the representative parties, when in fact those governments may not be representative and the shape and origins of the states themselves are likely to be at issue. International theorists and area specialists have their part to play here, in righting the balance against institutionalized tendencies to preserve the status quo.

Ultimately, however, if the continued division of humankind into hard-and-fast populations with rights of their own is to constitute some kind of progressive social order, as well as retain a degree of stability, then one fundamental principle must prevail, and that is equality; because self-determination as everyone's birthright derives from the idea of constituted states as the analogue of free individuals, and equality is a value to which individuals attach at least as much importance as to their freedom.

Perfect equality between the populations of states is practically unachievable, and perfect equality itself too much like sameness for most of us. Still, a great deal more could be done than modern political conditions have achieved or promise for the future. Eliminating weapons of mass destruction everywhere—a step toward *negative* equality in what are already counterproductive instruments of power—would remove a significant object for demagogic self-aggrandizement for either individuals or groups. With more equal material endowments for peoples in geographically separated societies, there would be no pretexts for such self-aggrandizement anyway, and no special security in states themselves, nor any magnet for terrorist egomaniacs dedicated to bringing down "great powers" in public view. Under these conditions, there would be no cause called "human rights" as such, because human rights themselves would begin to be fulfilled—or properly speaking, restored. With more space in the world given to non-human living nature—a space made secure by human invention—a fuller human identity would be possible.

For the future we may also assume that the curiosity and restlessness which impel individuals to seek other horizons will not diminish. It can be harnessed for moral ends, as the example of technical assistance shows. Cosmopolitan exchange brings intermarriage and miscegenation, and so, ultimately, an end to racial exclusion. But it is also most enjoyed, I would argue, by people with strong and deep roots. By becoming more alike and equal in concrete (material, demographic, territorial) terms, the inheritances of *states* would make *societies* stronger, and weaken the identity-destroying effects of globalis/zation. And making territorial states smaller, and dependent on local, community-based use of technology, would help to anchor their inhabitants in stabler values. Between extreme conceptions of property as unshared and unaccountable because individual (whose name is greed), or state/collective (whose name is war), the middle way is a conception of property as local and provisional—whose name is community.

369

The putative equal agency of states in conventional international theory, diplomacy, and international law rests, I have argued, on an uncritical acceptance of sovereignty in its internal (political) and external (diplomatic) forms. Present states are neither physically uniform nor equally representative of the peoples they confine; sovereignty has been exposed as a travesty of independent human agency. But sovereignty mitigated by the changes I have proposed would lose much of its rigidity and its force. If all societies were to become liberal-democratic (which I have suggested is no longer a fanciful hope), then governments would be less likely to act abusively, unilaterally, and be more open to working for their citizens' well-being. If all societies were subject to "intrusive" inspections to guard against the secret acquisition of weapons of mass destruction (inspections whose modalities, I have argued, are tried and tested), then much mutual suspicion would cease to be generated under the cover of "domestic jurisdiction." If all societies were to recognize the damaging effects on the natural environment of intensive economic development—effects which cannot be confined within the physical borders of states—then cooperation to repair the damage for the benefit of all would be feasible (on which the scientific consensus, worldwide, is overwhelming, and through the UN Climate Convention negotiations has become increasingly understood). If all societies were interpenetrated with each other in an organized way for cooperative and constructive purposes (which I have suggested should be pioneered in aid as technical assistance), then international understanding and trust could become the norm. And if for all these purposes, forms of political status not subject to traditional sovereignty were temporarily instituted, then state sovereignty itself would be further weakened. Real diplomatic immunity—not to cover up official wrongdoing, but to facilitate actions beneficial to all humanity—should, I suggest, be conferred on individuals engaged in public foreign aid as technical assistance, international environmental and security monitoring, and the prosecution of extreme crimes. In all these senses, the power to change things for the better in the universal states system passes through our ability to change our attitudes and expectations toward each other. Making state agency meaningful but limited may ultimately be the best way to the transcendence of states themselves.

The shape of states in the far future is, as Kant said, unforeseeable, but given constructive applications of human will, unimportant precisely to foresee. A world state is either oppressive or a contradiction in terms; a world without formal divisions is the ultimate expression of human freedom. The status of states in this millennium or the next is of interest only in this light. As the historian Linda Colley has written: 'The past matters. But, in regard to countries and peoples, the past contains the seeds of many possible futures."[86]

Left-over Power

Still, what use, you might ask, would centralized state institutions, in a world of weakened divisions, retain? What "left-over power" for governments would there be? What quality of life is *not* envisaged among the possibilities of liberal democracy?

My answer lies in the contemporary cliché "full employment"—which is really a euphemism for employment, in a phase in history in which human beings' major activity has become ritually threatened by governments. The key socioeconomic question of our time, as of any time, should be not who gets to work for money and who does not, but what kind of work most deserves to be done. In this light, the true purpose of government is to organize everyone's productive activity under states conceived as home.

The question is before us today because the Industrial Revolution has led increasingly (and not unjustifiably) to the allotting to machines of important human tasks, while the lightning efficiency of electronic transactions has turned economics into a Faustian profession. The moral worth of work has been eroded by corruption under state cover in the South, and a masquerade of democracy in the name of economic freedom in the North, where the privatization of public services has provided the means to enrichment of a callow few. This systematic promotion of greed has gone hand in hand with the development of "service industries" of questionable economic or even practical value, and the encouragement of economic migration from already fragile Southern societies or the export of onerous and toxic industrial production to them.

Yet without human effort allied to creativity, organized life for human beings in the states system would itself be impossible. Work cannot at once be the norm and not the norm in society; the result is *anomie*, Durkheim's word for the breakdown of the collective values which hold society together. Using state privilege to promote a purely economistic version of freedom is, as Susan Strange argued, illogical and hypocritical, because without public support for states as a focus of social stability, the secure property targeted for alienation by neoliberal financiers and their allies in government would not exist in the first place.

So Marx was right, I think, in one important respect: an essential part of human dignity is the capacity to contribute to society through one's work, while from a capitalist point of view, where potentially everything is for sale, their work is all people have to offer. Having read Kant, Marx was prescient of a world entirely given over to states; but he also perceived that states could retain a basic attraction in themselves, by providing a framework for the organization of human relations conceived as property relations, where labor is the key property (in the ontological, as well as the material, sense) of individual worth and social identity. These baby ideals of socialism were thrown out, at the end of the Cold War, with the bathwater of Soviet Communism, and we have been living with the consequences ever since.

None of which is to concede agency to states in their own right, still less moral agency; it is merely to argue that in the world as a whole, moral agency itself cannot operate unless some things are considered generally not for sale—of which the first is work conceived as a contribution to society. The material services which sustain civilized life, and the skills required to provide them, are the only things for the foreseeable future which enable a state fairly and freely to be considered a person's home—since history, culture, and tradition transcend the territorial boundaries of states. The universal states system, after the failures both of Communism (from a libertarian point of view) and capitalism (in terms of justice and equality) can no longer develop. It can only, for the foreseeable future, be reformed. And then, at some later date, the system itself may disappear.

With this in mind I have argued that there is a special duty incumbent on our wealthy Northern societies to help poor Southern ones, to ensure that financial investment bears fruit there—which is best effected by paying Northern citizens to go and work in the South. For a generation or more, that will be one legitimate recourse for Northern governments in their own duty to organize useful work for their citizens. Another, which can be shared between North and South, is the extension of renewable energy production in support of secure social life and material well-being: work which is creative without being destructive of the natural environment, and where Northern technology and skills can complement Southern climatic conditions and needs. Indeed many countries called "less developed" today can, with their unspoiled natural beauty, become the envy of everyone on earth once the peace and economic security of their peoples is assured.

But in general, for people under formal states, the assurance of employment is vital, as a concrete test of government accountability, as a minimal justification of the states themselves, and to aid progress beyond the states system. Here there is still a strong case for the public (that is, collective) ownership of the infrastructures of communication, energy- and service-provision, and the institutions of health and welfare, in all states, by the citizens of those states, for their good. These need be the only large enterprises in modern society, but without them there is no modern society at all. In the real world, in the world as a whole, work cannot be bargained over. On a true-to-life view of things it is not a choice. The left-over power of government, when all on the matter of human rights has been said and done, is to organize the work of everyone for a life which is more creative, more social and more secure—to make a democracy of necessity.

* * *

Life in the states system throws up all these moral concerns, it seems to me, as the first dim and muddled perceptions we receive of our modern world situation, lost somewhere between society and institutions, as one generation after another since the early twentieth century has striven to rebuild the shattered walls of civilisation. But what the *universal* states system implies is something different again: an idea of permanent order, of order for order's sake; an end, in a sense, to change. And I think this is perhaps the greatest moral concern of all, outweighing every piecemeal partial one that may arise. Already we inhabit an earthly prison that we shall not escape, so to speak, with our lives. Why double it with a prison of our own making? Moral concerns dictated and circumscribed by permanent institutions are poor shadows of the great ideals and imagined beauties of the historic human mind; at best, they only hint at change which will leave the universal states system in the dust of the past. So in disarmament against sovereignty, in human rights as solidarity across frontiers, and in ecology as the material reform of settled society, I am merely proposing forms of action to save us, for the foreseeable future, from making a prison of established states. To the prison of our mortality we must not add another out of fear and pride.

Kierkegaard once devoted an essay to the view, half-humorously expressed, that repetition was a valuable human capacity.[87] I hope, dear reader, for your sake that I have not overdone the demonstration already. But what exactly did Kierkegaard mean? Apparently, with his serious side, that we should live in the world as it is, even if we wish to change it; or rather, especially if we wish to change it. Living in the past, he said, meant continual sorrow for what was lost; living in the future the uncertainty of continual surprise. Living in the present was the only way to live life to the full, even if this meant continually starting afresh from one's mistakes.

What Kierkegaard intended was not a counsel of resignation, but an encouragement to find meaning in the life we are given—but as the beginning, rather than the end, of change. "Repetition is epiphany that sometimes grants the old again, as new, and sometimes grants something radically new."[88] Repetition is what we do, day by day on rising, as we strive to glimpse on the world's face the lineaments of peace.

Notes

1. Runciman, "Moral responsibility and the problem of representing the state," pp. 46–47.
2. *Ibid.*, p. 48.
3. Joseph Rotblat, *Nuclear Radiation in Warfare* (London: Taylor and Francis for Stockholm International Peace Research Institute, 1981), p. 139, second emphasis added.
4. Finnis, Boyle and Grisez, *Nuclear Deterrence, Morality and Realism*, p. 86.
5. John Keegan, *The Mask of Command* (London: Penguin, 1988), pp. 343–44, emphases in original.
6. E.g., Morton A. Kaplan, *System and Process in International Politics* [1957] (Huntington, NY: Krieger, 1975); Anatol Rapoport, *Fights, Games and Debates* [1960] (Ann Arbor: University of Michigan Press, 1997); Thomas C. Schelling, *Strategy of Conflict* [1960] (Cambridge, MA/London: Harvard University Press, 1980).
7. This was official NATO strategy after 1967 under the name of "Flexible Response." The other sacrificial hostage, US forces in Europe, could be likened to the "poor bloody infantry" sent to their deaths in the First World War by their callous general officers.
8. Shakhnazarov, "Effective factors of international relations."
9. See above, chapter 1 note 56.
10. See George F. Kennan, *The Nuclear Delusion: Soviet-American Relations in the Atomic Age* (London: Hamish Hamilton, 1984), and Barton Gellmann, *Contending with Kennan: Toward a Philosophy of American Power* (New York: Praeger, 1984).
11. The usual exception cited here is Israel. Leaving aside the post-1945 alignments, which became those of the Cold War, Israel is arguably the only small territorial state with a democratic tradition for which a rationale for nuclear deterrence can be mounted, given so many hostile neighbouring societies. But first, there is no official, declaratory policy of nuclear deterrence in Israel. Then the supposed democratic exception glosses over its deleterious history for Palestinian Arabs. The positive Israeli image has also been progressively undermined by the absorption into Israeli society of Sephardic refugees from Arab-majority societies, or migrants from the

United States and former Soviet Union (people either lacking experience of democracy, or with a racist axe to grind); by the tentative Palestinian steps away from terrorism and toward a separate democratic state; and by the pro-democracy uprisings in North Africa and the Middle East. This last development promises to overturn entirely the notion of Israel as an embattled bastion of freedom in the region—and by the same token, weaken the Israeli case for extreme measures of defense.

12. For a positive case for functionalism see Mark Imber, "Functionalism" in David Held and Anthony McGrew (eds.), *Governing Globalization: Power, Authority and Global Governance* (Cambridge: Polity, 2002), pp. 290–304.

13. The Russian national group comprised, by the late Cold War, barely half the total Soviet population (53.24 percent, calculated from Basile Kerblay, *Modern Soviet Society*, tr. Rupert Swyer [London: Methuen, 1983], table 10; or 52.4 percent, with 60 percent of membership of the 1981 Soviet Communist Party, as argued in David Lane, *Politics and Society in the USSR* [2nd ed. Oxford: Martin Robertson, 1982], table 7). Hélène Carrère d'Encausse estimated that as early as 1974, Russian birth rates had declined to 15.6 percent per annum (below the Soviet average), from 33 percent in 1940 (above the Soviet average). See "Graphique I. Géographie démographique de la population soviétique—natalité %" in d'Encausse, *L'Empire Eclaté: La Révolte des Nations en U.R.S.S.*(Paris: Flammarion, 1978), pp. 78–79.

14. *UN Treaty Series* vol. 1946, I (2) (b) (k) and p. 3. The former Soviet Union was not a legal "party" to the Convention.

15. The Soviet Union was declared dissolved at the Belovezhskaya Pushcha meeting of the leaders of Russia, Belarus, and Ukraine on December 8, 1991. At a special UNSC meeting of January 31, 1992, an official Russian government statement of intent of December 24, 1991 was accepted, leading to the takeover of all the former Soviet commitments and privileges, including the nuclear arsenal. *Keesing's Record of World Events* 1992, vol. 38, p. 38744.

16. An issue much discussed at the time was the risk that former-Soviet nuclear scientists would sell their services to the highest bidder. This fear has always seemed to me misplaced. First, most scientists have some loyalty to, and pride in, their profession, and also can find work in related areas to their specialism. It did not follow that without a country, Soviet nuclear scientists would prostitute themselves to foreign governments. Some would have been able to find continuing work in Russia, even if they did not already regard the end of the Cold War as reason enough to give up working on nuclear weapons. Some even crossed the old Cold-War divide and emigrated to the United States. Since 1991 there have been reports of the leakage abroad of former-Soviet nuclear materials and technology, but many of these (generally quite limited) shipments were discovered and stopped, and their significance is debatable. Contrary to popular myth, reliable nuclear weapons are extremely difficult and hazardous to produce from scratch: they require a well-funded, long-lived project run by a large team of workers in special (including medical) facilities, deriving its materials from an extensive nuclear technological program, and culminating in detectable explosive testing. A few scientists with disparate skills, working secretly and on their own, can achieve nothing of significance, whatever their level of nuclear knowledge. True, the Pakistani scientist Abdel

Qadeer Khan caused great mischief (beginning with the nuclear-weapon
program, based on uranium enrichment, set up in Pakistan under his super-
vision); but he benefited from ample, apparently Libyan, petrodollars to
procure equipment from abroad before he could make use of the centrifuge
data he had stolen from Holland. He also seems, eccentrically, to have been
on a one-man proliferation mission, passing the data and derived technology on
to China, Libya, Iran, and North Korea—all the while under the protection of
his own government. This is an extremely grave case; but in my view if the
relevant authorities (including Western ones) had had the right priorities,
Dr. Khan's nefarious activities could have been interdicted at an early stage.

17.   *UN Treaty Series*, vol. 729 (New York: United Nations), emphasis added.
18.   John Simpson, *The Independent Nuclear State: The United States, Britain
      and the Military Atom* (London: Macmillan, 1983), p. 54.
19.   See, for example, Desmond Ball, "Can Nuclear War Be Controlled?" Adelphi
      Paper 169 (London: International Institute for Strategic Studies, autumn
      1982)—a prospect the author describes as a "chimera," p. 38.
20.   As an illustration of this argument, in India in 1997 the Hindu Nationalist
      Bharatiya Janata Party campaigned on an aggressive foreign policy platform
      aimed at transforming the country into a "declared nuclear-weapon state"—in
      the process denying the official version of the one Indian nuclear test
      (in 1974, at Pokharan) as a "peaceful nuclear explosion." Within weeks of the
      BJP's electoral victory, five new nuclear explosions were ordered, leading to
      a similar riposte in Pakistan—the first nuclear tests in that country. In this
      way two "nuclear-weapon-states" were declared almost overnight. Indian
      criticism of the NPT had originally borne a Gandhian stamp of non-violence.
      But this stance also had much to do with political rivalry in India and China
      for leadership of the world's poor. There was an India-China border war in
      the Himalayas in 1962; then came the first nuclear test in the People's Repub-
      lic in 1964, followed by PRC accession to permanent UNSC membership.
      The Pokharan explosion of 1974 was therefore, in my view, designed to kill
      two political birds with one stone. Strategically it was directed at Beijing,
      declaring Indian nuclear-weapon *capability*, while toward the Security
      Council it served to express Indian dissatisfaction at the non-recognition
      of India as a great power. But neither of these messages would have had any
      effect, had the official version been accepted that the test was "peaceful."
      This description was a bluff, which the BJP's actions later exposed. I think
      that the same calculated ambiguity, aimed disingenuously at maintaining
      nuclear-weapon capability while professing the opposite (but this time actu-
      ally under the NPT) characterizes the development of the Iranian nuclear
      program after 1979, which became heavily focused on the indigenous
      engineering of uranium enrichment. In support of this judgment I would
      mention the following factors. i) Iranian oil reserves are among the largest
      in the world, obviating the need for a new large-scale domestic source of
      energy. ii) One learns nothing, in technological terms, about power genera-
      tion from its nuclear forms that cannot be learned from non-nuclear forms
      (concerning turbines, pumps, heat-exchangers, transformers, etc.)—and so
      there is no specific developmental, educational case for choosing *nuclear*-
      power generation in Iran. iii) The environmental (low-carbon) argument for
      nuclear, as opposed to fossil-fuelled, energy is a strong one in the minds of

some international specialists. But it has never figured in Iranian government declarations, even though the Iranian president who did the most to develop the national nuclear program (Mahmoud Ahmadinejad) built his own political career on a reputation for ecology. iv) The IAEA-safeguarded nuclear power program centred on Bushehr in SW Iran, which was eventually realized in 2011 after long delays, came with a full guarantee of external (Russian) supplies of low-enriched uranium (2–4 percent of U^{235} for power reactors)—at a time, moreover, of low prices for raw uranium worldwide; which left the case for a domestic Iranian uranium-enrichment program to supply Bushehr as very weak from the start. v) Technically, all one learns about uranium enrichment from developing it oneself (inevitably at enormous expense) is how to do more of the same process; there are no practical spinoffs. Meanwhile, in order to raise the level of enrichment to weapons-grade (80 percent plus of U^{235}), all one needs to do is turn up the power in the plant over a period of time, and multiply the collection points (centrifuges), as the Iranian government did at Natanz and Qom. vi) The Iranian enrichment program was founded using centrifuge data supplied by Dr. Abdul Qadeer Khan and obtained by criminal deception (see note above). vii) Nuclear installations have also been built in Iran with no technical relation to the safeguarded, civil nuclear energy program—including a heavy-water reactor, an outmoded and inefficient model which nevertheless produces large amounts of plutonium. (Enriched uranium was used at Hiroshima, plutonium at Nagasaki.)

21.   For details, see Richard Kokoski, *Technology and the Proliferation of Nuclear Weapons* (Oxford: Oxford University Press for Stockholm International Peace Research Institute, 1995), ch. 4.

22.   See www.iaea.org www.opbw.org www.opcw.org

23.   Speech of March 8, 1983, in Orlando, accessible at www.nationalcenter.org/ ReaganEvilEmpire1983. html

24.   Kant, *Perpetual Peace*, Preliminary Article 3 in Reiss (ed.), pp. 94–95.

25.   *Ibid.*, Sixth Article, p. 96.

26.   This may require ending all large-scale activities involving nuclear fission, including the production of electrical energy for civilian economies. Even leaving aside the indissoluble link between fission in "civil" power reactors and the materials and principles of nuclear weaponry, I think we should not, in a civilized society, have to ask anyone to work in the conditions required by the cleanups of nuclear accidents like those at Chernobyl and Fukushima.

27.   Erik Voetens, "The practice of political manipulation" in Emanuel Adler and Vincent Pouliot (eds.), *International Practices* (Cambridge: Cambridge University Press, 2011), p. 271.

28.   See www.icc-cpi.int/

29.   E.g., in the Horn of Africa—Ethiopia and Somalia under Haile Mengistu Mariam and Siad Barré respectively.

30.   Ian Brownlie in Brownlie (ed.), *Basic Documents on Human Rights* (2nd ed. Oxford: Clarendon Press, 1981), p. 15.

31.   See above, chapter 12 note 36.

32.   Extending to "1) internal propaganda, 2) governmental monopolistic control of both the source and flow of public affairs information, 3) refinements in techniques of physical torture, 4) improvements in psychological torture

techniques, 5) the new social science of behaviour modification (by chemical and surgical methods), 6) the perfection of miniaturised surveillance equipment—much of it invented . . . for economic espionage and sabotage, but now adapted to political ends, 7) the development of military and police information systems for the storage and rapid retrieval of the individual's identity and political biography." Harry M. Scoberg and Laurie S. Wiseberg, "Human rights and Amnesty International," *Annals of the American Academy of Political and Social Sciences* 413, May 1974, p. 15.

33. Maurice Cranston, *What Are Human Rights?* (London: The Bodley Head, 1973), p. 66.

34. See above, chapter 9 section 9.4.

35. See above, chapter 9 section 9.5.

36. Cf. Hitti, *History of the Arabs*, parts II and III.

37. Olivier Roy, "Révolution post-islamiste," *Le Monde* 12 February 2011, my translation.

38. *Ibid.*, mentioning Algeria and Iran.

39. Frantz Fanon, *Peau Noire, Masques Blancs* (Paris: Editions du Seuil, 1952).

40. Azar Nafisi, *Things I've Been Silent About: Memories* (London: Heinemann, 2009), pp. 312–313.

41. Henry Shue, *Basic Rights*.

42. The exceptions were Japan (1957–58), France (1950–68, 1981–89), and the three Scandinavian countries and the Netherlands from the early 1970s on. Based on *Development Assistance Committee Reports* 1985, table 26; 1990, table 24; 1995, table 4; 2000, table 4; and 2002, table 4 (Paris: OECD).

43. Tomohisa Hattori, "The moral politics of foreign aid," *Review of International Studies* 29 (2), April 2003, pp. 229–47.

44. The modern source of the *potlatch* account is Marcel Mauss, *Essai sur Le Don, Forme Archaïque de l'Échange*[1928], in English as *The Gift: Forms and Functions of Exchange in Primitive Societies*, tr. Ian Cunnison (rev. ed. London: Routledge and Kegan Paul, 1966).

45. See above, chapter 6, section 6.2.

46. Hammerstad, "Population movement and its impact on world politics," p. 247.

47. From 1960 to 1980 between a third and a half of overseas OECD aid personnel in technical assistance were French. In **1964**: 44194 individuals out of a total of 86302. **1969**: 47562/111932. **1974**: 32759/76832. **1979**: 23136/73462 (*DAC Reports* 1970–94). The French share of OECD technical assistance then declined, while remaining the highest as a proportion of donor population. Exact measurement from French sources like INSEE of the number of French *co-opérants* in service in any one year is however difficult, owing to their engagement under different ministries and contracts, occasionally in the *DOM-TOM* (French overseas departments and dependencies).

48. See Jacques Adda et Marie-Claude Smouts, *La France Face au Sud: Le Miroir Brisé* (Paris: Karthala, 1989).

49. See reference to Daniela Krosnak's critique above, chapter 9 section 9.2.

50. See Nicholas Rengger, "On 'good global governance,' institutional design and the practices of moral agency," in Toni Erskine (ed.), *Can Institutions Have Responsibilities?*, pp. 207–217.

51. P. A. Reynolds, *An Introduction to International Relations* (1st. ed. 1970), p. 260.

52. On the environment in international relations, see Brian Baxter, *Ecologism: An Introduction* (Edinburgh: Edinburgh University Press, 1999); Andrew Dobson, *Green Political Thought* (4th ed. Abingdon/New York: Routledge, 2007); and Mathew Humphrey, "Green political theory" in Duncan Bell (ed.), *Ethics and World Politics*, pp. 181–199.

53. *North-South: A Programme for Survival*, Report of the Independent Commission on International Development Issues (London: Pan Books, 1980), ch. 9.

54. For a broader economic but equally pessimistic view of the prospects for less-developed societies, see Ray Kiely, "Inequality and underdevelopment in world politics" in Beeson and Bisley (eds.), *Issues in 21st Century World Politics*, pp. 190–201.

55. For example, in the Sahara's case, by channelling fresh water from northern Europe. Already in parts of the Arabian peninsula, intensive pumping of deep groundwater (the accumulation of aeons of rainfall) has made agriculture possible in formerly-desert areas. This practice has also induced micro-climatic change—since evaporation from plant life will precipitate locally - and so is partly self-sustaining. Deep groundwater is not, however, unlimited, a fact which means that supplementary outside sources would be needed to recover the much-larger area of the Sahara. In mainland Australia—a very large island—the refoliation of the interior would require the intensive desalination of seawater, but again could prove self-sustaining.

56. In July 2012 there were power failures in twenty of India's twenty-eight states; in the north and north-east the entire electronic supply grids broke down. This was "the largest electrical blackout in history, affecting an area encompassing about 670 million people, or roughly 10 percent of the world's population" (*New York Times* 31 July 2012). At the time of writing the Indian government retains, near Mumbai, a prototype fast-breeder reactor, of a type almost universally abandoned on grounds of safety, feasibility, and economy. Such a device in theory both produces and recycles nuclear fissile material, but in reality it is completely unproven. A catastrophic accident in this reactor, moreover, would release the radioactivity of many Chernobyls, since it typically contains far more radioactive material than even a large conventional reactor. The continued use of this toxic white elephant of the electrical industry testifies to the perverse belief of successive Indian governments in technological solutions to the overwhelming problem of administering Indian society, and the misguided aspirations of the middle classes who support them.

57. In 2009 I visited ten provincial towns in two states of India (Gujarat and Punjab), interviewing prospective students for UK vocational courses. The vast majority of my interviewees sought education in the UK as a means to at least temporary emigration. None gave criticism of India as a reason for wishing to leave.

58. Galbraith, *A Life in Our Times*, chapters 21, 26–27.

59. Dalrymple, in his "search for the sacred in modern India," includes a site in Pakistan. Dalrymple, *Nine Lives*.

60. See Crawford (ed.), *The Rights of Peoples*.

61. See Peter Lomas, "Attitudes of the nuclear threshold countries" in Jozef Goldblat and David Cox (eds.), *Nuclear Weapon Tests: Prohibition or*

Limitation? (Oxford: Oxford University Press for Stockholm International Peace Research Institute and Canadian Institute for International Peace and Security, 1988), pp. 311–319.

62. Survival International, *Disinherited: Indians in Brazil* (London, 2000), p. 9.
63. BBC TV *Human Planet*, 3 February 2011, my translation. In the film, groups of rain-forest people are shown being observed from the air, from a light plane, at a distance of about a kilometer through a long camera lens. There are estimated to be about eighty such loose kinship groups. "Uncontacted" should not be interpreted in an over-idealized way—only to refer to peoples who have not *directly* come into contact with people from modern society, except in insignificant numbers within the forest. On this see further www.survivalinternational.org
64. See Garrett Hardin, "The tragedy of the commons," *Science* 162, no. 3859, 13 December 1968, 1243–1248.
65. Rousseau, *Du Contrat Social*, 3.1. The argument is well explained in Bertrand de Jouvenel, "Rousseau's theory of the forms of government" in Cranston and Peters (eds.) *Hobbes and Rousseau: A Collection of Critical Essays*, pp. 484–497.
66. These terms—meaning "transparency" and "reconstruction" respectively— were used by Gorbachev to define his project to reform the Soviet Union.
67. On this episode and the "Cultural Revolution," see Jung Chang and Jon Halliday, *Mao: The Unknown Story* (London: Vintage, 2006); or the more sympathetic but nonetheless revealing eyewitness accounts by Maria-Antonietta Macciocchi, in her *De la Chine* (Paris: Editions du Seuil, 1974).
68. See Xu Youyu and Hua Ze (eds.), *In the Shadow of the Rising Dragon: Stories of Repression in the New China*, tr. Stacy Mosher (New York/London: Palgrave Macmillan, 2013).
69. Data in this section are based on: http://unstats.un.org/unsd/snaama; and historically, *UN Statistical Yearbook* 48, table 8; 49, tables 2 and 8 (New York: UN, 2004, 2005); *UN Demographic Yearbook* 53, table 3 (New York: UN, 2003); *2004 Revision Database*, UN Department of Social and Economic Affairs at http://esa.un.org/unpp
70. Historically, Tutsi-Hutu intermarriage in the Great Lakes was apparently not unusual, though in modern times it became entangled with conflicts over land. See Jan Vansina, *Antecedents to Modern Rwanda: the Nyiginya Kingdom* (Oxford: James Currey, 2004), and Alex de Waal, "The genocidal state: Hutu extremism and the origins of the "final solution" in Rwanda," *Times Literary Supplement* 1 July 1994.
71. Under the Belgian mandate, ethnic competition based on status and occupation was embittered by the introduction, in the 1930s, of national identity cards stating the bearer's ethnicity—either Hutu, Tutsi, or Twa. Also, the Jesuit *Pères Blancs* missionaries in charge of education in colonial Ruanda/ Urundi favored, up to the early 1950s, the tall, fairer-skinned Tutsis as a "natural élite" akin to Europeans; this is quite clear from the diary evidence published in Ian Linden, *Church and Revolution in Rwanda* (Manchester: Manchester University Press, 1980). This stance was then reversed, with the Christian mission supporting the Hutu as an underdog people: a change reflecting the replacement of older French Jesuits, with their aristocratic roots and nineteenth-century ideas of race, by younger priests imbued

with "liberation theology." Little wonder, however, if the inheritors of these contradictory policies were confused and resentful at independence.

72. René Lemarchand, *Rwanda and Burundi* (London: Pall Mall Press, 1970), parts 2 and 4.

73. A figure of one hundred thousand actual perpetrators of the genocide was suggested by Gérard Prunier. This is roughly comparable to the number of arrests by the post-genocide government in Rwanda. See Prunier interview with Fergal Keane, *PBS Online* at www.pbs.org.wgbh/pages/frontline/shows/rwanda/etc/interview.html and Keane's eyewitness account, *Season of Blood: A Rwandan Journey* (London: Penguin, 1996).

74. A conclusion also reached by Jared Diamond in his *Collapse: How Societies Choose to Fail or Succeed* (London: Allen Lane, 2005), ch. 10.

75. The Rwandan president Paul Kagame underlined the common threat in the crises by being the first African leader to offer a contingent of African Union peacekeeping troops for Darfur. Owing to the restrictive UN mandate, however, the AU peacekeepers eventually sent were ineffective, being too few, inadequately armed and supplied, and prohibited from taking on the government-sponsored *janjaweed* militias who were carrying out the atrocities.

76. Alex J. Bellamy, "Peace operations and humanitarian intervention" in Beeson and Bisley eds., *Issues in 21st Century World Politics*, p. 149.

77. The latter was the verdict of the UN investigating commission to Darfur in 2004. See *Report of the International Commission of Inquiry on Darfur to the United Nations Secretary-General*, UN Document S/2005/60, 25 January 2005. On Sudan see also Alex de Waal, "Counter-insurgency on the cheap," *London Review of Books* 5 August 2004, pp. 25–26; and (less satisfactorily) Gérard Prunier, *Darfur: The Ambiguous Genocide* (London: Hurst, 2005). On Rwanda, see *Independent Inquiry into the actions of the United Nations during the 1994 genocide in Rwanda*, UN Report S/1999/1257 in English, p. 1, and Dallaire, *Shake Hands with the Devil*. More generally see Geoffrey Robertson QC, *Crimes Against Humanity: The Struggle for Global Justice* (3rd ed. London: Penguin, 2006).

78. On the colonial Congo see Adam Hochschild, *King Leopold's Ghost: A Story Of Greed, Terror and Heroism in Colonial Africa* (Boston, MA: Houghton Mifflin, 1998).

79. Mainly for coltan and tantalum (used for capacitors in digital electronic devices), tin, tungsten, and gold; see the report *Coming Clean: how supply-chain controls can stop Congo's minerals trade fuelling conflict* (London: Global Witness, 2012).

80. In 2013, the Save the Children Fund ranked the DRC as one of the most dangerous places in the world to be born. Save the Children Fund, *State of the World's Mothers—2013*, esp. pp. 33–37, available at www.savethechildren.org/

81. On the latter see Jerome Lewis, *The Batwa Pygmies of the Great Lakes Region* (London: Minority Rights Group, 2000).

82. See above, chapter 11, section 11.2.

83. For a more sceptical view, see John Breuilly's "Case Study 3" in Baylis, Smith and Owens (eds.), *The Globalization of World Politics* (6th ed. 2014), p. 397.

84. See in this connection the admirable study by Ishtiaq Ahmed, *The Punjab Bloodied, Partitioned and Cleansed: Unravelling the 1947 Tragedy through*

Secret British Reports and First-Person Accounts (Karachi: Oxford University Press, 2012).

85. Contemporary Argentina, in the light of the massacre of the indigenous population in the nineteenth century, may be regarded simply as a European colonial society, with a rival and therefore undecidable historic claim to the British one over the islands (which lie, moreover, outside the limits of any modern Argentine claim under the UNCLOS—Law of the Sea—Treaty). This was a Fascist colonial society too, for much of the twentieth century—culminating in the 1982 invasion of the islands and the disastrous war. One can debate whether the war was diplomatically avoidable; but for certain, the British intervention saved the helpless islanders from the torturers of the Argentine military junta, who had launched the invasion as a distraction from their own bloody and ruinous rule. All of which makes the war a shameful, rather than a heroic, episode in Argentine history. In my view, the best thing for Argentines for the foreseeable future would be the recovery, through democracy, of their dignity and sense of self-worth as a society, and the overcoming by legitimate means of their geographical isolation, which has fuelled extremism in the past. Once democracy is securely established in both Argentina and the Falklands/Malvinas, the question of their peoples' association can be more calmly viewed.

86. Linda Colley, *Acts of Union and Disunion*, p. 152.

87. "Constantine Constantius" [Søren Kierkegaard], *Repetition: An Essay in Experimental Psychology* [1843] in *Repetition* and *Philosophical Crumbs* tr. M. G. Piety (Oxford: Oxford University Press, 2009), p. 4.

88. M. G. Piety, "Introduction" in *ibid.*, p. viii.

Index

For Product Safety Concerns and Information please contact our EU
representative GPSR@taylorandfrancis.com Taylor & Francis Verlag GmbH,
Kaufingerstraße 24, 80331 München, Germany

Batch number: 08158441

Printed by Printforce, the Netherlands